Praise for China Hands

"Mr. Lilley's insider accounts of U.S.-China relations from the Nixon years through Tiananmen Square are vivid and frank. But it's his gripping hour-by-hour telling of the events surrounding the student-led rebellion on June 4, 1989, that deserves to be turned into a movie. *China Hands* is an adventure story worthy of John le Carré but without his moral ambiguity. James Lilley always understood what he was fighting for and why it was worth it. The U.S. remains the pre-eminent power in Asia. China is not free yet, but it is freer." —Melanie Kirkpatrick, *Wall Street Journal*

"While rich in the telling of anecdotage, this story gains mostly from its unusual perspective." —Gavin Scott, *Chicago Tribune*

"Mr. Lilley is now on his third career, as an Asian expert at the American Enterprise Institute, and a regular as a TV talking head and op-ed commentator. He remains a problem-solving pragmatist. Like his long-dead brother Frank, he does not see military might as the ultimate solution (thought it is nonetheless a card that should not be discarded). When he left China two years after the Tiananmen massacre, his final report stated, 'Our effort should be to bend China, not to break it or change it fundamentally . . . China is what it is, not as we want it to be.'" —Joseph C. Goulden, *Washington Times*

"Skillfully weaves together the personal and the political, leaving no doubt of the impact the two had on each other . . . the most riveting part of this book focuses on the Tiananmen Square massacre, which occurred while [Lilley] was ambassador to China. It's a harrowing tale, graphically reported by brave embassy staffers who witnessed the carnage." —Andrew Nagorski, *Newsweek International*

"A survey of post-imperial Chinese history, a compendium of American blunders in troublesome nations, and it has some pretty good locker-room tales about spies." —Chaim Estulin, *Time Asia*

"*China Hands* . . . offers real insights and insiders' information about many of the most important and tumultuous events of the second half of the century . . . *China Hands* is too smart to sink into a simplistic us-against-them world view. Lilley saw the clear lines between what he was fighting for and what he was fighting against, but he also knew the complexity of the real world . . . By refusing to take the easy road, Lilley's story is ultimately more than just a political or historical one; it is a human one . . . By showing us the real individuals along with the grand flow of history that surrounds them, James Lilley provides a stunning view of American involvement in Asia that no one else could possibly have given. —Andrew J. Weber, *The Asian Reporter*

"[An] excellent book . . . Lilley gives a vivid account that surely adds to the historical record of the Tiananmen episode."

—Richard Halloran, *Far Eastern Economic Review*

"[Lilley's] candid account is a must-read for students of Asia and intelligence work."

—*Publishers Weekly*

"This is both a warm and moving personal account of businessmen, soldiers, spies, and diplomats all in one family. The Lilleys, particularly my friend Jim Lilley, know a lot about China; and all readers will find their experiences to be of great interest. They served and they made a difference."   —President George H. W. Bush

"This is the extraordinary memoir of a man whose life encapsulates America's involvement in Asia over the past seven decades. His book not only contains a wealth of new detail about American intelligence operations and diplomacy, but also conveys a sense of what it felt like to be part of these historic events."

—James Mann, author of *About Face, Beijing Jeep,* and *The Rise of the Vulcans*

"*China Hands* is a splendid memoir—as engaging as it is informative. Lilley, intelligence officer and later U.S. ambassador to China, South Korea, and representative to Taiwan, is literally an Old China Hand—or at least the scion of an Old China Hand. He weaves together family history, Asian history, intelligence work, and foreign policy in a manner that will surely enchant any reader interested in the evolution of northeast Asia over the last 90 years."

—James Schlesinger, former Director of Central Intelligence

"A fascinating account of an extraordinary life and career in espionage and diplomacy between America and Asia during and after the Cold War. Lilley takes the reader inside the CIA, White House, and other U.S. government agencies, all around Asia, and illuminates events previously shrouded in secrecy. This is a memoir of a dedicated professional and patriot, having grown up in China and serving most of his career centrally involved in U.S-China relations. A significant contribution to the history of the era."   —David Shambaugh, George Washington University and The Brookings Institution, author of *Modernizing China's Military*

"Ambassador James Lilley and his family have been intertwined with China's last century in so many interesting ways that a narrative of their history is like a series of vivid dioramas documenting Sino-American relations. Written simply, elegantly and frankly, *China Hands* offers a marvelous and accessible way for specialist and neophyte alike to follow China's usually unpredictable and always fascinating progress since Lilley's father first traveled up the Yangtze River in 1917."

—Orville Schell, Dean of the Graduate School of Journalism at University of California Berkeley and author of *Virtual Tibet* and *Mandate of Heaven*

CHINA HANDS

NINE DECADES OF ADVENTURE, ESPIONAGE, AND DIPLOMACY IN ASIA

Ambassador James Lilley

WITH JEFFREY LILLEY

PublicAffairs

NEW YORK

Dedicated to Frank Lilley—who died young and pure

so that we could carry on.

Copyright © 2004 by James Lilley and Jeffrey Lilley.
Published in the United States by PublicAffairs™, a member of the Perseus Books Group.
All rights reserved.
Printed in the United States of America.

No part of this book may be reproduced in any manner whatsoever without written permission except in the case of brief quotations embodied in critical articles and reviews. For information, address PublicAffairs, 250 West 57th Street, Suite 1321, New York, NY 10107.
PublicAffairs books are available at special discounts for bulk purchases in the U.S. by corporations, institutions, and other organizations. For more information, please contact the Special Markets Department at the Perseus Books Group, 11 Cambridge Center, Cambridge, MA 02142, call (617) 252–5298, or email special.markets@perseusbooks.com.

All photographs are courtesy of the author unless otherwise noted.

BOOK DESIGN AND COMPOSITION BY JENNY DOSSIN. TEXT SET IN ADOBE CASLON.

Library of Congress Cataloging-in-Publication data
Lilley, James R.
China hands : nine decades of adventure, espionage, and diplomacy in Asia / James Lilley with Jeffrey Lilley.
p. cm.
Includes index.
ISBN 1-58648-343-9 (pbk)
1. Lilley, James R. 2. Diplomats—United States—Biography. 3. Diplomats—China—Biography. 4. United States—Foreign relations—China. 5. China—Foreign relations—United States. 6. United States—Foreign relations—1989- 7. United States—Foreign relations—Asia. 8. Asia—Foreign relations—United States. 9. China—Politics and government—1949- 10. Asia—Politics and government—1945- I. Lilley, Jeffrey. II. Title.
E840.8.L48A3 2004
327.73051′092—dc22
[B]
2003069035

10 9 8 7 6 5 4 3 2 1

CONTENTS

Note to the Reader   *vii*
Map: China and Its Neighbors   *viii–ix*
Prologue   *xi*

PART I
GROWING UP, 1916–1947

1   "Where the Daisies Cover the Country Land"   3
2   Only a Memory   24
3   Americanization   35
4   An Anguished Cry   47

PART II
INTELLIGENCE OFFICER IN ACTION, 1948–1968

5   A Ready Recruit   65
6   A Covert Foot Soldier   77
7   On the Edge of Conflict   97
8   Running the Secret War   106
9   Of Coups, Floods, and Failures   119

PART III
CHINA OPENS UP, 1969–1981

10   Reading the Tea Leaves   135
11   Breaking Down Walls   152

12 Kissinger's Man in China   169
13 Good Fortune   196
14 Riding a Wave   213

PART IV
DIPLOMAT IN ACTION, 1982–1991

15 Righting the Balance   227
16 The Golden Years   249
17 Pushing for Change   264
18 "Through the Blur of Our Tears"   282
19 Stepping on a Volcano   297
20 Small Victories   335

    Epilogue   373
    Acknowledgments   383
    Notes   385
    Bibliography   402
    Index   406

Note to the Reader

In this book we are using the Wade-Giles system for the standardized transliteration of Chinese cities such as Kiukiang, Peking, Tientsin, and Tsingtao, as well as for well-known Chinese leaders like Mao Tse-tung and Chou En-lai and Taiwan leaders such as Chiang Kai-shek and Chiang Ching-kuo. Other Chinese names and places are written using the newer pinyin phonetic spelling system.

The CIA has reviewed this material. That review neither constitutes CIA authentication of information nor implies CIA endorsement of the authors' views.

The opinions and characterizations in this book are those of the author and do not necessarily represent official positions of the United States government.

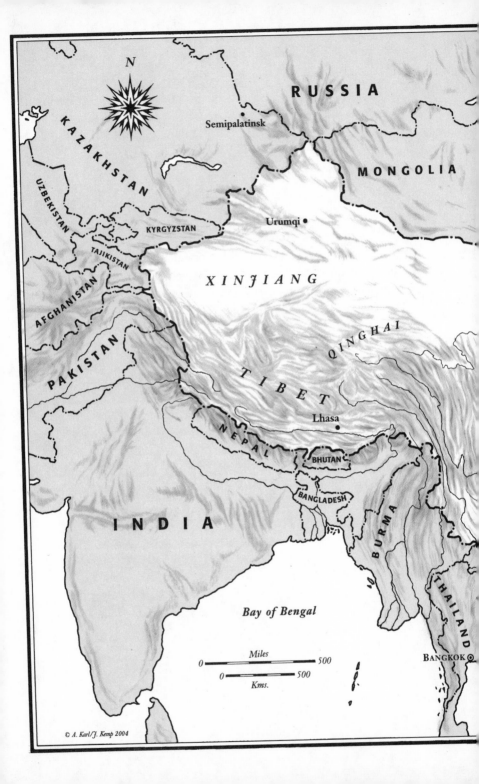

During a government career spanning four decades, James Lilley served in the CIA, White House, State Department and Defense Department. The only American to have served as the U.S.'s top-ranking diplomat in both Taiwan and China, he also served as the U.S. ambassador to South Korea. He is currently a senior fellow at the American Enterprise Institute in Washington, DC. He and his wife Sally split their time between Washington and Lewes, Delaware.

Jeffrey Lilley is a writer and journalist whose work has appeared in the *Far Eastern Economic Review*, *Sports Illustrated* and the *Wall Street Journal*. He is currently working on a democracy building project in the Kyrgyz Republic in Central Asia. When he's in the United States, he lives in Silver Spring, Maryland. He is married with two sons.

PROLOGUE

O N THE MORNING of June 7, 1989, I faced a roomful of anxious staff and dependents in the snack bar of the U.S. Embassy. They had cause to be apprehensive. The Tiananmen massacre of Chinese citizens by People's Liberation Army (PLA) soldiers had occurred three nights earlier. Peking was under lockdown. There was loose talk of civil war between rival factions of the army. Foreign residents were clearing out of the city. To make matters worse, we were getting credible reports of sporadic killing by PLA soldiers continuing to fire on groups of students and other citizens opposed to the government crackdown.

I had convened this staff meeting of about seventy people to explain the procedures for voluntary evacuation. It was time to get Americans out of Peking. We had arranged for charter planes to fly out any dependents who wanted to leave. Families wanted to stay together, and the group included embassy officers who had just risked their lives to report on the brutal situation in Tiananmen Square. Understandably, there wasn't much enthusiasm for leaving. But I urged dependents to consider it. We had been fortunate on June 4 that no Americans had been killed. I didn't want to push our luck.

As I was completing my talk, the "pop-pop-pop" of gunfire rang out. Embassy officers jumped from their seats and quickly shuttered the windows. A staff member came on the embassy speaker system to warn people not to leave the building. Women in the audience huddled with their children, and some started to cry.

We soon found out that Chinese troops withdrawing from central Peking had opened fire at the upper floors of a nearby diplomatic compound, raking apartments with multiple rounds of automatic weapons fire. A number of American families lived in the international compound, which included the apartment where my family had lived during our first tour in Peking in the early 1970s. In all, ten U.S. Embassy apartments were hit with more than a hundred bullets. Americans escaped harm, but just barely. In our former apartment on the top floor, bullets came crashing through a bedroom window. An alert Chinese amah threw herself over the two American children she was watching to protect them from bullets and falling glass. She may well have saved their lives. Supposedly, came the official line, the Chinese forces were looking for a sniper, who had killed a soldier in the retreating column.

"I think the Chinese are trying to send us a message," I said after the firing had died down. The shots were like a series of exclamation points at the end of my appeal to convince dependents to leave on the evacuation flights.

.   .   .

My wife Sally and I had arrived in Peking a month earlier to take up our new posting. Buoyed by a tour in nearby South Korea, where we had witnessed the democratic transformation of that country, we were looking forward to the Peking posting as a chance to further strengthen Sino-American ties that had been steadily growing since the early 1970s. My selection by President George H. W. Bush as U.S. ambassador to the People's Republic of China was the pinnacle of my government career as a specialist on China.

It was a personal milestone for me as well. Sixty-one years after being born on the Shandong Peninsula southeast of Peking, I was returning to China to serve as America's highest-ranking diplomat. The country had defined my family's life since 1916, when my father stepped off a boat in Shanghai harbor to work for Standard Oil. He ended up working in China for nearly thirty years. Three of his four children were born in China, and my two older brothers both returned to China before I did. But my association with the Middle Kingdom was the longest and most enduring. By 1989 I had observed China for nearly four decades from the vantage point of twelve different postings in Asia, in the process evolving from a CIA officer on the front lines of the Cold War into a participant in the formulation of American policy toward both mainland China and Taiwan.

Now I was in the middle of a country that seemed to some to be on the brink of civil war. The alleyways of Peking were filled with confused and frightened people, Chinese citizens who were angry at the central government. This latest action clearly showed there would be no democratic transformation in China. Her leaders had emphasized this on the evening of June 3 when troops were ordered to retake Tiananmen Square. Embassy estimates put the number of dead at one thousand to two thousand. It has been called, and it was, a massacre.

Back in America, the news was broadcast throughout the country. Courtesy of CNN and the other major American broadcasters, American viewers had been tuning in to the world's first televised revolution, which began with student demonstrations in Peking in April. The aspirations of Chinese students for more openness and an end to cronyism and corruption were crushed when the tanks rolled into central Peking.

As the American ambassador on the ground in Peking, I took to TV in those tumultuous days after June 4 to try to explain what had happened in China and how we were responding. I wanted to make the point that the United States had to stay engaged with China for strategic reasons. America, I insisted, could contribute in constructive ways to a more open China. I also acknowledged that, in the short term, we had to react to the killings and subsequent arrests.

Apparently, my comportment impressed a few people back home. In July 1989, I received a letter in the diplomatic pouch. It was postmarked Baltimore, Maryland, and had been written by a man named Bob Emig. I was used to receiving cables from the State Department and letters of support from family and friends, but this man's name was unfamiliar. I opened the envelope and started to read the handwritten note: "My congratulations to you for a job well done under extremely difficult conditions. Our prayers go with you," Mr. Emig had written. At the end of the note, Mr. Emig asked if I was related to "China-hand Frank Lilley (Yale '43)."

Yes, I was related. Frank was my older brother and had been a model for me in all that he did. Frank was a world-record swimmer, a Chinese linguist, and an Army officer who had served in China and Japan. A deep-thinking and sensitive person, Frank was philosophical about life and its predicaments, and from an early age he recorded his thoughts and impressions in diaries and letters. His musings revealed a young man trying to come to terms with a world of hardship. In September 1940, at the age of 19, as war raged in Asia and heated up in Europe, he poured his thoughts and concerns out to my parents in a letter from Yale, where he was studying: "There is so much that is mysterious, unknown and unexplainable in life; that is why, in spite of sadness, I suppose life is so fascinating and people hate to give it up so. The only aspect of life that we can really be sure about is that it is all a struggle, every bit of it. To struggle against sorrow, suffering, disillusionment, discouragement, ill health, and to keep alive is after all the real fiber of life."

I followed Frank at Phillips Exeter Academy and Yale, in the study of Chinese language, and in the choice of government service, so many of the steps I took in life carried the echo of Frank's footfalls. Even though I kept my thoughts about him largely to myself, his memory had a way of catching up to me during my posts throughout Asia. It was as if Frank wanted to make sure that I was doing all right. It made sense. He had been that kind of big brother, always looking out for me.

It turned out that Bob Emig had served with Frank at Fort Bragg in 1943. They kept in contact through their early years in military service, but then lost touch. More than forty years later, Bob Emig saw me on TV or read about my involvement with the tumultuous events in China and made the link.

This memoir, too, is an attempt to make connections. It tells the story of my family and China in the twentieth century, beginning with our roots on the Shandong Peninsula and continuing with my work in Asia as a CIA officer and diplomat. It is also the story of fulfilling a mission and a destiny. The mission was to look out for America's interests and help build a stable and, where possible, more democratic Asia. The destiny bequeathed to me by my brother Frank was to survive and make a contribution.

I

GROWING UP

1916–1947

1

"WHERE THE DAISIES COVER
THE COUNTRY LAND"

MY FAMILY's connection with China began in the shadow of the picturesque peaks that line the country's great waterway, the Yangtze River. There, in 1917, in the heartland of a country known by its people as the center of the world, my father was traveling upstream on a Chinese junk. Along the way he recorded the family's first images of life in the Middle Kingdom, a place that we would work in and around for the next nine decades.

From his perch on the junk, my father admired the Yangtze's dramatic scenery and noted the exotic names of some of its gorges—ox liver, wild duck, and horse lungs. At the Wushan Gorge, "the great gloomy gorge of the river" as he called it, cliffs rose up over the Yangtze to heights of a thousand feet and channeled rapids that could break a boat into pieces. "Awe-inspiring in its massive ruggedness," my father wrote in his diary of the trip. During the journey upstream, a hundred laborers, trudging at times along narrow paths carved into the limestone rock, used ropes to haul the boat against the current. Later my father heard gunshots that signaled the start of a battle between armies of opposing warlords. Exotic scenery, perilous rapids, backbreaking labor, and brewing conflict—my father recorded it all.

Frank Walder Lilley II had arrived in China a year earlier. After dropping out of Cornell University, he had gone to California to "seek his fortune." But destiny drew him farther afield. After reading in a local newspaper that the Standard Oil Company was looking for single men to go to China, he sent in an application. When he was accepted, he joined a growing corps of marketers, or "classmen" as they were called, for John D. Rockefeller's Standard Oil Company of New York, or SOCONY. The men were sent all over the world to sell oil and oil products. They were part of America's expanding economic empire.

The commitment my father made to work for Standard Oil was excessive by today's standards. He agreed to learn Chinese, work without vacation, and stay unmarried for three years. But at 26, sporting a mustache and a piercing gaze, he was eager for adventure. And without a college degree, he was happy to have a steady job.

SOCONY employees called their work "selling oil for the lamps of China," and it became an almost messianic mission to spread light around China and make profits for "the company." The sign of SOCONY was a flying red horse, and it came to be recognized around the country. In those days, in a phrase that conjured up thoughts of empire, it was said that Standard Oil's holdings in the world were so vast that the sun never went down over the business.

That scenic ride up the Yangtze dropped my father off in Wanxian, a city in China's interior in eastern Sichuan Province. His job was to sell kerosene and other oil products to the Chinese multitudes. To do this, he established a network of Chinese sales agents to peddle oil products to the villages and towns in his district. Like his fellow SOCONY managers working in remote locations, my father had to learn quickly how to distinguish between locals he could do business with and those he should stay away from. On the trip up the Yangtze in 1917 he got a taste of what he was in for. "One of the coolies punched a hole in one of the tins and poured out ½ a tin of oil," my father wrote in his diary. "We discovered the theft when the oil was being put back on the junk and after much arguing made the no. 1 coolie pay $1 for the oil. A great deal of this goes on here and we wanted to teach the crowd a lesson."

The business was time-consuming and demanded patience. Success in securing reliable and trustworthy Chinese agents depended largely upon how well the manager understood Chinese customs and ways of doing business. The American managers and their Chinese agents differed like night and day—both on the surface and in more substantive ways. The managers wore Western suits and fedoras. The agents wore skullcaps and dressed in Chinese collarless shirts and long gowns. History, language, and culture were completely different. China was thousands of years old. The United States of America was not halfway through its second century. The Chinese wrote in characters and spoke in rising and falling cadences, while Americans used an alphabet and conversed in a monotone.

But there were much more subtle differences as well. If a manager was successful in dealing with the Chinese, he earned the Chinese moniker of a "keeper of the custom," meaning one who understood Chinese rites and practices, such as figuring out family ties, lining up allies, acting deferentially, and avoiding humiliation of others. This made him an "honorable adversary," a description that revealed a dislike and distrust of foreigners.

.   .   .

China was in a state of upheaval when my father arrived in 1916. Several years earlier, a bloodless revolution had toppled the country's last emperor, a six-year-old boy named Pu Yi. The breakdown of the imperial system was followed by the rise of a republican form of government in 1912, headed by a president and based on provincial assemblies and a national parliament. But real power rested with powerful military governors or regional warlords. The republican government collapsed several years later, and an era dominated by warlords ensued. Along the Yangtze, in a microcosm of what was happening throughout China, warlords vied for power, and robbers and ex-soldiers controlled passages of the river and preyed on traders. In fact, for periods of time in 1916, shipping companies stopped sending boats up parts of the Yangtze because lawless bands along the banks were shooting at anything that moved.

My father's first respite from these challenges of work and turmoil came in late 1919 when he was allowed three and a half months of home leave. Three years of living alone in the backcountry of China had made his thinking clear on one thing: He needed a wife. And he had to work fast at finding one since the boat journeys across the Pacific would take up almost half of his allotted vacation time. Fortunately, during those years in the interior of China, he hadn't been just selling oil. He had also spent time selling the idea of himself as a husband to a schoolteacher he had met before leaving for China.

Inez Bush came from Monroe, New York, an area of rolling farmland and lakes about forty miles northwest of New York City, where my father's family had moved from Canada in the early part of the century. While Inez had dated other people in my father's absence, when he returned and asked for her hand, Inez, beautiful but an old-maidish 25 years old, accepted. My father never did ask her father for permission. Since he came from a strict Catholic family and my mother's family was Protestant, both sets of parents were opposed to the union. My parents solved the problem by eloping. And by deciding then that formal religion would be minimized in their new family's life even though the strong Catholic strain would live on in Grandma Lilley.

My oldest sibling, Frank Walder III, was born in 1920 in Wuhu, a port city on the Yangtze about two hundred miles inland from Shanghai. Following Frank's birth my homesick mother returned to the United States with her newborn son. But after several months of washing clothes, cooking meals, and doing chores at her parents' home in Monroe, she headed back to China, more appreciative of the house staff that came with the posting. My brother Jack was born two years after Frank on the next home leave in New York. Elinore, born in 1924 in Chefoo (present-day Yantai on the tip of the Shandong Peninsula), broke the line of boys. I, the last of the four, was born on January 15, 1928, in the German hospital in Tsingtao. By that time the family had already been living for two years in Tsingtao, a Yellow Sea port on the Shandong Peninsula where I was to live the first eight, very happy years of my life.

．　　　．　　　．

Tsingtao's history ties in directly with the era of foreign domination in China. Since the late eighteenth century, when England started to sell opium to China in return for teas, porcelain, silks, and other decorative goods, Japan and the European powers had taken advantage of China's fractured political system and weak military to carve up the country's cities into commercial sectors. For their companies, these stronger countries arranged trading privileges, and for their citizens, extraterritorial rights, which allowed foreigners to be judged by their own national laws for crimes committed on Chinese soil. America followed her European rivals. In 1844, Caleb Cushing, the personal envoy of President John Tyler, negotiated access to Chinese ports and similar extraterritorial rights for Americans.

These kinds of privileges ultimately led to President William McKinley's Open Door policy in 1900. Ostensibly designed by the United States to protect China from being carved up, this declaration actually served to preserve the status quo of a subservient China open for trade on favorable terms to outside countries. Seeing the American declaration as an attempt to curtail their commercial involvement in China, foreign powers already in China for the most part ignored it and continued their business activities. Competition for a better foothold in China ultimately led China's two most powerful neighbors, Japan and Russia, to fight the Russo-Japanese War in 1904–1905. Japan's victory in that war fueled its push into China in the early twentieth century.

Germany's conquest of Tsingtao in 1897 is a good illustration of the imperialist practices of the day. The pretext for the German takeover was the murder of two German missionaries by Chinese bandits in a town on the Shandong Peninsula. Germany dispatched three cruisers to Tsingtao, which had one of the finest natural harbors on the coast of China. After Chinese soldiers evacuated Tsingtao upon orders of the German emperor, the German military occupied the town.

Bargaining from an inferior position, China concluded a ninety-nine-year lease of the bay area to Germany. Thus began the Germanization of the village of Tsingtao. German engineers laid out roads lined with linden trees and connected to sewers, constructed bunkers on the coastline, and built sturdy brick houses. The town's most distinctive landmark became the Lutheran Church built on a high point overlooking the harbor. To this day you can see the German houses on Tsingtao's hillside, with their fading yellow and red trim and overgrown gardens, standing solidly a century after they were built.

Germany's remaking of Tsingtao came to a halt in World War I, but imperialist practices didn't. Japan, which opposed Germany in the war, saw an opportunity to extend its foothold in China past its control of Manchuria, which had been won from the Russians in the Russo-Japanese War. Together with a small force of British troops, Japan captured Tsingtao in 1914 and a year later wrangled from the weakened Chinese government complete control over the Shandong Peninsula.

After the end of World War I, China hoped to regain the German concession of Shandong and rid itself of the yoke of extraterritoriality. But at the Paris Peace Conference in 1919, which was supposed to.enshrine U.S. president Woodrow Wilson's favored principles of national self-determination and territorial integrity, the Chinese were told they had no claim on Tsingtao because the treaty they had signed with Japan in 1915 was binding. Protests against the unjust decision started on May 4 in Tiananmen Square in front of the Forbidden City palace complex in the center of Peking and spread across China, giving birth to the eponymous movement that was a landmark in the development of Chinese nationalism and that would be echoed in later events in China, including the student demonstrations in 1989.

The May 4th movement had roots in the Boxer Rebellion almost two decades earlier. That rebellion was fueled by resentment toward the presence of foreigners in China—be it the Japanese military in the north, German missionaries in the west, or British and American businessmen in the ports. It wasn't called the era of the gunboat, oil can, and Bible for nothing. Heir to a tradition of martial arts and shamanism, the Boxer movement, I Ho Ch'uan in Chinese ("righteous, harmonious fists"), reached its peak when the Boxers occupied the capital city of Peking and Tientsin in the summer of 1900. The Boxers attacked Christians, both foreign and Chinese, and looted the legations in which foreigners lived. An international army soon came to the rescue of foreigners trapped in Peking and squashed the rebellion. In victory, the foreign powers solidified the status quo trading arrangements, and, with the Boxer Protocol of 1901, forced the Chinese government to pay indemnity for damages and acquiesce to a strengthened foreign military presence in the legations. A battalion of the U.S. 15th Infantry, which had been part of the international army, returned to China in 1911.

The Chinese people stewed, but without a competent central government, China was powerless to change its fate. It was left to depend on other powers, mostly acting in their own self-interest, to address its grievances. In 1922, alarmed by Japan's growing presence in China, two of those powers—Britain and the United States—pressured Tokyo to cede control of Tsingtao back to China in accordance with provisions of the Washington Conference, which tried to settle outstanding territorial issues stemming from World War I.

So by the time my family moved to Tsingtao in 1926, it had been under Chinese control for four years, but the presence of foreigners still shaped the city. Though there were no longer many Japanese troops in the city, Japan remained the dominant outside power in Tsingtao. Its businessmen made up the core of a 15,000-strong Japanese community. Other foreign communities were the British, Germans, Canadians, Russians, and, of course, Americans.

The Russians were a curious lot. They were European-looking but didn't enjoy the same privileges of work, housing, and lifestyle of the other foreign communities. Many had been stranded in China after fleeing the Bolshevik Revolution of 1917 and were stateless. In the hierarchy of nationalities that characterized life in Tsingtao, the Russians were one step up from the Chinese. They were poorer than the other Westerners, lived more frugally, and had to scramble to make ends meet. Many worked service jobs for foreigners: operating the city's dry cleaners and cafés; working as musicians and hairdressers; and giving music, dance, and art lessons. The foreign community and even the Chinese generally looked down on the Russians for their marginal existence as stateless refugees. I remember that when my brother Frank wanted to tease my sister Elinore, he would call her a Russian girl and say she had been adopted.

.　.　.

In the post–World War I period, Tsingtao entered what was for us a golden age. The city's natural deepwater port attracted businesses from around the world, and the Strand, its crescent-shaped beach, became a prime tourist attraction. From an obscure fishing village at the turn of the century, by the mid-1930s Tsingtao had turned into a bustling port city of 450,000 people. It was home to American lumberyards, a British cigarette factory, a German brewery, and a Japanese brick plant. Silk, flour, and peanut oil were also produced in the city.

On the diplomatic front, Britain, Germany, Japan, and the United States maintained consulates in Tsingtao. The city contained ten churches to serve the various faiths of the foreign communities, and the local newspaper was published in three languages: Chinese, English, and Russian. In the summer, Europeans from other parts of China flocked to Tsingtao's tourist attractions. Vacationers enjoyed the beach, frequented the fine restaurants, played golf at the country club, and laid bets on ponies at the racetrack. No wonder *The Tsingtao Times* touted the city in a 1928 tourist pamphlet as the "Riviera of the Far East." The same article went on to say unabashedly: "If ever there was justification for Old World imperialism, Tsingtao, the Magic City, located on the coast of Shandong Province of China, certainly provides that justification."

My father's posting to Tsingtao was a reward for ten years of work in less attractive outposts like Wuhu, Ningbo, and Chefoo, where the amenities were fewer and the foreign communities smaller. And though his salary was modest by American standards, we lived like kings. Our house, #8 Chi Tung Road, was a spacious German-style three-story structure built halfway up a hillside. It had two balconies on the second floor and a porch on the first. We had a staff of six: a cook, a houseboy, the houseboy's helper, an amah who watched over the children, a wash amah who did the laundry, and a gardener who cultivated vegetables and flowers in our greenhouse and the plot next to the house. Little wonder my mother stopped being homesick!

The good life for me in Tsingtao started with amah, a tiny woman with bound feet who took care of me. She seemed entirely selfless, a servant whose work defined her life and who asked for little in return. I guess that she was between 40 and 60 when she lived with us, but maybe she didn't even know her exact age. We did know that she had fled stifling village life for opportunity in the city, and she occasionally spoke of family in her home village. She may well have left children behind.

Amah, who wore her hair in a bun and dressed in traditional Chinese jackets, came to us originally as wash amah, but when my parents fired that woman, she was elevated to this more prestigious position. However, we children insisted on teasing her by continuing to address her as wash amah. One day my sister demanded to see wash amah's bound feet. She dutifully complied, unwrapping first the white cloths around one foot and then the other to expose gnarled stubs with the toes broken and folded under. Elinore was horrified by the sight.

Wash amah hobbled around the house, but she attended to my every need. She wiped my bottom and combed my hair, all the while bantering to me in Shandong street talk. We were inseparable. She even provided comfort when I had a bad dream, as at night she slept on a cot in the third-floor hallway, just outside my room. Wash amah's tender care of me mirrored the comfortable environment that surrounded my family in Tsingtao.

Freed from the work of taking care of small children, my mother enjoyed life in Tsingtao. She met often with other American and European women for bridge, gossip, or golf. She looked forward to Saturday night, when she and my father would join friends for dinner and dancing at one of the cafés or restaurants near the Strand.

While I remember my father as a distant figure in our family, my mother was warm and loving. She doted on us. And for a woman who had never left her native New York State before the age of 25, she developed quite an interest in her new surroundings. She enjoyed expanding our horizons beyond Chi Tung Road and used to tell us stories that she had learned about famous—or infamous—Chinese personalities.

I remember one story about the former warlord of Shandong Province, Chang Tsungchang, one of the more colorful characters from the period of upheaval and civil war that we were living through. Chang was subordinate to the Manchurian overlord Chang Tsolin, whose fiefdom included Shandong. He was notorious for his licentious behavior. He used to travel with countless concubines. One of his more vulgar nom de guerres, I learned later, was "old eighty-six coppers," which referred to one of his anatomical boasts. To protect him on his journeys, Chang employed 4,600 White Russian mercenaries in his private army. This elite cavalry served as Chang's personal bodyguard. But these soldiers were powerless to prevent the assassination of their leader. According to the legend of the day, Chang was assassinated at a railroad station in Jinan, inland from Tsingtao. His last words as he expired on the platform were reportedly, "Pu hao" (No good).

In Tsingtao, life was decidedly "hao" for us kids. Sometimes it was hard to tell that we were living in China. Frank, Jack, Elinore, and I attended the American School in Tsingtao, which was housed in a former mansion. It provided instruction in English to about forty-five students from kindergarten to eighth grade. Because of lack of space, two or three grades had to study in the same classroom, but we enjoyed the camaraderie. I spent many hours on the playground and participated in the school plays. Best of all I remember being secretly in love with Miss Nelson, a teacher at the school who had red curly hair and was the apple of my young eye. In contrast, my teacher, Miss Linke, was a stern, methodical German woman, not sweet and pretty like Miss Nelson, who soon married a Mr. King Paget, a dashing young employee of Standard Oil who raced a Snipe class sailboat with my brother Frank as crew. I was crestfallen.

At home, we ate waffles, celebrated Halloween, and watched movies starring Laurel and Hardy and Ginger Rogers and Fred Astaire. Elinore studied piano with a Russian musician. For fun we boys ran around with our Canadian and American friends. When we got adventurous, we took excursions to Laoshan Mountain outside Tsingtao and explored the old German forts dug into the hillsides. During the summer, we had it especially good. We would go to the Strand in the morning and stay all day. For lunch, the cook would make a batch of fried chicken, and the houseboy would hand-churn ice cream. Then the houseboy would hail a horse-drawn carriage, load it up with food and tableware, and set off for the Strand. On the porch of our beach cabin, while we sat in our bathing suits, he would set up a makeshift table, spread a white tablecloth, and serve us fried chicken and ice cream.

It was a big thrill when U.S. Navy ships would anchor in Tsingtao harbor, their base for summer maneuvers in the 1930s. I remember the flagship of the U.S. Asiatic fleet, the heavy cruiser U.S.S. *Augusta*, docking at Tsingtao's port, accompanied by other ships in the fleet. They were huge, mighty, and filled with strapping sailors. For American kids so far from home, these ships made us feel patriotic and proud. We used to venture around the town, hoping to catch up with sailors on shore. Some kids even got invited to spend a day on the ships—that was like a dream come true.

Another thrill came one day in 1934 when I was about six years old. My older brother Frank called me to the wall enclosing our compound. We scampered up the wall, careful not to cut ourselves on the broken glass, which was strewn along the top of the wall to deter curious types. Gongs were clanging, and a woman was wailing. We peeked over the wall onto Chi Tung Road and saw a long procession of Chinese walking up the street. In the middle of the crowd of policemen and soldiers was a Chinese man with his hands tied behind his back. "He's a bandit on his way to execution," we heard the Chinese bystanders remark. The woman was his mother, and she was running alongside the procession. "You can't do it. You can't execute my son!" she cried to the authorities. But her own son, the bandit, dismissed her pleas with a shake of his head. "Never mind. It's fate," he said, and walked on. I couldn't understand it at the time, but the whole scene underscored a fatalistic view of life that had been inculcated in the powerless Chinese masses over the centuries.

.   .   .

I remember an American piano player who used to play at one of the city's hotels. His name was Whitey Smith. Whitey sang all sorts of songs, but the lines from one song stick in my head to this day: "Take me where the daisies cover the country land, we'll make hay in the sunshine, we'll make love in the rain." Tsingtao in the 1930s was that kind of place for our family—a city of flowers, sunshine, and fun. Chinese fatalism had no place in our lives.

Frank was responsible for much of our happiness in those days. Though he grew up in China, Frank was entirely American in his exuberance for life and his enthusiasm for organizing activities, and Tsingtao, with its idyllic beaches and international community, was a splendid playground for his schemes. Frank would walk the rest of us kids down to the beach, take us out in a sailboat, or chaperone us to the movies. After reading an issue of *Boy's Life* magazine, he organized a Boy Scout troop and recruited an American missionary to be the troop leader. The troop used to meet on the third floor of our house.

My sister tells of the time when—still a toddler—I fell down and cut myself badly on the head. Wash amah, crying hysterically, was helpless. My parents were not home, and no one knew what to do. Ten-year-old Frank took charge. He scooped me up, placed me on the front of his bicycle, and peddled to the German Hospital. After a German doctor had sewn me up, Frank and I rode back home.

That was my older brother to me—a protector rising to the occasion. In many ways, he was larger than life. As the youngest boy, I adored him and wondered how I could ever be as good as he was. In fact, in sports both of my brothers set standards that I would never equal. While my mother doted on me, she was enamored of Frank and Jack, and I think she sometimes couldn't shake the thought of me as "Little Jimmy," a tender moniker that, nevertheless, carried with it the understanding that the main focus was always on Frank and Jack and their exploits. Faced with an age gap of six and eight years with my older brothers, I ended up spending more time with my sister Elinore, who was just three years older. At least she wasn't a better athlete than I was!

To this day I remember an embarrassing experience in Tsingtao, which characterized early on the differences between my brothers and me. There were no sports teams at the American School so Frank put together a soccer team and arranged a game with our main rivals, the German School. No doubt some of the storm clouds brewing in Europe had drifted over Tsingtao because there was little love lost between the German and American kids. Sometimes Frank, Jack, and other American boys would take on the Germans boys in impromptu wrestling matches, but the more physically mature Germans always got the better of the Americans. So Frank, organizer that he was, came up with the idea of a soccer match in hopes that the game would be more competitive than the wrestling matches.

Too young to play, I got as close to the action as I could by watching the game from beside the American goal. The match turned out to be hard fought, and the game was scoreless, when a German boy boomed the ball toward the American goal. Inexplicably I stuck out my arm and blocked the shot. A huge argument ensued with the Germans demanding that the shot be counted as a goal. The Americans ended up conceding the goal and lost the game. I was so shamed.

I guess that was my way of trying to make a contribution. When I look back on myself at that time, I see a young boy who felt that life was beyond the reach of his skinny arms. While everybody around was doing something exciting, I felt that I was watching and doing little. I couldn't keep up.

·   ·   ·

Tsingtao remained calm from 1926 to 1936, the decade we lived there. As children, we lived in a kind of bubble, insulated from what was happening in wider China and largely unaware of Chinese resentment of foreigners. We did receive news of bitter infighting between Chinese Nationalist forces and Communists, but like other foreign enclaves in China, Tsingtao remained protected from the outbreaks of violence. In our daily lives, the Chinese were all around, but their lives were largely separate from ours. At the Strand we didn't see Chinese because they weren't allowed to swim in our section of the beach. In the case of our house staff, we had friendly contact with them, but we knew little of their personal lives.

Despite our limited personal contact with Chinese people, we had a bird's-eye view of Chinese society. Outside the walls of our compound we caught glimpses of Tsingtao's colorful street life, a completely different world of vendors, puppet shows, and funeral and bridal processions. And then there were the ubiquitous rickshaw drivers who laughed and cursed as they picked lice out of their jackets.

Nevertheless, things were starting to change in our complacent world. Throughout recent history, Tsingtao's prime real estate had been an inviting target for countries wanting to expand in China. Though the walls that surrounded our house may have allowed us to live in peace, they couldn't hold back the desires of the most rapacious of those foreign powers—the Japanese.

I got my first glimpse of a formidable Japan in 1934 at, of all places, a swimming competition. In summer the Edgewater Mansion Hotel on the Strand used to hold races for adults. The swimmer to beat in 1934 was a muscular Japanese sergeant. But few dared give him a race except 13-year-old Frank. The swimmers took off from the pier at the hotel and aimed for a buoy three quarters of a mile away. The Japanese soldier swam breaststroke. Frank swam freestyle. While the other racers fell behind, Frank battled the burly soldier and hung close to him around the buoy, but couldn't match his powerful adult stroke. The sergeant ended up winning the race by 150 yards.

I was standing on the pier where they finished. The Japanese ser-

geant swam his last strokes, rose from the water, and strode purposefully away. I can still vividly remember Frank coming out of the water,
his face gaunt and body sagging from the exertion. He collapsed on the
pier in front of me, his chest heaving. I was just six years old, and I got
scared. I had never seen such a spectacle. There in front of me, I
thought my brother was going to die.

The scene of him gasping for breath on the beach left me with a
sense of disquiet. Frank, the organizer extraordinaire and leader of our
band, had all of a sudden become mortal, and that realization was at
odds with my understanding of Tsingtao as a place somehow untainted
by the unpleasant side of life.

Other hard lessons were to come. With the benefit of hindsight, I
see that Frank's race with the Japanese soldier reflected the times: an
unprepared America taking on a dedicated Japan in China. This could
have been a metaphor for Japan's takeover of China, which would soon
disrupt life in Tsingtao and upend the city's peaceful way of life. Of
course it would be Frank, my personification of the idyllic life of Tsingtao, who informed the family of the impending Sino-Japanese conflict
taking shape in northern China.

Frank departed for boarding school in 1934 just a few months after
his race with the Japanese sergeant. Because there wasn't a suitable
high school in the city, my parents chose to send him to the Pyongyang
Foreign School (PYFS) in Pyongyang, Korea. Jack joined Frank at the
PYFS in January 1935. The strictly Christian fundamentalist school was
a peculiar choice on my parents' part as they had elected not to send us
to church services, and in Tsingtao we had little religious instruction
apart from attending Sunday school. But there were few options for
high school in China. The available choices were far away, either in
Shanghai, Japan, or Korea. As it was, to get to the school it took my
brothers more than 40 hours of traveling by ship to northern China
and then by train down the Korean peninsula to Pyongyang.

Virtually all of the foreigners in Pyongyang in the 1930s were there
as missionaries or educators with a Christian sense of mission, part of
the strong American and Canadian Christian communities in north-

east Asia. By the mid-1930s, Western missionaries had founded four schools in Pyongyang alone. The Pyongyang Foreign School itself was founded in 1900 as a high school for the children of missionaries living in Japan, Korea, and northern China. My brothers were some of the few students of "business people." Fresh from the carefree social atmosphere of Tsingtao, they chafed at the school's puritanical rules, which, among other things, carefully controlled contact with girls.

Though Frank disagreed with living life under strictures, he was irritated more by the hypocrisy he saw in his fellow students. Many of the missionary kids would proclaim what good Christians they were and talk about how they went to church and said their prayers. But Frank remarked to us in his letters that they were often poor sports, ill-tempered, and bad-mannered in their daily lives. Frank made no bones about his resentment of these kids. "Don't worry," he wrote to my parents in February 1936, "these missionaries here haven't converted me yet." But Frank wasn't so much holding out as searching for a better way. Though just 15, he felt matters deeply and had a visceral reaction to perceived wrongs and injustices. He seemed to have the opinions and thoughts of an older person. For example, in Bible class at PYFS Frank rejected the teacher's instruction that a man couldn't be considered good if he didn't believe in Christ. A man, Frank wanted to believe, was good if his acts were good, even if he didn't proclaim himself to be a Christian.

As Frank adjusted to life at his new school, he didn't forget me and wrote often. He figured that in a couple of years I would be following in his footsteps, and he wanted me to be prepared for boarding school. So he wrote that I better learn to like vegetables because they served a lot of them at PYFS. He also encouraged me in my violin lessons and told me to pay closer attention to my spelling. Sometimes he gave me pointers on how to improve my swimming. He was always encouraging and supportive. "With a little practice, you ought to make an Olympic champ," he wrote me in 1937. "Lots of love from your big brother, Frank." I loved receiving his letters.

·　　·　　·

When my brothers arrived in Pyongyang, they found it larger than Tsingtao, with several six- and eight-story buildings and many taxis and streetcars, but it was a gritty, gray city under the heel of Japanese occupation. In Tsingtao we were still somewhat unaware of Japan's intentions in China, but Frank kept us clued in from his vantage point in Korea, which Japan had annexed in 1910 and which was closer to the center of Japanese military activity in northeast Asia. Frank sensed impending war from his reading of the local papers and his observations of the Japanese military in Korea, and he conveyed his thoughts to us in Tsingtao every week in his letters.

Indeed, at school he and the other students were often very close to demonstrations of Japanese military might. Across the river from PYFS, the Japanese had their major military airfield in Korea. Several times a week during classes, Japanese dive-bombers executed dry runs over the school, aiming for the school's athletic fields as the target for their imaginary payloads. Then, at night, searchlights would light up the sky over Pyongyang for night runs, and students would run to black out their windows.

In downtown Pyongyang, Japan's oppressive colonial policy was even more evident. When Frank and his friends would wander into town on a free day, they would see harassment of Koreans by the Japanese in the city's markets. Since Japan's annexation of Korea, many Korean farmers had chosen to protest the loss of their country by wearing white clothes, the traditional color of mourning in Korea. This practice of silent protest infuriated the Japanese authorities. Periodically, Japanese policemen on horses carrying buckets of red paint would make runs through the produce markets in Pyongyang. Armed with long paintbrushes that they wielded like lances, the Japanese policemen would smear paint on any Koreans wearing white clothes.

By the time Frank got to Pyongyang, the Japanese were turning their tactics of intimidation on the local community of Western missionaries. In January 1935, Japanese authorities called down two American missionaries, Samuel Moffet, the pioneer Western missionary in Korea, and Dr. Douglas McCune, head of Union Christian College. The Japanese demanded that the missionaries follow Japanese custom and force the Korean students at their schools to pay homage to the Japanese emperor at the city's Shinto shrine. The missionaries refused. The Japanese threatened to close the Christian schools in retaliation.

Meanwhile, in northern China, the Japanese military was moving ahead with plans to break China's hold on her own northern provinces. In the fall of 1931 the Japanese occupied Manchuria, and by that winter they had set up the puppet state of Manchukuo to extend their sphere of control. "It's a clever way, which the Japs are using to take northern China," Frank wrote caustically in December 1935. "An autonomous government. Baloney!"

In early 1936, the conflict with the American missionaries reached a head when the Japanese extradited Dr. McCune from Korea because he had refused to accede to their demands about worshipping at the shrine. Later that year, Moffet, who had been in Korea for forty-five years, left the country on four hours notice. In April 1936, Frank, having just returned to school from spring vacation at the house of American missionaries in Sunchon in southern Korea, wrote us about the worsening situation: "I think the Japs are getting ready for war in Manchuria—huge troop trains go through here all the time, but nobody is supposed to know it. We saw one huge troop train coming up from Sunchon. We hardly dared look out the windows they watched us so closely."

Frank's words in 1936, written from the tiny room he occupied in the boys dormitory at PYFS, proved prophetic. A little more than a year later, the Japanese military machine began rolling into northern China from Manchuria. Those troop trains that Frank saw had delivered their cargo.

.   .   .

The Sino-Japanese conflict broke out in the summer of 1937 in the small village of Lukouchiao west of Peking, near a junction of the Peking–Hankow railway. The Japanese had had their eye on the rail line, which was the only remaining access to Peking not under Japanese control, and had been sending troops to the area for military maneuvers. The railway line was of strategic significance, but it was the nearby Lukouchiao Bridge that carried significant historical importance. It was one of China's most beautiful monuments, made out of stone eight hundred years earlier and decorated with parapets adorned by marble lions. Admired by the first Western visitor who had crossed it in the thirteenth century, the bridge was known in his honor as the Marco Polo Bridge.

The battle near the Marco Polo Bridge the night of July 7, 1937, was sparked by a confrontation between a Japanese Army unit returning from a training exercise and Chinese troops garrisoned in the nearby city of Wanping. It is not clear who fired the first shot or shots, but at least one Japanese soldier fell dead in the first moments of the clash. When the Chinese showed unexpectedly tough resistance, the Japanese responded with mortar and artillery fire and called in reinforcements. Over the course of a two-day battle, scores of bodies were reported floating down the nearby Yungting River. World War II had been ignited in Asia.

By July 10, the Japanese were pouring troops into the area from their stronghold in Manchuria. In a few short weeks, a full-scale war was under way. The Chinese armed forces, a ragtag collection of mostly indifferent soldiers, some of whom were under the command of the Chinese government in Nanjing and others commanded by local governors and warlords, were no match for the sophisticated Japanese military machine. But the clash at Marco Polo Bridge and the ensuing conflict did spur the Chinese to join together against the outside invader. Later in the summer of 1937, the Chinese Nationalists and Communists, at each other's throats in a bitter civil war for control of China for the past ten years, agreed to join forces against the Japanese. They called their union the Second United Front, the First United Front having been organized in the 1920s with help from the Soviet Union to combat the warlords and roll back the foreign presence. The Second United Front was preceded and, some say, produced by an incident in 1936 that my father witnessed.

One historian has called it "the most bizarre experience ever to befall a modern chief of state." The incident happened in the western city of Xian, the capital of Shaanxi Province, and captured headlines around the world. In December 1936, Generalissimo Chiang Kai-shek, the leader of the central government and Nationalist forces, hoped to deliver a final blow against Chinese Communist forces in western China, where they had encamped after Mao's famous Long March in 1934 and 1935 across twelve provinces and 6,000 miles. Chiang flew into the city of Xian, but he was promptly kidnapped by Chang Hsüehliang, the warlord of Manchuria (and son of Chang Tsolin) ostensibly allied with Chiang Kai-shek, who was supposed to lead the final offensive. Tired of civil war, warlord Chang wanted to forge a united front of Nationalists and Communists against the Japanese. The best way, he decided, would be to get rid of the Generalissimo. After all, some reports had it that Chiang Kai-shek was actually in cahoots with the Japanese against the Communists. Good and bad, friend and foe, often proved to be opaque in China.

At about this time, my father was traveling in Xian, checking on Standard Oil agents. He told me later about what is now known as the "Xian Incident" and how he had thought a war was going to break out in front of his eyes. The air was electric with tension as days passed with China's leader under arrest and supposedly awaiting execution. SOCONY's Chinese agents in Xian were frightened, babbling gossip about the disorder that might ensue: bombings, looting, and rape.

Chiang Kai-shek was eventually saved by a constellation of forces coming together from far and wide. Communists in Moscow, who at the time exerted considerable influence in China, as well as some prominent Chinese Communists saw the prospect of chaos if Chiang Kai-shek were killed. They were most concerned about a resurgent Japan and so wanted China to be as strong as possible. There was no other leader in China with Chiang's stature, they reasoned. Only he had the power to forge a united front even if he didn't want one. So Chou En-lai, at that time a leading figure in the Chinese Communist Party and someone who himself had narrowly escaped death at the hands of the Nationalists in Shanghai, came to Xian and convinced warlord Chang to let the Generalissimo go. In exchange for his life and continuance as head of the central government, Chiang Kai-shek had to agree to abandon his campaign against the Communists and promise to support a united front.

For forging the second front, Chang Hsüehliang is said by some to have changed the course of Chinese history. But he didn't get any reward for it. Instead, Chiang Kai-shek returned to Nanjing, the capital of his government, with the cowed Chang in his custody. He ended up putting the mutinous warlord under house arrest for fifty-four years.

Chiang Kai-shek even took the warlord to Taiwan when he fled the mainland in 1949. In 1990, when Chang Hsüehliang turned 90, he was finally allowed to leave Taiwan, fifteen years after the death of Chiang himself. Rather than go back to the mainland, where the Chinese Communists were enticing him to return, he went to Hawaii and the U.S. mainland and started looking up old girlfriends. He lived to the ripe age of 101, outlasting virtually all the other principal actors in China's dramas of the 1930s, including Chiang Kai-shek, Mao Tsetung, and Chou En-lai. Chang died in October 2001 in Hawaii. In an obituary, the *Economist* magazine called him "a Chinese enigma." He was outlived only by Madame Chiang Kai-shek, who finally succumbed in 2003 at the age of 106.

.   .   .

By nature, my father was a serious and reserved man, qualities that, one would think, would lend themselves to promotion in his line of business. But by the 1930s he had realized that he wasn't shooting up Standard Oil's corporate ladder. My mother always blamed the company's new management, which promoted friends, many of whom were graduates of Colgate or Syracuse. Men who had attended the Ivy League colleges, surprising as it may sound in this day and age, didn't have as good a chance in the company.

But bad timing also played a role in my father's stagnant career at Standard Oil. In the late 1920s, he had been ready to quit the company and get into the business of importing American cars to China, but the stock market crash of 1929 decimated his savings and forced him to stay on with SOCONY. Resigned to his role as a mid-level manager peddling lube oil to Japanese-owned factories and mills in Tsingtao, my father settled for doing his allotted job and enjoying his leisure time. Who wouldn't like coming home every afternoon for lunch with the family? And then taking a nap before heading back to work? There was never work to be brought home from the office, to boot. Often on his afternoon breaks, my father would go horseback riding. On the weekends there was socializing and golf, often with one of his major Japanese clients, Mr. Takahashi, who built the Tsingtao course. The leisurely pace of life also allowed time for my father to pen verses and make drawings of life in China, many of which were published in the *Meifoo Shield,* an informal Standard Oil journal. It was a comfortable existence, and my father took advantage of it.

I know this for a fact because when my father got wind that Standard Oil wanted to move him northward to the more industrial city of Tientsin, he enlisted me in a ploy to gain sympathy from his boss, Mr. Fred Twogood, the general manager of SOCONY in China and one of those "Colgate men." The plan was hatched when we were in California on home leave in 1935. My father decided to make a courtesy call on Mr. Twogood. At the boss's house, I was prompted by my family to tell Mr. Twogood how much I was going to miss living in Tsingtao. Sniffles and all. Mr. Twogood surely wouldn't refuse a seven-year-old boy's plea, right? That was wishful thinking. We moved to Tientsin the next year, and Mr. Twogood earned the lifelong resentment of my parents.

In later years each one of us, from my father on down to me, looked back on our years in Tsingtao as the happiest of our lives. Thereafter in China, life became more spartan. In Tientsin, we stayed in a hotel instead of renting a house in order to save money so that Frank and Jack, supplemented by scholarships and educational insurance, would be able to attend the best boarding school in the United States. That was my father's consolation for a professional career that hadn't worked out—he would send his children to the best schools he could afford.

2

ONLY A MEMORY

URING THE tumultuous summer of 1937, my family was enjoying
Dsummer vacation in Beidaihe, a popular seaside resort for foreigners on the Yellow Sea. The war was being waged all around us, but
from our protected enclave the closest we got to it was seeing Japanese
planes overhead on their way to bomb our new home, Tientsin, which
fell to the Japanese in early August. After taking Peking shortly thereafter, the Japanese set their sights on Shanghai to the south, the commercial capital of China.

In late August, Frank, now 16 years old, and Jack, who had just
turned 15, began a long journey to the United States to go to boarding
school. They left Beidaihe by train on August 17 and made an unscheduled stop in Tangku, the port city that serves Tientsin. Tangku had
been captured by the Japanese at the end of July and was bustling with
activity. They found themselves in the middle of a Japanese resupply
operation. Troop ships and armaments were arriving from Japan, and
there were Japanese soldiers everywhere. After spending one night in
the port city, Frank was relieved to get out.

The train traveled next to Tientsin. My brothers were safe there, enjoying the kind of bizarre sanctuary that foreigners had carved out for
themselves in so many cities in China. Aside from sporadic firing in the
city and food rationing in the shops of the foreign concessions, the war
had had limited effect on the foreign communities. The Western community had carefully insulated itself from the bloody conflict by insisting that the combatants conduct their battles elsewhere. In fact, during
the battle for Tientsin in late July, when French authorities in the city

learned that Japanese soldiers had shot and killed a Chinese person from a vantage point in the French concession, they refused the Japanese Army permission to cross through the French compound. Not wanting to incite Western condemnation, the Japanese dutifully obeyed and sidestepped the French concession in their military operations. For the Americans, the 15th Infantry regiment, one of the two American military forces in China, was an additional form of insurance. As a result, foreigners were able to continue to enjoy their usual summer diversions. My father, in fact, was asked by his manager in Tientsin to cut short his vacation in Beidaihe and return to Tientsin, where Standard Oil employees were working around the clock. He refused.

My brothers lodged at the Court Hotel in Tientsin for four days. They ate and slept to their hearts' content, went swimming at the country club, and caught several shows at the local theater. Only once did the sound of firing interrupt Frank and Jack's last days of summer vacation.

By mid-August the battle for Shanghai, China's leading port city, was raging. Any rules of civilized warfare were discarded. The Japanese bombed residential sections of the city, causing the deaths of hundreds of civilians, and the Chinese mounted fierce resistance, including air raids on Japanese naval ships docked outside the city. But the Chinese operations against the Japanese were characterized by folly as much as ferocity. On August 15, Chinese airplanes dropped errant payloads on the foreign concessions in Shanghai instead of on Japanese warships in the harbor, killing more than 1,100 people, including eighteen foreigners of various nationalities, and wounding another 1,400. The U.S.S. *Augusta*, which we had so often seen in Tsingtao on ceremonial visits, sailed to Shanghai to evacuate American women and children. U.S. Marines rushed ashore to help the international settlement, which held thousands of Westerners. On August 20, the chaos of war hit the *Augusta* when Chinese planes inadvertently bombed the ship. One sailor was killed and seventeen wounded. American citizens were the next victims of Chinese pilot error. The ocean liner *President Hoover* was docked at the mouth of the Yangtze River, north of Shanghai, after bringing in Marine reinforcements from Manila. It was now waiting to assist in the repatriation of American refugees from war-torn China. But on August

30, Chinese pilots mistakenly bombed the *Hoover*. Three passengers and one crewmember were killed when a bomb struck the ship's deck.

The *Hoover* limped into Kobe, Japan, where my two brothers joined hundreds of American refugees on board the ship for the trip across the Pacific. They had traveled by train up through northern China and down the Korean Peninsula and then by boat across the Sea of Japan. The President lines usually offered passengers a life of luxury with shuffleboard competitions, fine dining, and, yes, the possibility of shipboard romances. But this time my brothers found the casualties of war were being counted among the Americans. Frank wrote in a letter about an American woman on board who had lost her husband in the August 15 bombing of the foreign concession and was frantically trying to track down the whereabouts of her son at summer camp in Tsingtao.

In China, a slaughter was just beginning to take form. Japanese restraint gave way to all-out brutality in places like Nanjing. After capturing the ancient Chinese capital in early December 1937, Japanese forces went on a six-week rampage that according to Chinese and Japanese estimates left between 200,000 and 300,000 Chinese dead. I remember hearing from Standard Oil friends about something terrible happening. In fact, the Japanese armed forces used inhumane methods against the Chinese in Nanjing. Japanese soldiers tortured, raped, and executed vast numbers of Chinese in one of the bloodiest massacres in modern history.

.   .   .

We learned from a family friend that the Japanese methods in Tsingtao, my family's beloved former home, were more surreptitious and less vengeful. The Japanese had always gotten along quite well with the other foreign communities. They ran shops in the business district, and their huge cotton mills outside the city provided a major source of business for my father's company. The few Japanese soldiers in Tsingtao were friendly to American kids, and when we were living there in the 1930s, I remember them handing out candy whenever a group of us went to watch their maneuvers on the parade grounds.

Relations between the civilian Japanese and Chinese in Tsingtao had long been strained, and they deteriorated completely when war broke out in the summer of 1937. One morning during that summer, to the surprise of the Western community, the Japanese Navy evacuated the entire Japanese population of several thousand from Tsingtao back to Japan. They left vacant their electric light plant, textile mills, and shops. The Chinese stepped in to keep Tsingtao running, but soon there were rumors that the Japanese would be returning in force.

In late December, in order to hamper any Japanese occupation of the city, the Chinese authorities decided to sabotage Japanese property. A group of Chinese soldiers came to the Standard Oil offices and plunked a large bundle of bank notes on the manager's desk for a thousand cases of the highest quality kerosene. Off they headed to the textile mills. They covered the machines and looms with cotton soaked in kerosene and set fire to the mills that evening. The cotton mills' huge chimneys were dynamited at the base and collapsed in a heap. After the destruction of the textile mills, fearful of the wrath of Japan, many Chinese fled into the countryside, mostly on foot with a few pushing wheelbarrows or riding ponies.

For the first week of January 1938, Tsingtao was like a ghost town, a city living in limbo, waiting for the return of the Japanese. In the absence of law enforcement, the British established a special police force composed of European residents to keep order. Chinese petty thieves and ne'er-do-wells were rounded up and put in jail.

On January 10, the Japanese returned in force. An armada of ships arrived in Tsingtao harbor, and hundreds of Japanese planes flew escort so low that you could see the faces of the pilots if you were watching from the hills. The Japanese came marching into town, led by the recently evacuated residents, including my father's client and golfing partner, Mr. Takahashi. This leader of the Japanese community had evidently been doing work on the side for Japanese intelligence, I now realize.

But something had changed in the atmosphere, and there was little sense among the Europeans in Tsingtao of seeing old friends. In one of their first acts, the Japanese took the handful of Chinese prisoners arrested by the special police force several days earlier and shot them one at a time. Then they dumped the bodies in the street.

In his last journal entries before leaving Japan for the United States in September 1937, my brother Frank remarked on the beauty of the Japanese coast along the Inland Sea. His next recollection followed swiftly: "Soldiers everywhere." It was hard for Frank to reconcile the Japan of natural beauty, of friendly Japanese soldiers doling out candy, and of amicable Japanese businessmen in Tsingtao with the Japan of military might, colonial oppression, and brutality. Japanese national pride had somehow been turned inside out in Tsingtao itself, altered from the harmless arrogance of a Japanese sergeant striding victoriously out of the water in 1934 into the purposefulness of Mr. Takahashi walking forcefully down the road to reclaim Tsingtao in 1938.

In April 1938, the U.S. 15th Infantry pulled out of Tientsin. With fewer Americans left to protect after the evacuations, the 15th Infantry had lost its *raison d'être*. There was probably no one sadder about this than the soldiers themselves. They had to say good-bye to their Russian and Chinese girlfriends and to a life of uncommon luxury, which included cooks, maids, houseboys, a golf course, and race track. As the American soldiers passed through each concession on their farewell march, I watched the British, French, and Japanese troops lined up along the road to say farewell to them. The band was swell, but the occasion was sad.

The departure of the 15th Infantry signaled the end of an era in China. The foreign enclaves, for decades a part of the landscape in China, were coming to a close. Extraterritoriality was becoming a thing of the past. For families like my own that had grown up in the idyllic and comfortable world of legations and international concessions, something was irrevocably lost.

Back in the United States at Phillips Exeter Academy in New Hampshire, my brother Frank mourned the losses in China. He followed the war in the newspaper and on newsreels. The news came fast that fall of 1937 and winter of 1938: the battle for Shanghai, the bombing of Nanjing, and the burning of Tsingtao. In his diary Frank rued the destruction of his childhood homeland: "I suppose China will never be the same again." Yet part of him refused to believe that all he read and saw about China was true. There were too many good memories tied up in places like Tsingtao, Tientsin, and Beidaihe. "I dream about China every night, and I hate it when I wake up and find myself here. I wish I could sleep forever and dream about China," he wrote in October 1937.

The last great memory I have of Frank in China was during the summer of 1937 in Beidaihe. Always thinking outside the box, Frank hit on the challenge of swimming eight miles from the beach at Beidaihe to the industrial city of Qinhuangdao up the coast. He convinced Jack to go along with him. They started swimming at 5:45 in the morning with my father and me riding alongside in a rented sampan. Frank made it to Qinhuangdao in five hours, and Jack straggled in twenty minutes later. Everybody in Beidaihe marveled at what the young teenagers had done.

One could say that the legend of Frank Lilley was born from that eight-mile swim in July 1937. It was a legend that came back to me almost forty years later when a Chinese cadre who accompanied us in Beidaihe asked me if I had ever heard of the "great swim" by the American boys in the summer of 1937.

That swim in the peaceful waters of coastal China, isolated from nearby war, captures for me the spirit of the time my family spent in China in the 1930s. For us kids, China was filled with possibilities for interest and adventure. We took our lead from Frank, especially me, the youngest of the family. Frank's zest for life wowed us all, even my parents, and the comfort of our life in Tsingtao was fertile soil for his energy and budding idealism. During those years, my mother and father watched their eldest son outstrip all their expectations. Each time Frank amazed them with some feat of athleticism or achievement, they basked in his reflected glory.

.   .   .

In the midst of the growing turmoil in China, my father was exiled farther inland by his company. In the fall of 1939, my mother and I returned from an extended home leave and joined him at his latest post in Kiukiang on the Yangtze River. It was as if my father's career was going back to where it started—the hinterlands of China. Except that he was now a twenty-year veteran of Standard Oil.

I had just spent a year in America, in part because my parents wanted to "Americanize" their China-grown children. When my father returned to China after home leave in the summer of 1938, my mother and I, after leaving Elinore to board at Dobbs Ferry School in Tarrytown, New York, remained in the United States and rented a house on the Bush family farm in Harriman, New York, next door to where my mother grew up and forty miles from New York City. It was beautiful country of hills given to dairy farming. I was a skinny little boy who became fascinated with American baseball. I listened to the broadcasts of the New York Yankees games on the radio and followed the exploits of my favorite player Joe DiMaggio. My cousin Peter Bush and I were inseparable, dreaming baseball, playing one-on-one, and in rare instances visiting Yankee Stadium in New York to see the mighty Yanks play.

I didn't want to return to China, but return we did, my mother and I. We took the train from New York to Chicago. It passed through Harriman. My little cousin Peter Bush and his family waved flashlights and lamps on the farm as our train sped by in the night. China seemed like the other end of the earth. And it was.

Kiukiang was an ugly, forlorn city on the Yangtze River. The main part of the city consisted of a collection of two- and three-story gray cement buildings on the waterfront, called a bund, surrounded by thatched huts, which spilled down the riverbank. Japanese soldiers had torn the wooden beams out of the buildings for firewood. The foreign population in the fall of 1939 was made up of several missionaries and fewer businessmen. In contrast to the bustling SOCONY offices in Tsingtao and Tientsin, there were just two American employees in the dusty port of Kiukiang. Business was very slow. The Japanese were squeezing Standard Oil out of business. As part of their drive to control the heart of China, Japan had outposts in virtually all the small towns that dotted the Yangtze banks. My father's job was to hold the fort—to protect SOCONY properties from further encroachment—and he did his best to cultivate the resident Japanese army officer, whose troops guarded the port.

On our trip back to the U.S. in 1938, I had seen firsthand one outcome of the Japanese drive to control China. For the first leg of our journey we took a Japanese boat headed for Kobe. I remember seeing many white wooden boxes stacked up to the ceiling in the vestibule of the boat. There were 300 to 400 of them. Each was covered in white cloth and contained the ashes of a Japanese soldier who had been killed in China. A thin wooden strip attached to each box had a name, rank, and date of death written in Japanese characters.

The boxes sat in the vestibule for the whole trip. When we docked in Kobe, my mother, Elinore, and I stood perched up high at the railing of the ship, surveying the activity in the port below us. We spotted an elderly Japanese couple walking up to the boat. A Japanese military officer proceeded toward them with a box in his hands. The officer handed the box to the couple. The couple accepted the box and bowed to the officer. There were few words exchanged, and the elderly couple, presumably carrying the ashes of their son, showed no emotion as they turned to walk away.

Though I was just ten years old, that scene has stayed with me to this day: the rigidity of the ceremony, the lack of emotion, and the solemn air of acceptance on the part of the elderly couple. As a foreigner living in a China increasingly occupied by Japan, I was in a position to observe Japanese people and their customs. Like my brother Frank before me, I was both attracted and repelled by what I saw. But I came to see more clearly that there was something evil rooted in the actions of the Japanese government.

.   .   .

In Kiukiang, I used to wake up to the sounds of small Japanese tugboats and skiffs at work on the river, transporting troops and equipment to and from the Yangtze River outpost. I spent much time alone playing with my toy soldiers and concocting stories about two soldiers named Frank and Jack. The highlight of my day was playing baseball with Taki, a private in the Japanese Army who lived in the barracks next to our house. Taki was short and bow-legged, clean shaven and with a smile of gold teeth. The two of us—an American kid and a young Japanese enlisted man—would play catch in the backyard, talking little because neither of us spoke the other's language. But we had great fun, and I looked forward to every morning when I would rush outside to find Taki resting under the oak tree in our backyard, smoking a cigarette before we began our game.

Taki sometimes brought a comrade who could speak English, and the three of us would sit under the tree and talk. They always wanted to know about America. As we had just returned from a one-year home leave, I was full of stories. I would tell them of the immensity of the land and of playing games on the farm with my relatives. They, in turn, would tell me about a Japan I had never heard of—a country of gardens and parks and of happy, lazy holiday afternoons. They never talked of their life in Kiukiang. When I asked them what they did and why they were in Kiukiang, they would change the subject or become silent.

One day my parents announced to me that they would be having to tea Lieutenant Takahashi, the Japanese liaison officer in Kiukiang (no relation to my father's former golf partner in Tsingtao). My father had to deal with Lieutenant Takahashi to get business done. I can remember his face very clearly. It was thin except for a slight puffing in the cheeks and around the mouth, which gave him a perpetual pout. He wore thick, horn-rimmed glasses on a broad, flat nose.

My parents and Lieutenant Takahashi discussed various topics: the grade of pottery in the city, the prospects for next summer in the mountains, and the possibility of a cold winter. Then, after a short time looking at our photo albums of America, the lieutenant got up and remarked that it was time to leave. He thanked us for an enjoyable afternoon and turned to walk out the door. As he left, he said abruptly, "Ours is an army of discipline. There is a strong mutual respect and feeling between men and officers. No sacrifice is too great. This is what makes our army unconquerable." He then bowed and left the room. My father let go a long, low whistle in a sign of relief. My mother smiled. "It's rather strange how they act," she said. "So methodical, so polite. You can't really hate them, but the way he talked frightened me. It seems their ideas cover a lot more ground than just China alone."

Taki didn't frighten me at all. He was my best and only companion in Kiukiang. We continued to play baseball. I would hit the ball to him. He would catch it, and then we would switch. One day, as Taki darted around the backyard scooping up the ball, Lieutenant Takahashi entered our backyard and strode toward the house. But when Taki shouted to me to throw the ball, Lieutenant Takahashi spun around quickly and stared straight at him.

The lieutenant released an angry torrent of words at Taki. Taki did not waver, but I could see by his face that he was very frightened. I heard several obscene words in the lieutenant's speech, words that I had heard used by soldiers in the streets. He then began striking Taki across the face and neck with the side of his hands. These were not routine blows but powerful, hateful strokes. The lieutenant then pointed toward the gate of the compound, kicking Taki and motioning him to leave. He turned abruptly on his heels and headed for our house. As he passed me, he gave a polite smile and said, "How unfortunate such incidents have to happen before your young eyes."

I turned and walked away. I saw Taki disappear out our back gate. I suddenly felt tears well in my eyes. I did not know quite why I felt that way. Was it my anger at Takahashi or my concern for my only friend? I never saw nor heard of Taki again.

.　　　.　　　.

In January 1940, shortly after the incident with Taki and the lieutenant, I left drab, frozen Kiukiang for boarding school in Shanghai. I was put on the American gunboat U.S.S. *Luzon* for the trip down the Yangtze to Shanghai. The *Luzon* was the flagship of the Yangtze River Fleet, a detachment of three flat-bottomed U.S. Navy gunboats that patrolled the river in accordance with the remaining extraterritorial military rights that had been granted to foreigners decades before. The presence of the American gunboats on the Yangtze was by now largely symbolic, but they also served as platforms for intelligence collection.

On the ship I was doing my own sort of intelligence collecting. I would listen in on conversations and try to find out as much as I could about the sailors on board. I guess you could say I got an early start in the intelligence business. Spurred by my fascination and delight to be traveling on a gunboat of the U.S. Navy, I learned the names of the boat's American officers. There was Admiral Glassford, Marine Major McHugh, and Commander Overesch. Also on the ship was the American ambassador to China, Nelson Johnson. As we went down the river, Chinese Nationalist artillery pieces started firing at Japanese freighters sailing near us. They missed wildly, but some of the shells landed periously close to us. Several American officers in the wardroom traded comments about the Chinese forces' feeble attempt to counter the Japanese. I listened in: "A poor show put on for us," remarked one officer. Another countered, "But it's good to know they are still able to fight." A sense of pity and helplessness underscored the general feeling of the American officers. "These Chinese guerrillas really need our help, but what can we do?" concluded an American officer.

By the fall of 1940, the Americans' time in China was running short. Because of the worsening situation and the deterioration of U.S.–Japan relations, the U.S. government ordered the evacuation of all American women and children from China. After twenty-five years in China, the Lilley family was clearing out and heading back to safer shores. Within the space of four years, from 1937 to 1941, all of us would be gone from China. My brothers had sailed to the U.S. in 1937. My sister had returned to America in 1938. My mother and I finally departed China in 1940, and my father joined us in 1941.

Elinore later wrote a poem about her ship leaving China. It's a poem about the breaking of a bond. It's something we all felt in one way or another when we left our home of twenty years.

The milling Chinese on the wharf become familiar and old friends.
I can't leave them now.
Please God. Let me stay.
I'll do anything if I can only stay.
China is only a memory now.
I have left it forever. It is unreachable except in my thoughts.

China was "only a memory" in more ways than one. The country was gone from our daily living, our early days there never to be recaptured. But the country was also soon to be transformed, something I would find out in dramatic ways when my connection to China resumed a decade later.

3

AMERICANIZATION

WHEN WE returned for good from China in 1940, I entered the eighth grade at a school in Ridgewood, New Jersey, where my parents rented a house near my mother's sister. Counting the Shanghai American School and the four schools that I had attended in New York and New Jersey during our extended home leave from the summer of 1938 until the fall of 1939, it was my sixth school in two years.

The moving around took its toll. There was fleeting exposure and constant adjustment to new environments. I was new and, consequently, strange to my classmates. We came from very different backgrounds, and in an effort to conform I tried to put my childhood experiences in China behind me and become totally American. But I found it hard to make friends; I think it was in those early formative years that I became a loner. I didn't feel comfortable joining groups, nor did I feel I fit in well with the social hierarchy I encountered. Part of that hierarchy was based on how successful a boy was at popular sports. Despite my dreams to the contrary, I didn't have a future in baseball. Those other two staple sports of America, basketball and football, were new to me, and I showed little promise. I was skinny and not very well coordinated. When I despaired, I remembered my brothers telling me that losing in sports was due to a lack of confidence: "You have to think you are going to win," they would repeat to me. But I didn't have their gifts. Frank was a driven and disciplined athlete who went on to set a world record in swimming at Yale. A superb natural athlete, Jack was a three-season star at Yale in lacrosse, soccer, and swimming. Where my brothers conquered, I seemed just able to survive.

I had been reminded of my frailty during our stay on the farm in Monroe that first summer back in the U.S. in 1938. While playing with my cousin Pete Bush, I caught two terrible cases of poison ivy, including one patch around my eyes that temporarily blinded me. I had never encountered poison ivy in China and didn't have the immunity to it that my cousin seemed to have. Then one day on the farm when I was kicking the soccer ball with Frank, I put my hand up to shield my face and broke my arm for the third time, having done it twice already in China.

When I reflect back on those first uninterrupted years in the United States, I remember it as a time for my "Americanization." If I did feel a bit out of place in my new surroundings, life was, nevertheless, quiet and normal. Academically, American schools in China had prepared me well, and I excelled, though I probably came across as a bit of a nerd. We lived in a peaceful American environment, made more so because President Roosevelt seemed intent on keeping America from entering another world war. I had my passion for baseball, and I became fascinated with soap operas on the radio that would come on as 15-minute segments and had names like "The Goldbergs" and "When a Girl Marries." But, though my world was safe, it was not immune from periods of loneliness, separation, and loss.

In the winter of 1938, we learned that my paternal grandfather had died in New Jersey. I had gotten to know Grandpa Lilley when he visited us in China in 1935. He was a white-haired patrician who looked like President Roosevelt, and the Chinese had treated him with great respect because of the resemblance and because of his age. I remember that my parents let my brothers go to the funeral, but I had to stay on the farm in Monroe against my wishes, and alone. I climbed into bed on a cold winter night. Snow swirled outside the window, and as I gazed into the dark, snow-filled night, I thought an apparition was looking through the window at me. Could it be Grandpa Lilley's spirit?

Nine months later, feelings of loneliness and separation returned. One afternoon in September 1939, Frank and I were left alone on the farm in Harriman. I watched sadly as he packed up his bags and then walked down the long hill leading to Route 17 to catch a bus to take him to New York and then on to Yale University. I have learned to hate good-byes since that time long ago.

Something in these two losses—the death of my grandfather and the departure of my brother—echoed to me the plight of China, which was being chewed up in the war in Asia. And the echoes would carry forward in the coming years as Frank's life began to mirror the destruction in Asia.

·　　·　　·

I had gotten to know Frank, once again, while living on the farm. We hadn't seen much of one another since he had left for boarding school several years earlier. During the summer of 1939, I was 11, and he was 18, and we seemingly lived in completely separate worlds. But it was grand having him around. By now Frank was an angular 6'3" with a thoughtful gaze and tight smile. While I was learning all I could about baseball and the New York Yankees, Frank practiced the piano, read books by the dozen, and did the haying with Uncle Peter Bush, my cousin's father. Everyday he dove into nearby Walton Lake and swam long distances.

Frank had thrived during the two preceding years at Exeter Academy. He played center halfback on one of Exeter's finest soccer teams, but it was in swimming that he had excelled. Exeter's swimming program in those days was one of the best in the country. On a team that had some of America's most heralded schoolboy swimmers, Frank had held his own. With extraordinary competition pushing him in practice, Frank developed into a crack sprinter. In the hallowed annual meet against archrival Andover his junior year, Frank swam the anchor leg on Exeter's victorious 200-yard relay team. The relay win brought Exeter from behind to win 34–32 and garnered Frank a mention in *The New York Times*. In his senior year, Exeter trounced Andover 43–23, and Frank led the way. He won the 100- and 200-yard freestyle relay races. In the 100-yard freestyle, he equaled his school record of 55 seconds set a week earlier against the Harvard freshmen team. Jack also chipped in at this Exeter–Andover meet by swimming the freestyle leg on Exeter's victorious medley relay team. By the time he graduated from Exeter, Frank held three pool records and had been accepted by Yale, which had one of the top swimming programs in the United States.

But Frank was more than just a successful athlete. Though he was popular on the Exeter campus, he seemed wary of adulation. He observed the sniping that went on in school, particularly when it was aimed at less gifted classmates: "It makes me awful sore to hear fellows class other fellows as 'good guys' or 'shits.' Just cause a fellow isn't athletically prominent and is quiet he's called a 'shit'," Frank wrote in his diary entry for May 2, 1938.

While at Exeter, Frank took Jack under his wing. He had been watching over Jack since 1935 when they both attended boarding school in Korea. Jack had hated the Pyongyang Foreign School, especially the food, and had tried to run away, but Frank had dragged him back. From there they had gone to the Shanghai American School for a year before heading back to the U.S. for boarding school. Jack and Frank both entered Exeter in 1937, with Jack a year behind in the sophomore class. But their careers there couldn't have been more different. A mischievous personality who starred on the playing fields but not in the classroom, Jack found himself on probation in the winter of 1939 because of poor grades and arguments with teachers. With the best of intentions, Frank tried to steer Jack straight and assuage my parents' concern about their wayward middle son. We have a photo of Frank, standing erect in his Exeter swimsuit, the old-fashioned kind that looks like a wrestler's garb. He gave the picture to Jack while the two were still at Exeter, and at the bottom of the picture, in his flowing longhand, he encouraged Jack to take advantage of his days at Exeter. "Your turn is coming up this winter and I fully expect to see that 100-yds. freestyle record fall," he wrote. "Your best year at Exeter is coming up so make the best of it. Remember, don't squander your time for that is the stuff life is made of." It was sincere, with Frank sounding more like a father than a brother, but poor Jack got appendicitis that year and was knocked out of swimming.

I followed Frank and Jack to Exeter, starting as a 10th grader in the fall of 1942. Given the age difference between me and my brothers, I never overlapped with them, but I did compete in the same sports. I played center half on the soccer team and swam in the winter. Though I lagged behind my brothers in athletic ability, I was elected a captain of the 1945 swim team and helped lead it to an undefeated season, including a victory over Andover. I had a good frame, having grown to 6'3", but there were big expectations to live up to. All the while I swam at Exeter, Frank's record of 55 seconds in the 100-yard freestyle stood on the wall above the pool. During my senior year, against Andover, the team Frank had fared so well against, I took second to the Andover captain in the 100-yard freestyle. But like my brother, I swam the anchor leg in the 200-yard freestyle relay, which we won.

When judged in comparison to my brothers' more exceptional careers—Frank's achievements and Jack's troublemaking—my years at Exeter were unremarkable. I studied hard and developed into a good student. Like my classmates, I participated in the routines of prep school by joining clubs, living in a dorm, and, because of the war going on, choosing a service preference—I chose the Marines—and helping out in the local community. Because the war effort had taken much of the region's workforce, we were called upon to help local farmers gather in the apple harvest. In our dorm rooms we followed the progress of the war's battles on maps tacked to the walls.

But those "unremarkable" years at Exeter helped to give me a sense of who I was or, rather, of who I wasn't. By the end of my senior year, I set my sights on attending Yale. In my case, the apple certainly didn't fall far from the tree, and, in fact, fell right on top of the other apples. Frank had graduated Yale in 1943, and Jack received his degree in 1944. But at just 17, I felt I wasn't ready for study at a university. "If I go to college I realize I'll have to work and learn but in my present state of mind I'm not so sure I'd be willing to resign myself to that task," I wrote to my parents in January 1945. "I haven't gotten any particular objective in life as yet and have nothing towards which to work." A wanderlust was creeping in. "I'm afraid that I want to get out and do things while I'm young. Drive about the country, go to foreign parts and see for myself what goes on in the world."

Hoping that time and experience would help me mature, I opted for an Army specialized reserve training program at Clemson College in South Carolina, which combined college courses with military training. I started in the fall of 1945. In the interim between Exeter and Clemson, I took a summer job as an ordinary seaman on a SOCONY oil tanker that plied the ports of the East Coast. Part of my motivation was to get away from the cloistered, isolated life of Exeter and see how others lived and worked. It wasn't glamorous. I washed the decks and pulled shifts in the boiler room and on the bridge, but the time on the ship did allow for rubbing elbows with the first mate and discussing girls with the mess boy and cook. There was also opportunity for healthy introspection. "Figured out a guy's got to be—sincere, conscientious about everything he does, energetic, self-possessed, at ease at all times," I wrote in a diary entry for that summer. "I've sure as hell got a long way to go!"

After my stint as a deckhand, I headed up to Canada for adventure with my Exeter roommate. There I found a French Canadian girl. I must say that in these days I did manage to attract girls, and having just spent three years at an all-male school, I was very attracted to them. The French Canadian girl spoke no English, but my Exeter French paid off. At the end of the trip, for some reason, I got separated from my roommate, who had all of our money. I ended up hitchhiking all the way from Ottawa to New York City, but before I left Ottawa I read about the U.S. dropping atom bombs on Hiroshima and Nagasaki and Japan surrendering. My reaction was that I had to get to New York as soon as possible. I arrived penniless—but in time for the victory parade.

. . .

In my writing and tendency for self-appraisal, I was similar to Frank, the family's first scribe. But there were also clear differences. I could let my hair down, so to speak, while Frank seemed serious most of the time. In letter writing, while I limited my thoughts to a page or two, Frank would go on for ten. I was usually unsentimental and focused on what I was going to do. Frank used his written communications as a place to pour out his thoughts about the world and the dilemmas he faced.

One subject that consumed him was whether to join the military. For Frank, it became part of the bigger question of the state of the world, something he had become increasingly concerned about since his days at Exeter. His election as president of the Exeter class of 1939 gave him a pulpit from which to express his views. In his graduation speech, he painted a grim picture of the world on the verge of war. No doubt images of war-torn China were in his mind when he told his audience: "Is it not safe to say that the strain of national and international uncertainty, strife and disagreement upon world affairs has almost reached the breaking point? [It is] an age when men distrust each other, an age when men have no control over their desires and an age when men resort to wholesale butchery to accomplish their desires." He ended the speech on a dark note by quoting the last part of "Dover Beach" by English poet Matthew Arnold:

for the world, which seems
To lie before us like a land of dreams,
So various, so beautiful, so new,
Hath really neither joy, nor love, nor light,
Nor certitude, nor peace, nor help for pain;
And we are here as on a darkling plain
Swept with confused alarms of struggle and flight,
Where ignorant armies clash by night.

With that speech, Frank was asking himself: Would he go with the flow and serve in the armed forces or would he follow his heart? When he enrolled at Yale in the fall of 1939, Frank registered for Army ROTC (Reserve Officers' Training Course). He had a keen sense for apprehending world events, and news of the Nazi juggernaut rolling through Europe reverberated loudly around the campus. He saw no way for the U.S. to avoid entering the war. By taking a military science course for several years and participating in military drills, he would receive a reserve commission as a second lieutenant when he graduated.

But inside, my brother was deeply conflicted. The military science course didn't interest him, and he voiced grave doubts about war in his letters and diaries as the U.S. came closer to fighting the Germans. In June 1940, the newspapers carried front page coverage of the British withdrawal from Belgium. Eight hundred ships took English, Belgian, and French troops across the English Channel at Dunkirk under constant bombing and firing from the Germans. But when he read the news reports, Frank couldn't distance himself from the loss of life and pain caused by war. "The news reports are so smug and strategic; they make no mention of the horror, suffering and hell that is going on," he wrote in his diary entry of June 3, 1940. "I don't know what to think about this question of war."

Frank wanted to be a conscientious objector but doubted his ability to carry through on a commitment that went against the convention of society and his own intense ambition. It was a battleground he would revisit time and again throughout his Yale career. In his dilemma he found solace in religion, and he started to attend the meetings of Dwight Hall, Yale's on-campus Christian Association. Frank kept a Bible handy and would refer to the example of Jesus for inspiration. In a fourteen-page letter to the family on September 18, 1940, that stands as a testament to his deeply held beliefs, he wrote of the need for a change of mind in humanity: "I know you will say that it is idealistic and impractical but not until some men have the guts to stand up and even die for these ideals, as Christ did, will there ever be an end to the wars."

He put pressure on himself to be part of that change. "I shall always try to be on the side of right and truth, no matter what it costs me," he had written to my parents and me three months earlier. "Perhaps when the real showdown comes I'll chicken out and run along with the rest of the crowd although my conscience or what ever you want to call it, tells me differently; I know the survival of the fittest rule holds true with humans as well as with animals, that it's either you or the next man and that if you don't push yourself no one else will, but it seems to me that is the main trouble with the world today. If people could only be just a little more kind towards their neighbors, give them just a little more consideration, even sacrifice a little of their own pleasure for that of others and try to see the other fellow's point of vue [sic] so much of the suffering and war and hatred that is prevalent today would be wiped out."

But Frank disappointed himself when it came down to standing up for his principles. "I don't think I have the guts to remain a pacifist through the coming years," he wrote in that long September letter. "When the time comes [for me to be called into active service], I think I would take the easier course of accepting the duty regardless of my beliefs against war; so few people ever understand the case of a true and sincere conscientious objector; friends call him a coward, leaders brand him a traitor, and whether he will do any good in bringing the nation to see that war is futile is very doubtful. But I am still convinced that wars will never stop until men of high position are courageous enough to refuse to fight under any circumstances."

At the beginning of his sophomore year, Frank resolved to stay with the ROTC program at least through the spring, but his decision brought him little peace. He continued to think through all of the complicated issues regarding war and peace. A large part of him was morally opposed to war. Yet Frank was too smart and practical not to see the need for the U.S. to stop Hitler's war machine. So many young men, he thought, were being killed because of the orders of one man, Hitler. "The only sure thing today is that we better arm and arm fast. . . . It doesn't seem that a moral question exists any longer; it's merely a question of finding out how we as a nation can best save our hide," he wrote in that September letter to my parents. The two sides of Frank—the sensible student of international politics and the sensitive pacifist—clashed with one another.

.   .   .

I remember driving up from New Jersey with my parents to see Frank and Jack in New Haven on December 7, 1941. That afternoon, while I lingered outside the car, my parents talked to Frank about whether to continue in ROTC or become a conscientious objector. My father tried to persuade Frank to stay with ROTC. Frank was clearly tortured by this contradiction in himself and said he was undecided. Driving back from New Haven through the beautiful Connecticut countryside, we heard on the radio that Japan had bombed Pearl Harbor. Frank's future was then decided. He stayed in ROTC.

Frank's exuberance, a hallmark of his youth, was slipping away. Though he enjoyed success in the conventional sense almost everywhere he went, he continued to question the value and worth of accolades and whether he really deserved them. I had seen this side of him earlier. Those times when he didn't achieve success, he could be unpleasant. When he did, he was almost remorseful. At Yale, he had picked up where he had left off at Exeter. He became part of a remarkable university setting, a setting that, as one classmate has described it, exerted "an awesome, pervasive presence." It was a formal place where students wore jacket and tie to meals, classes, and even to football games. There was the solemnity of Gothic structures and the tranquility of residential colleges whose ivied walls enclosed hidden green courtyards.

One of those solemn gothic structures was Yale's gymnasium, which stood twelve stories high and towered over the campus. The swimming pool was sunk into the ground floor, and Frank spent many hours training there. He was elected captain of the freshman swimming team, which had an undefeated season in 1939–1940. Two years later he swam on a world-record-setting relay team in the 400-yard freestyle relay. Frank was one of a bevy of talented swimmers who broke every Yale swim record during this grand season and beat defending national champion Michigan to win the NCAA title. But Frank didn't give himself any credit. After helping to set the world record at the Michigan meet, he berated himself in his diary for swimming the slowest leg. In fact, Frank had so exhausted himself with worry and his Yale routine that two weeks prior to the Michigan meet he landed in the infirmary, fatigued, depressed, and unable to sleep.

Frank seemed to be reaching out in his letters. "It's a funny thing about our family," he wrote in April 1942 to Elinore, "we're all so restrained . . . we seem to be afraid to show our emotions to each other, afraid to be friends with each other, afraid of each other. A barrier exists which I think should be broken down. . . . We don't talk enough with each other and do things enough with each other . . . and reveal our inner thoughts to each other. All of us seemed to be ashamed of them, which is really very silly."

For so long Frank had been the beacon of the family, the doer, the accomplisher, the resilient one who led the way. It's as if the family didn't have the vocabulary to understand his philosophical outpourings. We were inclined to independence, and, with each one of us doing his or her own thing, hard-pressed to understand or respond to Frank's needs. We saw that he was a serious man, perhaps too serious. But outwardly he was fine. He remained active and social and helpful. In 1942, he was elected president of Dwight Hall, the Christian Association on campus, and later that year he was tapped to be a member of Yale's most prestigious secret society, Skull and Bones, an honor accorded in those days to only fifteen young men each year. Frank hoped his selection would be a boost. "It will make me less introspective . . . give me a much needed feeling of self-confidence," he confided in his diary. His code name was Eeyore, from *Winnie-the-Pooh,* and he and his fellow members wrote humorous critiques of one another and hashed out the problems of the world in their hideaway on the Yale campus.

But even as he was productive or, perhaps, because he was doing so much, Frank grew anxious that his duties were distracting him from his goal of developing himself into a less selfish person. "I am a person who only cares about beating out his fellow men. . . . I am beginning to see the futility of it all. All my life I have forced myself to do what I think I ought to do rather than what I like to do," he wrote in his diary on January 23, 1942. Two years earlier in a letter to my father, writing about his career at Exeter, Frank had expanded on the conflict within himself: "I guess I might have been called a success at Exeter," he wrote. "But in my own mind there was something vitally lacking. . . . I achieved my main aim of getting into college, but there was something terribly insincere in the way I went about it, and it bothered me. . . . I am not boasting when I say my motives would not have bothered most boys, but I've found in my experience thus far in living with myself that I tend to be an idealist and a philosopher in everything I do; for me what is important is not what I do but the way I do it. The motivating force behind my actions must be in accordance with my ideals . . . or I am not happy at all."

As a result of his brooding, Frank became more introverted, too absorbed in his problems and the problems of the world. The legendary Yale swimming coach Bob Kiphuth took to calling Frank "old philosophical, sentimental Lilley." To some of his classmates he was a model individual, an observant and aware young man, who strove to make himself a better person; others saw him as a strict, pious, and over-earnest classmate who didn't have enough fun at Yale.

As late as April 1942, Frank was still agonizing over his role in ROTC. The great crisis of conscience over military service had never been resolved in his mind. Events had just sped up. After the Japanese bombing of Pearl Harbor in December 1941 and America's subsequent declaration of war, Yale adopted a three-year degree program to help get its graduates into the armed services more quickly. Frank became caught up in the war effort and remained in ROTC despite his reservations.

In January 1943, following his accelerated graduation several weeks earlier with the Yale class of 1943, Frank went to Fort Sill, Oklahoma, to get training as a second lieutenant in the artillery. A series of military bases followed: Fort Bragg, North Carolina, back to Fort Sill, and then to Camp Mackall, North Carolina. Frank felt like a fish out of water. "English poetry doesn't help me to remember that the recoil system of the 105 mm. Howitzer is hydropneumatic, constant, long and floating piston type," he wrote to my parents in January 1943. For Frank, the routines of military life, with its rigidly controlled schedules and close living quarters, were stifling. Despite a desire to mix better with those around him, he felt ill at ease. "Here, there is little solitude—the dreamy, sensitive, romantic, non-aggressive person has no place—the work is a succession of immediate, external, 'little' things," he wrote to Elinore on September 24, 1943.

Then in May 1944, by this time commissioned a second lieutenant and qualified as a field artillery instructor, Frank was infused with a new enthusiasm when he was selected by the Army to study Chinese at the Yale Chinese Language School in New Haven. He was to be part of U.S. military assistance to the Chinese Nationalist Army under Generalissimo Chiang Kai-shek. After completion of the course in the summer of 1944, Frank did some more language training and then sailed to India in the fall of 1944. After a few weeks at an American Army base there, he went into China to work as a field artillery instructor at a training center in Yunnan Province in southwestern China.

4

AN ANGUISHED CRY

ABOUT THE TIME Frank arrived back in China in January 1945, I was signing up for military service. Though I adored Frank, I was growing up in my own way, and the ways we went about joining the armed forces highlighted our different approaches. I made my decision as a matter of fact. The war was still going on when I volunteered along with most of my Exeter classmates. To serve in the armed forces during wartime was considered a badge of honor. It was a given that we would sign up. That was it. For me, the only remaining question was which branch of the military I would be accepted into. As it turned out, I failed the physical for the Naval Air Corps because I got a case of the mumps in the spring of 1945. I then chose the Army reserve program at Clemson with high hopes of contributing to the war effort.

That effort was making good headway in both Europe and Asia. Fierce fighting spearheaded by the Normandy invasion of June 1944 was pushing the forces of the Third Reich back toward Germany. In China, with the help of Western allies, including the Americans, the Chinese were finally making some progress against the Japanese. General Claire Chennault's Flying Tigers were making air raids on Japanese positions from western China. In January 1945, American-trained Chinese troops opened up the Burma Road, permitting supplies to flow from the allies to Chinese Nationalist forces in the interior of China. Their success helped spur the opening of six military training centers in western China to help prepare the Chinese Nationalist forces to drive the Japanese from China. Frank was serving at one of those centers.

In addition to assisting the Nationalist forces, selected members of the American military in China were conducting talks with the Chinese Communists in an effort to help build a sustainable united front between Chinese Nationalists and Communists against the Japanese. Eight years after my father had witnessed the Xian Incident, efforts were still being made to bring the Chinese sides together. To this end, a group of nine U.S. military representatives, called the Dixie Mission, moved to Yenan in Shaanxi Province to hold talks with the Communist leadership in their holdout in the summer of 1944. But the possibility of a coalition was fraught with obstacles. While American military observers determined that Mao's 8th Route Army was a viable fighting force that could make a difference in the Allied war effort in China, Chiang Kai-shek refused to countenance a united front with Communists or any U.S. military hardware going to Mao Tse-tung's rival forces.

U.S. general Joseph Stilwell, as field commander of the Chinese Army in Burma, had been a strong advocate of widening the base of Chinese support in the fight to defeat the Japanese. President Roosevelt appeared to back his top general in the east when he proposed to Chiang in July that Stilwell be put in command of all China's armed forces. It was unusual because no American had ever before directly commanded the forces of an ally. But Chiang Kai-shek couldn't swallow a foreigner being in charge of China's military. In a test of wills with the Generalissimo, the American President gave in and decided to throw his weight behind Chiang, his main, though mercurial, ally in China. General Stilwell was recalled to the U.S. in October 1944. His replacement, General Albert Wedemeyer, took a much tougher position toward the Chinese Communists in Yenan.

.   .   .

The reverberations of this political infighting reached all the way to the field artillery training center (FATC) in Yunnan Province. Frank had come to western China, along with thirty other officers, hoping to energize the Nationalist war effort against the Japanese. Indeed, the training program had been instituted under the command of General Stilwell himself. At the FATC, Stilwell's crack Burma Theater Chinese troops worked as demonstrators beside the American officers. But Stilwell's departure took the wind out of the training center's sails. The planning for the center had never been ideal. It turned out the 105 mm American-made howitzers sank in the region's many rice paddies, and the small Chinese mules were not strong enough to haul the 200-pound barrel of the 75 mm howitzer. In addition, by May it appeared the Japanese war effort in China was showing cracks. Japanese troops were redeploying to defend Japan, diminishing the FATC's *raison d'être*. In June 1945, Frank complained to Elinore of nothing to do. "This theater is dead," he wrote.

In the absence of meaningful work, my brother and his colleagues took long walks in the mountains. The FATC was located in one of the most scenic areas of China, a region of lush valleys and high mountains. Oak trees grew beside banana trees. Rice paddies were cultivated at the foot of 10,000-foot-high mountains. Hot peppers grew on vines. The slow pace of work afforded my brother the chance to enjoy his exotic surroundings. "Kunming weather is the best in China . . . air is soft, flowers budding, sky clear. Last night the moonlight was so brilliant that I took my bedding to the top of a mountain behind the camp and slept there. When I awoke this morning, the sight of the whole valley met my eyes," Frank wrote to Elinore in April 1945.

The natural beauty was a good antidote to the frustration my brother was feeling. The Chinese troops at the training camp, who were mostly young conscripts from the countryside, were in poor condition—malnourished and badly treated. Many had never seen anything mechanical before, let alone a howitzer. Relations between Chinese soldiers and officers were strained. Medical care was insufficient, and dissatisfaction among the American officers was considerable. "Civil strife runs high although as yet there is no open revolution," Frank wrote in April. The soldiers "are sick, poor, undernourished and ill-clothed; they cannot fight even with our equipment for these reasons. Power, money and education are in the hands of the few. . . . The problem is political, economical, social, medical, religious and educational."

In his duties as liaison officer for a Chinese battalion, Frank ran up against lack of discipline, a corroded command structure, and unfriendly Chinese. "The Chinese battalion commander is poor—he runs around in his jeep with singsong girls and cares nothing about train-

ing," Frank wrote in July 1945. In the letter, Frank vowed he would curtail the battalion commander's escapades by cutting his gasoline al-
lowance. On another occasion, Frank and another soldier were out on
patrol when shots rang out. They jumped out of the their jeep and hid
behind it. "We came here to fight the Japanese and to help the Chinese," Frank wrote to my mother, "and the Chinese are fighting us."

During these months in Yunnan, Frank started smoking a pipe. He
would take long walks in the countryside and write in his diary for an
hour each day. He told his roommate Walt Beckjord, a fellow lieutenant, that he was seriously considering becoming a missionary after
he got out of the army.

For a further diversion, on the weekends Frank and his fellow
American officers would travel seventy miles to the provincial capital
of Kunming. Frank looked forward to these trips because of the chance
to eat better food and to see familiar faces. Many Westerners had
sought refuge in Kunming as a result of the Japanese advance into
China. When 6'3" Frank walked down the street, he invariably saw a
familiar white face. One day in early June 1945, Frank and Walt Beckjord met up with an American acquaintance of Frank's named Dick
Weigle, who was in charge of the American Field Service in Yunnan, a
humanitarian organization. Weigle invited the two young lieutenants
to a dinner that evening at the house of a well-to-do Chinese merchant. "We have this small group," Weigle explained to my brother and
Beckjord. "It is very confidential, and people will get hurt if the nationalist leaders find out. The group is preparing to call for a coalition
government to be controlled by moderates instead of the KMT [Kuo-
mintang, or Nationalists], on the one hand, or communists, on the
other hand. You are free to come if we can trust you not to talk about
it." The gathering lasted four or five hours and consisted of two American colonels and a wide array of Chinese, including two Chinese professors and a Chinese businessman from Hong Kong. My brother and
Beckjord presumed the American colonels were sympathizers with the
departed Stilwell. The Chinese cited a number of friends whom they
considered good people who had gone over to the Communist side.
They were hoping that these people, if convinced of the possibility of a
workable coalition government, would come back.

The idea of a coalition government didn't die, though my brother never went to another clandestine meeting. After the war, the Americans attempted to use General George Marshall to broker an agreement between the two warring sides in the Chinese civil war but had little success. Mistrust ran too high.

· · ·

During the summer of 1945, with the war effort winding down, Frank had applied to and was accepted by the U.S. Military Government School. He hoped to find a more constructive line of work in the army's post-war efforts to rebuild Japan. In late July he left China and headed back to America.

Frank arrived unexpectedly at my parents' apartment in New York City in August shortly after the dropping of the atom bomb on Japan. My sister opened the door of the apartment to find Frank standing there in his uniform. He was fatigued and anxious. At night he couldn't sleep. He was consumed by religion and confided that he wanted to become a minister. But his mood swings indicated someone who was torn up inside. By his own admission, worry was quickly making him an old man.

Many years later Elinore learned details that helped us to make some sense of Frank's distressed state. A close family friend named Claire Lintilhac, who had served as a missionary nurse in China in the 1920s and 1930s, told Elinore that Frank confided in her shortly after arriving back in New York from his tour of duty in China. He told Claire that he had been living in barracks that were next to a cell used to torture Communists. At night he would hear the screams of the prisoners being tortured. When Claire related the story to my sister years later, she said that Frank had told her that when he was leaving China his commanding officer had told him, "You have heard and seen nothing." Walt Beckjord later recalled hearing about Chinese Communist prisoners being tortured in a valley some distance from the FATC, but the rumors of torturing near the FATC were never substantiated.

Whatever really happened in China, Frank returned to the U.S. a distraught man. Evidently, the experience of seeing China torn apart by the war with Japan and then subject to an impending civil war took a heavy toll on him. His sensitive nature made him more prone to feeling the agony and suffering. And only now do we in his family see that his depressed state, which took root in his university years and was characterized by exuberant highs and tormenting lows, was a condition that today is treatable with medication and counseling. Unfortunately, in those days psychiatry as a medical field was still in its infancy. Indeed, the Yale University health officials who looked after Frank when he checked himself into the infirmary for exhaustion were only just beginning to recognize its importance in the assessment and treatment of students. There was not much they could do for him.

.   .   .

I remember meeting Frank in a restaurant in New York City in November 1945 after I joined the Army program at Clemson. I was impressed by his officer status, but for some reason this time I wasn't intimidated by him. We were both in uniform. I came up from behind and pulled his ears. He looked at me sadly and then reproached me, saying people would never understand an enlisted man pulling an officer's ears.

Maybe I pulled his ears because I was bored. I had arrived at the Army reserve program two months earlier and was finding out that military life didn't suit me very well. At least not peacetime service. The wars in both the European and the Pacific theaters were over by September 1945. There was no glory left to be had. Just a mediocre education and military training for a war that had ended. When I got the opportunity, I jumped at the chance to accelerate my service. After my superiors gave their assent, I quit the reserve program after four months and enlisted for a year of active duty in the U.S. Army. That way I could get to university more quickly and get the G.I. bill to cover expenses. That university would be Yale, where I had been accepted in the spring.

Sitting beside Frank at the restaurant was Nan, the love of his life. Their short time together is the stuff of romantic novels. Frank met Nan Viergutz on the train to San Francisco in September 1944. He was on his way to attend the Defense Department's Monterey Language School for extra work in Chinese before shipping out to China. Nan, just nineteen years old, was heading back to Mills College in San Francisco to continue her studies. When the train crossed the Rocky Mountains in the middle of the night, Nan developed a nosebleed. She hopped off her top bunk and walked along the narrow corridor to the ladies' room. My brother, who was standing in front of the ladies' room, asked Nan if she was all right. The two started talking and ended up spending much of the next three days together conversing on the train or strolling the platforms of the stations where the train stopped. By the time the train arrived in San Francisco, a chance meeting on the train had blossomed into a full-fledged romance. They courted in San Francisco while Frank waited on his departure papers. The young couple visited Fisherman's Wharf and looked out at the sunset over the Pacific Ocean from the Top of the Mark. A month after arriving in San Francisco, my brother proposed to Nan. He promised her that they would get married when he returned from China. "It was a fairy tale thing," Nan said years later of their meeting and courtship. "We shared the same philosophical, dream-like turn of mind."

Frank kept his promise to Nan, and they were married with little advance notice on a sunny day in mid-September 1945 in Washington, D.C. Because the wedding was held so suddenly, I was unable to get permission to leave my military unit at Clemson College.

.   .   .

For the five years of the war my father worked for the Red Cross in New York City after retiring from Standard Oil. But once the fighting ended in Asia, he was called back by Standard Oil to work on contract as a consultant in China. The company wanted him to survey the damage done to SOCONY facilities for war claims against Japan. So my mother and father arrived in Shanghai in 1946.

Although the war was over, all was not quiet in China. China had survived the Japanese occupation only to be engulfed in a civil war between the Nationalist, or Central, government led by Chiang Kai-shek, also known as the Kuomintang or KMT, and the Communists led by Mao Tse-tung. Indeed, soon after the defeat of the Japanese forces, there was a rush for control of Manchuria, which, with its heavy industrial base built up by the Japanese, was considered a key to re-

building China's economy. The Central government's forces raced to
northern China to take control of an area that had been under Japanese
rule for fourteen years. The U.S. ferried a number of these troops by
aircraft into key areas. Eager to extend their influence, the Communists infiltrated their own agents and soldiers into Manchuria with
support from the Soviet Union.

After Japan's sudden surrender, in accordance with the stipulations
of the Yalta Conference of 1945 (at which the Soviet Union agreed to
enter the war in Asia and to recognize the Nationalist government in
China in return for favorable territorial concessions), the Soviet Army
had occupied huge swaths of territory in Manchuria and taken over
North Korea, where it put its own man, Kim Il Sung, in charge. In
Manchuria, the Soviet Army sealed off Japanese factories, ostensibly
with the intention of handing them over to the Central government.
But the Soviets ended up carting much of the heavy machinery back
across the border as war booty. During this time my father was surveying Standard Oil property in Manchuria and wrote to us about the
stripping of Manchuria's industrial assets. In the industrial city of
Mukden (today's Shenyang), Red Army soldiers blasted holes in the
walls of factories to drag machinery out and load it onto trains. The
same pillaging happened all over Manchuria. Where there had once
stood a rubber processing factory or hydroelectric plant, after the Soviets were done pillaging the industrial centers of Manchuria, only shells
of buildings were left. The Soviets also refused to allow Nationalist
troops entry through the major ports of Dairen and Port Arthur. At the
same time, they let their Chinese Communist brethren slip into
Manchuria from the south.

The American military tried to get a strategic foothold in China in
order to influence the outcome. The U.S. Navy established its Western
Pacific Fleet headquarters in my old hometown of Tsingtao. In Shanghai, 13,000 U.S. sailors and soldiers arrived during the fall of 1945 to take
up new posts on the Chinese mainland. Their first task was to disarm
the one million Japanese soldiers who had been left stranded at their
posts in China when the Japanese emperor surrendered to Allied forces.
In late 1945, many Japanese soldiers were still at their battle stations in
interior China, manning radar installations or on patrol in cities.

Meanwhile, the U.S. government was engaged in a delicate game of diplomacy, trying to negotiate a coalition government between the Chinese Nationalists and Communists while still favoring the approach of the noncommunist Central government. Headed by General Marshall, the U.S.-led Truce Commission succeeded in getting the warring sides to agree to several cease-fires, but the goal of reaching a political agreement was unachievable. There was still too much mistrust between the two sides. Marshall withdrew his mission in January 1947, later declaring it impossible to arrange a peaceful solution to the Chinese civil war. Though it officially adopted a policy of noninterference, the U.S. government clearly favored Chiang Kai-shek's Nationalist government and continued to provide it with both material and political support.

On the battlefield, the Central government's forces initially held the upper hand. With U.S. support in the form of ships and planes ferrying troops to key ports and cities, the Central government extended its control throughout north China. The highpoint of the Nationalist campaign against Mao's guerrilla army came in March 1947 when the KMT forces seized the Communist capital of Yenan. But the Communists' war of attrition and guerrilla tactics eventually carried the day. In 1948, Communist forces captured the northern cities of Mukden and Changchun.

At the same time that the Chinese civil war was being waged in the north, American civilians and some soldiers were enjoying life in port cities like Shanghai and Tsingtao, which were coming back to life after their wartime hibernation. The prospect of spending time in a semi-Europeanized city with plentiful distractions in the form of Russian and Chinese girls sent many Americans on a spending spree. To catch a bit of the action, local entrepreneurs scrambled to get their businesses going again. White Russians emerged from their wartime hovels and reopened cafés on the cities' thoroughfares. Chinese-run bars opened in their old spots along the water. Within six weeks of the Japanese surrender, a stringed orchestra was playing in the lobby of the Palace Hotel in Shanghai.

Slowly, foreign businessmen returned to these cities as well. But whereas in the past Americans had had to compete with the Japanese,

British, and Germans to make money, in post-war China the American businessman was unrivalled. Americans found they had the market pretty much to themselves. The challenge of making order out of chaos, however, was a huge one. Inflation was so high that beggars in Shanghai were seen carrying wads of Chinese bank notes in their hands. On one day of routine shopping in 1948, my mother spent 38 million Chinese dollars, the equivalent of $26 U.S.

Though he had been assigned to the SOCONY Shanghai office, my father spent most of that first year in Manchuria assessing claims against the Japanese for destruction of Standard Oil property. He even earned a mention in CIA files during one trip to Manchuria. While on assignment in Mukden, he checked in with the local American military intelligence operation, which had taken over the old Standard Oil Company compound. My father apparently so impressed the American army captain with his extensive knowledge of China that his name wound up in CIA files as a possible contact. I found his name five years later when I was working at early CIA headquarters near the Reflecting Pool in downtown Washington, D.C.

My father's travels around China in the post-war period not only impressed upon him the great damage done to the country during the war, but also engendered in him sympathy for the Communists. He came to see Mao's Communists as the only force capable of ridding the country of endemic corruption and disunity. "They are disciplined and tough," my father would say. "And China needs this harsh treatment." When he would start to talk about his support of the Communists, we would jokingly call him Chairman Mao.

.   .   .

Back in the U.S., Frank tried to pull himself up. After his depressing experience in China, he put his hopes in the U.S. government's program to reconstruct Japan. He began his studies at the School of Military Government in Far Eastern Affairs in Charlottesville, Virginia, in the fall of 1945.

In Charlottesville, Frank and Nan were able to have a honeymoon of sorts. They had time to catch up, to talk about the dreams they shared, and to explore the world of ideas. On occasion, they would wake up in the middle of the night, eat oranges, and discuss things like the nature of truth, the subconscious, and values. "It was an astonishingly rarified time for me," Nan recalled years later.

But Nan noticed changes in Frank as well. He was consumed with formal religion and with becoming a minister and showed less interest in his often chaotic and uncontrolled world of ideas. It was as if he were looking for something to hold onto.

In December 1945, Frank began the long trek back to Asia, this time to Japan. But before departing from Seattle, he unexpectedly called Nan, who was back at Mills College in San Francisco, and asked her to come up to Seattle to stay with him at Fort Lewis. He needed Nan's company. They walked around the military base in the cold, gray winter weather. It was a quiet time, and Frank was subdued, but he held out hope that as soon as Nan finished her degree, she would be able to join him in Japan during the summer of 1946.

Frank arrived in Yokohama harbor on a rainy day in mid-February. He found a country under American military occupation, and he also saw firsthand the destruction wreaked on Japan by the war. Frank had long held a conflicted view of Japan. The serenity and ascetic beauty of the traditional culture was counterbalanced by the bestial nature of its military. In 1946, he encountered a Japan, both its good and bad sides, utterly destroyed by war.

From the boat, little war damage was evident, but Frank noticed that the Japanese people looked much poorer. The American soldiers on the ship threw cigarettes at the Japanese gathered on the pier until U.S. military police on shore commanded them to stop. "Once ashore," he wrote to my mother on March 5, 1946, "the bomb damage was terrific to behold—blocks and blocks with nothing but frames of buildings and usually not even that."

But the damage in Yokohama would pale in comparison to what Frank would see at his posting. He was assigned to the 76th Military Government based in Kure, a former Japanese naval base that itself was almost entirely bombed out during the war. Kure also happened to be a suburb of Hiroshima. We have a picture Frank took of Hiroshima's cityscape in 1946. Only there is no city. Just mounds and mounds of dirt and debris, and several craggy, lifeless trees, and even fewer buildings.

Frank wrote less frequently and, when he did, he expressed a sense of loneliness. He pleaded with Nan to leave school and come join him, but she chose to stay and complete her last year. Frank tried to throw himself into his work as a detachment commander. He made trips around the western tip of Honshu Island and discovered that many American soldiers and officers were supplementing their income by engaging in black market operations and then sending the money home. Worse still, it appears that some of the soldiers had forged Frank's name to get approval for money orders to wire money back to the U.S. The environment—an impoverished Japan with a wealthy American presence—was ripe for speculation, and it's no secret that American soldiers took advantage of the favorable conditions. Though his trips gave him the opportunity to see beautiful areas of Japan untouched by bombing, the cumulative effect of having to deal with black marketeering and of being in such a destroyed region of the country must have weighed heavily on my brother's already burdened mind and spirit.

On May 13, while driving to see a British sergeant, Frank seemed preoccupied to his passenger, a first sergeant in the 76th Military Government Company. Frank handled the jeep erratically, passing trucks on the wrong side of the road. While discussing details about a party he was planning for the enlisted men, Frank had to ask the British sergeant several times to repeat what he had just said. That night at his billet Frank declined to socialize with his roommates. He appeared morose and despondent, according to his roommate, and seemed "to be concentrating on some problem."

On the morning of May 14, 1946, my brother appeared at the supply room of the 76th Military Government in Kure. According to the staff sergeant working in the room, Frank seemed to be in a great hurry and looked down the whole time. He asked to check out a carbine. The staff sergeant asked Frank if he needed ammunition. Frank said, "No, I don't need any."

About three or four weeks earlier, Frank had withdrawn a carbine and six rounds of ammunition from the same staff sergeant. At that time, he had asked whether he could see a round of .45-caliber pistol ammunition as well. In his deposition, the staff sergeant recalled Frank weighing a pistol cartridge in one hand and a carbine cartridge in the other, lifting them and examining them carefully. "He seemed very quiet and thoughtful at the time," the staff sergeant wrote later.

Now, Frank had returned for a carbine. While he was walking back to his room with the carbine in one hand, he encountered the American first sergeant from the day before. Frank greeted him. "This is a beautiful morning, isn't it?" he said. As the two men exchanged small talk, Frank opened the bolt of the carbine, looked into the breech, closed it, slung the carbine over his shoulder, and walked away.

Later that morning Frank's body was discovered on a stone path in a courtyard outside his living quarters. Lying next to his body were the carbine and an empty cartridge case. A note was found in Frank's room, addressed to Nan and to my family, saying "My own selfishness has made me useless to you and society. Carry on—you've all been wonderful. Frank."

.   .   .

I was an 18-year-old private at Fort Dix in New Jersey, carrying through on my commitment to serve a year in the Army, when I found out about Frank's death. My platoon was in uniform in military formation when a Red Cross representative asked if he could see me. The man didn't say anything as we drove up to New York City to my parent's apartment on West 23rd Street. But when I entered the apartment I knew something had gone wrong. My mother was sobbing, and my brother Jack broke down as he talked on the phone. Frank had died in Japan—that was all we knew. Only later as the proceedings of the military investigation into his death were made known to us did we find out that he had ended his own life. The investigation turned up nothing untoward in his life. There was no cover-up. He had no secret sins nor private agenda.

Six days before he died, Frank gave me some advice in a letter he wrote to my mother: "I really think a year's training in the army will be fine for Jim." Though I had already been accepted into Yale, he suggested that I attend West Point. Then he connected my life to the future course of events in the world: "The world's future, it looks to me, will depend on who can most successfully use the force of arms—this is true whether you like it or not—and even so West Point's discipline is good for business. West Point has the discipline, which most of our educational institutions lack, and discipline is needed for success in any field."

In that fourteen-page philosophical treatise that he had sent to my parents in September 1940, Frank had written: "I believe that some men must be martyrs to the cause, must first rise up against the beliefs of their fellow men, must like Christ, be willing to die for their beliefs. Then and only then, it seems to me, will there be any chance of convincing the masses that war is an evil, which must be outlawed as a method of settling international disputes. I don't have the guts to do it though. I value my own life, my own future, the respect of my friends too much."

I believe that Frank, deep down inside, must have felt that he had surrendered to the material demands of the world. Here he was, a pacifist by conscience if not conviction, encouraging me to go to West Point to get a military education and accepting matter-of-factly the militarization of the world. His idealism and his pacifist leanings found no place in his final writings.

Frank had once written to my father that one of the greatest questions a man must face is determining to what extent he is going to accept his environment and to what extent he is going to combat it. That had been Frank's lifelong personal struggle, and he had never been able to resolve it.

Though we cannot make sense of such an end to a promising life, I have tried to see Frank's final action as the anguished cry of a man in a deep depression who came to believe that he had outlived his usefulness to the world. He must have felt helpless and powerless to live in the world the way it was. It was the only selfish act he ever committed.

Because of Frank's death, I wasn't sent to serve in Germany but was instead detailed to Fort Kilmer, New Jersey, so that I could be near my parents. I was no longer "Little Jimmy" but a young man starting to make his way in the world. Frank's death was a deep hurt, but I didn't speak of it much and instead went forward with my life. I guess you could say that I internalized his death while at the same time trying to draw lessons from it. Frank became a compass for me, and I would often reread his diaries and letters in the coming years. One lesson that I drew from his death was that it was dangerous to get too attached, too emotional, or too aspiring. Frank had been a dreamer, pacifist, and philosopher who had felt deeply and who had died young. I developed differently, eschewing romanticism and excessive emotion and inclined to deal with facts and forces as they presented themselves. I felt it was important to stay away from disillusionment.

I said good-bye to Frank, at least in a formal sense, on October 5, 1947, during my first fall at Yale. That was the date when Yale held a memorial service for Frank and fifteen other graduates who had served as deacons while at Yale. The men were being honored posthumously for their service to the country in the Second World War. The service was held in Yale's Battell Chapel, a Gothic structure in the center of campus. Elinore and her husband, Bill Washburn, a good friend of Frank's from Yale whom she had married in July 1945, drove down from Boston to attend the ceremony. The Battell Chapel Choir sang two anthems, and on display were a new altar and stalls, both part of the dedication of the chapel's apse to the memory of the men. "The service was a fine one, wonderful music and appropriate to the circumstances," I wrote to my parents later. Then, with one eye focused on taking advantage of my time at Yale and the other trained on a fast-changing situation in the world, I carried on as best I could with my life just as Frank had asked us all to do.

II

INTELLIGENCE OFFICER IN ACTION

1948–1968

5

A READY RECRUIT

FOR THE SUMMER of 1950 I took a job on a farm in Rushford, Minnesota, to get in shape for my last season of soccer at Yale. I spent the long summer days weeding corn, harvesting hay, and mending fences. On the morning of June 25, I was working in a cornfield when the farmer who had hired me drove by on a tractor. "There is a war on in Korea," he shouted to me. "It broke out today." The news of that far-away war changed the direction of my life or, rather, returned me to a predestined course of action. From my location in a small town in the heartland of America, I felt the forces of history pull me back to Asia.

I had started at Yale three years earlier in February 1947. Like a good number of students in those post-war years, I came to university on the GI bill. Yale was more than a welcome change from the stultifying life of a soldier during peacetime. Walking among those massive Gothic buildings—the great Sterling Library and the cathedral-like Payne and Whitney gymnasium—was exhilarating. I jumped back into sports and took a wide array of courses, including American history, English, religion, and science classes. Plus, I was finding that being an older student had its advantage. I was no longer an enlisted soldier but a Yale student. Girls whom I hadn't heard from for a year started to write again.

My first year I swam on the freshman team and set my sights on making the varsity the next year. Bob Kiphuth, who had coached both Frank and Jack on Yale's storied 1942 National Championship team, was still at the helm of the university's vaunted swimming program. Knowing that I would have to work hard to make the team, I dove into

Kiphuth's weight-training program in the spring and took a summer job as a lifeguard at Black Point, Connecticut, where I swam everyday. But my hopes for swimming were set back the next fall when, as a member of Yale's freshman soccer team, I tore up my right knee in a game against, of all teams, my alma mater, Exeter. I had an operation to remove the damaged cartilage and missed the swimming season. It was the first of two knee operations I would have at Yale. My junior year in a game against West Point I injured my left knee. It, too, had to be operated on. (I eventually left Yale shakier on my limbs, with matching half-moon scars on both knees running from my lower thighs to upper shins.)

By training hard and strengthening my knees on the farm in Minnesota, I was able to make it through my senior soccer season. My teammates seem to have recognized my three-year struggle with injuries because they elected me captain of the team for my senior year. We had an excellent season, finishing 9–2–1 and winning the Big Three crown by defeating Harvard and Princeton and then the New England Championship at the end of the season. I was cited for my "full time yeoman service" to the team. My play wasn't overwhelming. As center forward, I scored just one goal, but I did stay healthy. For being Big Three champions, we each got a gold soccer ball memento. Mine would come in handy in a couple of years.

China didn't engage me much during those first years at Yale. In fact, buoyed by the end of the war and an interest in Russian literature, I had veered toward things Russian. I started studying Russian in my first year at Yale, believing that if America wanted peace, it needed to understand the Soviet Union, which was a prominent member of the UN and the main competitor to the U.S. on the global stage.

China had fallen off my radar screen, although my parents had written me from Shanghai about the deteriorating situation through 1948—when they returned to the U.S. Indeed, I had turned down a chance to join them after my first semester at Yale. The country had continued to suffer through its post-war period of tumultuous change, which culminated in 1949 when Mao Tse-tung and the Communists swept to power and established the People's Republic of China. News of the fall of my "hometown" of Tsingtao came in June 1949 when I was at Air Force ROTC summer camp in New York State. Tsingtao's fall would prove to be one of the final nails in the coffin of Chiang Kai-shek's Kuomintang forces after the Communist takeover of Shanghai, Tientsin, Peking, and Nanjing earlier in 1949. In the months leading up to Tsingtao's capitulation, while Communist forces closed in on the port city, the U.S. Navy waited off the coast, ready to assist in the evacuation of Americans but resigned, along with the rest of the U.S. government, to the eventual victory of the Communists. By the time Mao's forces were at the city gates, KMT supporters, government employees, and army personnel had already fled the city by boat or defected to the Communist side. Many headed south for Taiwan, where Chiang Kai-shek reestablished the Republic of China at the end of 1949.

But the import of those events in China didn't register with me until that summer day on the farm in Minnesota. "Maybe this will push the price of grain up," the farmer had said to me at lunch later that day. But I was too caught up in my own thoughts to think about the price of grain. Asia, the continent I was born on, was once again caught up in conflict. The world was dividing into two camps: the Soviet-led communist bloc and the U.S.-led democratic grouping of nations. I wondered what the outbreak of war between communist North Korea and Western-oriented South Korea would mean. Where would China fit into this puzzle of international relations?

I came back to the Yale campus that fall determined to learn more about Communist China's role in the world. Though I stayed with my declared major in English and Russian literature, I switched my focus to Asia in my senior year. I read Edgar Snow's book *Red Star Over China*, which was a sympathetic portrayal of the Communists, and I remembered my father's favorable view of Mao Tse-tung and the Communists. They were agrarian reformers with support from the long-oppressed peasantry, he had insisted. Those "liberal" assessments of the Chinese Communists clashed with the point of view I heard in a class called "China Among the Powers" taught by David Nelson Rowe. A supporter of the Republic of China on Taiwan, Professor Rowe made no bones about his squabbles with the so-called liberals up the road at Harvard, who were viewed as favoring the People's Republic of

China. In his lectures Rowe attacked scholars like John K. Fairbank and Edwin Reischauer for their positive view of the Communists as a force that China needed. With their contrasting opinions on China, Rowe and Fairbank not only stoked the Yale–Harvard rivalry, but also, and more importantly, staked out early ground in the debate over China policy that continues today.

I didn't know much about Communism, but I knew its adherents were opposed to America's power and ideals. That belief was hammered home for me when swarms of Chinese infantry stormed across the Yalu River separating China and North Korea in October 1950 and sent UN forces, which had entered on the side of South Korea, retreating southward across the 38th parallel dividing the two Koreas. The U.S., which made up the bulk of the UN forces, and China were now at war on the Korean Peninsula.

But not every member of the senior class on the Yale campus that fall was caught up in thinking about a new world war with China. Most of my colleagues didn't want to countenance another war so soon after the last one had ended and preferred to concentrate on enjoying their final year at college. An entry in our 1951 classbook puts it simply: "The world situation that fall, headlines to the contrary, was still a matter of little importance." This was written, incidentally, by my classmate Peter Braestrup, who was later wounded in Korea while serving as a Marine officer and then became one of the preeminent war correspondents of our time while working for *Time*, the *New York Times*, and the *Washington Post*. About the class of 1951's ambivalence toward the breakout of the Korean War and mixed feelings toward the likelihood of military service for graduates, Braestrup wrote, "We were the class of '42, only we had had no Pearl Harbor, and God no longer seemed to be a co-pilot."

I, however, felt compelled to try to make a difference.

.   .   .

By the 1950s, Yale had had a long association with U.S. government intelligence collection. After all, Nathan Hale ("I regret that I have but one life to give for my country.") was Yale's first unsuccessful spy. Because of their high intellectual caliber and language abilities, Yale graduates were considered attractive candidates for intelligence work. Yale had played a part in the formation in 1942 of the Office of Strategic Services (OSS), which was created to carry out intelligence gathering and paramilitary operations against Germany and Japan. From Yale's class of 1943 alone, Frank's class, at least forty-two young men had entered intelligence work, with most going to the OSS. Many of these men stayed on after the war and helped form the core of the new Central Intelligence Agency, which took over the duties of the OSS in 1947.

The connection between Yale and the new CIA started at the top. Yale's president for most of the time I was there, Charles Seymour, was on close terms with Allen Dulles, a top OSS official in World War II and after 1953 the head of the CIA. Seymour's daughter actually worked for the OSS in Europe during the war. During my time at Yale, recruiters on campus for the CIA included the varsity crew coach as well as eminent professors.

One of those professors invited me to see him on a fall day in 1950. He ushered me to sit down in his dark, wood-paneled study. It was late afternoon, and the room was in shadows. The walls of the study were lined with leather-backed volumes on Renaissance history, the Chinese classics, and English literature. The professor smoked a pipe. Between puffs, he made his pitch. Even though I barely knew who he was, he clearly knew of me and what I had been doing at Yale. "You were born in China. Your family saw the collapse of China," he started out. "And here at Yale you are a Russian major?" he asked quizzically. He tried to dissuade me from a career in the diplomatic service or corporate world by mentioning that I hadn't taken any business or accounting courses at Yale. The State Department, he told me, was stuck in cement. "Look at what you are interested in and consider intelligence. It's a growth industry." He then talked about the crucial role intelligence had played in past wars and the exciting nature of the work. He explained that people were needed who had been exposed to foreign environments. I was sold even before he got to my personal qualities. "Besides," he added, "You are a leader. As captain, you turned the soccer team around."

Like so many of my fellow students at Yale, including an English major and wrestler from Wallingford, Connecticut, named Jack

Downey and a sophomore from South Bend, Indiana, named George Witwer, I was excited by the prospect of an adventurous career and by the idea that I could contribute to efforts to stem the tide of communism. It was a good cause, and I believed that the United States and its values were worth fighting for. In the foreword of that same 1951 classbook in which Peter Braestrup gave voice to ambivalence on campus was a chilling sentence: "We face the realization that the very civilization we have trained ourselves to foster has been placed on the verge of destruction. The challenge to each of us as individuals cannot be overemphasized." I quickly signed up for the CIA. So did about a hundred of my classmates.

.   .   .

At Yale, I was reminded often of my brothers and their time there. Coaches remembered both Frank and Jack, especially Kiphuth. The record plaque at the pool in the Paine Whitney gymnasium still featured the world record of 3:26.6 in the 400-yard freestyle relay that Frank helped to set along with Dick Kelly, Ed Pope, and Howie Johnson in 1942. I walked the same campus paths my brothers had and studied with some of the same professors. But the most vivid reminder I had of Frank in those days was the toll that his death was taking on my family.

My father became even more removed and introspective after Frank's death. He felt he had let Frank down by not communicating more, especially during those difficult years when Frank was so confused about military service. My father spent a good deal of time in his remaining years—he died of a heart attack in 1961—thinking about what he could have done differently and trying to reconcile himself to the loss of his eldest son. He was wracked by guilt over not sensing Frank's desperate, depressed state: if only he had been more supportive of Frank's faith in Christianity, from which sprung, my father believed, Frank's pacifist beliefs.

On July 4, 1946, just seven weeks after Frank's death, my father had found himself on business in Tientsin. But he quit the city and retreated to Beidaihe, the beach resort on the coast where my family had spent our summer vacation in the fateful year of 1937. My father seemed to be looking for some solitude away from the big celebrations, which would go on in Tientsin. The nature of Frank's death was very much on his mind. "If I had been more understanding at that point, I might have helped him in his most crucial moment. My heart aches terribly," he wrote to the family from Beidaihe. "There were times when I was silent when we might have opened our hearts to each other." He continued: "His last prayer was most likely for forgiveness. In that last prayer he asked that we bear our grief with fortitude and humble pride. That we fulfill our various missions in life in the best tradition, and, if by his example, we are inspired to better things, he will not have died in vain."

Perhaps my father chose to visit Beidaihe precisely because it reminded him of Frank. "I'm going down for a swim now," he closed out his letter about Frank. "To the sea he loved and where he spent many happy, youthful hours."

With the death of Frank, my mother lost the greatest love of her life. After my father died, she lived alone in Del Ray Beach, Florida, before moving north to stay in Washington, D.C., and later Andover, Massachusetts, where she died in 1983 at the age of 89. Occasionally, she would pull out old letters, many of them the ones Frank had sent to her and my father when he was at boarding school, Yale, or in the Army. One Sunday in 1974, in the course of packing to move into a new apartment, she found Frank's letters in a pile of boxes near her front door. She stopped to reread them. "Life was not the same after he left us. It seems sometimes like a dream. Please keep the letters together and read snatches slowly," she wrote to us.

Notwithstanding the toll Frank's death took on my parents, it may have sidetracked my brother Jack for life. He was probably the one who was affected most by the loss and attempted to show it the least. From that summer day in 1937 when Frank and Jack swam the eight miles to Qinhuangdao and on to Exeter and Yale, Jack strove to keep up with Frank in sports. In other ways he set himself apart from Frank, particularly in his indifference to studying and his penchant for pranks. Frank may have helped Jack from getting kicked out of both Exeter and Yale, but that assistance might also have prevented Jack from learning lessons on his own. In retrospect, Jack didn't have much of an opportunity to shape his own life. Frank convinced him to go to Yale when he probably would have been better off at a different school, like Princeton, where he could have made his own mark and been with many of his Exeter friends. Then, when Jack wanted to leave Yale sooner to become a pilot during World War II, my father dissuaded him. As a result, Jack never saw combat as a Marine pilot. A few years later, when he wanted to fly for General Claire Chennault's airline, Civil Air Transport, my father again intervened and persuaded him not to leave his job at Standard Oil.

Jack was the kind of guy who compelled people to take notice when he walked into a room. In his prime, he was 6'2", broad-chested, and handsome with dark eyes, dark curly hair, and a gentle smile. Some people said he could have been a double for the film star Tyrone Power. At Yale, he became an all-American in soccer and all-Northern in lacrosse. Jack was a natural, but he was also impulsive. That impulsiveness carried over into his personal life. During my senior year at Yale, he was in a rush to get married while on home leave from his work for Standard Oil in the Philippines. He found a girl—in fact, an old girlfriend of mine—and married her in three months. I remember this well because at the last minute he asked me to be his best man for his wedding, which was on the same day in the fall of 1950 that the Yale soccer team was scheduled to play against the University of Pennsylvania. I was torn between my commitments, but ultimately chose to honor Jack's request. Yale lost the game, one of our two losses that year, and Jack divorced the woman seven years later.

In post-war China in the late 1940s, Jack had lived it up. Like many other American bachelors in Shanghai, he acquired a Russian girlfriend. To my mother's horror, incidentally. He was one of those American ex-servicemen, young and ready to fight, who had come to chaotic China. Jack developed a reputation as a hard-drinking brawler. In tribute to his pugnacity, he became known in Chinese cities as "the black Irishman."

One night in Wuhan in 1948, Jack's willingness to fight landed him in trouble. In a nasty bar fight he punched a Chinese man and sent him tumbling down a flight of stairs. He had to leave China shortly thereafter.

After continuing his career with Standard Oil in the Philippines, Hong Kong, and Vietnam, Jack was transferred to Colombia, where he ended up living for thirty years. He had five children by two marriages, but professionally he never really succeeded. Jack and his second wife Ellen returned to the U.S. in 2001. In 2002, suffering from the effects of dementia, a form of Alzheimers, and other ailments, he entered a Veterans Administration hospital in Fayetteville, North Carolina. The last time I saw him in November 2002, I think he recognized me, but his mind was almost gone. But when I showed him an album of old pictures, he saw our home in Tsingtao—and said "Tsingtao." Jack passed away at the age of 80 in the early morning of January 1, 2003. He lives on in his children.

Perhaps Jack and Frank are back together now after fifty-seven years, looking down on us. I like to think of them as young and agile, swimming or playing soccer. Frank is straining with effort. Jack is the natural one.

.   .   .

My entry class at the CIA was made up of graduate students, medical doctors, former war pilots, and young college students looking for adventure. I met one of those college kids, fellow Yale student George Witwer, early on during training, and we ended up getting an apartment together in Arlington, Virginia. George and I and the rest of our class spent the summer of 1951 learning CIA tradecraft in a Washington setting. It was a bizarre mix, and I'm still not sure what I took away from the training.

One particular task had us in Georgetown, then in neighborhoods predominantly African American, "casing" the area. We were told to describe the flavor of the area and what kinds of people lived there. I wonder what the black residents thought when they saw white guys in khakis and collared shirts snooping around. I say snooping because, as intelligence officers in training, our instructions were to find potential safe houses (where we could meet with agents), report on dead-drop sights (where material could be deposited for later pick-up), work on signaling with hypothetical agents, and identify escape routes. We had little sense what we were doing and ended up detailing a long list of irrelevant facts.

In retrospect, I see now that one of my more useful intelligence tools was in my suitcase when I arrived from New Haven. That was my United States Air Force (USAF) uniform. Having gone through the reserve officers training program at Yale, I had been commissioned in June 1950 as a second lieutenant in the USAF. So I was legitimately in the service, and that uniform would help to create a cover for my work as an intelligence officer in the coming years. In war situations, you get better access, run fewer risks, and accomplish more when you wear an officer's uniform.

Fortunately, the whole summer wasn't spent casing Georgetown and listening to dreary lectures. There was ample time to enjoy life in the nation's capital, and George Witwer turned out to be a good companion. The only son of a successful insurance executive, George had come east for boarding school and college, but he retained a Midwestern manner. He was soft-spoken, energetic, and had a love for cars. Actually, George loved all sorts of machines, and he was usually fiddling with the latest model camera. At Yale, he was on the *Yale Daily News*. But restless and with a desire to do something patriotic for his country, George dropped out of Yale during his sophomore year. He came to Washington without a job and ended up staying for a short while in the spare bedroom of friends of his parents, the Booths, who had a house in Arlington.

Like many American families in those days, the Booths had been caught up in the war effort. The former manager of a travel agency, Waller Booth had joined the OSS at its inception and during World War II had worked behind German lines in Spain, North Africa, and France, where his exploits included parachuting into German-occupied France and getting 800 Ukrainian soldiers fighting for the Nazis to defect to the Allied side. When the Korean War broke out, then Lt. Colonel Booth left civilian life once again. Working for the CIA in Korea, he infiltrated into North Korea by boat, landing on an island in Wonsan Bay. There, he planned escape routes for American soldiers taken prisoner when the Chinese swept across the Yalu River in November 1950. Wally Booth was an authentic hero.

Waller Booth also happened to have two very attractive daughters, Lee and Sally, whom he didn't get to see often. So when he received orders to go to Korea in late April 1951, his youngest daughter, Sally, a senior at The Baldwin School in Bryn Mawr, Pennsylvania, came down to say good-bye. Sally was a vivacious beauty, who happened to have no plans that Saturday evening, so George invited her to come to a party.

Sally and I met at the party. However, with an age difference of five years between us, neither of us dwelled long on that first acquaintance. But the wheels were in motion for the start of not one but two relationships. Not long after, George spotted a picture of Sally's older sister, Lee, on a bureau at the Booth residence and was smitten. And while destiny had a Booth girl in store for each of us, both George and I were having too much fun to think exclusively of the two sisters at that point.

George and I were "gentlemen on a spree" that spring of 1951. He had an MG sports car, and we covered the town. We watched French movies, listened to the latest songs, and went to parties. Our CIA tradecraft even came in handy. One thing we enjoyed about training were the cover stories we came up with to mask our identities. We were not CIA officers but Department of Defense officials or foreign service reserve officers working for the State Department. So, in order to spice up conversations with young women, George and I made up a character named Jack Larimore. Jack did special assignment work for the American president. He was a James Bond figure, a devilishly handsome linguist who carried out secret missions in the Soviet Union and China. And we were terribly jealous of him. In front of girls we were trying to impress, George and I would have fake arguments over which of Jack's exploits in Russia and China were true and which were only rumors. The CIA secretaries we dated were probably onto our wild stories, but they played along for the benefit of pulling the legs of the more naïve and trusting girls in our social network.

When summer rolled around, we remembered the Booth sisters over in Arlington. The problem was that Lee, then at Smith College, was engaged to a fellow at Harvard Law School, and George would soon be headed overseas for a posting in Vietnam. He feared he would lose any chance at Lee. We had to call on our intelligence backgrounds once more. George's first scheme was to use my acquaintance with Sally to find out if Lee was even interested in him. I was to be his "principal agent" and report back. But I failed because when I returned from a date with Sally, I had lots of information about Sally but not much about Lee. The clock was ticking for George.

So George launched scheme number two. "Listen, Jim," he said, "I know that as your case officer I shouldn't get too close to our target, but this is an emergency. You bring Sally out of her parents' house and set her on the brick wall of their driveway. I will be lying on the floor of the car so I can hear your conversation. Leave your cigarettes in the glove compartment, and every so often go over and open it to get a cigarette. I'll leave notes suggesting that you follow up on this or that."

The covert operation worked, and Lee fell for George. She broke off her engagement, and in October, just six months after George saw the photograph of Lee on the dresser, the two of them were married. I think Jack Larimore was invited to the wedding, but he couldn't make it because he was on some secret mission in Siberia. But, alas, George would never have a chance to rival Jack. While George's marriage to Lee signaled a start to his wedded life, it also marked the end of his career as an intelligence officer. The CIA wanted unmarried officers for certain jobs. Slated to go to Hanoi, George instead took Lee to New Haven, where he resumed his studies at Yale and then began a career in journalism.

George likes to joke that his "principal agent" performed miserably in the early attempts to woo Lee. I may well have disregarded my case officer's instructions, but I had an excuse: I had fallen in love as well. My relationship with Sally blossomed that summer. We took walks in the moonlight in Arlington and enjoyed the popular musicals of the day, particularly *The King and I*. Unlike George, though, I wasn't ready to get married. I stayed single and received orders to depart for Japan in November. Sally, then a freshman at Smith, came down to say goodbye to me in New York. As a token by which to remember me, I gave her the gold soccer ball I got at Yale for being a member of the 1951 Big Three champions. We would not see each other again for more than two years.

6

A COVERT FOOT SOLDIER

O N NOVEMBER 7, 1951, I stepped off a Pan Am Strato-Cruiser at Haneda Airport in Tokyo. I was 23 years old and ready to begin work as an undercover officer for the CIA. As we came down the ramp, American crewmen from a group of B-29s lined up on the runway gave us a mocking hitchhiker's thumb—they wanted to get on our plane and catch a ride back home to the U.S. Instead, they were heading to drop their payloads on North Korea.

Asia was in turmoil when I arrived in 1951. I understand now that as I descended from the plane in Tokyo, Frank's words to me in 1946 about the world's future depending on "who can most successfully use the force of arms" were coming true. The Chinese Communists had defeated the U.S.-backed Nationalists in part because they understood better how to motivate the peasants and fight a guerrilla war. War was now raging in Korea, where U.S. and South Korean forces were still battling the Chinese and North Koreans for control of the Korean Peninsula, and in other parts of Asia Communist insurgencies were gaining traction among the underprivileged populations of ex-colonial nations. The French were losing ground in Vietnam; British-ruled Malaya was facing a powerful Communist insurgency; and Indonesia's Dutch masters were on their way out. In the Philippines, America's "showcase for democracy," the government was under attack by the Communist Hukbalahap, indigenous groups of Filipinos who were originally organized to fight the Japanese in World War II. Frank's words also echoed halfway across the world in Europe, where the Iron Curtain had been lowered, separating the democratic Western world from the Communist Soviet bloc.

Stepping off the plane, I was now a foot soldier in America's covert efforts to keep Asia from being dominated by Communist China, an enigma to the U.S. since Mao Tse-tung and the Communists had taken power in 1949 and shut China's doors to much of the outside world. While those crewmen in the B-29s were using bombs to fight the Chinese in North Korea, my weapons would be radio intercepts, secret agents, and liaisons with foreign powers. To enable me to carry out my underground activities, I was given a cover job in the U.S. Air Force while in the war zone in Korea. At other times, I posed as a civilian employee of the Department of the Army.

CIA covert operations against China in the early 1950s were three-pronged. The first prong called for the U.S. to support a purported 1.6 million Kuomintang guerrillas left stranded in mainland China or on its fringes after the Communist victory. This operation was largely carried out in cooperation with Taiwan's intelligence services. The second prong was a so-called "Chinese Third Force" of former Nationalist officers. This group, which professed loyalty to neither Chiang Kai-shek nor Mao Tse-tung, was being trained on the islands of Saipan and Okinawa for eventual reinsertion back into mainland China with the hopes of inciting a popular revolt against Mao's government. Finally, the third prong of CIA policy was to undertake unilateral (as opposed to working with intelligence agencies of other countries, namely, Taiwan) clandestine intelligence gathering on the People's Republic of China. Since the Chinese Communists had destroyed much of the KMT's equipment and uncovered the majority of its agents, there was precious little information coming out of China. The CIA proposed to use communications intercepts, air reconnaissance, and human agents to redress the problem.

Until the outbreak of the Korean War, the Truman administration had taken a mostly "hands-off" policy regarding Taiwan. Both the State Department and CIA had predicted that Taiwan would be seized by Communist China by the end of 1950. Still smarting from the KMT's collapse in the Chinese civil war, the Truman administration was reluctant to provide substantial aid to the island nation. And the U.S. government had no intention of helping Taiwan militarily. President Truman had reiterated the government's position that U.S. forces would not be used to defend Taiwan. Taiwan, the president implied, lay outside America's security perimeter in Asia.

But the start of the Korean War radically altered America's position vis-à-vis Taiwan. Communist plans for control of Asia had to be thwarted, Truman reasoned. He committed the U.S. to assist South Korea, and, in a move that showed the administration's determination to defend Taiwan, he instructed the U.S. 7th Fleet to dispatch naval forces into the Taiwan Strait. This decision gave new life to Chiang Kai-shek's tenure on Taiwan. There was increased military support for the island nation, and covert activities directed against China got a shot in the arm. The CIA started to receive virtually unlimited funding for its collaborative efforts with Taiwan's intelligence and special operations units. As the war in Korea progressed, Taiwan became the principal base for launching clandestine military operations against mainland China. The hope was that robust clandestine efforts would sap China's resources and force it to divert manpower from the war in Korea.

I was slated to participate in the third prong of intelligence activity by going into paramilitary operations in Korea, but I got a rude awakening while still in Japan when a Chinese American doctor took a look at my knees and told me that paramilitary activity, which included parachute training, was not an option. My superiors then decided to move me to Taiwan to take advantage of my limited Chinese-language ability. "But you were born and raised in China," they protested. Yes, I was, but that just meant that I could speak Chinese like a four-year-old. I had mastered the vocabulary to count, eat, swear, and defecate.

In May 1952, after a few months of managing a translation unit staffed with Chinese men and women in Yokosuka, Japan, I was transferred to a small intelligence unit on Taiwan to help with the training and insertion of intelligence agents into China. Our CIA unit in Taiwan had connections with Taiwan intelligence, which was known as the Pao Mi Chu (PMC) and headed by General Mao Jen-feng, who had succeeded Tai Li, the legendary intelligence chief for the Nationalists in mainland China who had been mysteriously killed in an airplane crash on the mainland in 1947. Our immediate contact in Taiwan was Eddie Liu, the interpreter for Tai Li and Mao Jen-feng, who had helped to organize a joint Taiwan–U.S. office to run intelligence operations against the mainland. I worked closely with the PMC not only to select the agents but also to plan the missions.

For much of my time on Taiwan, I worked with David Semmes, a Princeton graduate, who was an excellent case officer. Semmes, who had two more years of experience than I had, was thorough and disciplined. He had dropped agents into North Korea in 1950 and had accompanied bombing missions over North Korea. During this period, he nearly died of encephalitis.

My first task was to prepare a team of Chinese agents from Taiwan for an airdrop into Manchuria. We selected two men in their twenties who were originally from northern China. A similar team had fallen apart at the last minute the previous fall when one member refused to parachute out of the plane. Working with Taiwan intelligence, we replaced the reluctant agent with a hardened peasant who couldn't wait to go on the mission. I then retrained the team and accompanied them through Tokyo to Seoul. To make sure there was no evidence of American participation in the covert action should the team be caught, we recruited foreign pilots to ferry the Chinese agents from Seoul into China on C-47 transport planes. In accordance with instructions, I stayed on the ground in Seoul.

After a first mission was aborted because the aircraft ferrying them missed the drop zone by more than a hundred miles, my team successfully parachuted into Manchuria in October 1952. With the war on the Korean Peninsula still under way, we hoped they would be able to give us helpful information on Chinese troop movements on the Chinese–Korean border. They came up once on the radio, and then we never heard from them again. We guessed they assimilated into Chinese society or had been caught.

.   .   .

During the fall of 1952 on one of my training trips to Tokyo, I ran into my old classmate from Yale, Jack Downey, who was doing similar work with the Third Force of former Nationalist officers. Downey was working with another CIA paramilitary specialist named Dick Fecteau. A month after my mission infiltrated into Manchuria, Downey and Fecteau sent their agents up in a plane. Their agents' main mission was to make contact with a dissident general and send back reports on the strength and movement of Chinese forces. The nine agents parachuted into Manchuria and were captured almost immediately. One broke down under interrogation. The agent then agreed to radio back to Seoul to request that the CIA plane return to bring him back. Downey and Fecteau and two American pilots took off to rescue the agent. When the Americans neared the drop zone and swooped to make the agent pickup with a scooping contraption consisting of a pole extending from the door of the plane, Chinese Communist military forces waiting in ambush shot the plane down. The two American pilots died in the crash, and after a hail of gunfire, Downey and Fecteau were captured. At the CIA units in Japan and Taiwan, we knew we had lost the plane, and we assumed the worst about the four Americans. Several months later, the CIA informed the families of Downey and Fecteau that their sons were missing and presumed dead in the crash of a flight from Japan to Korea.

But the Chinese had other ideas about what they would do with the two CIA agents. For them, the capture of the Americans was a propaganda coup that they intended to exploit in this era of hostility between the two countries. After holding the Americans in solitary confinement for two years, during which time they were subjected to forceful and repeated interrogations, the Chinese put the men on trial for the world to see. At the show trial, Downey was characterized as "the arch criminal of all U.S. prisoners." The Chinese sentenced Fecteau to twenty years in prison. Downey received life in prison for espionage.

Downey and Fecteau's capture was one of the most glaring examples of the CIA's failed covert policy against China in the early 1950s. Shortly after the two CIA officers were lost in Manchuria, those of us working clandestinely in Asia recognized that covert operations, including missions like Downey's into China, were not revealing much about the closed-off Middle Kingdom. Contrary to CIA predictions, our missions were unable to locate or exploit the kind of discontent among the Chinese population that could be used to establish intelligence bases in China. The Chinese were not willing to side with outside forces. The missions were also costing a lot of money.

The two other prongs of the covert policy didn't fare much better.

The mission to train Chinese guerrillas on the islands of Okinawa and Saipan skidded to a halt before any successful missions were carried out on the mainland. One of the biggest failures occurred with the third prong on the Chinese border with Burma, where a garrison of former Nationalist soldiers attempted several times to penetrate into China in hopes of sparking a wider revolt. One goal of the forays was to force the Chinese Communists to fight a two-front war in Korea and in the south in Yunnan Province. The troops on the Burmese border, who numbered more than 10,000 in 1953, were led by a former Nationalist general in the civil war, General Li Mi. Supplied with weapons by Taiwan and aided by several American advisors, Li Mi led his troops across the border in the summer of 1951, only to be met sixty miles inside China by stiff resistance from the People's Liberation Army. They were rebuffed. Two other forays over the next two years met similar fates. Eventually, under pressure from the United Nations, Taiwan pulled out most of its soldiers from Indochina.

One explanation for our lack of success was that security was too tight in Communist China. Another reason was that our intelligence partners on the Taiwan side were a defeated and demoralized group, who, though they might have worked effectively during World War II, lacked the motivation to work clandestinely against a formidable enemy on the mainland. If they once did have good intelligence contacts on the mainland, those sources had evidently dried up by the early 1950s. I remember our intelligence partners in Taiwan telling us that they had high-level penetrations in the Soviet Embassy in Peking and in the Chinese military, but nothing of importance ever came from these sources. As time passed, we came to see our Taiwan partners more as refugees, dependent on the U.S. for work and pay. This was not a productive situation for collaboration.

The CIA was also swindled by elements of the Chinese Third Force, the second prong of CIA efforts against China. Desperate for information, the CIA had linked up in the early 1950s with these disaffected Chinese because they claimed they had reliable intelligence networks on the mainland. But the Third Force elements stranded outside the mainland were high on reporting and low on access. U.S. intelligence officers in Hong Kong and Taiwan thought they were getting firsthand reports on conditions in China, but the reports turned out to be embroidered versions of articles from provincial Chinese newspapers concocted in Kowloon apartments. We discovered that, like Taiwanese intelligence, they didn't have credible sources on the mainland. The CIA had been "had."

By the time the CIA cut off these "pseudo" agents from CIA payments and sent them back to their previous professions as barbers, newspapers sellers, and manual laborers, damage had already been done. As punishment for catching American case officers paying off Chinese Third Force agents in the lobby of a popular Hong Kong hotel in 1951, the Hong Kong Special Branch (HKSB), the island's British-run security service, kicked out the offending case officers and put the CIA on a tight rope in Hong Kong. The HKSB forbade the CIA from getting mixed up with paramilitary groups trying to operate in China and also prohibited it from penetrating communist organizations in Hong Kong, contending that such delicate operations in a British colony were their bailiwick.

Yes, the British were our allies, but having been granted a ninety-nine-year lease on the New Territories by China, they were sensitive to anything that could upset Peking about the way Hong Kong was being run. They were dismayed by the CIA's decision to work with what they deemed questionable agents. Such contacts carelessly managed, the British reasoned, risked provoking the mainland.

As a young case officer, I drew two lessons from the CIA's missteps: that there were, in fact, no reliable stay-behind networks of agents in China and that the smooth operators who sold these alleged networks were basically crooks. I also understood that the best information CIA was getting on Communist China was coming from technical intelligence gathering as opposed to human intelligence collection. Interceptions of Chinese military communications off the coast turned up better information that we could then corroborate through our own technical intelligence.

But I still thought good work could be done on the ground, and I believed that the CIA would have a better chance of collecting intelligence if we contacted people who had recently been in China or who were going there. As I surveyed my options, I decided that my time would be better spent "closer to the action." I pinpointed Hong Kong, the European outpost on the fringes of Communist China, as my new base of operations and came up with a plan to go undercover. Actually, in CIA parlance, I went under deep cover by shedding any connection with the U.S. government and assuming a new identity. My superior, a thoughtful and resourceful officer, approved, and by May of 1953 I had rented a small flat on the peak in Hong Kong and had enrolled as a language and literature student at Hong Kong University.

．　　　．　　　．

When I arrived in Hong Kong, the "red" menace seemed to be spreading all around. Eastern Europe had been forcibly absorbed into the communist sphere, and in Asia it seemed that Marxism-Leninism was expanding from a base in China. Many Americans referred to the People's Republic of China as "Red China," a name that conjured up masses of faceless Chinese waving red banners and denouncing the United States.

Hong Kong was the best listening post into "Red China." It was, as the long-distance telephone ad used to say, "The next best thing to being there." The island-colony was roiling with action in 1953. Unlike on Taiwan, there were many trade and transportation links to the mainland, and because of its location, Hong Kong was a crossroads for Chinese of all stripes. It was a base for agents from China and Taiwan and, therefore, served as one of the few places where the two sides could rub elbows, and, if the situation called for it, pass on communications to each other's governments. Wealthy capitalists from Shanghai sought refuge in Hong Kong after the Communist revolution and spent much of their time trying to find a way off the island. Furthermore, refugees were streaming in from the mainland. Since 1949, more than one million Chinese had arrived in the city and its surrounding territories. There were an estimated 300,000 squatters in Hong Kong and its territories. Most of the refugees, the majority of whom were farmers and laborers from southern China, came in search of work and a better livelihood. Amazingly, with its improving economy and free enterprise methods, Hong Kong was able to accommodate most of them.

The British colony also accommodated me and my double life. During the day I was a student at Hong Kong University, poring over classical Chinese texts such as *The Doctrines of Filial Piety* and *The Spring and Autumn Analects*. At night I was a case officer looking for targets of opportunity in the streets, bars, and hotels of the city. I directed my efforts at engaging the local Chinese communities, particularly refugees who represented valuable sources of information on conditions in China. At the same time, we tried to recruit from among the refugees for agents willing to return to China to work for us. In contrast to the agents whom we were trying to insert clandestinely into China during the Korea War, some of these refugees, who still had relatives in China with whom they communicated, were able to return to China legally and were thus less conspicuous as information sources.

I started out working with the Pao Mi Chu, Taiwan's intelligence apparatus. I worked under "deep cover," meaning that I kept my true identity a secret from the Chinese people with whom I worked. I used aliases when I contacted agents or met with counterparts in Taiwan intelligence. The one I used most often was "John Wright." I would meet with agents in hotel rooms or in safe houses, apartments that had been scouted beforehand to make sure they were not under surveillance by the Communists' huge underground apparatus in Hong Kong. We debriefed refugees and travelers to China, placed agents on ships going to Chinese ports, and helped establish a base in Macao to take advantage of the flow of Chinese between Macao and the mainland.

When the PMC's agents returned to Hong Kong, I debriefed them for information on popular attitudes toward Communist control, identification of military units, and living conditions in the cities such as availability and prices of commodities. But it was an uncertain business. Most of the agents rejected as too heavy and bulky the RS-1 radios that we gave them to transmit information. Other times, the agents failed to come through. One agent from Tientsin balked at returning after I had debriefed him. He said life as a spy was lonely and that he would only return if we supplied him with an agent-wife. Unfortunately for him, the girl he had in mind would not join him on his return trip. She eventually did join him, but we never heard from them again and surmised that they both had been "turned" by the Communists who wanted to use her to get more information on our techniques and infiltration methods.

In the course of my work, I was learning that we could accomplish far more by debriefing travelers or people returning from China than we could by planting frightened resident agents in the country. The resident agents naturally tended to be fearful of getting caught. Travelers, on the other hand, moved more freely and without that fear. Using debriefings, I started to gather useful information for the CIA about what was going on in China. Unfortunately, in those days CIA was obsessed with the idea of a resident agent with a radio no matter what the level of his access or his ability to survive. They focused on process over substance.

Like my father before me, who developed the acumen to select good agents to work for Standard Oil, I started using my judgment to determine who and what was bona fide. My work was made easier by a contact in Taiwan's intelligence organization. (Yes, we spied on them as they did on us.) He told me of deception and of schemes to get money out of us by the PMC apparatus in Hong Kong. Radios for agents were never delivered. Resident agents in Canton turned out to be fictional. And Hong Kong-based principal agents were skimming money off agent payments.

.   .   .

A spy's life isn't complete without some romance, and a bit of that happened in Hong Kong as well. During my six-month stay, I met a lovely Chinese woman from Peking. Her name was Ms. Lee, and she attached herself to me fairly quickly. I was quite enamored of her, but the intelligence officer side of me became suspicious when she said she could help me get to Peking to become a student there.

However, any chance of pursuing the romance—and of following up on my suspicions—ended suddenly when one of my shipboard agents who was supposed to be reporting on Chinese submarines and warships was caught smuggling guns and ammunition into Hong Kong. It turned out that he was being used by the PMC without my knowledge to carry out the activity. The British authorities caught him and charged him with a capital offense punishable by death. It would be only a matter of time before his interrogation led to me since I had met with him several times. My involvement with this agent would have made it look as if I had been flouting HKSB's restrictions on CIA activity in Hong Kong.

I left Hong Kong quickly before, as we used to say, "the landlord hauled me in." Ms. Lee, however, remained in Hong Kong and popped up at odd times in my career, still a mysterious character, hoping, it seemed to me, to capitalize on our previous association. But I managed to fend her off.

Ms. Lee was a dalliance, not a future. I had been living on my own for two years in Asia and was ready to settle down. So when it was time to leave Hong Kong in December 1953, I booked a flight to Paris, where I met three CIA colleagues from Japan. We were looking forward to living it up in Europe, but I also had another purpose in mind. Sally Booth was now a junior at Smith and spending the year in Paris studying at the Sorbonne.

Sally met us at the airport. She was an excellent tour guide, though my colleagues and I didn't care to see any of the sights. We preferred to sit in the cafés and drink beer. I guess we were decompressing after the tensions of working clandestinely in Asia. Sally was as vivacious as ever. And nervous. We hadn't seen each other for two years. Nevertheless, in Paris she invited me to spend Christmas with her family in Frankfurt, Germany, where her father was serving as a colonel in the U.S. 7th Army.

Given Sally's familiarity with living overseas and her connection to the intelligence profession, she seemed like a natural partner. Besides, I was in love, as I had been since meeting her at that party two years earlier in Washington. I proposed during our stay in Germany, and Sally accepted with one caveat: that we wait until the spring after she had turned 21. At 20, she felt too young to get married.

My brother Jack was the best man at our wedding, which took place on May 1, 1954, in Andover, Massachusetts. I remember when I cabled Jack to tell him of the wedding. "MARRYING SALLY SOON," the cable read. Jack asked, "Is Jim marrying a Chinese girl?" The wedding was a great occasion. We chose Andover because my parents and Elinore and her family were all living in a big Victorian house not far from

Phillips Academy Andover, and the actual wedding ceremony was in the Phillips Academy Andover chapel. The Booths flew in from Germany. George Witwer came with Lee, who was pregnant with their second child.

Our honeymoon in Bermuda was extended for a few days when Sally and I got drafted to "star" in some publicity photographs for a hotel. Somebody at the hotel had apparently spotted us on the beach and liked what they saw. For running in and out of the surf and playing catch with a ball, we got to stay several days for free at the hotel.

Following the extended honeymoon, Sally and I began our life together. Our first tour was in Japan, where we lived first in Tokyo for six months and then moved to Kyoto. Professionally, I spent my time trying to penetrate the Chinese Communist political movement in major Japanese cities and trace its activities back to China, but our efforts were hampered by never being able to recruit an agent in the inner core.

My most vivid memory of Japan, however, is a personal one. In the spring of 1956, we took a scenic boat trip down the Inland Sea of Japan. The boat docked in Kure, the suburb of Hiroshima where my brother had ended his life in 1946. I had the address of the house where Frank had lived. We walked down the narrow streets of Kure, past low buildings with walls surrounding them. At one of the buildings we stopped and entered the courtyard. In a mixture of English and Japanese, with Sally helping on the Japanese portions, I asked if anyone remembered the American lieutenant who had died there ten years earlier. A cook stepped forward and said, "I remember him." He then led us to a path in the courtyard and pointed to a spot on a pathway inside the walled compound. Nobody spoke until the cook said, "I heard the shot and ran outside. I was the person who found his body."

Afterward, Sally and I visited Hiroshima. The city was still in ruins from the atomic bombing eleven years earlier. It was a desolate place with only a few people walking around. On the boat back to Kyoto that evening, we found we were nearly out of money. We pooled the few yen we had and shared a fried egg and a dish of peanuts.

The two places, Kure and Hiroshima, were linked in my mind by the thread of destruction: the end of my brother's life and the death of

70,000 Japanese at Hiroshima. Only nine months separated the two events. It's a connection that I have thought about for a good number of years. Frank lived adjacent to Hiroshima with the knowledge that his country had caused that destruction, and yet he understood, and I know he understood, that it was done to save lives—other lives. All that horrendous disfigurement and obliteration for the purpose of saving lives. Imagine how skewed the world must have looked to his young, idealistic mind.

That visit to Kure was a pilgrimage of sorts, and it signaled, perhaps, a break with a painful past. I was now sharing my life with Sally. Over the span of the next five decades, we would raise three boys and live in nine Asian countries. She has been an invaluable partner and friend, and committed wife and mother. While I immersed myself in the politics and power structures of Asia, Sally delved into the languages and culture of the countries we lived in. During our time overseas, Sally studied four Asian languages—Japanese, Thai, Chinese, and Korean—learning them well enough to converse with house staff and do shopping. That goes along with the French and Spanish she already knew, languages that helped us in the diplomatic communities in which we were immersed.

.   .   .

By the mid-1950s, the U.S. was confronting China along its periphery, from the Korean Peninsula down to the Taiwan Straits and across to Southeast Asia. American military forces in South Korea, Taiwan, and South Vietnam were holding the line against an expanding communist presence. On the covert side, in less visible but no less important battles, Chinese and American clandestine forces were facing off in places such as the Philippines and Indonesia. The Chinese Communists were trying to turn local populations against their former Western colonial overlords. The PRC's chief instrument was the overseas Chinese populations.

The Chinese Communists were building on work they had done during World War II when, in the process of developing guerrilla forces to resist the Japanese, they had recruited and organized a large number of sympathizers and supporters in ethnic Chinese communities throughout Asia. After the war, these organizations directed their efforts against the newly reestablished colonial governments in Asia—the Dutch in Indonesia, the British in Malaya, the French in Indochina, and the Americans in the Philippines. The Communist victory in China in 1949 gave these subversive Chinese forces ideological impetus and material support.

The problem for the Chinese Communists was that these movements, composed almost solely of ethnic Chinese, came up against indigenous, anti-colonial movements that were deeply suspicious of Chinese underground organizations operating with support from China. The underground Chinese forces were also hurt by the perception among the indigenous populations that Chinese communities in Southeast Asia controlled a disproportionate amount of the business and wealth of those countries.

In July 1958, I arrived in the Philippines and entered this atmosphere of bubbling activity. My assignment was threefold: First, find out what the Chinese Communists were doing in the local Chinese communities and negate their efforts; second, make connections in the communities; and, third, collect information from the Chinese mainland in order to get answers to some of the big questions of the day: Had there been a Sino-Soviet split? How were the Chinese reorganizing their society? Would the Chinese strike out militarily against Southeast Asian countries or Taiwan?

To prepare for my clandestine work, the CIA had given me my first formal Chinese language training. No longer would I have to rely on the "pidgin" Chinese I had learned as a child. I studied at the Institute of Far Eastern Languages Chinese Language School at Yale, the same school Frank had attended fourteen years earlier. Yale dominated the study of Chinese language in the U.S. in those years, and the school's textbooks were used everywhere. In 1958 the school was still being run by Dr. Henry C. Fenn, a master scholar of Chinese, whose dictionary of 5,000 characters bore his name and was used by thousands of Chinese-language aspirants. Those five months of Chinese study in New Haven were the true beginning of a lifelong labor to learn to read and speak Chinese.

In accordance with CIA procedure, I was assigned a cover position at an official U.S. organization in Manila as a middle-level Chinese affairs officer. In my hours outside this role I carried out my dual functions for my cover organization and CIA: developing contacts in Manila's small but influential Chinese community.

The task of intelligence gathering in the Philippines was made easier because the operating climate included a government favorable to the U.S., many American-educated leaders, and substantial American investments and commercial interests. The leaders of Manila's 90,000-strong Chinese community knew the U.S. had considerable influence in the Philippines because the CIA, and by extension the U.S., had been credited with helping reformer Ramón Magsaysay defeat a growing Communist movement and get elected president in 1953. The Philippines and the United States were also linked by common security goals. In the past, we had cooperated in fighting the Japanese, and during my posting we shared a common interest in curbing Chinese Communist expansion.

The leadership of the Chinese business community in Manila exhibited conflicting and shifting allegiances to Taiwan and mainland China. In reality, the local communities exploited the threat from Communist China in order to keep themselves established. The Chinese community leadership at that time was split between two Chinese Chambers of Commerce—the Federated Chamber of Commerce headed by the Yang family and the General Chamber of Commerce under the influence of the Hsueh, or Sycip, family. The Yang family was more pro-Taiwan, whereas the Hsueh family was more susceptible to the PRC's indirect influence. The Hsueh family was an interesting phenomenon—a sort of Chinese balancing act. They had three successful sons. One son was an American citizen in accounting; a second son was a Filipino citizen in the law; and the third son was a Chinese citizen in commerce. To make matters even more interesting, two of the Hsueh boys had married Yang daughters. I kept in contact with both sides and still do to this day. The divisions between the families were never that deep. A common heritage in Fujian Province and a shared need for survival and prosperity outweighed any differences arising from the political leanings of the two families.

·　　·　　·

Using a variety of methods, we started to blunt Chinese Communist activity in the Philippines. Through recruitment of agents in the community, we learned about the anti-Taiwan activities of the Communist underground in the Philippines. Chinese Communist intelligence efforts included a smear campaign against the wife of the Chinese Nationalist (Taiwan) ambassador as well as a campaign to taint with charges of corruption the Taiwan government's youth outreach programs to young Chinese in the Philippines. Agents for the PRC were also trying to turn Filipino political leaders against Taiwan by depicting the mainland as the rising and morally clean power in Asia.

When a Chinese-language newspaper under PRC influence ran a stream of articles attacking the U.S., we countered by organizing a briefing for American businessmen at which we explained the Communist backing for the newspaper. Some of the American businesses responded by withdrawing their advertisements from the newspaper. But not all the jousting was through words. When a Chinese Communist agent in Manila—a highly placed employee at a Chinese-language newspaper—tried to defect to our side, he was found murdered, his body dumped into Manila Bay.

In the fall of 1958, we helped bring Chinese Nationalist Air Force pilots to Manila in an attempt to prove to the local Chinese population that we were succeeding in the struggle against the Communists. These tough, U.S.-trained pilots had battled their Communist counterparts in a series of air clashes during the Quemoy crisis in August and September 1958. The Taiwan pilots, flying U.S. F-86 Sabrejets with air-to-air sidewinder missiles—the first time this weapon had been used in combat—had overwhelmed the PRC pilots, who were flying Soviet-built MIG-17s. According to Taiwanese press reports, the Taiwan Air Force lost just one plane while shooting down more than thirty MIG-17s. When the pilots came to Manila, they brought evidence of their high-flying victories. They showed documentary footage of the air clashes to a roaring crowd of overseas Chinese, who applauded wildly when Chinese Communist aircraft exploded on the screen.

Peking and Taipei had been sparring since 1949 over a Taiwan-controlled group of islands just off the coast of mainland China, about a hundred miles west of Taiwan. The fighting had started because

China wanted to neutralize the islands, called Quemoy and Matsu, which had been used as a base for the Taiwan military as well as a launching pad for CIA-assisted covert operations against the mainland. Chairman Mao sparked the August 1958 crisis by ordering an artillery bombardment of the islands. Then U.S. Secretary of State John Foster Dulles (brother of CIA director Allen Dulles) warned ominously in late August that if China took the islands, it would risk widening the conflict. Soviet Premier Nikita Khrushchev upped the ante in October when he said that an attack on China would be considered an attack on the USSR.

The artillery bombardments continued into December but at a reduced level. Eventually, the PRC settled for the status quo—a well-armed Republic of China presence at the doorstep of Fujian Province. The air victory over Quemoy and Matsu was significant because it signaled a victory over Communist aggression. Chinese attempts at air superiority and artillery bombardments had been rebuffed by first-class Taiwanese pilots and U.S. logistical support. The Taiwanese anointed the pilots as their newest heroes.

For twenty years after the initial crisis, the Peking government continued bombarding Quemoy every other day, dropping up to thirty shells each time. The shelling finally came to a halt in 1979 when China and the U.S. established formal diplomatic relations and Marshal Ye Jian-ying offered a nine-point reconciliation proposal. The important fact is that, more than forty years after the initial crisis, the islands remain in Taiwan's hands.

· · ·

In order to find out what was happening inside China, we started a few modest operations from the Philippines, such as sending local Chinese back to their ancestral areas of Fujian Province for visits. We flew our Filipino-Chinese agents into Hong Kong, where we procured permits to enter the mainland from travel agencies. Before going into China, our agents left behind their Philippine passports or residence cards in Hong Kong. But the document switching didn't really fool the Chinese. The PRC's security services, which oversaw the travel agencies, had to sign off on granting travel permits and most likely allowed the overseas Chinese to go because they represented sources of revenue and were considered possible fodder for conversion to communism.

So both sides were trying to use the overseas Chinese for their own purposes. I think we got the better deal. Inside China, our agents were able to observe targets, such as radar stations and airfields, but this information was only of marginal value. More important, we began to receive firsthand reports from these agents of the disastrous effects of Chairman Mao Tse-tung's Great Leap Forward, which was undertaken in 1958.

Mao was applying drastic means of social and economic engineering in an attempt to propel China in just fifteen years to the hypothetical advanced stages of Communism. He proposed to increase agricultural production by a massive mobilization of rural labor into work communes. Rather than provide incentives, like making a wider range of consumer goods available to the peasants, the Chinese government applied brute force in the form of excess labor in order to increase productivity in the countryside. There would be more hands enlisted in close planting, digging irrigation ditches, and reclaiming land. It was meant to be, in short, a revolution in the countryside, powered by the zeal and ardor of Chinese peasants. To help boost industry, peasants were exhorted to build backyard iron smelters.

But natural catastrophes and mistakes in carrying out the policies led to a series of poor harvests and an acute food shortage in China's rural areas. In the face of such hardship, local government officials, feeling pressed to meet the high goals of Mao's economic plan, nevertheless continued to requisition inordinate amounts of grain from the countryside and inflate production statistics. It is estimated that 20 to 30 million people died of malnutrition and famine because of Mao's absurd policies. We got a picture of the tragedy from our Chinese agents and from a look at the mail pouring in from the mainland. Heart-rending letters to family and friends in the Philippines depicted the desperate conditions, disillusionment, and fear of the people. We filed all of this with Washington.

In vivid contrast, Edgar Snow, author of *Red Star Over China*, went to China during the time of the Great Leap Forward and wrote a book entitled *The Other Side of the River*, which depicted the Chinese as working hard to build a new, happy, and prosperous China. He completely missed the massive starvation of the Great Leap Forward, the rioting in the countryside, and the peasantry's flight to urban areas.

Ultimately, though, the legacy of my work in the Philippines probably lay in my decision to denude our Manila unit of many of its Chinese assets. Shortly after I arrived, I ended an ongoing bureaucratic turf war among CIA posts when I decided to move most of our Chinese operations to Hong Kong. The move made operational sense because Hong Kong was the base of the CIA's covert work against mainland China and the place where the CIA had working penetrations of Chinese Communist organizations, such as the Bank of China and the China Resource Corporation. In Hong Kong, the agents would also get closer American supervision.

I had to smuggle one of our most important agents back into Hong Kong in the course of this move. This agent ran a network of Chinese agents working in Communist organizations in Hong Kong. To return to Hong Kong, though, we had to get past British authorities, who had kicked him and his CIA case officer out of Hong Kong several years earlier when their activities became too noticeable. For my part, I didn't feel much heat returning to Hong Kong because I had "eluded" capture several years earlier. To disguise our agent, an emaciated chain-smoking Chinese, I dressed him in the uniform of a sergeant in the U.S. Air Force. The suit hung on his thin body like drape curtains on a rod. He looked no more like a U.S. Air Force sergeant than a man on the moon. I put on my U.S. Air Force lieutenant's uniform—it did, indeed, come in handy in nonmilitary circumstances—and after a week layover in a safe house in Okinawa during which the agent taught me the fundamentals of Mahjong, we boarded a plane bound for Hong Kong. There were some tense moments when we walked past the British border guards at the Hong Kong Airport. A 6'3" pale-faced foreigner with his diminutive Chinese counterpart. They regarded us curiously, but we made it. Outside the airport, the agent took off the uniform and quickly melted into the Chinese crowd.

It was a successful operation at the end of a decade that had seen multiple failures in intelligence activities and covert operations. As a young case officer, I had learned important lessons working with refugees and overseas Chinese and had passed on valuable information on turmoil inside China. The operating climates in Hong Kong and the Philippines, though, had been generally favorable to intelligence work. The challenge in the next decade would be to learn to work in "hostile" environments.

ON THE EDGE OF CONFLICT

O UR EFFORTS to battle China covertly began to take a back seat to an expanding conflict in the heart of Southeast Asia. There, in the former French colony of Vietnam, the U.S. was helping South Vietnam fend off communist infiltration from the north. We didn't want our South Vietnamese allies to be the next domino to fall. I got my first experience of life in this new, more hostile region in 1961 when I was assigned to serve in Cambodia, another former French colony and Vietnam's neighbor to the west. Gone were the sympathetic governments and local cadre of American supporters that I had gotten used to working with in places like the Philippines and Hong Kong.

Despite a generous U.S. aid program that had pumped around $200 million into Cambodia since 1955, the Cambodian government was becoming increasingly anti-American. The country's leader, Prince Norodom Sihanouk, who had championed the cause of Cambodian independence since 1945, was opposed to the U.S. position in Vietnam and was fanning anti-American feelings among the population in a bid to stabilize his country's position in the region and cozy up to China. A cunning manipulator who saw himself as a God-king, Sihanouk was seeking Chinese help to ensure his country's survival as an ostensibly neutral state against pressure from the U.S. and its Southeast Asian allies, including Thailand and South Vietnam.

A small country caught between these two larger and more powerful neighbors, Cambodia was then relatively well-off economically: It had a food surplus and exported lumber, rice, and rubber. But it had no industry to speak off and little infrastructure, just a few good roads and one railroad. Its population of five million people was mostly poor and uneducated.

I recall landing in Saigon in September 1961 and staying at the famous Continental Palace Hotel. Late that evening Sally and I looked out at the street scene below us. The square was silent, with a lone soldier patrolling the deserted area. It was a quiet interlude at the beginning of a violent decade in Southeast Asia. We were told that we would have to fly to Phnom Penh the next day as Route 7 from Saigon was too dangerous. The Vietnam War was already encroaching upon us. Ironically, as I would soon find out, a more hostile operating environment provided excellent opportunities for intelligence gathering.

.   .   .

For our intelligence operations in Cambodia, we developed the standard two-pronged approach: cover what the Chinese mainlanders were doing in Cambodia, and then use assets in the ethnic Chinese community in the Cambodian capital of Phnom Penh to report on events in the PRC. In the early 1960s, the ethnic Chinese community in Cambodia numbered around 300,000 and was split between those who supported Taipei and those favoring Peking. Fortunately for us, unlike the Philippines, travel between China and Cambodia was both legal and commonplace. In light of our work in Manila, which indicated that the mainland was entering an unstable period in the aftermath of the Great Leap Forward, Cambodia was a promising platform to gain intelligence on China.

But we had to overcome a few obstacles along the way. First of all, China had considerable momentum in its relations with the Cambodian government. Peking could draw upon the fact that through the centuries there had been peaceful relations between the two countries, with China being the accepted senior partner. In 1958, on the heels of a trip to Cambodia two years earlier by China's star diplomat Chou En-lai and disbursement of a $20 million Chinese aid program, the two countries established diplomatic relations. Taiwan responded by removing its diplomats from Phnom Penh shortly thereafter. In terms of carrying out intelligence gathering in Phnom Penh, we faced formidable foes in not only the Soviet and Chinese embassies but also Cambodia's large pro-communist Vietnamese population. All of these forces worked against our intelligence activities by shadowing us, discrediting our mission, and criticizing our personnel and projects.

An increasingly antagonistic relationship with Prince Sihanouk's government took a turn for the worse when we committed a major intelligence gaffe in 1962 by combining two separate intelligence operations in one location in Phnom Penh. In CIA parlance, we "crossed safe house." One of our CIA case officers, a Chinese American, used a safe location to meet with a local Chinese agent. Meanwhile, working in conjunction with our South Vietnamese allies in Saigon, another CIA case officer used the same house to handle a Vietnamese agent. Unfortunately, South Vietnam's intelligence organization was thoroughly penetrated by the North Vietnamese, and thus the liaison operation run with the South Vietnamese contaminated the unilateral operation we were running with the Chinese agent. When the Cambodians were tipped off to the presence of the Vietnamese agent, the Cambodian police closed in on the safe house and nabbed the Chinese agent and our case officer. It was a mistake in operational judgment, and we paid for it. Not surprisingly, the Cambodians protested vigorously and held the Chinese American CIA officer in detention for ten days. A nervous U.S. Embassy ordered a shutdown of our intelligence operations. We eventually sent our case officer home and removed our other Chinese American case officer by having him feign illness. We got a seat for him on an official flight to Saigon and put him on the plane all bundled up as if he were fighting a bad case of the flu.

Despite the embassy's order, I maintained contact with certain crucial agents in Cambodia, some of whom were understandably jittery about continuing to work. With the two Chinese Americans gone, I was the only person left in the unit who had enough Chinese to handle them. I met with the agents to reassure—and pay—them. With safe houses no longer an option, I had to meet with the agents in my house after dark. The decision to use my residence went against the modus operandi of clandestine operations, but I had no other choice. Our agents made the risk worthwhile. Basically loyal and dependent on us, they were highly effective in these dangerous times.

.   .   .

Working with and through our remaining agents, we continued to get important information on the devastating consequences of the Great Leap Forward. From travelers, letters, and debriefings of returnees we learned firsthand of widespread starvation and of the Chinese government's decision to lower food rations to the population. We began to understand how the massive reorganization of the commune system had contributed to the tragic results. We concluded that the Chinese authorities were still in control but that they were considered predatory and hostile by growing segments of the population. On the basis of our intelligence, we believed that there would be some kind of social explosion in China ignited by the economic hardship.

We were right. In May 1962, in a desperate attempt to flee deteriorating conditions, tens of thousands of refugees from southern China stormed across the border fences between Hong Kong and China. With its problems documented on TV and in newspapers for the world to see, China lost ground in the arena of international opinion. The PRC's claims of advancing the cause of the common man suddenly rang hollow. Working with the British colonial authority in Hong Kong, which was concerned about adding to the island's already swelling population, the Chinese succeeded in repatriating more than 25,000 of the refugees back to China. The two governments eventually brought the situation under control but only after great human suffering by the Chinese people.

The question then came up of whether the U.S. and Taiwan could exploit this volatile situation by air-dropping 150-man armed teams into China to organize an opposition force. My experience in the 1950s in Hong Kong, Taiwan, and Korea told me this would not work. Sure enough, the few exploratory operations run from Taiwan were quickly captured and "neutralized." Bad as the situation was inside China and despite some wistful longing on the part of some Chinese to welcome back the U.S., the overall climate was not conducive to the introduction of an external force. In September 1962, the Chinese military took no chances, however, and poured reinforcements into the coastal area across from Taiwan. The movement of forces was first perceived as indicating an imminent invasion of Taiwan. Only later did we find out that the Chinese had moved in troops to keep a lid on restless segments of the population in Fujian Province and to prepare for any military exploitation of the situation by Taiwan.

In Phnom Penh we soon found ourselves wondering if the U.S. was going to be attacked by the Soviet Union. During the tense days of the Cuban Missile Crisis of October 1962, we staked out observatory positions around the Soviet Embassy to see if Soviet diplomats were burning documents or preparing to evacuate. We would have taken these as signs that the Soviet Union was getting ready to do something drastic.

.　　　.　　　.

In Cambodia's tense environment, we did have some operational successes. A low-level Chinese diplomat defected. He was smuggled out to Saigon in the back of a small car but not before he told us about the workings of the Chinese intelligence apparatus in Southeast Asia, including the identity of key people in the Chinese Embassy's intelligence branch, such as the party chief and senior intelligence officer, a man whom I would run into at two later stages of my career.

We also successfully recruited a Cambodian diplomat to work for us in Peking. Since the U.S. lacked any diplomatic representation in China, the idea was to make the agent our resident "asset" in Peking, reporting on conditions in China. We recruited the midlevel Cambodian diplomat while he was in Phnom Penh and trained him in secret communications. He was sent to work in the Cambodian Embassy in Peking, but the operation failed because he could not master the communication techniques we had taught him. Furthermore, his reports were superficial and useless. The lesson of this failure was that you cannot rely on an unsophisticated asset to do your reporting even if he is a "resident" agent in country.

Penetrations like the one with the Cambodian diplomat took a lot of time, effort, and skill to cultivate. But they were usually worth the effort. They not only led to a better understanding of local hostile forces but also garnered reliable information about communist leadership around the world. The most valuable penetrations in terms of divining Chinese intentions often came not from Chinese agents but from communist party members of third countries. These penetrations had excellent access to leaders in both Moscow and Peking. For example, an FBI operation using an American Communist Party penetration took the FBI into the Kremlin at the highest level. From early on, this contact shed light on Soviet–Chinese difficulties. Luck and ingenuity also played roles. To our good fortune, some of our penetrations in Latin American and Middle Eastern communist parties ended up being trained in Peking for subversive work overseas. In another instance, the CIA manufactured a communist party faction in a Middle Eastern country. Our agent representing this sham party was dangled in front of the Chinese. They took the bait, and our agent ended up in Peking discussing political action with leading Communist Party members. Such operations gave us worthwhile insights into the workings of the Chinese government.

My tour in Cambodia came to an end in fact with the arrival of Chinese president Liu Shaoqi on an official visit in May of 1963. With his country more dependent than ever on his neighbor to the north, Prince Sihanouk had to do everything right for his Chinese friends. Prior to the visit, in a move reminiscent of internment camps during wartime, Sihanouk rounded up most of the pro-Taiwan Chinese community, including many of our agents, and put them in an enclosed area under armed guard. As a warning to any opposition movement, Sihanouk's henchmen dragged a retarded and physically deformed Cambodian man into the street, accused him of a plot against President Liu Shaoqi, and executed him in a gruesome way.

The environment for our operations progressively worsened. When we learned that two of our most important agents, men whom I had met with in my house at night, had been deported to China from the enclosure, I began to feel the web closing tighter around me. It was clear that Sihanouk was collaborating with the Chinese against a large portion of the Chinese community and against our assets. I had become "vulnerable," so for the second time in my career I had to leave a post early. But not before I threw myself a farewell party to which Sally, totally unwitting of the circumstances behind our leaving, and I invited Cambodian government officials, left-wing media people, and foreign diplomats. Almost everybody showed up, perhaps to celebrate that I was leaving town voluntarily. I suppose that amidst this entire fanfare I was in a way daring them to touch me—a CIA officer relishing his diplomatic cover one last time.

Before I left, I made sure the information channels remained open. We made contingency plans for some of our agents to be "picked up" by friendly Western powers and managed through their intelligence arms. We also set up letter drops in Hong Kong. Agents could write their reports in the secret script we had taught them and then send them to Hong Kong for collection. The result was that our intelligence production actually increased after 1965.

.   .   .

We headed back to the U.S. in 1964 after a tour in Thailand, which was cut short because I contracted hepatitis. After two weeks in the hospital, I convalesced at home in Bangkok, but when it was time to return on the boat to America, I was still very weak. With no house staff to help take care of the children, Sally had her hands full on the two-week trip across the Pacific Ocean. For the first time she had to take care of our three boys by herself. Douglas, born in Manila, was then five years old. Mike, who was born during an interlude back in the U.S. in 1961, had just turned three, and Jeffrey, born during our short stay in Thailand, was just nine months old.

Still battling hepatitis, I had my own dark, artificially lit cabin, where I occupied myself with a model of a combustion engine that someone had given us before we left. I spent my time trying to put it together, but never quite succeeded. Sally would pass through my cabin from time to time and check on me, whom she called "The Birdman of Alcatraz," before going to the cabin she was sharing with the three boys. Sally kept the two older boys busy with activities on the ship, tended to me, took care of a crying Jeffrey at night, and did laundry incessantly—everybody's clothes, Jeffrey's diapers, and my sheets, which I was still soaking with sweat. To free herself to do the laundry, she followed the same routine: bathe and clothe Jeffrey, make sure the older boys were occupied, and then drop off Jeffrey at the ship's infant day care, a small cabin with a wall of drawers on each side to stash babies in. She would then go to the nearby laundry room in the bowels of the ship and wash the clothes to the rhythm of the boat's sway.

The routine on the ship was a change from the more comfortable lives we had led in Southeast Asia and the Philippines, but Sally didn't complain. She was supportive in the ways she had to be, and that has been one of the secrets of my professional success.

Sally's support of me in Cambodia even included a stint working furtively to take pictures of visiting Chinese president Liu Shaoqi's delegation when I was out of town. Much to the chagrin of senior American officials at the U.S. Embassy, who wanted no hint of trouble during the visit of the Chinese president, Sally climbed up to the roof of the U.S. Embassy and photographed President Liu 's motorcade as it passed below.

When we arrived back in Washington, I received a dose of humbling reality. Our reports on the huge costs of the Great Leap Forward, which had seemed so important to us in the field, appeared to have had minimal impact in the corridors of American power. That was because Cambodia and internal developments in China were secondary to the war brewing across the border in Vietnam. In our next posting in Laos, I myself would be caught up in this war, totally absorbed in a struggle on the flanks of the Vietnam War.

.   .   .

In the summer of 1998, after a thirty-five-year absence, I returned to Cambodia to monitor elections. I found our old house as well as the former American Embassy. Both buildings were broken down but still standing. Cambodia had gone through one of the cruelest genocides in human history during the period from 1975 to 1979. With Chinese support, the communist Khmer Rouge killed hundreds of thousands of Cambodians. Hundreds of thousands also died of starvation and disease. Estimates of the dead range from one to three million, out of a 1975 population estimated at 7.3 million. Cambodia became "the killing fields."

In 1998 I saw new, modern hotels built by corrupt and wealthy overseas Chinese with the complicity of the Cambodian government. The Royal Palace had been restored, but the government, nominally a constitutional monarchy, was still suppressing dissent and murdering opponents. While I was there, I learned that a pro-PRC Chinese from Los Angeles had fled the U.S. for Cambodia after being implicated in the election scandal of 1996 in which the Chinese government working through overseas Chinese had contributed money to the Democratic Party. It had been a clumsy attempt by the Chinese government to influence American politics, and it was illegal. I found out the offending character was working with ethnic Chinese who were in the hotel business as well as reportedly running the drug trade.

On that same trip back to Cambodia, I saw Prince Sihanouk again. He was riddled with cancer, emaciated, and mostly bald. Finally proclaimed king again after an odyssey that included exile in Peking and house arrest under the Khmer Rouge, whom he had initially supported, he was now protected by North Korean thugs. He kissed me on both cheeks and seemed to treat me as an old friend, but his eyes gave him away. They shifted warily, the sign of a suspicious man.

8

RUNNING THE SECRET WAR

THE TELEPHONE call came into the CIA Station in Vientiane, Laos, at the end of a sweltering summer day in August 1965. An Air America H-34 transport helicopter carrying CIA personnel had crashed into the Mekong River, north of Vientiane. I scrambled to respond to the emergency. As acting chief of the CIA Station, it was up to me to help set up a rescue mission and file an initial report immediately. There were seven people on board the chopper, including the CIA's base chief for our outpost in northwestern Laos as well as a colonel in the Royal Lao Army, our allies in the battle against communist Lao forces and their North Vietnamese backers.

The helicopter had been returning to Vientiane from the CIA's outpost in Nam Yu, but monsoon clouds closed in while the chopper was making its approach to the capital along the Mekong River. The pilot lost visibility and dropped so low that the helicopter blades hit the water. The helicopter flipped over and sank in the swollen Mekong, we learned later during our investigation into the crash. While water poured in through the doors and windows, the passengers trapped in the back cabin of the chopper struggled to get out. Our up-country officer Lewis Ojibway, a gigantic, lumbering Native American who had once been a sparring partner for Joe Louis, drowned in the panic along with three others. Amazingly, the American pilot, Bob Nunez, survived even though he didn't know how to swim. Nunez had managed to grab a floating log outside the sinking chopper. He held onto the piece of wood and let the Mekong's strong current carry him. Hours later, he was found fourteen miles downstream, exhausted but alive.

Some time after we arrived at the area of the crash site, the Lao vil-lagers told us that the Lao colonel had been spotted wandering in the nearby woods. When we questioned them further, the villagers said that the *phi,* local spirits who inhabit the woods, had seen the colonel. We were incredulous, but we checked out every report. We never found any sign of the living colonel. Days later, his body washed up on the Mekong River bank.

I had arrived in Laos three months prior to the crash to join the CIA's effort to fight a guerrilla war against the Lao communists, known as the Pathet Lao, and their North Vietnamese allies. While our mission regarding the conduct of the guerrilla war was clear, there was much about the Kingdom of Laos, like Laotians' belief in the *phi,* that was a mystery. Indeed, the helicopter crash—with its tragic conse-quences, the mystery of the *phi,* and the Mekong—set the tone for an intense, gut-wrenching, and often bizarre tour of duty in Laos.

I was sent to Laos because my superiors in Washington had been impressed with my reporting on China and wanted to get me involved in a different kind of clandestine work. If before I had focused on get-ting intelligence on China, now I would assist, under diplomatic cover, a covert paramilitary operation. In terms of language, I left Chinese be-hind, but my French, learned at school and honed in Cambodia, came in handy as Laos had been a French protectorate and the elite, includ-ing government officials and military officers, spoke French.

.   .   .

When I arrived, the CIA station in Vientiane was a small operation, numbering about thirty to fifty people, with about half working as paramilitary officers in the field. Those of us in Vientiane did not actu-ally fight. Our primary goal was to help and guide the paramilitary of-ficers in the field as they worked with the local Lao and ethnic tribes. In conjunction with these field officers, we trained and supplied the Laotian guerrilla forces, mainly through a base in Udorn, Thailand, and bases in Pakse, Savannakhet, Long Tieng, and Nam Yu in Laos.

Laos is a long, thin, landlocked nation in the center of Southeast Asia. It is roughly hourglass shaped, surrounded by Burma, China, and Vietnam at its swollen top, flanked along its sides by Vietnam and

Thailand, and bordered to the south by Cambodia. The country's long eastern border with Vietnam gave it strategic importance. In the 1960s, Laos was a sleepy, underdeveloped country with few roads outside the capital of Vientiane. More than 90 percent of Laotians were illiterate, and it seemed that many of the people preferred to relax rather than work. Most of the labor was performed by communities of Chinese and Vietnamese brought in during the French colonial period. Our house staff was entirely Vietnamese and Thai. Laotian reluctance to change was well known among U.S. Agency for International Development (USAID) workers, who had been in the country since the 1950s trying to introduce modern ways of growing crops. There was the famous, perhaps apocryphal, anecdote about the Lao farmer who had been given a batch of fertilizer that would double his crop yield: So he worked only half as hard. Instead of inducing the Lao to become more productive farmers, AID programs, especially the delivery of food aid, ended up making the Lao dependent on the Americans to feed them. As the Lao saw it, rice fell from heaven, delivered by helicopters.

.   .   .

For several years before I arrived in Laos, the U.S. had been engaging in a game of hit-and-run warfare with the communist forces in Laos, while adhering in policy pronouncements to the Geneva agreements of 1962. These Geneva agreements reiterated the country's position in the 1954 Geneva Accords as a neutral state and called for all foreign military forces to be withdrawn. The last stipulation was aimed mainly at North Vietnam but also at the U.S., which had been deploying more and more regular U.S. Special Forces and CIA paramilitary specialists into Laos. An International Control Commission (ICC) composed of Canadian, Indian, and Polish representatives was sent to Laos to monitor adherence to the Geneva Accords.

In order to maintain compliance with the agreements in Geneva, the U.S. initially pulled out Air Force aircraft as well as uniformed military advisors. But the CIA officers, military equipment, and personnel didn't go far. They were restationed just across the Mekong River at the U.S. military base in Udorn, Thailand. Secretly, in circumvention of the agreements, the CIA kept several of its key officers up-country in Laos to help prosecute the guerrilla war. In addition, a crack group of Thai policemen trained by a CIA paramilitary specialist stayed behind to assist the CIA officers. Looking like Lao and speaking Lao, these Thai paramilitary specialists or PARU (for Police Aerial Resupply Unit) operated radios and trained field commanders of the Laotian guerrilla forces. For their part, the North Vietnamese violated the peace accords on a much greater scale. They withdrew forty soldiers past the checkpoints, leaving an estimated 5,000 to 7,000 soldiers behind in Laos.

Under a plan devised by Bill Lair, a CIA senior paramilitary officer based in nearby Thailand, the CIA had agreed in 1960 to finance the training and equipping of 1,000 Meo tribesmen to serve as a guerrilla force against the Pathet Lao and North Vietnamese forces. The Meo, or Hmong as they later came to be called, were one of the largest ethnic groups in Laos. They held a historical antipathy toward the Vietnamese, whom they perceived as trying to dominate Laos, and also didn't care much for China, from where they had come in the eighteenth and nineteenth centuries. Known as fierce fighters, the Hmong, who numbered about 250,000 in the 1960s, jealously guarded their independence from any interlopers. They lived in the mountains.

In 1960, Lair determined that the Hmong were ripe for partisan war against the communist Pathet Lao and their allies in Laos, both of whom favored a "neutral" Laos that was linked to North Vietnam. With CIA assistance, two bases, one secret and one overt, were established in central Laos for what came to be known as the "secret army." The secret base was about ninety miles north of Vientiane in Long Tieng. The overt base was set up at Sam Thong, a USAID-operated hill tribe refugee center in central Laos. The head of the "secret army" was a colorful Hmong named General Vang Pao. Vang Pao, in effect, wore three hats: He was a general in the Lao Royal Army in charge of the country's 2nd Military Region north of Vientiane; he was a Hmong tribal leader; and he was commander of the CIA-supported guerrilla forces. By the mid-1960s, Vang Pao controlled a force of about 10,000 Hmong, mostly grouped in strike forces called special guerrilla units.

In more ways than one, Vang Pao, even though he was our closest ally, represented the other world that was Laos. A former sergeant in the French colonial army in Laos and a career military man, Vang Pao believed that to retain his strength he had to have sex every night. Therefore, wherever he went, he brought several young Hmong brides with him. He also had a lingering faith in tribal medicine. When I was in Laos, I heard the story that when Vang Pao was shot in the shoulder in a skirmish with the Vietnamese, he refused to have surgery. Instead, he demanded that a witch doctor be brought to him. The doctor arrived and performed several incantations. Smoke circled around Vang Pao. The witch doctor put his mouth on the wound and sucked hard. Then he spat out pieces of metal into a brass receptacle. Vang Pao raised his arm, waved, and said, "To Hell with Western medicine." Or something to that effect. The next day the Hmong general was in terrible pain, and his arm was worse than ever. He finally consented to let an American doctor operate and remove the bullet. Such incidents were part of the war in Laos and the mystery of the country.

But however ethereal the Hmong seemed, there was no disputing their attachment to the Americans who were helping them. On many occasions the Hmong tried to rescue downed American pilots. During one rescue attempt forty miles into North Vietnam in June 1965, one of Vang Pao's finest officers, Colonel Vongrasamy Thong, was hit in the abdomen by ground fire while standing at the door of the helicopter he was riding in. Thong eventually died of his wounds. Other rescue raids were more successful. In one instance, with Hmong help and the assistance of friendly Laotians, the CIA orchestrated a surprise raid on a Pathet Lao prison camp in central Laos. We were able to rescue an Air America pilot and a Filipino crewman. In another case, a downed American Air Force pilot in central Laos was about to give up hope of being rescued when the bushes in which he was hiding parted. An Asian face appeared in the breech. The pilot said, "I hope you are who I think you are." The face broke into a wide grin. It was a Hmong, and the pilot was rescued.

.   .   .

Vint Lawrence and Tony Poe were two of the American CIA officers who worked closely with the Hmong. I came to know both of them. When I arrived in 1965, they had already been on the ground in Laos for several years and were well on their way to going down in

CIA folklore as paramilitary legends. They were among the key CIA officers who remained behind in Laos in circumvention of the Geneva agreements of 1962.

Poe, whose full name was Anthony Poshepny, was the more colorful of the two. He was a hard-drinking, profane veteran of paramilitary wars around the globe. A U.S. Marine veteran of Iwo Jima, Poe arrived in Laos in 1961 after stints training Muslim separatists from southwest China, Tibetan Khampa guerrillas, and anti-communist forces in Indonesia. Perhaps Poe's most famous claim to fame was that he had helped the Dalai Lama flee Tibet in the spring of 1959, a step ahead of the People's Liberation Army's blazing guns as the story goes. Poe was the quintessential "cold warrior" against communism; he traveled lightly and went wherever he was ordered. He cared little for local customs or languages; he was interested in training men to fight. Because I knew of his reputation as a soldier of fortune, I was surprised when I saw Poe reading *The Wall Street Journal* when I visited his outpost in northwestern Laos. I found out later that he had a college degree in history and English.

Poe added to his reputation as a swashbuckler when he was wounded in January 1965 on a mission in northeastern Laos. While providing artillery cover for a Hmong battalion that was retreating from the North Vietnamese, Poe and a small group of PARU and Hmong that he was commanding came under fire. When Poe's Hmong charges failed to halt the advancing North Vietnamese troops, Poe himself opened fire and decimated the North Vietnamese lines. Poe was under strict orders not to get involved in fighting, but he lived on the edge and had no plans to run away from action. As he and his troops were walking over to check the bodies of the North Vietnamese for possible intelligence information, three or four enemy soldiers jumped out of the bush and ambushed the group. Poe was hit in the hip. The other members of his search party were all killed. While lying on the ground, Poe unclipped his grenades and lobbed them at the approaching Vietnamese. He fended off the attack, thus clearing the way for a retreat. Using his M-1 rifle as a cane, he hobbled out to an evacuation site. Several Hmong fashioned a makeshift stretcher out of a poncho to carry him up a last hill to where the helicopter would land. Poe and thirteen wounded Hmong were successfully evacuated, and the legend of Tony Poe, the disobedient warrior, grew larger.

On one occasion, I received physical proof of Poe's unusual behavior. I had heard that Poe proved his kills of Pathet Lao by collecting their ears. The story has it that Poe also paid bounties of 5,000 kip (Lao money) for new pairs of ears. The ears piled up outside his hut in a green cellophane bag. One day early in my tour, Poe dropped a bag of ears on a desk in the front office as if those of us in Vientiane had doubted his performance. We did not. Nor did we find it necessary to examine the evidence. I also think he wanted to shock the new Ivy League CIA officer. He succeeded.

If Poe was the rowdy cowboy type, then Vint Lawrence was the cerebral and patient operative. Poe's junior by about fifteen years, Lawrence was recruited into the CIA in 1961 during his senior year at Princeton. While stationed among the Hmong, Lawrence took an interest in their family lineage, healing practices, and chanting. He studied their language and became conversant in Hmong. The Hmong used to say about Lawrence, "Il est tres réfléchi." (He is very thoughtful.) Lawrence's cables back to Washington were famous for their descriptions of the Hmong and for the lyrical style in which they were written.

Because of the nature of their work—training the Hmong to be a reliable and effective fighting force—both Lawrence and Poe had to live among the Hmong. They seldom left Long Tieng, where they lived in thatched huts with dirt floors and without electricity and running water. Much of their work was done discreetly because they had to avoid detection by the ICC monitors who periodically toured the countryside looking for violations by foreign countries, particularly the U.S. In those early years of the CIA's covert paramilitary program to support the Hmong, called by its code name Operation Momentum, both Poe and Lawrence made significant strides in building a working relationship with Vang Pao and his leaders and in making his irregulars into a tough fighting force.

Thus far in my intelligence work in Asia, I had not run into officers like Poe and Lawrence. They represented a breed of grassroots operatives who were as close to "going native" as you could get. In many ways, the two men took their cue from their boss Bill Lair, a native Texan who had been working for the CIA in Thailand since the early 1950s. Lair spoke Thai superbly. In fact, he was married to a Thai princess. Lair had worked himself into the Thai security community so well that the Thais made him an officer in their police corps. Lair was the man who had organized the Thai PARU into a fighting force.

For the CIA, Lair's position in Thailand was a boon. His status as a major in the Thai police was genuine, not a cover, and the Thais allowed him to maintain his American citizenship and continue his work for the CIA. In fact, the Lair-trained PARU were, in more ways than one, the shock troops of the CIA's covert operation in Laos. But Lair, like Poe, was also known to push the envelope sometimes. After learning in May 1965 that the Pathet Lao had captured an American pilot named Ernie Brace when he touched down in a hotly contested site in central Laos, Lair launched a full-scale assault on the retreating column to try to rescue the pilot. Lair called in American-piloted T-28 fighter-bombers. But he acted without approval from U.S. ambassador William Sullivan, a powerful figure who had to sign off on all operations in Laos. While the T-28s were strafing the trees and bush in an attempt to flush out the enemy, additional firepower showed up in the form of U.S. F-105 Thunderchiefs. Brace was not rescued and ended up in the infamous Hanoi Hilton, the Hanoi prison camp for American POWs. He was released by the Vietnamese after spending nearly eight years in prison. As for Lair, he almost got fired. One of the F-105 Thunderchiefs miscalculated and bombed a friendly village in an adjacent valley. The U.S. government had to pay compensation for the pilot's error. I remember a furious Ambassador Sullivan saying about Lair: "I would kick him out of Laos if he weren't so good."

. . .

Vientiane contained a community of middle-class Americans living respectable lives for the most part. They sent their children to school, socialized at parties, put on plays, and participated in scavenger hunts and wine-tastings. The American community took its lead from Ambassador Sullivan, who served in Laos from 1964 to 1968. He was an intensely patriotic man who understood the need for a sense of community among the several-hundred-strong American population in the midst of a dangerous situation. He believed in what the U.S. government was doing in Laos and made sure to boost the morale of the American personnel and their families. At July 4th parties on the U.S. Embassy grounds, he gave stirring speeches that eloquently called for support on the home front for America's role in Laos. He would talk about the need for wives to be understanding of their husbands who had to spend weeks up-country building roads, practicing medicine, teaching more efficient agricultural methods, or carrying out the paramilitary war in frustrating, primitive, and often sweltering conditions. His words of encouragement helped to engender a sense of belonging among the resident Americans, many of whom felt cut off from the rest of the world and isolated by anti-Vietnam War sentiment back in the U.S. I even got some negative flack from my own family. Several relatives who joined in the anti–Vietnam War fervor wrote me that they resented what I was doing in Laos. I replied that, since I did not tell them how to vote in the U.S., they should leave my part in the war in Southeast Asia up to me.

But there was also another side to life in Laos. Perhaps it was the combination of the dangerous environment, a permissive atmosphere, and Laos itself, but whatever the ingredients the mix of being in Laos had a potent effect. It could pull people downward. I saw this in our own CIA station in Vientiane and did my best, as deputy chief of station, to respond.

People with unresolved personal problems were especially susceptible, but that did not seem to be a necessary precondition. On one occasion, a communications officer fell for his colleague's wife and said he was ready to give up everything for his new love. We transferred the families out of Laos before anything happened. In another case, the Asian wife of an officer turned against her husband and was ready to go after him with a knife. Another time, when a young officer was up-country on assignment, his attractive blonde wife became infatuated with a male member of the couple's Thai house staff. She declared that she wanted to "chuck it all" and live with the young Thai in a house on stilts and fornicate for eternity. We were able to get her out in time as well. In a postscript to this particular drama, when I was back in Washington a few years later, I saw the woman and her officer-husband in a sporty convertible with the top down cruising through the city. They waved to me.

And then there were the infamous bars. The White Rose was a collecting point for visitors to Laos and some of the local expatriates, including CIA paramilitary types looking for "nonmilitary" action. One day one of our senior CIA officers briefed a visiting congressional delegation on the secret war up-country. That evening the delegation was taken to the White Rose for exposure to nightlife in Vientiane. Members of the delegation saw a large American man stark naked on the floor of the bar yelling, "I want it now!" A hostess lifted up her skirt and sat on his face. It was the same officer who had briefed the delegation earlier in the day.

. . .

By this time Laos was a country simmering on the edge of an increasingly "hot" war next door in Vietnam. Up until the mid-1960s, the Americans and North Vietnamese, not wanting to widen the conflict in Vietnam, had both maintained the fiction of a neutral Laos, a ploy that kept fighting to a considerably lower level than in Vietnam. But this pretense was crumbling fast. The North Vietnamese were making use of mountain passes to cross into Lao territory and shuttle supplies into South Vietnam. The bypass through Laos became part of the evolving network of footpaths and trails that came to be known as the Ho Chi Minh Trail. This allowed the Vietnamese to avoid fighting around the demilitarized zone separating the two Vietnams. It became clear that the North Vietnamese had no intention of complying, even slightly, with the 1962 agreements in Geneva. After surveying the changing situation in Southeast Asia from Washington, U.S. policymakers concluded that the small-scale, covert operation run by Bill Lair and company would have to be upgraded if the U.S. intended to halt the North Vietnamese advance into South Vietnam. In March 1965, at about the same time as the decision to escalate the military effort in Laos, the U.S. military undertook a sustained program, codenamed Rolling Thunder, to bomb North Vietnam. One of the main targets of American bombs was the Ho Chi Minh Trail.

As part of the enlargement of the U.S. paramilitary effort in Laos, more CIA case officers, including myself, as well as paramilitary specialists poured into the country. Better housing was built in Long Tieng and Sam Thong to accommodate the new personnel. A road was built to connect the two bases, and a new airstrip, part of which was fog-free in the mornings, was constructed in Long Tieng.

The seminal event in upgrading the strategic importance of the Laotian theater was the arrival of my new boss Ted Shackley in Vientiane in July 1966. It has been said that Ted Shackley transformed the CIA's operation in Laos from a country store to a supermarket. Shackley was a no-nonsense workaholic with a background in combating the Soviet bloc in Eastern Europe and the Americas. He had cut his intelligence teeth in places like Berlin and Miami in the early years of the East–West rivalry during intense events such as the Cuban Missile Crisis. A bespectacled man with blonde hair, he was organized, ambitious, and relentless. We used to say about him that "he had no intellectual fat."

Shackley wasted little time in outlining the new mission for the Laos CIA station. From an organizational standpoint, he began by reigning in the "free-wheeling" attitude and open-ended budgets that had existed under his predecessors. He instituted personnel reporting to keep track of up-country teams and introduced the use of flight logs so he could more closely monitor helicopter and plane flights. The changes irked CIA officers in Laos who had gotten used to a much more flexible system that seemed to fall in line with the Lao way of doing things. At the CIA station in Vientiane, we started working ten-hour days, six, sometimes seven, days a week. We flew all over Laos to check up on bases in different parts of the country. The days became a blur of work: following missions, devising strategies, and building support. I had a two-way radio the size of a small refrigerator beside our bed that would shake the mattress when it went off in the middle of the night with reports from various sites around the country. To this day, Sally says that it was not the radio but the beating of her heart that caused the mattress to shake. Activities outside work fell by the wayside. I failed to find the time to learn my lines for a role in the play *Tiger at the Gates* put on by the American diplomatic community.

When the time came for the performance, director Joy Zinoman had to prompt me on stage by whispering my lines. In those hectic months the only way I knew it was Sunday was because we had waffles for breakfast at home.

If the original goal of Operation Momentum had been to aid a Hmong guerrilla force that harassed the enemy, gather intelligence, and tie up North Vietnamese troops inside Laos, the new *raison d'être* became more of the same on a larger scale. When Shackley arrived in Laos, the U.S. government was engaged in a major buildup in Vietnam, which would bring the number of American troops there to about 500,000. More Americans, heavier weapons, and bigger aircraft, like the C-130, were brought into play in Laos to beef up the military presence and to deliver a blow to the North Vietnamese operating in northeastern Laos. The plan was to bleed the North Vietnamese divisions and force Hanoi to send in replacements, thus diverting manpower from South Vietnam.

In the southern part of Laos, where North Vietnamese convoys were streaming into South Vietnam via the Ho Chi Minh Trail, the goal was to use infiltration and ambushes by trained guerrilla teams of tribesmen, as well as heavy bombing with trained spotters on the ground, to disrupt the flow of supplies and troops. We devised a small radio, called HARK-1, for the illiterate Kha tribesmen. The radio doubled as a counter and had several buttons, with each button containing the silhouette of a truck or a soldier. The tribesmen would punch buttons corresponding to what they saw on the trail. The information was then transmitted to hovering aircraft, which in turn called in air strikes.

We used World War II–era B-25 and T-28 fighter-bombers to attack the trail because they were slower and had more hover time. Faster F-4 Phantom jets were used in northern Laos and North Vietnam, where antiaircraft guns were more formidable. One of the successes of the augmented air campaign came when a Hmong spotter on the broad plateau in central Laos called the Plain of Jars detected a cave opening. He called in an air strike, and an F-4 fired a missile into the opening of the cave. A huge explosion inside the cave blew off the top of the mountain. We had struck a hidden Vietnamese ammunition dump.

The hope was that the revised plan, which still paid lip service to the

Geneva Agreements by excluding the introduction of U.S. ground troops into Laos, would allow the U.S. to strike a heavy blow at North Vietnam without provoking full Chinese or Soviet entrance into the war. The division of the effort—with the Lao supplying the ground troops and the U.S. carrying out air strikes—remained the same; the campaign was just conducted on a larger scale. A secondary objective of our operation in Laos was for the friendly Lao forces to occupy as much territory as possible to enhance their negotiating position should a political solution to the Laotian conflict be found. The Pathet Lao backed by Vietnamese troops were still a dominant military force in the country, and we wanted to make sure that their power would be kept in check and that any resulting government would be open and subject to American influence.

9

OF COUPS, FLOODS, AND FAILURES

As TED SHACKLEY's deputy, I was in the thick of the action. Around me the CIA's presence in Laos grew from about thirty people in 1966 to 250 people in 1968. While Shackley spent the bulk of his time coordinating the paramilitary program in northern and southern Laos, I focused on improving our knowledge of the inscrutable and unpredictable Lao political scene.

Since 1960, political coups had occurred regularly in Laos. Rightwing strong men, the weak royalists, and communist-backed neutralists struggled for control of the government. Two half-brothers, Prince Souvanna Phouma, who leaned toward the West, and Prince Souphanouvong, who was a stooge of the North Vietnamese–backed Pathet Lao, vied for leadership of the country. But whoever got into power was faced with the prospect of maintaining the support of the generals of the Lao armed forces, some of whom had strong ties to, and made money from, the country's powerful opium magnates. Since the U.S. government was sinking valuable resources into Laos, we wanted to know with more certainty where the inchoate Lao political process was going. We wanted to limit the surprises. To this end, we recruited Lao agents who could keep us informed about what was going on in the National Assembly, the King's Royal Council, the Prime Minister's Cabinet, and the General Staff of the Royal Lao Army. The latter had its share of corrupt generals whom we needed to watch. The commander-in-chief himself was involved in the opium trade and in the summer of 1967 actually conducted an opium war against his Burmese rivals in the tri-border area of Laos, Burma, and Thailand using Lao-operated, American-made T-28s to bomb their factories.

One of my biggest operations involved ensuring a "favorable" outcome in the elections to the National Assembly in 1967. With more attention being focused on the war in Southeast Asia and with the National Assembly in Laos starting to play a larger political role in the country, we thought it was important for Vang Pao to have more of a say in the political governing of the country. We figured out whom to support without letting our fingerprints show. As part of our "nation building" effort in Laos, we pumped a relatively large amount of money to politicians who would listen to our advice. In the election, "friendly" politicians won fifty-four of fifty-seven seats. Ambassador Sullivan referred to me as Mr. Tammany Hall, an allusion to New York City's prodigious Democratic vote-getting machine of the late nineteenth century.

With the CIA's mission expanding so rapidly, our intelligence gathering and reporting efforts boomed. As CIA personnel, we had better access to parts of Laos than our State Department colleagues. In fact, few Foreign Service officers were even allowed to visit places like Long Tieng. The major exception was Ambassador Sullivan, who oversaw the whole military effort in Laos. But other than him, during my time in Laos, only a handful of State Department personnel made it up to Long Tieng. Sometimes, we were in the awkward position of "outreporting" our State Department colleagues in the embassy, who were supposed to be the experts in designated fields such as the Lao economy, politics, and culture. In some cases, their best sources for information turned out to be our paid agents. We had to be discreet in handling such touchy situations. Since I had worked with many of the Foreign Service officers at other posts in Asia, I was given the job of smoothing ruffled feathers. Sometimes I succeeded. Sometimes I failed. Whatever the outcome, my efforts helped Shackley to concentrate on the guerrilla war.

.   .   .

Occasionally, I even got involved in the guerrilla war. When Washington cabled in 1967 that they wanted the CIA station to commit more resources to stopping the North Vietnamese from infiltrating into South Vietnam through southern Laos, I took a personal interest in the problem. The Ho Chi Minh Trail had long been a source of irritation for the U.S. military, but in recent years it had become the main infiltration route. We also had reports that the enemy had set up bases in southern Laos. Our assets to address the problem were varied. On the "plus" side, we already had a CIA base in Pakse, a regional center located at the foot of the spectacular Bolovens Plateau in southern Laos, and a crack Lao regional commander in General Phasouk Somly. But General Phasouk's troops were of dubious use. Furthermore, the local Kha tribesmen were known for being passive and lazy. In short, we had no Hmong-caliber troops to work with in the area.

I helped with the operation. First, at the embassy in Vientiane, using our intelligence we made sure that areas designated for bombing by the U.S. military in Saigon were free of any villages. Giant B-52 bombers from Thailand then made carpet-bombing runs over the tri-border region of Laos, Cambodia, and Thailand. But the cagey North Vietnamese dug in under villages, knowing they would not be bombed. A lot of bombs ended up falling in empty areas. We also organized teams for after-action reports, but most of our teams were reluctant to go into dangerous areas and produced little worthwhile information.

At the same time, we recruited the Kha tribesmen to run road watch and sabotage missions on the Ho Chi Minh Trail, running north to south, and on the lesser known Sihanouk Trail, running east to west from Cambodia across the southern tip of Laos and into Vietnam. Paramilitary trainers formed the Kha into groups in the safe area of Bolovens Plateau, and then we transported them in helicopters to the trails. More often than not, the Kha returned triumphantly, with reports of a spectacular number of kills and minimal losses. We dutifully relayed the numbers to Washington, but we grew suspicious. We had no confirmation of the Kha's work. Unlike Tony Poe, they did not bring back ears. We decided to subject the Kha to lie detector tests. To convince them to submit to the Western contraption, we described the polygraph to them as some sort of voodoo, which would infect or even sterilize them if they lied. They consented, and under examination, it turned out that much of what they had been reporting was either false or exaggerated. I was led to believe that General Phasouk executed several of these tribesmen.

Finally, to interrupt the North Vietnamese supply lines running through southern Laos, we brought Nung people up from South Vietnam. The Nung were ethnic Chinese who had gained a reputation as fierce and reliable guards of our military installations around Saigon. We settled the Nung into a camp on Bolovens Plateau and trained them in team operations, grenade launching, and road watch duties. I visited them to get a sense of how the operation was shaping up. They had a picture of Sun Yat-sen on the wall of their dormitory and talked a good "anti-Communist" game. But when the time came to leave the safe plateau and go down into the jungles around the trail, the Nung balked, claiming that they had not realized that their mission would entail such risky and dangerous work. The few missions we tried with the Nung did not work, and we sent them back to South Vietnam, their reputation somewhat diminished.

Our experience with the Kha and Nung in Bolovens Plateau taught us that to be effective in Laos we needed to use natives of the area who would fight, not outsiders. It was a lesson that came back to haunt us the longer we operated there.

.   .   .

At the start of the Vietnam conflict in the early 1960s, some analysts in the U.S. believed that China was directly involved in Laos. China, it was thought, wanted to control Laos through communist surrogates because Laos could offer the PRC a land route through which Peking could project southward and dominate Southeast Asia. At times, we came across information to support a wider Chinese role in Laos.

There were reports that a CIA operative in northwestern Laos, near the Chinese border, had seen a Chinese general in a Laotian village. Why he was there or where he came from, we never found out. On another occasion, during my tour in Laos, we interrogated a North Vietnamese defector who had confidential information on a road being built by the Chinese through forbidding mountains and jungles near the border of Laos and China. The road project in northern Laos was one of China's strangest undertakings during the Vietnam War. We had thought the road was to be a thoroughfare for the Chinese People's Liberation Army to threaten Thailand, but the defector, who had been a cadre in the North Vietnamese Communist Party's operation in Laos, said the road was being constructed to get Chinese supplies to the North Vietnamese and Pathet Lao forces fighting in Laos. Only in 1973, when the road became a topic of conversation between Henry Kissinger, President Nixon's national security advisor, and Chinese premier Chou En-lai, did the mystery get unraveled. Curious to know why the road had been built but hardly ever used, Dr. Kissinger questioned the Chinese premier. From Chou's answers, Kissinger surmised that the Chinese had built the road during the Vietnam War not to threaten Thailand nor to help supply the communist forces in Laos, but to have a foothold in Laos in order to counteract the possible domination by its supposed ally North Vietnam over all of Indochina. Even during their partnership with North Vietnam against a common enemy, it appeared that Peking was wary of Hanoi. Six years after Kissinger and Chou's discussion, China and North Vietnam would fight a war on their common border.

In reality, the PRC was not very active in Laos. The Chinese Embassy was quite dormant, having little constituency with which to work because a large part of the local Chinese community in Vientiane leaned toward Taiwan and had close links with the Thai-Chinese, who were similarly inclined. Though the PRC was not a primary target of our activities in Laos, we wanted to take every opportunity to probe them for soft spots and increase our intelligence collection against them. Through my close contacts with Lao generals in Vientiane, we determined that there was a group of several hundred anti-communist Chinese soldiers in northern Laos near the border with China. They were being supplied by Laos with help from Taiwan's intelligence service. The Lao military asked me to help them equip and train the force. I queried Washington, but they turned down the request because it was considered too provocative to China. Also, I doubt that the anti-communist guerrillas would have been willing to move from their base area to engage Chinese troops head-on.

We were, however, able to tap Chinese military phone lines in northern Laos. Through these taps, we gained information on Chinese troop movements and on the road building in the Lao–China border area.

We occasionally tried to recruit Soviet bloc diplomats. And though we got some feelers, we had no takers. On one occasion we approached a Polish diplomat, who almost signed on to give us information, but his price tag was too high for what he had to offer. We had more success shaking up Soviet officials. At a late-night party we sidled up to an inebriated Soviet diplomat and discussed the possibility of working together. After he sobered up and realized what had happened, he was furious at us. He threatened to kill anyone who ever made a similar suggestion in the future. But the damage had already been done to his diplomatic career. I later learned that he was reassigned to Russia, where he remained under permanent suspicion.

Another incident with the Soviets concerned the North Vietnamese defector who had told us about the Chinese road project in northern Laos. To prove that the Chinese and Vietnamese were operating in Laos, we wanted to introduce the defector to the foreign community in Laos. At a cocktail party given by Mark Pratt, a Foreign Service officer at the U.S. Embassy, the Canadian, Indian, and Polish monitoring representatives of the International Control Commission showed up. In addition, a Soviet journalist, the TASS correspondent in Hanoi, happened to be in Vientiane, and he came to the party unaware that the defector would be there. During the party, the Soviet journalist sidled up to Pratt and confided in him, "I have sympathy for you Americans for having to deal with the South Vietnamese because if the South Vietnamese are as difficult as the North Vietnamese, you must have a real headache." Pratt didn't miss a beat. "Well, let's find out," he responded. Pratt called over the North Vietnamese defector and introduced him to the Soviet correspondent. "Here is one of your emissaries from Hanoi."

.   .   .

During the summer of 1966, the opalescent gray Mekong River lazed its way by Vientiane as usual. But toward the end of the summer to everyone's mounting alarm, the current of the Mekong accelerated, and its waters, now pink-brown in color, churned in the riverbed and slapped the riverbanks. Then the Mekong started to rise rapidly at a daily clip. Our American friends who lived in houses on the bluffs overlooking the river watched with fascination and trepidation as it rose the equivalent of four floors of a building in just a few days. Lao soldiers and students with help from USAID road engineers built new walls and sandbag dikes to halt the raging waters, but their efforts were in vain. After spilling over the embankment, the river flooded the entire downtown. Americans living near the river or in low-lying areas had to evacuate in three hours. By the time my embassy colleague Bill Maynes and his wife Gretchen were packing up their last belongings from their riverside villa, the water was already up to their waists. Eventually, the rust-colored mud of the Mekong would leave its imprint halfway up to the ceiling of the Maynes' house.

We took nine people, including four small children, into our house, which was built on high ground about a mile and a half away from the center of Vientiane. My youngest son Jeffrey called them his "refugees." We ate communal dinners, pooling the resources salvaged from the flooding houses, and then often the seven adults, avoiding the flooded street in front of our house, would climb over the chain-link fence to the house of Deputy Chief of Mission Coby Swank and watch films in the evenings.

Downtown Vientiane was inundated to knee level, and people got around by boat. The central market closed down. I ran a rice distribution center out of our house, getting bags to Lao friends who could distribute them to hungry people. As the water rose higher and higher, people had to think of new ways to get about town. Fortunately for us, the CIA ran the most reliable truck route in Vientiane. To get to work at the embassy, one had to adjust daily to a new set of conditions. Mostly, I used three modes of transportation. First, along with other embassy colleagues who lived on high ground, I would walk to the main road—basically an elevated, widened path between flooded rice paddies that were slowly beginning to wash out the road itself. From there we would climb into the back of a U.S. Army 2½-ton transport truck that would take us to the edge of the downtown, where we would dismount and get into narrow boats that would ferry us to the front gates of the embassy. We would then wade in our boots through the knee-high water to cover the final leg of our journey. Despite the embassy being four feet under water, our up-country work did not suffer.

As a result of such resourcefulness and the efforts of our administrative staff, we were able to man our command post in Vientiane twenty-four hours a day.

The flood brought with it the occasional fascinating sidelight. During the flood, an American Air Force officer told me of a story he had heard in downtown Vientiane. He wanted my help in taking action. The officer said an Australian magician in Vientiane had a cigarette lighter with the thumbprint of a missing American on it. The story only got more intriguing and bizarre. The thumbprint, he said, belonged to Jim Thompson, the legendary former OSS operative in Thailand who had organized Thai silk into a world-famous industry. Thompson had recently disappeared in Malaysia. The officer continued: The magician had a sixth sense and could visualize Thompson smoking opium and sitting in a small hut in northern Cambodia, tied up by his captors, the Cambodian communists.

I listened to the officer's outlandish story and then dismissed him as politely as I could. The next time I heard of the bizarre story was two weeks later when the U.S. military in Bangkok requested permission to cross into Laotian airspace to launch a rescue mission in northern Cambodia. It turned out that the officer had gone to Bangkok and convinced a senior American officer of the story's veracity. Suffice it to say that we blocked the attempt, but this anecdote, just like the Lao villagers' story of the *phi* seeing the Lao colonel after the helicopter crash in June 1965, carried with it the unreal element that often seemed to be hovering around events in Laos.

The flood lasted two weeks. While it was shocking to witness a city be paralyzed so quickly, the most terrifying part of the ordeal occurred when the water receded. Then the victims of the flood were uncovered. Many Lao lived in houses built on stilts, but there was no protection from the floodwaters for their pets and the livestock they kept tethered underneath their houses. Dead chickens, dogs, and pigs, as well as a few human corpses, littered the land.

.   .   .

In Vientiane itself, the battle scars of the past—and present—were a part of the daily landscape. We lived next door to the bombed-out shell of the former house of a Laotian general, Phoumi Nosavan, who had carried out a failed coup in 1964. Our Vietnamese staff was afraid to walk near the wall separating the two houses for fear of stepping on unexploded ordnance. On the morning of October 21, just as things were returning to what we might call "normal" after the flood, Sally was getting in the car with five-year-old Mike and three-year-old Jeffrey when they felt vibrations and heard a buzzing noise in the sky. They looked up and saw several planes coming in low as if they were getting ready to drop payloads. She gathered up the boys and hurried back inside the house, where they crawled under the dining room table as the house shook on its timbers, windowpanes cracked, and dust rained down. The squadron of six T-28 planes, it turned out, was led by the disgruntled former head of the Laotian Air Force, General Thouma. The planes were the firepower behind a coup attempt by Thouma. They strafed Vientiane's streets and dropped several bombs on the headquarters of the Laotian Army near our residence as well as the Vientiane airport and a military encampment, killing twenty-six people and wounding sixty-three. In the end, the bombings were more bravado than the beginning of an uprising. Thouma's coup petered out when there was no ground support, and he fled to Thailand, where, like General Phoumi Nosavan before him, he got help and sanctuary from friendly Thai conservatives.

I had reason to feel a bit sheepish when I returned home at the end of the day. The night before the coup, one of our up-country officers had called in on the radio to report that General Thouma was very drunk and railing against the corrupt Laotian leaders in Vientiane. The officer said Thouma was threatening to take action. But at the CIA station in Vientiane, we dismissed Thouma's threats as the ravings of a drunk general. We were wrong.

. . .

Of my various recollections of Laos one event stands out as illustrating both the triumph and tragedy of the U.S. presence there. As the war heated up next door in Vietnam, U.S. policymakers searched for ways to make waging war more costly for the North Vietnamese. In northeastern Laos, near the border with Vietnam, U.S. Air Force planners spotted a mountain that could be used to carry the air war more effectively into North Vietnam. In Lao, the mountain was called Phou Pha Thi, but we came to know the mountain by its military name: Site 85. It is a name that today, some thirty years later, still conjures up wishful thinking of what could have been avoided.

Site 85 was approximately 6,000 feet high. It was not the tallest mountain in the Lao Kingdom, but it had the distinct advantage of having a plateau at its very summit, and it was just 150 air miles from Hanoi. In 1966, the U.S. Air Force had installed a navigational beacon, known by its acronym TACAN, on the summit to help guide planes on their way into Vietnam. But in 1967, the Air Force wanted to upgrade the beacon with a new piece of electronic wizardry that would be able to provide all-weather capability for bombing in North Vietnam. The computerized gadgetry would be able to direct fighters and bombers precisely over their targets, even through heavy cloud cover, and then electronically release their bombs at the right instant. President Lyndon Johnson personally signed off on the plan, and the CIA was told to provide protection for the site. Several CIA paramilitary specialists and Hmong irregulars defended the summit, while scattered groups of Hmong guerrillas were stationed at the base of the mountain. Later a detachment of Thai PARU were added to bolster ground defense. U.S. Air Force personnel ran the actual site, but in a nod to the Geneva Agreements of 1962 forbidding the introduction of foreign military forces into Laos, the Air Force employees had to resign temporarily in order to work as civilians at the station in Laos. It was a clever yet cynical way around the agreements and would allow the U.S. to employ its latest technology in the war against North Vietnam.

In its first months of operation, the site paid huge dividends. From an altitude of 20,000 feet, U.S. Air Force and Navy planes dropped payloads right into Hanoi's backyard, onto railroads, airfields, barracks, and training grounds. But the buildup of Site 85 had forced us to stretch our Laos forces because they had to be used to protect its base. And, according to men like Bill Lair who had been on the ground a long time, such a site risked heavy retaliation from the Vietnamese once they discovered its location. Both Lair and Shackley insisted that the site couldn't be defended for long after it was discovered.

Sure enough, after several successful bombing raids, the North Vietnamese decided to strike back. In early January 1968 they picked the unlikely form of an air attack on Site 85. It was unlikely because the North Vietnamese Air Force was never considered a real threat. On January 12, they sent four antiquated, Soviet-made AN-2 Colt biplanes with cloth-covered wings and wooden propellers to attack the mountain. But the attack was fended off by gunfire and an Air America supply helicopter, which took to the air when the planes were spotted and chased after the slower biplanes. When the Air America helicopter caught up with one of the AN-2 Colts, a crewman on board fired off several carbine rounds at the Colt. The biplane lost altitude and crashed. Another Colt crashed and burned near the backside of the mountain. Washington was ecstatic over the air victory. A telegram arrived praising us facetiously as Snoopy shooting down the Red Baron. My job, shared with the Lao government, was to collect documents off the dead bodies and organize a big propaganda show in the stadium in downtown Vientiane to showcase the documentary proof of North Vietnamese military involvement in Laos.

The North Vietnamese, however, were not to be deterred. Despite shelling from the ground and bombing from above, by late February 1968 North Vietnamese workers finished building a road head that ended not far from the mountain's base. Given the buildup of North Vietnamese forces in the area, Shackley cabled that the mountain could not be held after March 10 and that the time to blow up the site was fast approaching. But he was told to hold tight by superiors at Air Force headquarters in Thailand.

The North Vietnamese struck on precisely March 10, using both strength and stealth to assault the summit of the mountain, where sixteen plainclothes U.S. Air Force men and two CIA men, as well as a forward air controller, were dug in. They fired artillery barrages at the mountain, and then sent a platoon of commandos to scale its side. The attack turned into a rout. Helicopters pulled off the two CIA officers, the forward air controller, and five Air Force technicians, one of whom was fatally shot through the bottom of the helicopter as it was taking off from the mountain. All told, eleven of the nineteen men on the mountain ended up dying.

Coupled with the Royal Lao Army's resounding ground defeat at the hands of the North Vietnamese and Pathet Lao forces at Nam Bac in north-central Laos in mid-January 1968, the disaster at Site 85 sent a shudder through the CIA station. Both Nam Bac and the assault on Site 85, it turned out, were part of a Vietnamese dry-season offensive into Laos. We realized we were no longer playing in the smoke-and-mirrors world of the "discreet war." Given a chance to attack stationary sites in Laos, the North Vietnamese mounted large-scale assaults, the likes of which the Royal Lao Army and Hmong had never seen. By this time, we estimated that the North Vietnamese had up to 70,000 troops in Laos.

The defeat at Site 85 was building to its climax at the time I left Laos in late January 1968. The offensive in Laos had coincided with the Tet offensive in nearby South Vietnam. Though the North Vietnamese and Viet Cong took heavy losses during the Tet offensive, their surprise assaults—carried out brazenly and openly—on cities like the ancient Vietnamese capital of Hue and inside the U.S. Embassy in Saigon further sapped the morale of the U.S. effort in Vietnam and emboldened the anti-war movement at home. It seemed that events were out of our control. In Laos, we started to feel powerless in the face of the sweeping North Vietnamese tide. By 1968, the North Vietnamese troops and Pathet Lao controlled 75 percent of Laos. As Bill Maynes, my colleague at the U.S. Embassy from 1965 to 1967, has said, it was like trying to stop a flood. But unlike the Mekong River, the North Vietnamese and their Pathet Lao comrades did not recede.

·   ·   ·

Our initial goal in Laos was laudable: to help the Lao fight the wave of communism that was infiltrating their country. Along the way, we took some hard losses. In October 1965, we got news that four men, including two bright, young CIA paramilitary case officers, Mike Deuel and Mike Maloney, both sons of CIA men, had been killed when their H-34 chopper crashed into dense jungle in southern Laos after an apparent mechanical malfunction.

I had gotten to know Deuel when I saw him in Vientiane, and had been impressed by his work ethic and charismatic personality. He was the kind of guy that legendary CIA officer Desmond Fitzgerald would have loved. Fitzgerald had once said that for the CIA he wanted "Harvard Phd's who could win a bar fight." Deuel wasn't a Harvard man, but he had graduated from Cornell and then served in the Marines before joining the CIA.

Deuel had been running road-watch operations in southern Laos since 1962. Maloney, a barrel-chested Irishman, was joining Deuel, and the two men were flying that October day so that Deuel could introduce Maloney to the tribal leaders with whom he would be working. Both men's wives were pregnant when their husbands died.

Deuel and Maloney's legacy of action and commitment to a difficult and controversial war left me with a strong feeling that they could not have died in vain. Good Americans, not ugly or quiet ones, made a difference. Like Jack Downey, my classmate at Yale who had spent more than 7,000 days as a prisoner in China when Deuel and Maloney's H-34 helicopter went down, they were the best America had to offer.

Deuel and Maloney were visiting Lao tribal leaders that fateful day, something that we began to do less and less of as the "secret" war continued. The U.S. had based its original plan in Laos on the Hmong, a hardy and fiercely proud people. But, perhaps, too quickly we lost sight of what had made the initial paramilitary efforts with the Hmong successful—keeping them at the forefront of military engagement with the Pathet Lao. Instead, as the war in nearby Vietnam escalated, the Hmong became more of a secondary consideration in the broader strategic plan of combating the communist threat in Vietnam. Well-intentioned efforts, such as settling displaced Laotians in villages along the Mekong River, contributed to the tribal people, especially the Hmong, becoming more and more dependent on U.S. assistance. Eventually, when Prince Souvanna Phouma agreed to enter into a coalition government with the Pathet Lao in 1973, the Hmong knew their days in Laos were numbered. When the Americans pulled out their military advisors in 1974, the Hmong understood that their hopes for a free Laos were dashed. After General Vang Pao left Laos with a CIA escort in May 1975, many Hmong fled across the Mekong River to Thailand, where they were housed in temporary refugee camps. In the years after the Vietnam War, 50,000 to 60,000 Hmong were resettled in the U.S. Yet even today in Laos, pockets of Hmong resistance to the communist government still exist, and Laos strictly controls visits by Hmong living outside the country. But the fact is that the Hmong were victims of the expansion of the war in Vietnam.

One day near the end of our stay, a Laotian general came unannounced to the front door of our house in Vientiane. My wife was home and invited him in. The general didn't linger. He told my wife, "Please always remember that we Laotians are grateful to you Americans because you are giving us time. You will leave, but, however long you stay in Laos, we are grateful."

Today, close to forty years later, Laos is still struggling to get out from under the Vietnamese and is now welcoming the U.S. back to help it become a productive country. Laotians currently view America's activity in their country in the 1960s and 1970s as a contentious and misguided chapter of Laotian history, but the United States is no longer seen as the enemy. The bombs we dropped certainly left a wound, but their impact is largely ignored today.

III

CHINA OPENS UP

1969–1981

10

READING THE TEA LEAVES

WHEN I returned to Hong Kong for a second tour in May of 1968, China was in the middle of Mao's last social engineering experiment gone mad, the Cultural Revolution. As in the 1950s, Hong Kong still provided Western intelligence agencies, including the CIA, the best access to information on China. The truth was that almost twenty years after the founding of the People's Republic of China, the U.S. remained estranged from the country and thus still handicapped in its ability to gather intelligence.

American diplomats, intelligence officers, and military personnel who collected information on China were less experienced with the country than they were with other nations and, therefore, vulnerable to schemes by resourceful Chinese middlemen. I had seen evidence of this during my first tour in Hong Kong in 1953. It was déjà vu in the 1960s when crafty Chinese in the New Territories were passing what they said were authentic Red Guard as well as intelligence documents to U.S. military intelligence collectors who naively defended their authenticity. Many turned out to be carefully crafted fakes. To prevent getting tricked again, Washington eventually developed, among other methods, a paper and ink test to check the authenticity of the documents.

The biggest obstacle, though, in intelligence gathering remained the restrictions that the British Special Branch had placed on CIA activities in the 1950s, including the prohibition on recruiting agents inside communist organizations in Hong Kong. Contacts with employees of Chinese communist-front organizations based in Hong Kong, such as the Bank of China, China Travel Services, China Resources Company, and the New China News Agency—the organizations that outwardly handled the mainland's investment, tourism, trade, and propaganda, respectively, but that also were intelligence fronts—were off-limits.

So, while China was reeling from the early stages of the Cultural Revolution, the CIA contingent in Hong Kong's downtown Central district had to content itself mainly with refugees fleeing domestic battles in China's major cities. But refugees were really one-shot deals: They told us what they knew, but were of little use in terms of providing continual streams of information about current and future developments on the mainland. It was as if the CIA had been confined to peering at China's troubled seas through a periscope or, to use a more apt metaphor, to reading tea leaves.

However, because of one exception granted by the British, a "walk-in" from one of the communist organizations, our periscope view wasn't as narrow as it might have been. Because we shared information with them, the Special Branch allowed us to continue to work with this agent, deemed a walk-in because he had voluntarily offered his services to us before the British prohibition. This middle-level official provided information on activities he was privy to, but because we didn't want to jeopardize this singular source of information, we declared him a "static" agent, meaning that we desisted from pushing him to give us leads on disgruntled superiors who might be susceptible to our advances.

.   .   .

While the CIA was at a disadvantage, it was not in the worst intelligence position in Hong Kong. In the late 1960s we discovered through inside information that nearly all of Taiwan's intelligence operations against the mainland had been compromised. We tried to inform the Taiwan intelligence agencies, but neither they nor our own people in Taipei were prepared to listen. I am sure they saw us as "breaking their rice bowls" with such damning information.

In this atmosphere of meager information, it turned out that the CIA's most successful operations against China happened outside Hong Kong. In perhaps one of the most important intelligence operations in the history of the CIA, in October 1961 Tibetan guerrillas had ambushed a Chinese Army convoy. From a truck in the convoy the guerrillas recovered twenty-nine issues of a secret military journal.

The top-secret documents, which covered the period from January to August 1961, were to be read only by senior-level field commanders in the People's Liberation Army (PLA). The journals shed light on the state of the military as well as on political and economic conditions inside China during a time of famine and the start of the Sino-Soviet split. Most importantly, the documents gave CIA analysts a valuable cross-reference to check the veracity of the official pronouncements that Peking was making. If China-watching was akin to reading tea leaves, then the Tibetan operation had uncovered a guide to identifying the different types of tea bushes in China.

Another main source of information came from analyzing provincial newspapers brought out by refugees or by Hong Kong Chinese visiting family members. By 1965 the provincial newspapers carried more and more articles on Mao's plan to launch a new campaign, grandly named the Great Proletarian Cultural Revolution, to root out disloyal elements in society and destroy his personal enemies.

The young activists of Mao's Cultural Revolution were known as Red Guards and wore red armbands to identify themselves. The Red Guards first appeared in July 1965 and were assigned the mission of ridding Chinese society of "bourgeois goods and ideas." They were mostly high school students or young university students. Ironically, the Cultural Revolution was anti-intellectual from its outset and would remain so, and to accommodate the goals of the movement, schools and universities across China were closed down in 1965 and 1966. Teachers were one of the first targets of the mass movement; they were denounced and paraded through the streets, and many ended up losing their jobs and lives.

Red Guard newspapers started to be published to get out the message. But as bands of Red Guards began to gather in major cities around China and assault the municipal Communist Party headquarters and the offices of the local Party newspapers, it became clear from a close reading of the Red Guard newspapers and from debriefings of refugees streaming into Hong Kong that Mao had unleashed the students as his shock troops. In an ironic turn of fate, the Red Guards, the engines of Mao's second revolution, started to attack functionaries of the Chinese Communist Party, the vanguard force of Mao's first revolution. We learned from refugees that the emotional frenzy of the Red Guards, who saw the world in stark, purist terms, fueled their conviction and radicalism. The irrationality of the Red Guards, combined with few limits on their use of force, led to catastrophic losses among the Chinese population during the Cultural Revolution.

Using the military journals from the Tibetan operation as a springboard for understanding the Chinese Communist phraseology, Hong Kong–based CIA analysts were able to decipher the real meaning behind the polemic directives of the Red Guards. Here is an example: We learned that the Red Guards' stance against "economism" meant that they opposed the use of money and other benefits to influence workers, a position of the "revisionists," who were, thusly, accused of "taking the capitalist road."

Analysts got so good at interpreting Red Guard pronouncements that they were often able to predict what the Red Guards were going to say in response to any event, at least this is what my CIA boss in Hong Kong, Bill W., contended. Those of us in his CIA contingent weren't surprised, therefore, when the anecdote filtered down to Hong Kong that Chinese premier Chou En-lai had written on a document, "If you want to know what's going on in China, ask the CIA people in Hong Kong."

Bill W.'s reports back to Washington were eventually packaged into a book titled *The Marco Polo Papers.* The book represented, in my view, the most objective and profound reporting on the Cultural Revolution to date for its limited audience of CIA officers and select Washington policymakers. Not only did the essays cover the origins of and motives behind policies followed during the period of Bill's tenure from 1964 to 1968, but they also reported on the turbulent state of affairs in Guangzhou, which, like other major Chinese metropolises, was being torn apart by factional fighting between rival Red Guard groups.

The title of the limited-circulation book, *The Marco Polo Papers,* was revealing for what it said about collection methods. Some historians believe that the Italian explorer Marco Polo never made it to the Middle Kingdom. They surmise that he collected his information about

China from the fringes of the country and from reports of travelers to China. So it was with the *The Marco Polo Papers*, a collection of analytical essays on the Cultural Revolution drawn from a thorough reading of Chinese newspapers and debriefings of refugees and visitors.

In the absence of direct information links with China, the CIA contingent turned to outside sources for help. One of the best sources in Hong Kong turned out to be a Hungarian-born Jesuit named Laszlo La Dany. His weekly reports on China, titled "China News Analysis," were read by analysts in Hong Kong. Father La Dany had lived for nine years in China before the Communist revolution. Once in Hong Kong, he set up a one-man research outfit, and, drawing on his contacts on the mainland, he produced one of the most authoritative publications on events in China for almost thirty years.

But brilliant as *The Marco Polo Papers* and La Dany's "China News Analysis" were, they still suffered from being a step removed from inside information on the Chinese leadership, its problems, and policies. The hard truth for Washington was that, as of 1968, the CIA had failed to develop any substantive operations outside of Hong Kong.

Given this situation, as deputy chief of the CIA contingent in 1968 I decided it was vital to break down the wall that separated the CIA from what were potentially the richest sources of information about what was going on in China—the Chinese mainlanders working for official Chinese Communist organizations in Hong Kong. Recruitment of these kinds of people could be key to intelligence collection efforts because, as trusted employees of the Communist Party apparatus, they had governmental permission to travel back and forth between China and Hong Kong. Agents inside official government organizations could give firsthand accounts of the developments of Chinese policy—the counterattacks, retreats, and offensives that were being orchestrated at the higher levels and carried out on the streets.

.   .   .

In those early days in Hong Kong as I pondered how to expand intelligence operations against China, the memories of my family's recent visit home to America were a sharp reminder that China wasn't the only country in upheaval. We had had a rough welcome back during our short four-month stay in Washington between assignments. I enrolled in Chinese language review training, but it was hard to study because of the distractions around me. Just a few blocks from my tutorial in a building on 14th Street, huge crowds of angry protesters gathered on the Mall and demanded that the U.S. pull out of Vietnam. On March 31, in the wake of the embarrassing Tet offensive, President Lyndon Johnson, who had engineered the American buildup in Vietnam, announced he would not run for reelection that fall. Then just four days later, Reverend Martin Luther King Jr. was assassinated in Memphis, Tennessee. Within hours of King's death on April 4, a wave of violence swept across the country. Washington, D.C., erupted in riots. I remember looking out the window of our classroom and seeing people racing down 14th Street, which became a main corridor of looting in the city. Our teacher told us to go home, and the building in which we studied was locked up.

Sally and I had rented a house across the Potomac River in Virginia. From our vantage point on the bluffs of the Potomac, we watched smoke rise from fires burning in downtown Washington. More than 700 fires ignited by arsonists illuminated the night as U.S. Army troops in full combat gear took battle positions around the Capitol and the White House. Incensed African Americans rampaged through the streets. In many cases, the police stood by helplessly, outnumbered and under orders to be restrained in their actions against the mobs. It seemed that the United States was coming apart at the seams.

Thus, 1968 had already shown itself to be a turbulent year in the making. In Washington I was concerned about the upheaval I saw, but I didn't confuse events in the United States with the Cultural Revolution in China. Violent events in China had been going on for years, involved millions of people, and were often orchestrated at the top, as in the case of Madame Mao's extremist faction of Red Guards.

Mao tried to stop the chaos he had unleashed and suppress the outbreaks of anarchy in the big metropolitan centers. Beginning in the fall of 1967 and continuing into the spring of 1968, there was a drive—at his behest—to restore order. Mao called on the PLA, which had been ordered to remain neutral in many previous clashes, to reestablish order throughout China, by force if necessary. The Army organized special vigilante groups to assist in halting street battles. In May, after several days of bloody clashes in Guangzhou between two rival Red Guard groups during which the groups threw stones, homemade bombs, and sulfuric acid at each other, the PLA finally intervened to quell the fighting. The Army imposed a dusk-to-dawn curfew in the city, and troops patrolled the streets in armored cars.

Mao's decision to turn to the PLA was the beginning of the end of the bloody reign of the Red Guards. The process of taking power back from the bands of renegade youths was a fitful one, but through 1969, which we nicknamed "The Year of the Gun," and into the early 1970s, power gradually returned to the Chinese government.

But fighting raged out of control in some places before the PLA was able to impose order. In late June 1968, those of us in Hong Kong got a graphic indication of the horrific toll the Cultural Revolution was taking on the Chinese people. Severe monsoon rains flooded the rivers leading into Hong Kong. Swept down to sea by the Pearl River, dozens of corpses washed up onto the shores of the New Territories, Kowloon, and Lantao Island. I sent case officers to investigate the gory scene. They reported back that some of the bodies had their hands tied behind their backs. Others showed evidence of bullet wounds in the backs of their heads.

Prior to the gruesome scene on the shores of Hong Kong and the surrounding area, refugees and border crossers had been telling us of desperate factional fighting in the city of Wuzhou, located on the Xi Jiang River near the border of Guangxi Province and Guangdong Province. The bodies, clearly the victims of a mass execution, confirmed that a bloody battle had taken place, most likely in Wuzhou. One account of the fighting from the newspaper of a Red Guard faction involved in the Wuzhou battles reported that more than 2,000 buildings were destroyed and up to 40,000 people rendered homeless. Seeing the washed-up bodies on shore, we could only imagine how many hundreds, or even thousands, of people had been killed in the senseless violence.

In Hong Kong we wondered for a time if events in China were out of the government's control. At the height of the chaos in Guangxi Province, the Chinese Central Government in Peking seemed powerless to stop the obstructing of railway cars going through the province. In some cases, the cars, filled with Soviet military supplies, were headed for Vietnam. But Red Guards, stirred up by anti-Soviet propaganda and eager to get their hands on weapons to use in clashes against other Red Guard factions, forced the trains to stop and stole their cargo. Appeals from Premier Chou En-lai and other Chinese leaders during the summer of 1968 failed to halt this looting. The prospect of an impotent central government and images of battles in places like Wuzhou led some observers to think the country was unraveling. Their nightmare scenario included millions of Chinese storming over the border into Hong Kong and the New Territories.

.   .   .

Hong Kong real estate prices had plummeted in 1967 when many wealthy Chinese, fearing increased instability on the mainland, fled the city for the safer havens of Switzerland, Canada, and the U.S. For us, this meant we were able to afford the rent on a house with a swimming pool on the opposite side of the island from the central business district. The house in Stanley Beach was a welcome respite from the hustle and bustle of downtown and the endless pressure of work. We invited friends and work colleagues over to relax by the pool, waterskied, and watched our two older boys play in Little League games at the nearby park.

Our comfortable situation in Hong Kong gave us the opportunity to invite my widowed mother, at the time living alone in Del Ray Beach, Florida, to visit us. She always looked back on her years of living in China as the best times of her life. We thought that by inviting her to visit us in Hong Kong we might give her a chance to reconnect with good memories of the past and to see her grandchildren. It was her first time back to Asia since she and my father had left in 1948.

During our early postings in Asia, my mother would occasionally advise Sally on the way to deal with the house staff. For example, she warned Sally from afar that one had to accede to the practice among cooks in Asia, called "cumshaw," of taking ten percent of the grocery money for themselves. When she arrived in Hong Kong in December 1969, my mother regained her Chinese persona! On shopping trips with Sally, she pointed out quality Chinese items, like furniture and jewelry that had been made during the 1920s and 1930 for foreigners. On their outings around Hong Kong, my mother recognized the names of shops that had relocated to Hong Kong to escape the communist revolution. And in one instance my mother even met an antique dealer whom she had known during her time in Shanghai twenty years earlier.

During the time she stayed with us, we convinced my mother to go on a trip to Cambodia with the American Women's Club of Hong Kong. At 74, she was reluctant to take a trip to a developing country with a group of people she didn't know. Despite her initial misgivings, she had a terrific time. She saw Angkor Wat and regaled her fellow traveling companions—who were also good listeners—with stories about living in China in the old days. The Chinese friends she made on the trip seemed to adore her.

We were very fortunate that my mother was with us in 1970 because Sally had to leave suddenly for the U.S. to receive medical attention. In January 1969, she had gravely injured her leg when she accidentally walked through a plate glass window. We were on our way to a party at the apartment of my old colleague Ted Shackley, whose family was safe-havened in Hong Kong while he was CIA chief in Saigon. As I was paying the taxi driver, Sally walked ahead, with her head down because she was engrossed in reading a letter from her sister telling of the latest news in the U.S. She did not notice that the plate glass panels she was heading for were not the entrance doors to the apartment complex. When Sally put her foot out to nudge open what she thought was the door, she broke through the glass, and the heavy sheet glass crashed down on her leg.

Over the course of the next year, Sally had three operations in Hong Kong and the Philippines to reconnect the tendon in her foot, which had been severed in the accident. Finally, at their wit's end because the wound would not heal, the doctors decided that Sally should go back to the U.S. for medical treatment. We asked my mother to stay on in Hong Kong, and she readily agreed. She became a mother of sorts again, taking care of the three boys while I went to work. She took them to birthday parties and generally oversaw the household. It was a godsend to have her there. After a successful skin graft operation, Sally returned to Hong Kong in April 1970, finally on the mend fourteen months after the accident.

·   ·   ·

In Hong Kong, we faced a massive effort on the part of China's Public Security Bureau (PSB) to track and neutralize "hostile" elements, chiefly the U.S. and Taiwanese intelligence agencies. The PSB's network of agents in China and Hong Kong included house staff, hotel clerks, maids, and taxi drivers, and while it wasn't airtight—the Chinese had to deal with unreliable and manufactured reports just as we did—it did stretch far and wide.

Shortly after my arrival in 1968, we made headway in targeting local Chinese Communist front organizations. Responding to appeals from my new boss Charley W., who had a good rapport with the British, the Hong Kong Special Branch relented on the prohibition against CIA conducting counterespionage. "If we are to survive as an intelligence gathering unit in Hong Kong, we have to do this," Charley said. The approach worked, but the British in Hong Kong told us our rear ends would be on the line if anything went wrong. They told Charley, "You will get no help from us, and we will drop everything," meaning that we would lose our access to the front organizations.

We started the laborious work of identifying vulnerable targets, developing access to them, and eventually approaching them covertly about the possibility of cooperating with us. Because of the widespread assault against Party members driven by the Cultural Revolution, we reasoned that the employees of these government organizations, like the Bank of China, China Resources, the New China News Agency, and some closely affiliated front companies, would be fertile grounds for recruitment. Indeed, in the aftermath of the brutality and extremism of the Cultural Revolution, a good number of Communist Chinese cadres in Hong Kong were disillusioned. Some, undoubtedly, had lost family members to the anarchy; others wondered if they would be the next victims. Through our network of Chinese agents in Hong Kong, we sent out feelers to them.

The New China News Agency, or Xinhua as it was known in Chinese, was the Communist Party–controlled media outlet that functioned as the mainland's mouthpiece around the world. In the late 1960s Xinhua was more than a propaganda front for Peking. In Hong Kong it was the headquarters of the Chinese Communist presence on the island. While a good number of Chinese organizations in Hong Kong and Macau were staffed by Hong Kong cadres, Xinhua was an attractive target because many of its employees were high-ranking Party members and intelligence officers from the mainland who, therefore, traveled back and forth regularly.

One contact proved particularly worthwhile. His information, which started coming to us in 1968, provided us with early indications that the Chinese were interested in opening up to the U.S. after nearly two decades of hostile relations. Our well-connected agent relayed to us his conversations with higher-ranking Communist Party figures in which they talked about the need for China to work together with the U.S. to oppose the increasingly belligerent Soviet Union.

During the Cultural Revolution, international relations had taken a back seat to the domestic agenda in China. During the height of the Revolution in 1966 and 1967, Peking recalled nearly all its ambassadors from around the world. The country slid into xenophobic isolation. In a sign of its withdrawal, China broke completely from its erstwhile communist ally the Soviet Union. After a period of close cooperation in the 1950s, when the Soviet Union helped China build its industrial base and the two countries presented a united communist front to the world, particularly during the early stages of the conflict in Vietnam, Moscow and Peking had had a sharp falling out starting in 1960. Ideological spats, territorial disputes, and China's wariness of Soviet "big power chauvinism" splintered relations between the two countries.

During the Cultural Revolution, China's relations with the Soviet Union continued to deteriorate. In August 1968, in an assertion of the Brezhnev Doctrine, which stated that the Soviet Union would come to the aid of other socialist countries when socialism was threatened, the Soviet Union intervened militarily in Czechoslovakia to squash a budding reform movement. Already smarting from the Sino-Soviet break in relations in the early 1960s, the Chinese saw the Soviet move in Eastern Europe as a direct challenge to socialist states who harbored ideologies that were at odds with Moscow. By 1969, around 200,000 Soviet troops were deployed across the border from Manchuria. Near Sinjiang in the western part of China, another 200,000 were massed near the border. I remember reading cable traffic in which high-level military intelligence officers in Washington were predicting a massive Soviet attack on China using tanks, aircraft, and, conceivably, nuclear weapons.

Fearing a Soviet invasion of his country, Mao concocted some bizarre defensive schemes. In one case, he ordered huge dirt mounds to be built across strategic access routes to important population centers and military installations, like at the confluence of the Huang Pu and Yangtze Rivers in Shanghai and near Shuang Cheng Zi, the missile test range in northwestern China. We succeeded in getting an agent inside one of these forts. He reported back that the mounds were about a hundred yards long and fifty yards high and often had moats around them. They seemed like medieval defense fortifications, except for the fact that they bristled with antiaircraft weapons. Mao's defensive tactics were certainly not revolutionary. In fact, when I heard about the forts, I was reminded of the well-defended tomb of the famous Chinese emperor Chin Shi Huang, which was built more than 2,000 years ago. I discovered by doing some of my own research that Native Americans had built similar forts with moats in parts of North America. About ten years later, while on board a Chinese naval vessel with Secretary of Energy James Schlesinger, I pointed out the famous mounds and recounted their history. This time, though, instead of antiaircraft guns, there were cows grazing on the raised ground. So much for Mao's strategic defensive schemes, which proved a grand waste of money and resources.

The Soviets didn't pour across the border in a huge invasion as anticipated. But in March 1969 the Chinese and Soviet militaries engaged in skirmishes along the northern border that shook the world. In Hong Kong we monitored reports of two clashes on March 3 and March 15 in the vicinity of uninhabited Damansky Island in the frozen Ussuri River. Around 100 Russians and 800 Chinese were killed. Several months later in August, the Soviets attacked three fortified Chinese positions near the border of Sinkiang Province in western China, sending tanks two miles into Chinese territory.

The erosion of its relationship with the Soviet Union was one of the major factors pushing the Chinese to pursue rapprochement with the U.S. Toward the end of the 1960s, China began to send out signals to the United States. Prior to the border clashes in October 1968, the Chinese Foreign Ministry had sent a peace missive to newly elected U.S. president Richard Nixon, who had shown signs of a new U.S. attitude toward China during his election campaign. An ardent anti-communist for virtually his entire political career, in the fall of 1967 Nixon had written in the journal *Foreign Affairs* that "we simply cannot afford to leave China forever outside the family of nations . . . in angry isolation." The article was the first public indication of Nixon's transformation—fueled by a healthy dose of realpolitik—from an adversary of Red China into a potential friend and collaborator.

On the basis of what it called "peaceful coexistence," the Chinese government proposed resuming in February 1969 the Sino-U.S. Ambassadorial Talks in Warsaw, which, until they were postponed in 1968, had served as the most reliable, albeit contentious, way to exchange information between the two countries throughout the 1960s. The talks had started after the Geneva Conference in 1954, but had yielded little other than demands and recriminations over seized assets and American prisoners in China. The cagey Nixon, who had approved a resumption of the talks before he became president, didn't respond to the Chinese offer because he was hoping to get Moscow's help in facilitating a withdrawal of American troops from Vietnam. If you are going to dance with Moscow, Nixon apparently reasoned, you don't invite Peking to the party.

But after a series of unsuccessful political overtures to Moscow and fearful that the Soviets were going to attack China in the wake of the March and August 1969 border clashes, Nixon started to act on a plan to use China in concert against the Soviet Union. During the fall of 1969, through intermediaries in Pakistan and via communications with Chinese diplomats in Warsaw (at a Yugoslav fashion show of all places!), Nixon floated balloons intended to show the Chinese that he wanted to open up channels of communication.

With our new contact in Hong Kong serving as a confirmation of sorts that the officially stated Chinese position matched the leadership's willingness, the U.S. responded in kind. In a speech in April 1969, Secretary of State William Rogers referred to China for the first time as the "People's Republic of China." Up until this speech, at the CIA unit in Hong Kong we used largely pejorative terms, such as "Chicoms" and "Red China," when referring to the Peking government, and while we didn't stop using the terms, there was a gradual evolution to calling China by its proper name or abbreviation, the PRC.

The thaw was under way. Pro-communist Chinese living in Hong Kong who had been scarce during the years of hostile relations started to turn up at receptions at Hong Kong social clubs. Most American diplomats, intelligence types, and journalists greeted the turn toward cooperation with great interest. The exceptions among intelligence officers were those involved in the Vietnam War. So consumed were they by their mission in Vietnam that they couldn't conceive of developments in the world that might overshadow the war. I remember having a conversation about the Sino-Soviet border clashes with a high-level CIA official from the Saigon office when he was visiting Hong Kong. While some of us truly feared a wider conflagration involving the two military superpowers, the CIA official could not relate to their significance outside of a possible connection to the Vietnam War, which in truth was a localized conflict in Southeast Asia. When I gave him my own jazzed-up version of an impending Soviet strike to provoke China, he responded, "I wonder how this will affect the war in Vietnam." His myopic view was symptomatic of the hordes of Americans who visited Hong Kong for a break from the war in Vietnam. They talked incessantly about "their war" and rarely, if ever, asked us about China, the emerging giant.

.   .   .

By contrast, many of us stationed permanently in Hong Kong had made our careers watching China, and the past two decades of relations between the U.S. and China had seen some of the chilliest weather of the Cold War. We felt we were on the verge of a great change in the relationship and of a significant movement of the world's geopolitical tectonic plates.

But we tempered our excitement about the prospects of a partnership with China against the Soviet Union by reminding ourselves of the doctrinaire approach of the communist leadership in Peking. We knew not to get romantic about the future. When dealing with China, it was important to keep one's head on straight. The thaw was founded upon practical considerations, foremost among them being the U.S. and China coming together to blunt the Soviet threat. In an ideological sense, however, the U.S. and China were still polar opposites. They despised capitalism, and we abhorred communism. In Southeast Asia particularly, where the Vietnam War was still raging, our national interests clashed, and we took every opportunity to best China and her communist allies.

One of these opportunities came at a Hong Kong safe house. Because foreigners, in this case our mostly white case officers, were too conspicuous if they conducted meetings with agents in public and semipublic places like parks and restaurants, much of our debriefing and planning took place in safe houses. Working like a hotel concierge, a safe house control officer in our unit kept an inventory of safe houses and made sure that they weren't too many in one location. To ensure a steady supply of secure apartments, he tapped into America's recent history in Asia: former American soldiers who had settled in Hong Kong after military service in Asia. These GIs, most of whom were of Chinese or Filipino descent, needed extra money to supplement their meager retirement pensions. A former GI had the advantage of being able to blend in well and could procure an extra apartment, particularly if he used as a cover story that he needed it for his alleged mistress.

During a meeting with one of our agents in a safe house, we obtained information that told of huge Chinese arms shipments going through Cambodia and into South Vietnam to help the Viet Cong. We also learned that the head of Cambodia's armed forces, Lieutenant General Lon Nol, was overseeing the shipments and taking a cut of the arms for the benefit of himself and his own army. In the late 1960s at the time when the arms shipments were at their highest levels, Lon Nol was a favorite of Peking. He was said to have a big picture of Chairman Mao over his desk in Phnom Penh. But we knew that Lon Nol was also a Cambodian patriot. Like their Laotian neighbors to the north, the Cambodians were strongly against Vietnam, whom they saw as the regional bully. Lon Nol was particularly upset that, in their effort to prosecute the war in South Vietnam, the North Vietnamese Army had occupied areas of eastern Cambodia. Our source told us that when the Cambodian Defense Minister traveled to Peking in the fall of 1969, he made a strong appeal to the Chinese to help him get the Vietnamese out of Cambodia. Lon Nol said he was willing to help supply the Viet Cong, but he insisted that Vietnamese troops belonged in Vietnam, not in Cambodia. The Chinese demurred. In Peking's eyes the North Vietnamese were fighting a war of national liberation against the American imperialists, and it was China's socialist duty and in the country's own interest to support its communist brethren.

The tiff between Lon Nol and Peking turned out to pay off, at least temporarily, for the U.S. Just six months after visiting Peking, in March 1970 General Lon Nol, in part bitter and disappointed at being rebuffed by the Chinese, staged a coup along with First Deputy Premier Sisowath Sirik Matak against Prime Minister Sihanouk and seized power. From Hong Kong we reported to Washington the first signs of a coup when we picked up information that commercial flights from Hong Kong to Phnom Penh were being canceled because the Phnom Penh Airport was closed. Once in power, Lon Nol turned from a supplier to the communist cause in Southeast Asia into an adversary. In an attempt to hinder the Vietnamese communists in their fight to take over South Vietnam, he tried to cut weapons supply lines through Cambodia to Vietnam. Then he cooperated with the U.S. military in its incursion into Cambodia in the spring of 1970, which hurt the North Vietnamese but did not drive them out. In this backdrop to the war next door in Vietnam, thanks in part to the reporting from our source, the U.S. briefly gained the upper hand at China's expense.

·   ·   ·

In those exciting times, a select few China-watchers in Hong Kong—diplomats, intelligence types, journalists, and academics—designed a tie to "commemorate" the struggle going on in Hong Kong that we faced everyday when we went to work. The tie featured obvious symbols of the Cultural Revolution. A black base color symbolized the dark times. Across the dark background were red stripes to represent the Peking communist "red party line." Arrayed across each "party line" were three animal heads, the most conspicuous actors in the struggle: a white-skinned pig, a yellow running dog, and a fat red cat. The white-skinned pig characterized the foreigners, the archenemies of the Chinese Communist Party; the yellow running dog represented the Chinese in Hong Kong who followed the foreigners; and the fat red cat symbolized the Hong Kong commercial magnates, many of them millionaires, who, despite making much of their wealth in a capitalist environment, bolstered their Chinese identity by mouthing Peking's line. Finally, in an indication of our belief that China would eventually emerge from the insanity and anarchy of the Cultural Revolution into better times, there was a silver lining on the back of the tie. Only a few members of this small, dedicated but informal group got the tie. As white-skinned pigs, we wore it proudly.

11

BREAKING DOWN WALLS

ONE OF THE highlights of our time in Hong Kong was watching Neil Armstrong walk on the moon. In July 1969, we gathered in front of the black and white TV in our den in Stanley Beach and watched the grainy footage of Armstrong descending the steps of *Apollo 11*'s lunar module. "That's one small step for man, one giant leap for mankind." His words echo even today.

On earth, our steps were not so momentous, but U.S.–China relations were breaking new ground. By the time our family returned to the U.S. in 1970 for a posting in Washington, things had started to move quickly, and the basis for rapprochement was being laid. The major public relations event was "Ping-Pong diplomacy." In April 1971, after continued behind-the-scenes maneuvering between the PRC and U.S. governments, the Chinese suddenly invited the U.S. table-tennis team, which was competing in Japan, to visit China. Then on July 15, 1971, while I was having dinner at a Chinese restaurant in Washington with intelligence colleagues from a neighboring country, I got a call from an excited Sally. President Nixon had announced on TV that he would make a historic trip to China to meet with Chinese leaders. "As I have pointed out on a number of occasions over the past three years," President Nixon said into the microphones from the Burbank studios of NBC in California, "there can be no stable and enduring peace without the participation of the People's Republic of China and its 750 million people." His trip, he told viewers across the country, would be a "journey for peace." It would be the first time a U.S. president had ever visited Communist China.

Nixon's announcement signaled a shift in superpower relations. Whereas before, particularly during the intense years of the Vietnam War, the U.S. was pitted against the Soviet Union *and* China, Nixon's announcement paved the way for a U.S.–China relationship, founded in part upon a common concern about Soviet expansion.

.   .   .

As I would learn later, the use of back channels and the personalization of diplomacy were the modus operandi for Nixon and Henry Kissinger, the president's advisor for national security affairs. The prospect of a Soviet Union bent on expansion and armed with nuclear weapons required new ways of thinking. Nixon concluded that ideology as the driving force behind much of the Cold War could be downgraded, and thus tensions diminished. Nixon said as much to Mao during his visit to Peking in February 1972: "What brings us together is a recognition of a new situation in the world and a recognition on our part that what is important is not a nation's internal political philosophy. What is important is its policy toward the rest of the world and toward us."

Such a dramatic and unexpected change of direction with the People's Republic of China both required, and engendered, subterfuge and secrecy. Nixon and Kissinger preferred to operate independently of institutions such as the State Department. Initially, in the early stages of making contact with the Chinese Communists at meetings like the Warsaw Talks, the executive branch worked side by side with the State Department. But by 1970 both Nixon and Kissinger regarded the State Department as a hindrance—Nixon, mostly because he was concerned about Democrats in the State Department, and Kissinger, because he thought secrecy would help him maintain room for diplomatic maneuvering as well as lessen the chance for leaks and public outcry.

To sidestep State, Kissinger worked through private channels like the CIA units in Pakistan and Romania, using CIA facilities and communication codes for these countries. They were good candidates for back channels to Peking in those days. Pakistan was closely allied with China in its struggle with its Soviet-backed neighbor, India, and Romania, having challenged the Soviet sphere of influence, had good relations with China. When Kissinger's staff at the National Security

Council was planning his first visits to Peking in 1971, they used the CIA contingent in Pakistan to arrange details of the trip. Then on his famous swing through Asia in July 1971, a trip concocted precisely for the purpose of getting Nixon's right-hand man to Peking, Kissinger faked a stomach ailment as an excuse to lie low for a couple of days. The CIA unit chief in Pakistan put into action a diversion plan, complete with a dummy motorcade and a substitute Kissinger, to get Kissinger and his entourage on a plane for Peking at four in the morning. The dummy entourage, meanwhile, headed for a private estate where "Kissinger," in reality the chubbiest member of the American security detail, was supposed to recover.

During early negotiations with the Chinese, Kissinger purposely limited the number of Americans present to reduce the risk of transcripts of the proceedings falling into the hands of bureaucratic competitors. Until he became Secretary of State in September 1973, Kissinger often did not allow State Department professionals with the requisite Chinese language skills to attend certain high-level meetings with the Chinese.

.   .   .

Back at CIA as the Deputy Chief of China Operations in the Far Eastern Division, I had mixed emotions about being home. For Sally and our boys, it was a good change and a chance to get used to being "American" again after spending most of the previous decade in Southeast Asia. The boys became transfixed with American football, and Sally learned to manage home and family without a cook or amah, and she enjoyed it. For me, while living in Washington had its distinct advantages like coaching the boys' soccer teams and rediscovering old friends and contacts, I couldn't help feeling as if the CIA bureaucrats in Langley didn't know what was going on in the field. And now I was one of those bureaucrats.

My immediate superior, curiously enough, was Ed B., a classmate of my brother Frank at Yale. Ed was extraordinarily bright and had served in Japan after the war. His distinction was that he had mastered the particularly difficult Okinawa dialect. At the CIA Ed had a reputation for being a mover and shaker. He called on me to supply expertise on

China and to draw on my history of China operations to get things done.

One program I worked on from Washington was a covert action to co-opt Chinese intellectuals who were disenchanted by the excesses of the Cultural Revolution. Through Chinese intermediaries in places such as Hong Kong and Singapore, as well as in European and American cities—in short, wherever there were concentrations of Chinese— we tried to stimulate thinking for reform in China based on democratic principles and free market forces. We also promoted the objective analysis of China's problems. Unfortunately, overseas Chinese were either focused primarily on their own financial gain, preoccupied with concerns about host country policies toward them, or politically dominated by fringe groups split between Peking and Taipei. It was a slow process, and we had to be patient.

Nevertheless, a few Chinese opinion makers did begin to talk more about a new Chinese identity not wedded to the ideologies and Maoist lunatic social engineering of the past, but based on historic Chinese principles of benevolence, collective responsibility, and pragmatic analysis.

Although the CIA's main mission in Washington was acquisition of secret information on China via covert means, I soon found myself involved in the surge of activity centered around defining a new diplomatic relationship with the mainland. Even before Henry Kissinger's first trip to China in July 1971, he had started turning the wheels of the Washington bureaucracy toward projecting a fresh U.S. relationship with China. Using authority granted to him by President Nixon, in November 1970 Kissinger ordered a series of studies on China policy from the State and Defense Departments, the National Security Council, and the CIA, addressing such issues as UN membership, Taiwan, and the impact of China on American policy toward the Soviet Union, Japan, and Southeast Asia. I became one of the two CIA representatives assigned in the interagency meetings to draft these long papers, known by their acronyms NSSM 106 and 107 for National Security Studies Memorandum.

The meetings were chaired by a laid-back and somewhat spiritual old China hand named Al Jenkins, who was Director of the Office of Asian Communist Affairs (ACA) at the State Department. The meetings were long on arguments, compromises, and endless drafts. The papers, however, were short on relevant policy recommendations.

One reason the NSSM policy papers didn't make much difference was that they were largely disconnected from Kissinger's own secret diplomacy, which was making great strides in putting the U.S.–China relationship on a more positive footing. As we bickered over the finer points of admission of the People's Republic of China into the UN, we had little idea of what was going on over our heads. Many of us were taken by surprise when the news of Kissinger's July trip to Peking was made public even though we represented some of the most informed and experienced China hands in the U.S. government.

Several times in these meetings I raised the question of how our improving relationship with China would affect Taiwan. In the face of opposition from both inside and outside the CIA, I maintained that we had to defend our interests in Taiwan and manage them against breakthroughs with China. I felt it was a delicate balance and that it shouldn't tip too far in either direction. My insistence on raising concerns about Taiwan irritated the other CIA representative on the panel. But my language concerning Taiwan got into the drafts of the otherwise largely ignored NSSM 106 and continued to be a key part of our new relationship with China.

Looking back now, I understand that our efforts on NSSM 106 were probably in part a diversion orchestrated by Kissinger and his staff. The diversion served two strategic purposes: corralling the nettlesome bureaucracy and distracting the press from covering the real target of secret diplomacy. Indeed, there were even press leaks of parts of NSSM 106 to the press, accompanied by much hand-wringing, but in the end it made no difference. We were a decoy.

But we were decoys with concrete contributions. We may have been pawns in a game of diplomatic chess with the Chinese, but I didn't feel as if we had been sacrificed. We had just been used by the knight to make a maneuvering position for the king.

The situations arising from Kissinger and Nixon's penchant for secrecy and control put some people in awkward positions, to say the least. Take Al Jenkins, the chairman on the NSSM 106 program. As ACA director in the State Department, Jenkins reported to Secretary of State William Rogers. But after Kissinger returned to Washington following his first trip to Peking, he asked Jenkins to head up a small working group in the State Department. Jenkins agreed and got permission for two members of his staff at the ACA office to do the hard work of preparing position papers for upcoming negotiations leading up to President Nixon's visit to Peking in February 1972. Kissinger told Jenkins that he should tell no one of this secret work, not even his bosses at the State Department, including Secretary of State Rogers.

Jenkins and his little group were given an obscure suite on the seventh floor of the State Department building, three floors above their ACA office. Besides Jenkins and his two handpicked assistants, Bill Brown and Roger Sullivan, no one else in the State Department was supposed to know what was going on. To keep up the pretense that things were running as usual in the ACA, Brown would make appearances in the office from time to time. Then after showing his face he would retreat back upstairs to handle the latest request from Kissinger's team at the National Security Council.

Brown and Sullivan worked ten- to twelve-hour days preparing papers on subjects like the Vietnam War, Soviet actions and policies, settlement claims, and exchanges of students, journalists, and athletes. The two men had free reign to draw on all resources in Washington, but they had to camouflage their requests for information. Because the men did much of the work after completing their day jobs, libraries had to be specially opened for them at night. Brown remembers photocopying documents at 3 A.M., then going home to sleep for a few hours before returning to start work at the ACA office the next morning.

So during the summer and fall of 1971, at the same time that Jenkins chaired the meetings of NSSM 106 that I was involved in, he was directing the work of this smaller, more elite group that, because of its direct link to Kissinger, could be guaranteed a hearing when the president wrote up his talking points. Kissinger actually commissioned similar secret studies from different agencies across Washington, including one from the CIA's Directorate of Intelligence. But people did not know what anyone else was doing. It was vintage Kissinger—secretive with multiple layers of similar work. "Henry Kissinger was having all kinds of people distill their wisdom, and then he would choose what he liked," recalled Brown.

.   .   .

I was taking stock of my options around this time. For two decades I had devoted my career to watching China from the fringes of Asia and from the vantage point of Washington. I was anxious to try something new, and I had to think creatively.

At the CIA, as part of my job as deputy chief in the China Division, I had played a role in some of the earliest planning regarding the establishment of a U.S. interest section in China, the preliminary American representation before the establishment of diplomatic relations. My input was part of a secret State Department memorandum on the options for a U.S. diplomatic presence in Communist China. Given that as of 1971 and early 1972 there hadn't been any breakthroughs yet in the relationship, the work was highly speculative and hashed over seemingly arcane questions such as: Would it be an interest section in the British or Swedish Embassies? One thing that became clear to me, though, was that, even if there were a big turn in the relationship that called for the establishment of diplomatic relations, there would be no role for the CIA in China for a long time. When I made the recommendation that I be part of the interest section, I was politely but firmly told that nothing like that would happen for several years. The Chinese wouldn't go for it, and the State Department wouldn't go for it. So that meant "no go" for me on getting into China.

So I came up with an alternate plan. If I couldn't get into China, I would do the next best thing: work in a country that had good relations with China. I chose Romania, a Balkan state in the middle of Eastern Europe. Because under the leadership of dictator Nicolae Ceausescu Romania had broken from the Soviet Union and aligned itself with China, I saw it as a three-corner shot: Use Bucharest to get from Washington to Peking.

By serving a tour of duty in Bucharest, I reasoned, I could at least prepare myself to work in China. Despite its independent posture, Romania remained a Communist dictatorship, a "denied-area country" in CIA parlance, where a case officer had to contend with travel restrictions and constant surveillance designed to trip him up, foil his plans, and, hopefully, embarrass him and his country. Operating in such a hostile environment required skills I didn't have yet. To equip myself, I would study Romanian and take special courses in "denied area" trade-craft. My superiors signed off on the plan.

As I prepared to go to Romania, confirmation of the new global alignment came with the announcement of the Shanghai Commu-niqué. Issued upon President Nixon's departure from China in late February 1972, the Shanghai Communiqué became the chief instru-ment on which a new relationship was built between the U.S. and the People's Republic of China. In it, China and the U.S. agreed upon four principles of international relations, which, in effect, directed the two countries' efforts against Soviet hegemony. On the controversial ques-tion of Taiwan, the thorniest issue in the bilateral relationship, the U.S. gave some ground. The Americans acknowledged, and said they would not challenge the position, that "all Chinese on either side of the Tai-wan Strait maintain that there is but one China and that Taiwan is part of China." Furthermore, the U.S. side said it would support neither military action by Taiwan against the mainland nor an independence movement on the island. As tensions in the region decreased, the U.S. said it would gradually withdraw its military forces from Taiwan. Fi-nally, in a severe blow to Taiwan, Nixon said he would work toward normalization with the People's Republic of China by the end of his second term.

The momentousness of the occasion for the United States perhaps can be best understood by looking at how Nixon communicated to Mao at their first meeting. Nixon said: "History has brought us to-gether. The question is whether we, with different philosophies, but both with feet on the ground, and having come from the people, can make a breakthrough that will serve not just China and America, but the whole world in the years ahead."

Things were happening so fast on the Washington–Peking front that Kissinger was moved to write Nixon in a memo that the U.S. stood a good chance of not only improving relations with Peking but also of goading Moscow into arms reduction as part of détente: "With conscientious attention in both capitals, we should be able to have our maotai and drink our vodka, too," Kissinger wrote to Nixon in early 1973.

In the wake of such dramatic developments, my assignment to Romania hardly looked fruitful. But I was committed to follow through on the plan. After a year at the National War College, I went straight into intensive Romanian language training at the Foreign Service Institute in Rosslyn, Virginia. At 45 years of age, I found that taking on a new language was a terrible ordeal. My teacher was a dedicated, hard-headed Albanian man. We students called him the "Iron Guard." He was intent on pounding into our heads the grammar, history, expressions, and vocabulary of this obscure language. I persevered and ended up getting a 3.3 grade on my final exam, meaning that I was able to use the language well enough to conduct work.

The position waiting for me in Romania was far from a dream job. Rather, it would seem like a demotion in status. Despite having fifteen years of experience operating under official cover, I was scheduled to be the number two CIA officer in Romania, working under a younger man with less experience. In Laos, I had been the number two agent in a 250-person station. In Romania, I was to be the second man in a two-man unit. Suffice it to say that should I run into any diplomats from my previous postings, my cover probably wouldn't hold up well.

Then destiny intervened. In February 1973, Peking and Washington announced the exchange of liaison offices as a first step toward the establishment of diplomatic relations. Kissinger called them "embassies in everything but name." Through a combination of my own efforts and deft intervention by Kissinger, I got myself headed back to China as a member of the first U.S. diplomatic mission in China since the late 1940s. Instead of self-imposed exile to a bleak outpost in Eastern Europe, I was slated to be America's first intelligence officer in the People's Republic of China.

Perhaps, if I had paid more attention to a gesture made by the Chinese in advance of President Nixon's visit, I might have had an inkling of China's softening toward the CIA. In 1971, the Chinese released CIA officer Richard Fecteau, shot down with Jack Downey over Manchuria in 1952. By the time the Chinese let him go, Fecteau, 43, had served nineteen years of a twenty-year sentence. (We now know that confidence had been built up to such an extent between the American and Chinese sides that during Kissinger's visit to Peking in February 1973 he and Chairman Mao engaged in an openly frank and humorous discussion about intelligence gathering.)

Once I heard of the opening of liaison offices, I seized the opportunity to put forward my name as a candidate for the Peking mission. It was a risky proposition. I realized that my tours in Laos and Hong Kong had identified me as a high-profile CIA officer to the media, to academia, and to both the Soviet and Chinese intelligence agencies. As if that weren't enough to compromise me, I assumed that the close friends and CIA associates of mine who were captured by the Communists in China and Vietnam may have revealed my name and background during interrogations. But I chose to push on with my plan to get to Peking anyway.

I was rebuffed by my superiors in the Far East Division at the CIA in February 1973. The mission in Peking, they said, was to be staffed purely by State Department officers in order to underscore the importance of a new relationship founded on trust. State would have no part of a CIA officer working undercover in Peking, I was told. Not to be deterred, I took my case directly to Bill Colby, the third-ranking person in the CIA as director general. "I'd like to give Colby a try on this," I remember telling my superior Charley W., deputy chief of the Far East Division and my former boss in Hong Kong. Colby had a reputation for being more adventurous and a creative turn of mind when it came to intelligence gathering. I made my pitch to Colby on a Saturday morning in March. I explained to him that I was the right man for the job because I had the language qualifications, knew clandestine operations, understood how the Chinese operated, and, no less important in such a politically sensitive area, got along well enough with the State Department. I also put in the downside: my high profile and the possibility of exposure. Colby listened to my pitch. "I like it," he nodded approvingly. "Tell Director Schlesinger your story."

I was incredulous at Colby's suggestion. Director Schlesinger was Director of the CIA James Schlesinger. I had never even met him before. But Colby was serious. I asked Colby, "When should I meet with Director Schlesinger?"

"Now," he said.

So I carried my thoughts up the ladder to the highest rung of the CIA. Schlesinger listened to me and then reached for the phone. "Get me Kissinger on the line," he said. As I sat in his office, Schlesinger briefed the president's national security advisor on my proposal.

"Henry," Schlesinger said, "I want my man in Peking, and I have him right here in front of me." The two men conversed for a while. Schlesinger closed out the conversation with a promise. "I'll have a memo to you right away," he said.

After hanging up the phone, Director Schlesinger turned to me. "If you give me a memo on why you should be in Peking, I'll get you there," he said.

Back in my office, I crafted a memo with the help of Charley W., who had a keen political sense. Together we put together a memorandum with phrases designed to cut through bureaucratic obstacles and inertia. I turned the memo in to Schlesinger. A great silence descended, and I began to wait.

While I waited, Kissinger went ahead with his end of the arrangement. On April 16 in New York, he told the Chinese ambassador to the UN, Huang Hua, that the U.S. would like to put one intelligence officer in the liaison office in Peking. To Chinese laughter, Kissinger said, "We will identify him so you can watch him. We promise he will undertake no other activity but to be a channel of communication."

The Chinese eventually agreed to a deal in which each country could station one intelligence officer in its diplomatic mission in the other country's capital. This placement of declared agents would be an indication of the closeness of the relationship since the CIA reserved that practice for allies. As Kissinger had promised, I was revealed to the Chinese. The deal, however, was not entirely reciprocal. My understanding is that the Chinese did not inform us directly of the identity of my Chinese counterpart in Washington. Only later did we presume that the Chinese "declared agent" was an English-speaking diplomat named Xie Qimei, a senior Chinese officer in the Ministry of Foreign Affairs.

.   .   .

Needless to say, the about-face from Romania to China was abrupt. Instead of living on the fringe of the Soviet Union in Bucharest, we would be headed for Peking and the heart of the Middle Kingdom. Also, I had to try to put aside the Romanian language, which had been drilled into my head for five months. I immediately started an intensive tutorial in Chinese to get my language skills up to speed. I had to keep a very low profile so that word would not get out around Washington, and particularly to the media, that I was going to China. Though I was declared to the Chinese, I did not want to be compromised in my dealings with other countries in Peking. Poor Sally had to continue with brain-numbing Romanian for cover reasons. She would arrive in China with Romanian on the tip of her tongue and not one word of Mandarin. To keep our departure as secret as possible, we had only one good-bye party given in our honor. It was hosted by my boss at CIA, Ted Shackley, and his wife. Sally and I were the only guests.

The move to China was wrenching for my family. While it represented the chance of a lifetime for me, it was a shock to our two younger boys who would accompany us, Mike, then 12, and Jeffrey, then 9. They would have to leave the friendly and free atmosphere of Chevy Chase, Maryland, for life in Mao's drab Peking. While I hurried around Washington, introducing myself, and in some cases reintroducing myself, to the State Department officers I would be working with at the United States Liaison Office (USLO), Sally attended to the melancholy details of disengaging the family from three years in the "land of milk and honey" as she always referred to the U.S. This included leaving our eldest son, Douglas, then 14, off at Phillips Academy in Andover, Massachusetts, where my sister Elinore lived with her family. In a coincidence of sorts, we rented our house to Richard Solomon, one of Kissinger's brightest aides on China. I guess that had I left my library in the house, it would have gone to good use.

.   .   .

In the midst of the flurry to leave Washington, I couldn't help but reflect on the Taiwan variable in the equation for U.S.–China rapprochement. Ever since the Communist takeover of the mainland, Taiwan had loomed as a divisive issue in Sino-U.S. relations. In his famous speech announcing the opening to China, Nixon had made sure to remember Taiwan. Though he used words that would not offend Peking and did not mention the island nation by name, Nixon left no doubts about his support for Taiwan. "Our action in seeking a new relationship with the People's Republic of China will not be at the expense of our old friends," the president had said. But by signing the Shanghai Communiqué seven months later in 1972, Nixon basically conveyed acceptance of the outcome of the Chinese civil war and the defeat of Chiang Kai-shek. The statement that the "U.S. side acknowledges that all Chinese on either side of the Taiwan Straits maintain there is but one China and that Taiwan is part of China" seemed to be pushing the inhabitants on Taiwan into a fait accompli. Indeed, in some of his private talks with the Chinese in Peking, Kissinger seems to have equivocated on earlier U.S. stands on Taiwan, particularly on recognition of Taiwan as a legitimate government. While the word "acknowledges" preserved an element of flexibility on the U.S. side, it turns out that Kissinger in private assured the Chinese that the U.S. recognized that Taiwan was part of China during his first visit to China, according to John Holdridge, a State Department China hand who accompanied Kissinger on these trips. Also, in translating the term "acknowledge" into Chinese, the term "cheng ren" for "recognize" was used by the Chinese, thus strengthening their version. I continued to mull over this statement. In general, I saw, along with some like-minded colleagues, few signs of compromise in the Chinese position on Taiwan. On the other hand, the Chinese acceptance of the communiqué and willingness to minimize the use of force against Taiwan were forms of progress.

The U.S. followed Japan's example of 1972 and transferred its embassy to Peking from Taipei, while maintaining a private, nongovernmental office in Taipei to carry on trade and cultural connections. In the ensuing years after the signing of the Shanghai Communiqué, the Chinese have never given up on their insistence that the United States agrees that Taiwan is part of China. It is a question of semantics, but an important one. We say in response, "No, we acknowledge the Chinese *position* that Taiwan is part of China." This distinction, which has had to be made again and again, has been a crucial justification for allowing us to maintain our support for Taiwan.

"Quid pro quo" diplomacy toward Taiwan and the People's Republic of China became a hallmark of Nixon's presidency. It was based on splitting hairs and also on concrete actions designed to reassure. In 1974, President Nixon approved the sale of advanced F5E fighters to Taiwan as well as the expansion of Taiwan representative offices in the U.S., but what was given with one hand was taken away with the other. In the same year, Nixon oversaw the withdrawal of nuclear-capable F4 bombers from Taiwan.

At a press briefing at the State Department following his third trip to China in February 1972, Al Jenkins recalls the State Department spokesperson responding to a reporter's question about the ambiguity in our relations with Taiwan and the People's Republic of China inherent in the wording of the Shanghai Communiqué. The spokesperson answered, "Yes, we have to preserve ambiguity in the interest of clarity." Perhaps that best sums up the tightrope that had to be walked. We had to retain a modicum of flexibility in order to defend old interests while formulating new ones.

In making historical decisions like the opening of diplomatic relations with China, Kissinger himself expressed remorse for what was happening to Taiwan. He wrote to Nixon in a memorandum dated March 2, 1973, "We should be under no illusions that our final step will be anything but painful—there are few friends as decent as our allies on Taiwan."

.   .   .

In July 1973 I departed for Peking on my own ahead of the family. I encountered the mysterious Miss Lee "by chance" in downtown Hong Kong. What a coincidence! Five years earlier she had suddenly appeared outside my office in Hong Kong, and we had chatted briefly. She had married an older British man, had given birth to two children, and was either looking for adventure or had been instructed to make a pass at me. I declined. This time in 1973 the conversation was even shorter. I lied to her and said I was on my way to Southeast Asia. The last I heard from her was a postcard from Los Angeles. Her old English husband had died, and like so many Chinese, she had moved to Orange County, California. Was she really fond of me or was there another motive? I leave that unanswered. But she certainly knew how to find me.

As the train pulled out of Hong Kong on July 16, 1973, I glanced at the nine black peaks of Kowloon outlined against the sky. "Today, perhaps, I will go beyond them," I thought to myself. I felt the same tightening in my gut and burning in my stomach that I used to feel before a swimming race. But my anxiety gave way to a feeling of being mesmerized by the changing landscape outside the train window. As the train chugged through the New Territories on its twenty-two-mile journey to the Lo-wu border post separating Hong Kong and the People's Republic of China, Hong Kong, bustling with its dominating skyscrapers and back-alley slums, gave way to vistas of mountains and trees and to scenes of pastoral life in small villages. Rice paddies surrounded rural hamlets of mud houses and narrow walkways.

I officially entered the People's Republic of China at 10:37 A.M. on July 16, 1973. PLA guards at the border took my passport and looked at my vaccination record.

"Are you American?" a guard asked me. "Are you with USLO?"

"Yes," I answered.

At Lo-wu, waiting to transfer to a Chinese train that would take me to Guangzhou, I tried my Chinese on a lady attendant in the waiting room.

"Where's the bathroom?" I asked.

Were my tones right? Would I ever be able to make myself understood in this language, I wondered self-consciously.

The answer came back swiftly, "Straight ahead. To your left."

I was on my way.

My excitement was not confined to the personal satisfaction of seeing if my Chinese worked. As a professional, I felt a substantial sense of accomplishment. As a member of USLO, I was one of a select few who had been chosen to represent the United States at its first mission in Communist China. When some of my USLO colleagues had walked across the border several months earlier, they became the first American officials to cross into China on permanent assignment in twenty-three years. When I traversed the bridge at Lo-wu in July, I became the first CIA officer to cross into China legally since 1949. I took these steps, mindful of my place in the tumultuous and often acrimonious history that linked the United States and the People's Republic of China. While I was entering Communist China freely on my way to become the first CIA chief in Peking, just four months earlier my Yale classmate and CIA colleague Jack Downey had crossed the same bridge in the other direction, headed for freedom after spending more than twenty years in Chinese prisons. Downey's release had been facilitated by President Nixon's public admission in January 1973, made at the behest of Chinese premier Chou En-lai, that Downey and fellow American Richard Fecteau were, in fact, CIA officers. Was I replacing him as the CIA representative in Peking?

The story of Downey and Fecteau is one of the most remarkable in the fifty-year history of the CIA. In captivity, Downey read as much as he could. He read Tolstoy's *War and Peace* six times in English, and then after teaching himself to read Russian, he read part of the original. He also read the selected works of Soviet leader Joseph Stalin in Russian, an experience that he described to me sarcastically as a "real treat." In one letter to his mother, he wrote that during a period of captivity he had done 23,000 calisthenics, run about 55 miles, and washed about 100 items of clothing.

Remarkably, the ordeal didn't kill the spirit of the two men. At the show trial, as the story goes, Fecteau, clad in shabby prison garb, was marched forward to the dock where Downey, whom he hadn't seen in the two years since they were separated after the crash, was already standing. Fecteau, known for his sense of humor, noticed Downey was wearing a new Chinese black padded suit, complete with hat and shoes. When the Chinese ordered Fecteau to take his place in the dock next to Downey, Fecteau, hoping to inject a little levity into the grim proceedings, sidled up to Downey and whispered, "Who's your tailor?"

After being released, Downey remarked that he did not think there was anything heroic about his long incarceration in a Chinese prison. About his two decades in Chinese prisons and the Communist indoctrination he underwent, he said in an interview with the *Yale Alumni Magazine* in 1983, "I can only tell you that I came home far more confident than when I went out of the limitations and flaws in the Marxist theory and the superiority of our system and society. It was an education. I remember saying when I first got home that it was mostly a waste of time, but I certainly learned a lot about myself and I had a chance to compare two societies."

To their great credit, both men returned to the U.S. to lead productive lives. They granted few interviews and refused offers to publicize their ordeal. Fecteau became an assistant athletic director at his alma mater Boston University, and Downey went to Harvard Law School and eventually became a judge in his home state of Connecticut. Downey actually ended up marrying an American woman who was born in the northern Chinese city of Shenyang, where Downey was held for the first five months of his captivity.

You could say that Downey's release marked the beginning of the end to an era of hostility, and USLO heralded the beginning of limited cooperation. Like a pair of bookends, Downey and I were cast from the same mold. But we encased in our lives completely different experiences with China. His capture and incarceration signaled the cold years of antagonism. My unobstructed entrance into China as a CIA officer was a direct result of communication at the highest levels. Over the past twenty years, while he had been doing calisthenics, washing clothes, and sweeping floors to pass endless hours inside a Chinese prison, I had been scrutinizing China from its fringes—tracking agents, running operations, and reading cables. As I moved up the career ladder at the CIA, he remained in China—as our mutual CIA colleague Don Gregg described—like a fly stuck in amber. Downey exited wearing the blue pants and shirt of a Chinese worker. I entered in khaki pants and a collared shirt with briefcase, ready to set up shop in Peking.

12

KISSINGER'S MAN IN CHINA

O N MY FIRST night in China on July 16, 1973, I met a garrulous American tourist named Bill. He probably doesn't remember me, nor do I really care to remember him, but my brief interaction with Bill became a defining moment in my experience in China.

Bill was a teacher, a good-natured, overweight man touring China as part of an educational program. It was just the kind of exchange between the U.S. and China that had become popular since Henry Kissinger and his Chinese counterparts had started broadening the range of contacts between the two countries.

I ran into Bill in the evening outside the Dongfang Hotel in Guangzhou where I was staying, and we decided to take a walk together in the neighborhood. Bill was full of impressions of China. He talked endlessly of visiting schools and of his conversations with Chinese teachers. Phrases like "I think that" and "I'm impressed with" prefaced his sentences. He was obviously overwhelmed by his visit to the Middle Kingdom. He didn't ask me any questions, and I volunteered nothing. We walked, and I listened until Bill became scared that we had lost our way. He panicked and temporarily surrendered his command of the conversation.

"I can't ask directions to the Dongfang Hotel because I don't speak Chinese," he explained, suddenly looking helpless in this land that he had been extolling only moments earlier.

I approached a passing Chinese pedestrian and asked how to get back to the hotel. "Oh, you speak Chinese," Bill said, struck by a moment of awareness. "How interesting." But he really wasn't that interested.

As we made our way back to the hotel, he picked up where he had left off—talking about schools, teachers, and impressions. It was "his" China that he described to me, a purely personal experience unadulterated by the views of anyone else. As with other Americans whom I have met over the years, curiosity about others was not his strong suit. Interacting with Bill I understood the difference between "what Bill thought" and "what Bill knew." Bill thought a lot of things about China; he didn't know many.

For some reason, many Americans think their personal experiences in China are fascinating and unique, and, like the Ancient Mariner, they must tell their tale to the end. Their idea is: I have seen China, and, therefore, it now exists. But this is a static view, shaped by subjective interpretation and woefully narrow in scope. Later I met American four-star generals who would get briefed on substantive issues before going into China. However, once they returned to the U.S. after their short trip, they would stop listening, thinking that they had China figured out. They became like one-way walkie-talkies that transmitted but didn't receive. In Bill, it was a harmless trait, but in generals it was dangerous.

In my approach to China, I tried to eschew romanticism and excessive emotion. The death of my brother played a role in my thinking. Frank had responded emotionally to China. To him, it was the greatest country in the world to grow up in, and when the Japanese overran it before and during World War II, he grieved for its loss. By contrast, in my "professional" approach toward China, I developed a certain remoteness in my scrutiny of the country and its motives. This remoteness was connected to the privileged surroundings of Tsingtao, my boyhood home on the Shandong Peninsula. We lived comfortable lives, and in contrast to Frank and my father, I was unaware at the time of the plight of China beyond our walls. China—its mountains, villages, people, and mud houses—made an indelible mark on me, but it was a visceral reaction. As perceived through my then immature eyes, China left little room for sentimentalism. Later on, as the country of my youth became the professional challenge in my adulthood, I studied China's language, culture, history, and literature, but—I told myself—it was mostly a professional acquisition and not an emotional involvement. I did not want to be destroyed the way Frank had been by becoming too attached.

One manifestation of what I call my "objective" approach toward analyzing China is that I did not feel guilty about the historical role of foreigners in China. The American guilt complex over wrongs done to China is often played upon by the Chinese. "We are weak," they say. "You have caused this, so you owe us. Give us something." I never bought this. Perhaps, I had an edge on understanding the Middle Kingdom because of my roots in China. I left China when I was 12 years old with an ingrained sense of the Chinese culled from interacting with wash-amah, hearing stories of my father's work with Chinese agents, seeing the country's weak position versus foreign powers, and other experiences. At that young age, I had begun to understand the Chinese as an appealing but manipulative people with kind of a raw, easily agitated nerve from having been squashed by foreigners.

My sense is that China's mixture of grievances derives from a self-centered nationalism—deeply rooted in the Chinese past—which can assume an anti-foreign tone or cast. This is not to say that there isn't genuine resentment against foreign behavior, which in the nineteenth century was deeply offensive to China. But one must not lose sight of the former because he is emotionally wound up in the latter. Here Bill's lesson comes back. He stands out as an example of Americans who desire to see "their" China as opposed to the one that exists. He was impressed by the country, but he did not seek to know it.

Later in my career, particularly during eventful tours in South Korea and China, I packaged the lesson from my encounter with Bill into a more concrete, transmissible format. When noisy reporters or prickly officials from host governments would ask me about a contentious issue or an emotional subject, I would often say, "There are three versions to the story: mine, yours, and the facts." It was an attempt to keep subjectivity out of the conversation.

I took my leave of Bill when we got back to the hotel in Guangzhou, but the encounter stayed with me. I would try to be "objective" in my work in China. But I also realize that embedded in my self-professed objectivity was a vein of subjectivity. I was choosing to view China through a certain prism—chiefly one defined by competition and by how China and America could find common interests and act on them. I guess you could say this was "my" mission in "my" China. Not exactly objective, but more so than some.

At the Peking Airport, Herb Horowitz, head of USLO's Economic Section, and Don Anderson of the Political Section met me. They accompanied me back to the Peking Hotel, a musty and cavernous Soviet-style hotel east of Tiananmen Square that had become home to most of the American diplomats in Peking. After a nightcap of scotch with my two new colleagues, I went to bed.

Horowitz and Anderson represented the best of the U.S. Foreign Service. They were capable, conscientious, and fluent Chinese-speakers. In fact, the USLO mission was an impressive collection of officers, handpicked by Kissinger and the State Department. Many of them had trained in Chinese language on Taiwan and had already served in Hong Kong or Southeast Asian countries with ties to mainland China. Like me, these political and economic officers had been waiting years for China to open up.

Out of the twenty-six original members of the USLO, seven, including myself, went on to become ambassadors. John Holdridge, a deputy to Ambassador David Bruce, the first Chief of USLO, later served as ambassador to Singapore and Indonesia. Nick Platt, chief of the political section, went on to become ambassador to Zambia, Pakistan, and the Philippines, while Herb Horowitz attained the rank of ambassador to Gambia. Lynn Pascoe, an officer in the political section, was ambassador to Malaysia, and Virginia Schafer, who headed up the budget and fiscal office in USLO, was named ambassador to Papua-New Guinea. Brunson McKinley, special assistant to David Bruce, became ambassador to Haiti.

In 1973, we were all trying to find our way in a new and unprecedented foreign experience. Fortunately, in those early days we were led by Ambassador Bruce, one of America's most accomplished and distinguished diplomats. When he was appointed by President Nixon to be the first Chief of USLO, David Bruce was 73 years old and had an impressive diplomatic pedigree, having served as the U.S. ambassador to Great Britain, France, and West Germany, three key posts in the world for the U.S. during the Cold War. Bruce remains the only American diplomat to have served as ambassador to London, Paris, and Bonn.

Bruce was honored to serve as head of USLO. Even though some may have perceived it as a demotion because the title didn't carry ambassadorial rank, Bruce saw the posting as the final adventure in a rich and varied diplomatic career. In fact, though USLO lacked the formalities of an embassy, such as being able to issue visas, it still carried out the basic functions of an embassy—consular, political, economic, and cultural.

Bruce took an interest in me from the start. A somewhat detached man, he nevertheless recalled that he had served in London in the Office of Strategic Services with Sally's father. In the spring of 1974, he showed confidence in me when he asked me to comment on a "think piece" he had written on the situation in China. It was beautifully written and, for a man not steeped in Chinese lore, observant. Bruce's experience in the intelligence field no doubt made it easier for him to be friendly with me at a time when the rest of the USLO staff, all foreign service officers, were wary of me, a CIA officer with the backing of Henry Kissinger, crashing their party.

The very nature of my position put me at odds with my Foreign Service colleagues, whose institution, the Department of State, Kissinger had been sidestepping since he began secret negotiations with the Chinese. Back in Washington, there had been resistance at State to my inclusion in the first mission. But Kissinger knew how to get his way. Al Jenkins, who had been named the deputy chief of mission at USLO along with John Holdridge, told me in secrecy that Kissinger had told the State Department powers-that-be that "Chairman Mao himself had approved me as part of an exchange of intelligence officers" in each other's capitals. The statement from Chairman Mao, whether true or not, seemed to silence State's opposition. I envision some awestruck diplomats walking away from the decisive meeting with Kissinger, shaking their heads in disbelief and thinking to themselves, "Chairman Mao personally approved Lilley?" I have always been impressed by Dr. Kissinger's ability to use just the right technique to get his way.

To be sure, Kissinger had his own reason to support my candidacy. He wanted to make sure that he would maintain a separate channel of communication in Peking once the State Department started running USLO. During preparatory talks in Washington regarding the establishment of USLO, Kissinger had said he wanted CIA technicians to be an integral part of USLO's communications system. In that way the State Department wouldn't have the ability to measure the volume of back-channel communications going on between Chinese leaders and the White House. He also wanted to have somebody in Peking who could be a link to the Chinese outside the U.S. diplomatic mission. I was to be his man.

Before I left for China, my friend and superior at the CIA Bill W. gave me some helpful advice: "When Kissinger asks you to do something, make sure that you do it in 24 hours." Kissinger himself also weighed in. He reminded me of my situation as a declared officer and told me that I shouldn't carry out any independent activity. The president's national security advisor said bluntly, "I don't want you screwing around with any two-bit, little Chinese militiamen." I got the message that any covert activity detected by the Chinese could jeopardize our new relationship with China. Put another way, there was nothing that I could do as an intelligence officer that would be worth the downside were I to be caught.

So the irony was I would be a declared CIA officer working in Peking like a normal, genuine diplomat, the kind I had been impersonating when I had worked for many years as a CIA officer under diplomatic cover. From the start, my unusual situation strained the relationship with State Department colleagues at USLO. I was declared only to Chinese officials at the highest levels. This information did not filter down to the lower levels of the Chinese bureaucracy. This worried some at USLO. In my first meeting with John Holdridge and Al Jenkins (who incidentally shared the deputy chief of mission duties because, the story goes, Kissinger had promised the job to both men), I was told that my cover as a lower-ranking political officer was flimsy and could jeopardize U.S.–China relations if I were "uncovered" by Chinese at the working level. Jenkins was particularly worried about my weak cover. To him, I was too articulate and, given my age—I was actually older than the heads of the political and economic sections—and numerous postings, resembled too much the profile of a senior political officer to pull off my cover. Why, Jenkins wondered, would such a high-profile person come here merely to serve as a channel? He even commented on how the ties I wore were too fashionable for a lower-ranking Foreign Service officer. That was the first time I had ever been complimented on my clothes!

But ruffled feathers were soon patted down, and my cover held up. After initially being placed in a small office alongside a secretary in the political section, I fought for and eventually got my own office on the third floor of USLO. Haggling with the State Department secured half of the communications room for CIA to use as the private channel back to Washington. In an important breakthrough, I got a wall put up separating the State Department's communications from CIA's. In addition, I got a darkroom that I shared with my State Department colleagues.

I was now set up to carry out Kissinger's back-channel communications with the Chinese leadership. Cables would come in from the White House at all hours of the day and night, but I didn't get to read a single one of them. I had been instructed not to. I was a glorified messenger, limited to alerting Ambassador Bruce to a communication. He would then take the cable and act on it himself, in the process sharing it with Holdridge and Jenkins.

During a trip to China in November 1973, Henry Kissinger and I spent some time alone together in the CIA cable room, leading my State Department colleagues to believe that I really was the "secret channel," privy to a private relationship with the president's trusted advisor. The truth was that Dr. Kissinger is a football fan and wanted to get the latest football scores, particularly of his favorite team, the Washington Redskins. The CIA communications equipment got the NFL scores quicker, and Dr. Kissinger and I were in there together looking at them as they came in.

.   .   .

In cables back to Washington, USLO provided the first steady stream of reports directly from China in more than three decades. By 1973 the violent stage of the Cultural Revolution had petered out, but the political infighting that precipitated much of the terror of the Cultural Revolution was continuing. Crudely speaking, because the ideological lines were not rigidly drawn nor the personalities easily

categorized, the "pragmatists" led by Premier Chou En-lai were battling the "radicals" with Mao's wife Jiang Qing at the helm. Chou En-
lai's group, which came to include Deng Xiaoping, generally favored a
downplaying of the harsh ideology that had wreaked so much havoc in
the 1960s and supported moving China away from isolation. In contrast, the "radicals" espoused "Mao Tse-tung thought" and called for
"carrying the revolution through to the end." To them, Western ideas
were still dangerous. Above the fray stood Mao himself, increasingly
infirm but still able to manipulate the players for his own ends.

A simple reading would have said that the U.S. should support
Chou En-lai and company because he represented the "good guys" in
the fight. After all, the Chinese premier had been instrumental in
pushing China to open a dialogue with the White House that eventually led to the establishment of diplomatic relations. That's probably
the way my American tourist friend Bill from Guangzhou would have
read the situation if he had been a young Foreign Service officer at
State. But the facts showed that Chou En-lai was a tough, confirmed
revolutionary with a violent past. He opened channels of communications with the U.S. not necessarily because he liked or admired Americans or our system but because China needed a counterweight to the
Soviet Union to survive. Chou also had to keep Mao's confidence by
supporting some of his far-out ideas. At the same time, Chou tried to
protect valuable friends from Mao's wrath without himself being identified as a counterrevolutionary.

The political battle between the two groups was carried on through
the media under the guise of campaign slogans. These sayings, written
in huge Chinese characters, were posted in public places around Peking
and the country for the masses to see. The popular slogan at the time
when USLO officially opened in July 1973 was "Criticize Lin, Criticize
Confucius." At USLO, the political section surmised the slogan to be a
"radical" salvo directed at the Chou En-lai group.

The links between the historical figures and current Chinese developments were well understood by those in USLO who were trying to
decipher this political war of words. But we wondered what the common Chinese worker, traveling to work on his bike early in the morning, thought when he passed by these slogans.

Unfortunately, we had virtually no opportunity to find out what the common "Chinese Man" was thinking. For Chinese citizens, contact with foreigners was strictly prohibited. In fact, the Chinese whom I saw seemed to be a cowed people. They rode their bikes en masse and wore drab Mao suits with the same cut for men and women. Training to become a barber in the People's Republic of China couldn't have taken long because there were only three different hairstyles in all of China—two for women and one for men. Chinese workers and peasants belonged to work-units, or "dan wei" in Chinese, that regulated almost all parts of their lives, including where they lived, traveled, and worked. On the weekends, Chinese citizens were required to attend political indoctrination sessions.

Peking was in large part a depressing city, its atmosphere made more oppressive by the limited interaction we had with Chinese. Occasionally, a clerk in a store would remember me from an earlier visit and would engage in a brief chat. Only after living there for three months did I get my first friendly acknowledgment. While I was riding my bike back to the Peking Hotel one evening in October, three little girls in red armbands waved and smiled at me. It was a milestone!

· · ·

At first I didn't know my role at USLO. As the supposed back channel, I had at one point envisaged late-night knocks on the door, hushed conversations, and clandestine messages. My actual routine was much less suspenseful. It became a hodge-podge of routine State activities and "passive" CIA tradecraft. Like the other Foreign Service officers in USLO, I gained information from reading the papers, talking to diplomats, collecting public reports, and observing what I could. Unlike them, I supplemented my work by marking what in intelligence parlance were called "targets of opportunities." I compiled a file of clandestine drop sights and Chinese surveillance techniques, devised coding systems to record information on the Chinese military, cultivated East European diplomats, and fended off what appeared to be Chinese provocations.

Long bike rides allowed me to get acquainted with different parts of Peking. They gave me a feel for the layout of China's capital city and a chance to observe the people and to scout out areas for possible contact with Chinese agents should that unlikely prospect ever come to pass. I didn't envision recruiting someone anytime soon. After all, Henry Kissinger had told me personally that he didn't want me "screwing around" with any potential agents. But I pushed the envelope a bit. I wanted to cover the ground for others who would follow me and leave behind an inventory of sights for agent recruitment and contact. I tried to detect surveillance patterns and discovered that, rather than follow me on my bike, the Chinese preferred stationary surveillance. As I rode or walked through areas of town that foreigners were likely to frequent, I might see a Chinese public security official track me with his stare. Or it could be a Chinese man eyeing me from behind a tree while I was at the Temple of Heaven.

In addition, I looked for places where a "bike toss" or "foot drop" could get information to and from a hypothetical agent. Or might there be a "brush" possibility at a busy street corner where you could receive messages from an agent walking by? Each week I sent back to CIA a report describing the overall operational atmosphere. I was heartened to see that when I came back to Peking in 1989 to serve as ambassador, some of my location notes were still in the files.

These long rides around Peking were probably the most pleasant part of my work. I explored back alleys, located historic places, and got a sense for how China operated. One day I might catch children lining up to greet an arriving foreign dignitary. Another day it might be a solitary ride to the Temple of Heaven, built in the fifteenth century, at whose massive marble altar Chinese emperors had once prayed at the summer solstice. Riding on crowded streets, I got closest to rubbing elbows with the common man.

As part of my passive CIA work, I also started to accumulate information on the Chinese military. I did most of this by memory, but I also devised a crude coding system to take down a long series of identification numbers, like those found on military vehicles, airplanes, and ships. When sent back to CIA, such information enabled analysts to figure out what type of military unit was stationed where and was helpful in deciphering military movements.

I decided that it would be handy to have a pocket tape recorder with me to record information when I was riding around Peking, but I didn't want to arouse suspicion. A white foreigner speaking into a portable microphone would definitely raise some hackles. So I set up a ruse to get people used to seeing me carrying the tape recorder. I started bringing it to my Chinese class and explained to my Chinese teacher how I was using it for language lessons. Then, in order to get the Chinese drivers who drove us back and forth to the office accustomed to it, I had my two sons play with it during car rides as if it were their toy.

I also talked to foreign diplomats, particularly East Europeans, who had better access to the Chinese than we had. I cultivated a Romanian diplomat, who informed us in advance that Deng Xiaoping would be made chairman of the powerful Central Military Commission of the Communist Party. In return for the helpful information, I tried to procure for the diplomat an oil heater that he had seen in an American catalogue. There was considerable haggling with CIA headquarters over the price. I ended up getting a cut-rate price on an oil heater from an American relative in the oil heating business, but it was still too expensive for the agency's tastes. On another occasion, an East European diplomat offered us "informations" about deposed Chinese leader Liu Shaoqi. As compensation he asked for a package of birdseed for his failing parakeet. It seemed a bargain, but an opportunity for cooperation fell through when we found out on our own that Liu had died. I fear the parakeet didn't make it.

In the absence of contact with Chinese, those of us at USLO who followed the political scene resorted to the storied tactics of "Kremlinologists," our diplomatic counterparts to the north in the Soviet Union who had devised ways—out of desperation mostly—to figure out what was going on in Moscow. To determine if a meeting at the Great Hall of the People was an important one, we recorded the number of limousines parked in front. To determine the rank of military personnel at such a meeting, we counted pockets on uniform jackets. Four pockets signified an officer, while two pockets indicated an enlisted man. To assess how well countries were getting along with Peking, we observed how the lineup of foreign guests changed. For example, on October 1, 1973, the national holiday of the People's Republic of China, I listened to the Chinese broadcast announcing the list of

distinguished foreign guests. Ambassador Bruce was lumped at the end
of the long list with—guess who?—a visiting Soviet official. We were
on the ground in China, but we were still very low on the totem pole,
roughly equivalent to the Palestine Liberation Organization, which
wasn't even a country.

We did have a few suspicious encounters with Chinese who indicated they wanted to help us. On one occasion a Chinese man accosted
a Scandinavian diplomat in a Peking park and gave him a stash of papers. The diplomat turned the papers over to USLO. We determined
that the Chinese man had been recruited in the U.S. years earlier and
sent back to China to work for American intelligence, but, mindful of a
possible provocation, CIA headquarters told me to stay away from the
man. On another occasion in an antique store in Peking, an old Chinese man led me to a corner. In his palm he spelled the letters O-S-S.
He then asked me if I knew of a Pete F. who had worked in Xian during World War II. He pushed into my hand an old photograph showing a young Chinese with a young American. He then pulled away.
There was, indeed, a Pete F. in CIA who had worked for the OSS in
Xian. Were these cases provocations or genuine attempts to make contact? I'll never know.

·   ·   ·

For the "State" part of my work, I performed consular duties, handled issues like housing and schooling, and monitored the political situation. For the latter, I agreed to listen to Chinese-language news
broadcasts each morning. The news content was dominated by the official Chinese view and rarely offered much insightful information. A
report, for example, on the Arab–Israeli War of 1973 would be highly
charged. After branding Israel the aggressor, the report would go on to
recapitulate a series of victorious battle reports on the Arab side. I always thought that to give my Chinese counterpart in Washington
equal treatment he should be assigned to monitor the children's television show Captain Kangaroo in the morning. It made as much sense
and was better written and acted than the Chinese news.

Considerably more time-consuming and substantive were my duties
that dealt with the American community. Finding a suitable school for

children of USLO employees and securing housing for Americans stuck in the Peking Hotel were pressing issues in those first months. We settled on the Pakistani International School for school-age American children, including Michael and Jeffrey, who had arrived in Peking with Sally at the end of August. Fortunately, instruction at the school was in English, albeit heavily accented Pakistani English. But that was about the only familiar thing for the six American children who started classes there in September. In the morning, as part of exercises involving the entire student body, students were divided into two groups under the names of the founders of modern Pakistan. In classes they addressed their teachers as "auntie" and "uncle" in Pakistani fashion. For break they rushed with their classmates—Pakistanis, Nepalese, Sri Lankans, Nigerians, and Ethiopians, as well as a few Swedes, Romanians, and Turks—for warm milk and biscuits. Athletic facilities consisted of a couple of Ping-Pong tables and a soccer pitch enclosed in a tennis court. At recess students from the school's eight grades played together inside the fenced-in court.

For our two children, used to the green parks and playing fields of Chevy Chase, Maryland, the Pakistani School was a sobering change. To their credit, the boys adjusted and became friends with students from all over the world. In just six months, Mike became one of the leaders of the school as the head of Iqbal House, one of the two groups named for the founders of Pakistan. It was a sight to see. As part of his duties, Mike would lead his "house" into the morning assembly, an American marching at the head of a potpourri of nationalities. Commands would be given, and then Mike would lead his house in the singing of the Pakistani national anthem. In Urdu. For his part, Jeff studied diligently and made friends with a diverse group of kids. Both boys held their own at the school's Ping-Pong tables. However, the next year we decided to start our own school for the eight American children based on correspondence courses from the U.S.

The biggest headache I had to deal with was the unpleasant living situation at the Peking Hotel. After several months of being cooped up in its musty rooms, some Americans began to lose their cool. Our family was stuck in two nonadjoining rooms, and the boys had little outlet for their energies. The hunt for apartments was painstakingly slow as the supply was woefully slim. In some cases I think that the ebbs and flows of the bilateral relationship dictated how fast the Diplomatic Service Bureau would release apartments. Unfortunately for the Lilleys, the lower rank associated with my diplomatic cover job put us in a lesser priority category. It was always a big day when we heard of an impending announcement that some apartments had become available. We had our hopes up in mid-October, but once again our name was not on the disbursement list. The boys were particularly distraught. Mike crawled under the bed, and Jeff sobbed.

Finally, I lost my patience and asked USLO to consider me at my true rank. There must be some advantages to being declared, I reasoned. But we didn't get an apartment until early 1974, and that was only because the previous occupant, a colleague of mine at USLO, had been obliged to leave China suddenly with his family after a tragic accident involving a young Chinese girl on a bike. But thanks to a helpful colleague from USLO, who allowed us to live in her apartment while she went on a two-month home leave, we were able to celebrate Christmas 1973 in a more pleasant place when Douglas, who had just finished his first semester at boarding school, came to join us.

In October, because the level of frustration among Americans at the Peking Hotel was rising, I agreed to be the point-person for complaints about the hotel. As ombudsman, I functioned as the "responsible person" on the American side in talks with hotel management. I got my first taste of dealing with hotel bureaucracy in October after the wife of one of our Foreign Service officers caused a stir at the hotel when she sent back a tofu dish to the kitchen and refused to pay for it because it stank. What would be a relatively minor incident in other posts suddenly assumed greater significance. The next day her action as well as her subsequent interrogation by hotel authorities became a major topic at our morning staff meeting. A meeting with hotel management was set for 6:30 P.M. that evening to discuss the incident. At the meeting, the American side, represented by me, and the Chinese delegation lined up on opposite sides of a long table with a white tablecloth and tea and peanuts, the usual format for official meetings, to discuss this weighty matter. It was a sticky situation, and we had been told by one of our Chinese employees at USLO not to push the issue.

At about this time in Peking the atmosphere had already been somewhat clouded by the U.S. Marine presence at USLO, for which they acted as security. To the Chinese, the Marines constituted a foreign military presence on Chinese soil, a touchy subject historically for them. To make matters worse, the Marines hosted lively Friday night gatherings every week at their makeshift bar, "The Red Ass Saloon," in one of the diplomatic compounds. In the few months since the Marines had opened up their apartment for social occasions, it had become the most popular watering hole in Peking for diplomats. The Marines were eventually forced to leave in the spring of 1974 following a bizarre misunderstanding concerning a flyer they put out about the formation of a softball team. They signed the announcement, which they sent out to diplomatic missions around Peking, with the names "Killer" so-and-so and "Sluggo," according to John Holdridge's account of the incident. The Chinese Foreign Ministry seized upon the circular to charge that the Marines were comporting themselves as "an organized foreign military force."

The Chinese were also upset that the Marines had had a birthday cake made to celebrate the anniversary of the Marine Corps. The icing on the cake apparently acknowledged the Marines' presence in China! Following the Marines' departure, we relied on Chinese policeman posted outside the compound for security.

After two meetings with Peking Hotel management over the course of a week, we put the "tofu-dish" incident to rest. In our meetings the Chinese delegation, a three-strong group comprising a senior cadre, translator, and scribe, laid out its position forthrightly: The American woman had shown disrespect to the Chinese workers by refusing to pay and then had added insult to injury by circling the offending dish on the restaurant chit, thus invalidating the bill. "This is the first time this has happened in over twenty years," the senior cadre told me gravely. "Since Liberation," he added. He was clearly making a political point. I listened politely and offered little resistance other than saying that in America circling something means nothing. I first paid the small charge on the outstanding bill and then went to the American woman's room to get her signature, which the Chinese said was necessary to revalidate the bill. Instead of engaging the agitated woman further on the matter, I forged her signature and returned the bill. The matter ended there. It was unpleasant, but I gained experience in negotiating with the Chinese and got some insight into what the Chinese consider sacred: an unsullied bill, respect for workers, and the righteousness of their own views. I also realized that these issues were far too small to let escalate. It was not my most daring James Bond operation.

.   .   .

Such were the frustrations of living in Communist China. However, despite the discomfort and isolation, I viewed myself as being part of an important mission that was advanced by my presence. Those of us working at USLO had a sense that we were making history. People back in Washington, we were sure, were reading our cables with great interest. There was a feeling that our work, no matter how mundane, was significant. We knew this because we had to remind ourselves of it every morning when we woke up in the grim surroundings.

We did have our stumbles and embarrassing moments. In those early days, we groped our way through trying to set up an American mission in a communist country. One particularly memorable experience came when I was assisting Bob Blackburn, USLO's administrative officer and senior consular officer, with the preparation of visa application forms. Blackburn took the standard forms used at U.S. diplomatic missions around the world to the consular division of the Chinese Foreign Ministry to get them translated into Chinese.

The form sets categories and visa eligibility requirements for foreigners who intend to visit the U.S. There was one section, however, which we let slip by unknowingly. It dealt with people who were ineligible for U.S. visas, including individuals with moral defects, such as prostitutes, as well as members of subversive organizations, such as the Communist Party. We found out about our faux pas when we got a call from an irate Chinese official at the Foreign Ministry. Translators had discovered the questions linking Communist Party members with subversive organizations and defective human beings. The official asked to see us immediately. John Holdridge hurried to his office. At the meeting, the Chinese interlocutor demanded an explanation. "You group Communist Party members with prostitutes?" he asked rhetorically, just beginning to gather momentum. "Did you not know that Chairman Mao Tse-tung and Premier Chou En-lai are Communist Party members? You equate them with morally defective people? Will they not be allowed to visit the U.S.?" Holdridge mumbled an apology and promised to change the offending section. Our administration officer Bob Blackburn got a severe tongue-lashing from Holdridge and then questioned me, the consular officer who spoke Chinese, on the slip-up. We goofed, and I had let Blackburn down. But to me it was still an amusing goof.

On the whole, though, I felt particularly useful in carrying out my cover job. Foreign Service officers usually equate consular work, which amounts to doing background checks, with drudgery. But in Peking my duties gave me a fairly broad exposure to China. In one case, I got an inside look at the perplexing and secretive modus operandi of the Chinese bureaucracy.

In 1974, while going over a list of Chinese aircraft technicians who were scheduled to travel to Seattle, Washington, to train at Boeing's facilities, I noticed that birth dates and birthplaces had been changed on some of the applications. I cross-checked the dates and places with the biographical information on the technicians' previous applications. Sure enough, dates, names, and places of birth had been altered. I called the consular division of the Chinese Foreign Ministry and asked them to explain the discrepancy. A consular official explained that the different information was due to the difference between the lunar and solar calendars.

I was suspicious and cabled the Hong Kong Consulate to send me up a lunar and solar calendar conversion table. The next day, even before I had received the conversion table from the Hong Kong Consulate, an official from the consular division of the Foreign Ministry called on me. His hasty visit, I believe, was prompted by the interception of my cable to Hong Kong. There was no longer any prevaricating or excuses for the altered information. He gave me new information on the Chinese traveling to the U.S. "Accept these names, dates, and places, and discount these other names," he said. I surmised that the Chinese were deliberately falsifying data on their applications. As for the motives behind the Chinese bureaucracy's machinations, I remain mystified. Perhaps they were supplying false information about their citizens so that we wouldn't be able to trace them. The Chinese were very secretive and didn't feel that they should give away information.

Falsifying information on visa forms was grounds for rejecting the applications. I alerted the State Department in Washington, but they said I should give out the visas anyway. Another time, when I was processing the visa applications of a Chinese delegation traveling to the UN in the fall of 1974, I noticed that the head of the delegation's passport was numbered 00001. It was Deng Xiaoping. I figured then that this man was upwardly mobile.

Another consular case allowed me to get a peek at what it was like to live in China. When I met Annie Hsiao in August 1973, she was 81 years old, a stooped but optimistic American woman who had lived in China through many turbulent decades. I was able to hear her amazing tale in the course of putting together her papers for emigration back to the U.S.

Annie was originally from Kansas, I believe, and had come to China in 1916 to work as a Baptist missionary not long after my own father arrived to work for Standard Oil. During World War II, with help from her Chinese friends, she hid for eight years from the Japanese Army occupying Peking. Annie married a Chinese man and had three children by him, but the onslaught of the Communist revolution and ensuing campaigns dealt her family severe blows. Her husband, probably because of his association with an American missionary, was jailed and died in a labor camp in the early 1960s. Her half-American children were similarly hounded. Her son Paul, who had become an English professor, was purged during the Cultural Revolution. Upon release from a reeducation camp, he swore he would never go back to teaching. "Too dangerous" were his words, Annie recalled. Instead, Paul worked at a lathe in a factory. Her eldest daughter spent fifteen years in prison because she had a hard time "conforming." She was caught praying, Annie said. Annie Hsiao's third child assimilated into Chinese society, putting distance between her and the American side of her family.

Annie lived alone in one room of the courtyard house that her family had owned before the revolution. There were eight families living in the compound when I visited Annie there in the fall of 1973. This was my first look at Chinese living conditions in that era. I saw how her Chinese neighbors cherished this stalwart and gentle American woman. They called her "laoye," a term of respect for the elderly.

Before China and the U.S. established diplomatic missions in their respective capitals, Annie had approached the British Embassy for help. She had lost her American passport and was officially considered a stateless person by the Chinese government. But without an American diplomatic mission in China to renew her passport and without the chance to obtain an exit permit to travel to Hong Kong because she was a stateless person, Annie had no opportunity to get back to America. In desperation, she even wrote to Henry Kissinger. I do not know if he ever saw her letter. Shortly after USLO opened, the British Embassy alerted us to her case.

The first time Annie tried to get into USLO in August 1973, the Chinese guards outside the gates stopped her. Beneath her pedestrian dress, they no doubt recognized a foreigner, but one without an American passport. Undeterred, she went to the British Embassy. I then got a car and picked her up. We drove her into the USLO compound, past the PLA guards. In October, Annie received an exit visa to Hong Kong from the Chinese government. Then in December, in an emotional ceremony at USLO, Annie Hsiao got her American citizenship back. She was dressed as usual: in a long, old-fashioned skirt with a Western-style blouse. Ambassador Bruce personally handed over her new passport. She clutched it tightly to her chest but retained her composure.

What I most remember about Annie Hsiao was that she did not show bitterness over the years she had been trapped inside China. She was sad about the death of her husband and the trials and tribulations that her children had had to endure, but she remained a remarkably tranquil person, secure in her religious faith. When we invited her to our apartment in December 1973 for Christmas Eve lunch, she was very grateful to be taken into an American home. She had not celebrated Christmas in years, she told us. The sight of the Christmas tree nearly broke her stoic resolve.

Shortly thereafter, I took Annie to the airport in Peking, where she got on a Boeing 707 jet to fly home. She had never flown in an airplane before. Annie and her son eventually resettled in the U.S. She returned to her home state of Kansas and, I believe, lived out the rest of her years there.

Other consular cases did not end up so well. I remember the case of a soldier from Oklahoma who went over to the Chinese side during the Korean War in the early 1950s. When he defected, this young soldier could barely read. He told me that he had a third-grade education. Yet the Chinese had wanted to showcase him by bringing him to Peking and making him into an English teacher. They eventually discovered that he was ignorant and uneducated. He ended up stirring vats in a chemical plant on the Shandong Peninsula. When he came into USLO after more than twenty years in China, he said he wanted to go home. We got him back to the U.S., but I later heard that his family in Oklahoma didn't want to have anything to do with him. He got a job pounding tent poles into the ground for a traveling circus. Eventually he returned to China, rejoined his wife, and adopted a daughter. Although I despised him as a turncoat, he did have interesting, firsthand stories of the struggles in a factory during the Cultural Revolution.

.   .   .

As American diplomats living in Peking, we were confined to a twelve-mile radius around the city. Only with special permission from the Diplomatic Services Bureau were we allowed to travel outside that limit. So when we received permission, we greeted the opportunity to visit other parts of China as a chance for new observations and as a holiday of sorts. Trips outside of Peking granted a respite from the charged political climate of the city and from its summer heat and winter dust storms. Outside of Peking, there seemed to be more latitude to do things, and new cities contained new—or old, in my case—sights to see. Wherever we went in China, though, throngs of staring Chinese greeted us. Many of them hadn't seen a white-faced foreigner in decades, if ever. When we were in Tientsin scouting old sites like Standard Oil houses and the U.S. 15th Infantry compound, I turned around to see a crowd of at least a hundred Chinese behind us. When we went forward, they followed; when we stopped, they halted. It was almost comedic. We soon learned that the best way to disperse the crowd was to turn the camera on them. That sent them scattering down the alleyways.

One of the first trips I made with my family was to Shanghai in the fall of 1973. My brothers Frank and Jack had attended the Shanghai American School in 1936 for a year before they headed off to boarding school in the U.S. I had studied there in 1940 while my family was stationed in Kiukiang, up the Yangtze River. In the 1930s, the Shanghai American School, or SAS as it was known, was a vibrant outpost of America in the foreign section of bustling Shanghai. SAS students attended church, played American football, and participated in the Boy Scouts. In 1973 the school's remaining buildings were shabby shadows of their former stately selves. I peered over the locked gate to get a glimpse of the old campus, but we couldn't get in. The buildings housed a military organization, and the playing fields were filled with makeshift housing.

By triggering memories of my brothers in China, the trip to Shanghai was just a preview of our family's summer vacation in 1974 at Beidaihe. There on the seacoast of China, just northeast of Peking, both sights and people recalled my family's time there thirty-seven years earlier. We rented a bungalow just up from the beach, and I could see the port of Qinhuangdao eight miles away, where my brothers had swum in the summer of 1937. But the view from the beach wasn't the only reminder I had of my brothers' exploits. It turned out that an employee of the Diplomatic Service Bureau, a Mr. Ge, remembered them, and had followed us to Beidaihe—or so it seemed.

Back in Peking, Mr. Ge stood out from other Chinese. I had seen him fairly frequently at the International Club, the chief diversion in entertainment-starved Peking. Foreigners and high-ranking Chinese cadres like Mr. Ge swam there, played Ping-Pong, and ate at the restaurant. At the club, I had noticed that Mr. Ge smoked cigarettes out of a holder, and in Beidaihe he wore Western-style bathing suits. He also spoke excellent English, peppered with slang expressions, and interacted easily with Americans. I learned later that he had been an interpreter with U.S. forces during World War II. Mr. Ge was clearly different, more relaxed than most other Chinese. For these reasons, he was a suspicious character, and I suspected he had an espionage role. So I wasn't completely surprised when I saw him in Beidaihe.

One evening there he approached me and said he had some extra tickets for the revolutionary opera "Azalea Mountain," which was showing at the local theater. He asked if we would like to go. I accepted, and Sally and I took the two boys to see the propaganda spectacle, which was full of clanging, high-pitched singing, and heroic deeds of Communist guerrillas. During the performance, Mr. Ge didn't seem terribly interested in the opera—he actually managed to fall asleep—but at the end he perked up when we started to talk.

He was blunt and to the point. To describe the opera, he used the well-known Chinese term "gou shi," which means "dogshit." Then he switched the topic.

"You know," he said, "there is a legendary story about two young American boys who swam from Beidaihe to Qinhuangdao in the summer of 1937." He called it "the great swim."

I was startled at the abruptness of his remark. Here was this unknown Chinese man suddenly bridging more than three decades of family history with me. I was intrigued.

"Yes, I have heard the story," I replied. "I believe those were my brothers, and I went alongside them with my father in a rented sampan." Then I figured I would further pad his dossier on me with some important family information. "One of my brothers," I told him, "went on to become a world record–breaking swimmer."

Mr. Ge expressed surprise at the coincidence. But given his background, I was convinced he knew beforehand of the connection between the two young swimmers and me. I am sure he had read my file from cover to cover. The following day he took us to a point overlooking the ocean called Eagle Rock to show us where the swim had taken place.

My suspicions were reinforced when I saw Mr. Ge again eleven years later in 1985 at, of all places, Vice President Bush's house off Massachusetts Avenue in Washington, D.C. In my role then as deputy assistant secretary of state for East Asian and Pacific Affairs, I was attending a reception given by Vice President Bush in honor of a high-level Chinese delegation visiting the U.S. During the reception, Mr. Ge approached the vice president and asked him about the whereabouts of a high-ranking Chinese defector to the U.S. named Yu Zhensan. "Where is he?" asked Mr. Ge. "What is he doing?" Vice

President Bush didn't know what his Chinese guest was talking about and referred him to me. When Mr. Ge raised the same questions with me, I politely cut him off. His questions confirmed for me that he was an officer of Chinese intelligence, and there was no way I was going to help him find out about a defector to the U.S.

We all particularly enjoyed trips to Hong Kong, an oasis of fun for adults and children alike. Kids went crazy over the toy stores, stocked with balls, models, and stuffed animals. Adults breathed in the comfortable accommodations and topnotch service of hotels as if they were enriched oxygen. For our family, though, it was a trip to the Soviet Union as much as forays to Hong Kong that showed us what we were missing in Peking.

Sally and I planned a trip through Asia to Europe for the month of August 1974. Since we had studied Romanian in anticipation of moving to Bucharest, we wanted to visit Romania along the way, something our Romanian friends in Peking had urged us to do. The trip began in Peking with stops along the way in Irkutsk, Moscow, Romania, and Denmark, and ended with a week in the U.S., where we deposited Mike as an eighth grader at St. Andrew's School in Delaware.

The first leg of our trip took us through northwestern China and Mongolia into Siberia on the Trans-Siberian Railroad. Sally and I and the two boys occupied one compartment for the three-day trip to Irkutsk. We all took in the many contrasts with China. We were struck by Mongolia's slow-paced life, rolling meadows, and prolific wildflowers, and the ubiquitous presence of Soviet troops. In Mongolia's capital of Ulan Bator, diplomats plus a good number of Mongolians dressed in traditional robes and leather boots came down to the railway station to watch the train come in, one of the big events in the city, it seemed. The tallest structure in Ulan Bator was a Ferris wheel. We then traveled through the forests and wooden villages of Siberia to Irkutsk, a lively and colorful city. Lake Baikal, huge and untamed, seemed to stretch forever to the north. Siberia, with its color, space, and fresh air, was a welcome relief from dusty, gray Peking. As Sally used to say about Peking, "Fresh air was our most missed commodity." We had always envisioned Siberia to be a dark and gloomy place, but compared to China it looked vibrant and alive.

At the Irkutsk train station, we were greeted by a busty, peroxide blonde Intourist guide in tight-fitting jeans. "Vair ees Meester Zhenkeens?" she asked us in her best English. We had no Al Jenkins to show for her, just the USLO deputy chief's daughter Sarah Jenkins who had traveled on the same train with us from Peking. The Intourist guide scanned Sarah, who was dressed in a billowy gown and had long, stringy hair. Sarah was part of the hippie generation. For the train trip to Irkutsk, she had chosen to ride in the hard seat section, where the Chinese masses sat. The Russian lady's face fell. It looked like the KGB had slipped up, and our guide ended up taking our family and Sarah around Irkutsk. Not quite the assignment she had anticipated.

.   .   .

During our short stay in the U.S. at the end of our travels across Asia and Europe, I met with USLO's new chief-designate, Ambassador George Bush. Bush was scheduled to take up his new post in October and was eager to collect as much information on China as he could. We met at CIA Headquarters and discussed how USLO operated, the restrictions that Americans lived under in Peking, and the political situation in China. Before I left, Bush asked me to have Sally call his wife, Barbara, who then invited Sally over for lunch at their house in Washington. Like her husband, Barbara was interested in knowing as much as she could about her new home. She plugged Sally for information about living in Peking. These two meetings—my discussion with George Bush and especially Sally's lunch with Barbara Bush— were the beginning of a special relationship with the Bushes.

During their tour in Peking, the Bushes were superb representatives of their country. Within an hour of arriving in Peking in the fall of 1974, they hosted a reception at their residence for all fifty-three Americans connected with USLO, including spouses and children. That same day, even before he went to the reception, George Bush came up to my office to greet me. I understood his personal greeting as a vote of confidence for what I was doing as the CIA officer on the ground in Peking. In another sign of his support for what CIA was doing in China, the next day Ambassador Bush invited one of the CIA communications technicians and his family, including two children, to have lunch with him and Barbara at the residence. Bush made this gesture before he had invited the deputy chief of mission or any of the section chiefs to have lunch with him. The Foreign Service officers were shocked and not very pleased.

Bush was a one-man wrecking crew of the isolation that had surrounded USLO in its first year and a half of operation. In one of his first decisions as chief of USLO, he decided that USLO staff should socialize as much as possible with the Chinese. That meant we would start to attend National Day receptions of the various countries represented in Peking. Technically speaking, because we didn't have formal diplomatic relations with China, the State Department thought it unwise to attend functions where U.S. diplomats might meet Chinese. But George Bush was determined to end that self-imposed rule. He himself led the way. Bush got to know the ambassadors from the Soviet Union, Ghana, and New Zealand. He played tennis at the International Club with other diplomats, and he and Barbara biked all around Peking, even to diplomatic receptions, arriving a bit dusty. Their gregarious personalities did wonders for USLO's morale and gave a positive image to America's presence in Peking.

During the fall of 1974, these boosts were sorely needed. Bilateral discussions between the U.S. and China had run aground upon the rock of Taiwan. The Chinese were putting pressure on Secretary of State Kissinger to normalize relations before 1976 in accordance with promises that they said had been made by both Kissinger and Nixon in earlier talks. Since both Mao and Chou En-lai were in failing health— Mao was very sick and going blind and Chou was in and out of the hospital with cancer—Vice Premier Deng Xiaoping became Kissinger's principal interlocutor. Deng was a hardened revolutionary who had been resurrected by Mao just a year earlier from the trash heap of the Cultural Revolution. He was a straight-talker without the loftiness of Mao or the elegance of Chou, but as deputy to Chou he had responsibility for foreign affairs.

In his negotiations with Deng in November 1974, Kissinger tried to have his cake and eat it too: normalization of relations with China while still maintaining diplomatic representation with Taiwan. Such a formulation was anathema to Deng because it spelled out a "one

China, one Taiwan policy." Deng was equally firm in his insistence that the U.S. abandon its defense commitments to Taiwan. Kissinger demurred, wanting to keep the defense treaty with Taiwan active as long as possible until normalization of relations with China. In a testy exchange at a meeting on November 26, 1974, in the Great Hall of the People in Peking, Deng remarked to Kissinger, "It still looks as if you need Taiwan." Kissinger tried to backtrack. "No," he replied, "we do not need Taiwan . . . What we would like to achieve is the disassociation from Taiwan in steps. . . ." But with the Republican Party already on the defensive because of Nixon's resignation in August 1974 over the Watergate scandal and conservatives adamantly against a sellout of Taiwan, Kissinger had little room left to maneuver. The U.S.–China relationship was hung up on the issue of Taiwan and seemed to be going nowhere fast.

.   .   .

At that time, I myself was in limbo. A month earlier, I had been exposed in the American media as a CIA officer working in Peking. Jack Anderson, a syndicated columnist, had a muckraking column entitled "The Washington Merry-Go-Round," and much to my surprise, in the October 30, 1974, edition of *The Washington Post* my name was there for the world to see. Beside the bold-faced print of "CIA Plant," Anderson had written: "Despite the sensitivity of U.S.–China relations, the Central Intelligence Agency has quietly placed an operative in the U.S. mission in Peking. He is James R. Lilley, a 'political officer' who has served in Cambodia, Thailand and Laos." I heard about the disclosure in a cable from Washington, but by the end of the day the news had traveled around the world.

Anderson had dug up my name with the help of a disaffected former Foreign Service officer named John Marks, who was about to come out with a book exposing the names of CIA officers who were working in U.S. embassies around the world. The exposures were an ugly business carried out by a bitter outcast. Anderson's information about me not only jeopardized my usefulness at USLO but effectively ended my career in clandestine operations for the CIA. Having been exposed publicly, I knew I would have to leave Peking. It would be an embarrassment to the mission to have a widely known CIA officer working there. I immediately told Ambassador Bush of my exposure and the need to leave. He appreciated my forthrightness and the way I placed the mission before the man—that is, USLO's reputation before my career. As it was, Ambassador Bush didn't want me to feel as if I were being pushed out. "Take your time," he counseled me. "Wait for a decent interval to pass." Sally and I had been planning to host relatives in the spring of 1975, and we wanted to carry through on our promise to have them visit. We ended up leaving China by train via Shanghai and Guangzhou to Hong Kong in March 1975, about six months after my exposure. My sister, Elinore, who hadn't been back to China since 1938, and Sally's sister, Lee, and her husband, my dear friend George Witwer, took the train with us. To avoid a big hoopla, we had told colleagues at USLO and friends in the diplomatic corps that we were just going on home leave.

Don Anderson, by this time the political chief at USLO, saw us off at the train station. He knew that I was leaving for good. As we prepared to board the train, Anderson handed me a letter from Ambassador Bush. As I would learn later, it was vintage George Bush to write a personal note, usually hastily and on a 3-by-5 index card.

The farewell card conveyed the sensitivity and warm-heartedness that is George Bush. On the outside of the envelope were typed the words: "do not open til the train has left Peking . . . ." In a letter addressed to Sally as much as it was to me, Ambassador Bush expressed his appreciation for my work and my willingness to take on any assignment. "No lousy job was beneath him; no big job too big for him," he wrote. As for Jeff, who had struck up a friendship with Ambassador Bush playing Ping-Pong, he wrote, ". . . if in any way, direct or indirect, I can be of help to this guy please please let me know." He closed with a heartfelt farewell to the three of us. "As you leave Peking tuck away into your heart of hearts the fact that you three have done well. You've made friends. You've given to your country in a tough assignment. Bar and I will miss you very much." I showed the letter to Sally. She started to cry.

George Bush's friendship and trust would prove to be of much assistance as I continued to carry out the "mission" of my life's work, though in a different role at the CIA and, eventually, in a different career.

13

GOOD FORTUNE

IN MY LIFE, two periods stand out when I was able to find a place for myself in the momentum of events. The first was my decision, precipitated by the outbreak of the Korean War, to change my academic focus at Yale from Russia to China, and shortly thereafter to join the CIA. The second decision occurred more than twenty years later when I thought of a plan to get to China as a member of the first American diplomatic mission in Communist China.

Shakespeare wrote in *Julius Caesar* that "There is a tide in the affairs of men/ Which taken at the flood leads on to fortune." If in each of these two pivotal decisions China was the "tide," then meeting George Bush in Peking in 1974 was the "fortune." With the benefit of hindsight, I see that the opportunity to work with George Bush profoundly influenced the rest of my career in government service. Serendipity played a role in bringing us together. First, Bush, a man better known for his role in domestic politics, chose to come to China in 1974 over more prestigious opportunities to represent the United States overseas. When I left China on that train in March 1975, however, there were no guarantees that our paths would cross again. His letter of appreciation might well have been the last communication between us. But the fortunate turn of events that had brought us together in Peking had not run its course. When George Bush, who had little active experience in the intelligence business, was recalled by President Gerald Ford to head the CIA, he became my boss for the second time.

.   .   .

Upon returning to the U.S., because Jack Anderson's column had finished my career in covert operations, I made the switch to the open, analytical side of CIA. I worked as the National Intelligence Officer (NIO) on China, the senior officer in the U.S. intelligence community for all matters concerning China. But the nature of the work—chairing interagency meetings, dealing with institutional biases, and churning out position papers—was tedious, time-consuming, and, I thought, largely irrelevant.

Furthermore, in the mid-1970s, the CIA was reeling from a serious institutional crisis. In the wake of the Watergate scandal and the defeat and disillusionment caused by the Vietnam War, there was increased scrutiny by Congress and the press of secret government operations. In response to this, in 1973 CIA Director William Colby had exposed the CIA's role in bringing down Chile's socialist government. Then in 1975 President Ford acknowledged the CIA's deep involvement in covert actions and set up his own commission to investigate the agency. Congress also appointed two commissions, one in the House and one in the Senate, to investigate the CIA's operations. Throughout the corridors of America's elected institutions, there was a call to rein in the CIA.

Inside the CIA morale was low, and employees had started to question the value of the agency's work and the importance of their roles. In my analytical work, I found it hard to get fresh perspectives on China from the outside because association with the agency could kill careers in academia. Perhaps the lowest point came on December 23, 1975, when the CIA station chief in Greece, Richard Welch, was assassinated outside his house in Athens after his name and job description had appeared in a letter to the English-language *Athens News*. The information on Welch may have come from a disgruntled CIA officer. With Welch's assassination, the whole business of revelations became not just annoying but dangerous.

Then, like a breath of fresh air, George Bush came back to Washington to take over the troubled agency in January 1976. Just as he had done in Peking, Bush brought his personality, energy, and intense interest to bear on his new position. At a time when the CIA was being pilloried in Congress, Bush invited the agency's congressional detractors, like Senator Frank Church of Idaho, to his home for dinner. Bush demonstrated a deep respect for the agency's intellectual brain trust, the hundreds of employees with master's degrees and doctoral degrees who worked in the Directorate of Intelligence. To show his solidarity with agency employees, he chose to keep his office at CIA headquarters in Langley, Virginia, rather than across from the White House in the Old Executive Office Building, where he could be closer to the president. Most importantly, in terms of getting the agency back on track, George Bush's professional leadership restored integrity to the CIA while balancing the necessity for secrecy in intelligence operations with Congress and the public's right to know.

In meetings he showed little pretense. When he did not know something, he asked questions. I will never forget the time during a briefing on strategic nuclear weapons when the briefer used the abbreviation MIRV, a term well known to intelligence types as multiple independently targetable reentry vehicle. Bush asked what a MIRV was. You could hear a collective gasp come from the room of smug employees.

When Bush started at CIA, there was much skepticism expressed about him. When he left fourteen months later, I saw tears in the eyes of some of the old, hard-bitten operators.

.   .   .

In early 1977, Bush resigned from the position of director of CIA to allow Jimmy Carter, who had defeated Gerald Ford in the 1976 presidential election, to name his own nominee. As a "normal" citizen, Bush had time to pursue opportunities closed to him while he served in government. One of those opportunities hearkened back to his final days in China in 1975. When Bush met with Deng Xiaoping to say farewell, at Mao's behest Deng offered the departing USLO head a trip back to China, anytime, anywhere, and with whomever he wanted. In 1977, he decided to take up the Chinese on their offer.

One of the meetings for the trip took place at my house in Chevy Chase. I set up the lunch with Ambassador Huang Zhen, head of China's Liaison Office in Washington, and his deputy Han Hsu. I tried to keep the luncheon meeting as low key as possible since the U.S. still did not have diplomatic relations with China. I asked Sally to prepare the lunch, and Jeffrey, then in eighth grade, came home from school to serve as the waiter.

In the friendly confines of our house, we had an extraordinary meeting with the Chinese. It was like old friends getting back together. Ambassador Bush and Ambassador Huang Zhen traded pleasantries, and the mood relaxed. When talk turned to the controversial subject of Taiwan, for instance, Huang used the term "mutual compromise," a much gentler formulation than the Chinese government usually applied. At one point, Bush leaned over the table toward Huang Zhen and said, "Mr. Ambassador, I want to tell you something I have told few people. I am going to run for president in 1980." It was a talent of George Bush to be able to make his interlocutors feel important. By letting the Chinese in on his future presidential plans, he brought them into his circle of confidence.

Over dessert of melon in the living room, the Chinese reciprocated. "Chairman Mao loved you," Huang Zhen told Bush. "And you never got to take a trip at the end of your stay. I would like to offer you the opportunity to take that trip."

After the Chinese left, George Bush turned to me. "Where do you think we should go, Jim?"

"Let's shoot for the moon," I said as thoughts of Tibet, the picturesque city of Guilin, and the Yangtze Gorges, through which my father had sailed sixty years earlier, came to mind.

But on the trip there would be no meeting with Chairman Mao. China's Great Helmsman died in September 1976, a year to be remembered in China for its cataclysmic events. Eight months earlier in January, Mao's longtime comrade-in-arms Premier Chou En-lai had passed away. Chou's death set off a huge outpouring of grief in April around the Martyr's Memorial in Tiananmen Square. Public mourning slipped over into demonstrations, which edged toward riots. Looking for a scapegoat on whom to pin the disorder, in April a quartet of radical Chinese leaders headed by Mao's wife Jiang Qing purged Vice Premier Deng Xiaoping of his posts. The political infighting continued when acting premier Hua Guofeng, fearing that the radicalized quartet of leaders would try to seize power, got the powerful backing of the military and had the "Gang of Four," as the foursome became known, arrested in October. Between Chou and Mao's deaths, as if to match the fractured political landscape of Peking, a devastating earthquake rocked the northern Chinese city of Tangshan in July. More than 250,000 people were reportedly killed.

.   .   .

Besides securing an invitation to China, that luncheon meeting at my house served the dual purpose of showing the Chinese that we saw them as good friends and that I was George Bush's trusted advisor on China affairs.

As we set about organizing the trip for September 1977, Bush invited along his close friends from the world of business and politics as well as the extraordinary personage of Lowell Thomas, the 85-year-old broadcaster and world traveler, and his new bride, Marianna, 36 years his junior. But I couldn't get permission to go, with objection coming not from the People's Republic of China but from the American side. While the CIA welcomed the opportunity to have me go into China and learn about places such as Tibet that few Americans had visited in the past three decades, the State Department had other ideas. The diplomatic arm of our government objected strongly to an intelligence officer visiting China. It would send the wrong signals, we were told. Finally, frustrated at the lack of movement, Bush picked up the phone and called Secretary of State Cyrus Vance.

"I want to take Lilley with me to China, and I'm getting resistance from your bureaucracy," Bush told Vance.

"Is Lilley known as an intelligence officer to the Chinese?" asked Vance.

"Of course he is," replied Bush.

"Then what's the problem?" Vance said.

The logjam was broken, and the bureaucracy overridden once more. I was on my way back to China, this time in select company. In fact, the trip turned out to be an introduction to several people with whom I would work in the next decade. In addition to George and Barbara Bush and Lowell Thomas and his wife, the group included James Baker III—Bush's long-time friend from Texas, who later served as Secretary of the Treasury in the Reagan administration and Secretary of State in the first Bush administration—and Chase Untermeyer, another Texas colleague of George Bush, who later was Director of Personnel in the White House, head of the Voice of America, and Assistant Secretary of the Navy during the Reagan and Bush presidencies. Others in the group were Hugh Liedtke, chairman of the board of Pennzoil, and his wife; Dean Burch, former chairman of the Republican National Committee and his wife; and *Washington Post* journalist David Broder and his wife. Our interpreter for the trip, furnished by the Chinese, was a brilliant young diplomat named Yang Jiechi, who had just arrived back in China from London. We nicknamed him "Tiger" because he was, in fact, just the opposite: kind and decent. He is currently serving as the Chinese ambassador to the U.S.

Lowell Thomas stole the show. Thomas, who had been one of the last foreigners out of Tibet in 1949, seemed to be on a mission to show his bride of a few weeks "The Heavenly Kingdom." To date the Chinese government had allowed few foreigners to visit Tibet, which it had forcibly occupied in 1951. In Peking, the Chinese tried as gently and then as persuasively as they could to discourage us from going. One creative ploy was for Chinese officials to say that they were concerned about Thomas's age and the fact that he wore a pacemaker to correct a slight irregularity in his heartbeat. Thomas prevailed in a test of wills with the Chinese. In a toast in Peking on one of the first nights, he told our Chinese hosts, "I happen to have been a mountaineer all my life, so when I go to high altitudes, I feel like I am going home, and besides I am on my honeymoon." With this statement, some in our group saw an opportunity for fun and suggested to the Chinese that Thomas was going to consummate his new relationship at 14,000 feet. Our Chinese hosts joined in the humor. All the while, Lowell insisted that he was of hale and hearty spirit and not intimidated by Tibet's mere 14,000-foot altitude.

But Thomas was disappointed in what he found in Tibet. There was little trace of his friends from his last trip in 1949, and Buddhism, the region's lifeblood, was obviously suppressed. The Dalai Lama had fled Tibet in 1959 after the Chinese used force to put down an uprising, but Thomas was hoping to get word of Tibetan acquaintances, who had served in the Dalai Lama's cabinet and remained behind. To his inquiries about the fate of such people, our Chinese hosts answered blankly, "They are gone" or "They are no longer here" or "They have disappeared." As the trip wore on, Lowell Thomas looked more and more depressed. During our time in Lhasa we toured monasteries, but we didn't see one Buddhist monk. When we attended social functions and meetings, there was a sea of green indicating the dominant presence of the PLA. Things came to a head when our hosts took us on a tour of the Tibetan Revolutionary Museum, a collection of hideous exhibits purported to show how the Dalai Lama's government had mistreated its own people. There were graphic photographs of people being tortured and expositions of children who had had their kneecaps broken and had been stuffed into jars. Our American group was revolted. At the front of the museum, in a section showing "imperialist" help to the Dalai Lama, there was a photograph of Lowell Thomas meeting with members of the royal court, including the Dalai Lama's finance minister. In the caption Thomas was identified in Chinese as an imperialist agent in the process of passing money to the traitors. The photo was from his last trip to Tibet.

At the end of the tour, at the habitual tea-drinking session in a museum antechamber, a Chinese host asked pro forma for any criticisms we might have. George Bush surprised them by asking to speak. "The pictures of children being tortured are distasteful," he said, "and Lowell Thomas is one of the most distinguished and respected journalists in America, and yet you have a picture describing him as an imperialist agent."

To cover his bases, after the trip to the museum Bush asked me to check with Thomas to see if he really did work with the U.S. government to help the Tibetans. I knew the Chinese had a copy of the book written by Thomas's son about their trip to Tibet in 1949, which described his father's cooperation with the Tibetans, so I wasn't surprised at his answer.

"You're damn right I did," Thomas told me. "I supported the Tibetans. And I would do it again, too."

I relayed the information to Bush. We both decided not to push the issue much further.

I know that George Bush was annoyed at the Chinese for taking us on the tour of the museum because by the end of our trip in China he had given David Broder an unclassified CIA report on Chinese repression in Tibet. In a story entitled "Tibet Under Peking's Control" that ran in *The Washington Post* after we got back, Broder cited the CIA report. Figuring that I was the person who "leaked" the report, the State Department exploded in anger at me. One foreign service officer said that he had studied minorities in China as an undergraduate and that he could not accept Broder's version. I was appalled at his naiveté. Chinese suppression in Tibet was very well known.

Fourteen years later, I returned to Tibet as the U.S. ambassador to China and got a glimpse of what the Tibetans were still going through. During a visit to Drapchi Prison in Lhasa, which was notorious for holding Tibetan political prisoners, I asked to speak with a prisoner. There had been reports of a death at the prison, and a year earlier forty-five Tibetans had been arrested for "counterrevolutionary activity." Our team of four American diplomats found the jail housing 300 prisoners orderly and clean, so clean, in fact, that it looked like the prison authorities had prepared for our appearance. The Tibetans, I was soon to learn, had also readied themselves for our visit. After our tour of prison facilities, a well-known prisoner walked straight at me from about twenty yards away and attempted to hand me a note. It was obvious what he was trying to do, and a Chinese guard grabbed for the note in our two outstretched hands. During the commotion, another prisoner snuck in behind our group and slipped a note undetected to one of the American diplomats. The Tibetans had circumvented their Chinese captors. We had the note translated when we returned to Peking. It said, "We are being tortured."

On the business front, the trip with President Bush was more of a success. Hugh Liedtke, the chairman of Pennzoil, met with Minister of Foreign Trade Li Qiang, and during a meeting with Deng Xiaoping at which Bush and I were present, Bush made significant headway in persuading Vice Premier Deng to allow American oil companies to work in China. At that point in 1977, Deng, who had been restored to his posts earlier in the year with the help of powerful backing in the military, was about a year away from introducing his initial plans for economic reform in China. An old oil man himself, Bush "sold" Deng on the concept of a "risk contract" in which U.S. companies would assume the significant costs of exploration for oil in places like the South

China Sea and then share the proceeds from production if oil were discovered. Deng liked the idea because it would allow China to bring
into the country free of charge the technology and capital needed to
exploit oil resources and then still share in the profits. Deng also knew
that his own oil people had oversold him on their capabilities, leaving
China with semi-submersible rigs that no one knew how to use and
jack-up rigs that had turned over in the Gulf of Bo Hai in northeast
China. The concept of "risk contracts" became the basis for joint ven-
tures in oil exploration between the United States and China.

Bush's meeting with Deng built on the acquaintance they had
formed during his posting in China and laid the foundation for future
meetings, including two more in the next three years that I would also
be privileged to attend. In spite of their diminished political statures in
1977—Bush being out of power and Deng having just returned to his
government posts from being temporarily purged—I believe that Bush
and Deng sized each other up as future leaders. Just as former President Nixon and Henry Kissinger had forged personal ties with Deng's
predecessors, Mao and Chou En-lai, Bush was developing a relationship with Deng that eventually became critical in sustaining
U.S.–China ties in troubled times and advancing them in better times.
When the two men ascended to the tops of their respective governments, their personal connection facilitated a blending of American
and Chinese interests into a workable formula. This congeniality of
leaders at the highest levels is, I believe, one of the keys to managing
the Sino-American relationship.

An added benefit of the 1977 China trip, and one that very few
people know about, is that it produced a nickname for George Bush. In
the 1970s in keeping with its desire to build an egalitarian society, the
Chinese government discouraged the use of official titles in addressing
people. Like its communist neighbor to the north, the Soviet Union,
China was proud to be a "dictatorship of the proletariat." So, for example, when a Chinese official, perhaps the highest-ranking person at a
commune, would introduce himself, he might say, "I am the responsible
person of Red Star People's Commune." Those of us traveling with
George Bush in 1977 soon found out that he was the "responsible person" in our group. When we went by sedan, he traveled in a Red Flag

limousine. So, in a friendly manner, we started to refer to George Bush as R.P. for "responsible person." The initials stuck, and in the succeeding years when he would write me a note, George Bush would often sign it "R.P." Barbara, who was with us on the trip to China, took a particular liking to the moniker and would write to us things like: "R.P. and I are just back from a sensational 6-day trip to Egypt and Israel."

. . .

By 1978 China was revving up for its modernization campaign. While Vice Premier Deng Xiaoping was not running the economic reform drive yet, his ideas about change were being discussed and debated in China. Aware of its need to industrialize, China was starting to court U.S. officials and businessmen more aggressively in hopes of getting American help in exploiting its vast but still largely untapped natural resources. Peking hoped to double its oil output by 1985 and by so doing increase the production of goods and services and also generate sufficient revenue from exporting oil to finance the import of Western technology.

As part of Secretary of Energy James Schlesinger's official delegation to China in the fall of 1978, I got a chance to see firsthand Chinese leaders articulate the new ways of thinking that were beginning to steer the economy. Just ten years ago these officials were mired in the muck of the Cultural Revolution, and now they were admitting China's backwardness and expressing hopes for a speedy normalization of relations with the U.S.

Our group investigated the prospects for U.S. cooperation in a range of energy-related issues, including coal, oil and gas, hydroelectric power, and high-energy physics. We were given excellent access to China's energy sites and, to our surprise, even got an unscheduled tour of a Chinese diesel submarine.

Schlesinger, a man of extraordinarily broad talents, was a favorite of China because of his strong anti-Soviet stance and because he had served in two influential positions in the Nixon administration: Secretary of Defense and Director of the CIA. In fact, in our meeting with Premier Hua Guofeng on November 4th, Hua pointedly called Schlesinger an "old, old friend." Then, after greeting the other members of our group, Hua, his hair combed back straight over his head and with an ever-present ingratiating smile, looked at me and remarked, "Mr. Li Li worked in the liaison office for a while, too." Hua was making a point that he knew who each of us was and that he was happy we had come to China. And to think that a year earlier the State Department thought that I would spoil a trip to China!

At our first stop in Peking, the head of the State Planning Commission, Yu Qiuli, a one-armed man with a rasping laugh, drove home the point that the Soviet Union was China's archenemy. The Russians, he said, were trying to take over the Middle East with its valuable natural resources. For China to be able to stand up to its adversary to the north, it had to develop its energy sector. "Energy is closely related to overall strategy," Yu said. "Our military hardware is affected if energy policy is not properly handled." Schlesinger knew that Yu was a Politburo member who was close to Deng, and, as the man in charge of energy, he also controlled nuclear matters. So, at the end of our meeting, he and I took Yu aside and asked him if we could visit one of China's nuclear submarines. Yu looked as though he were in mild shock. Pointing his finger upward toward the ceiling, he said that he would have to check "upstairs."

Several days later, while on a tour of China's oil fields in Manchuria, the Chinese told us that our schedule had been changed and that we would be visiting the port city of Dalian. I told Schlesinger that just south of Dalian was where the Chinese harbored their nuclear submarines. The man upstairs—in this case most likely Deng—may have spoken. The Chinese told us in Dalian that only three people could come to the port area to tour a submarine. Schlesinger took John Deutch and myself. At that time Deutch was director of the Office of Energy Research at the Department of Energy and later became Director of the CIA under President Clinton. There was another security man included, but he was not part of the official delegation. We left behind a few offended State Department employees and a curious American press corps that didn't know where we were going. In fact, the lead State Department representative threw a tantrum at me directly upon our return. The press took it more lightly, and at a dinner that night, Strobe Talbott of *Time* magazine led the press corps in a chorus of "Where, oh where has my Schlesinger gone?" to hoots of laughter. Though the tour was not of a nuclear submarine as Schlesinger had originally requested, the visit to the submarine was a historic event in the annals of U.S.–PRC military relations. It was the first time, I believe, that American officials had ever toured a Chinese submarine. The *Chiang Nan* was an eighty-three-yard-long diesel-powered R class submarine with a crew of fifty-six and room for fourteen torpedoes, as we learned that day from the ship's commander.

In Moscow the Soviets perked up their ears when they got word of our delegation's visit to China. They immediately seized on the visit as another sign of increasing cooperation between the CIA and China's special services. A TASS dispatch dated October 31, 1978, mentioned me by name. According to the news report, drawn largely from an article in London's *Daily Telegraph*, I was a crucial link in the pattern of heightened cooperation in that as a "leading CIA specialist on China" I had accompanied two former CIA directors to China within a year. They were right to suspect something, although substantive cooperation in the intelligence arena was still a year away.

In spite of cheery language on U.S.–China energy cooperation and our tour of a Chinese submarine, the Chinese still let us know loudly and clearly of the obstacles in the way of better relations. Head of the State Planning Commission Yu asked for the removal of restrictions imposed by NATO countries and Japan on technology exports to Communist countries, including the People's Republic of China. Yu reiterated that no government-to-government agreements on energy could be signed as long as there were no official relations between China and the U.S. But he added that agreements on a civilian basis between companies could be signed. It was a step forward, a continuation of the flexibility that Deng Xiaoping had shown to George Bush in their meeting on oil exploration a year earlier.

The Schlesinger trip was valuable in revealing a rapidly changing China. I observed from our talks in Peking that the technocrats were coming to power. There was less mention of ideology, and there seemed to be great anxiousness for modernization. Chinese officials turned more often to economic statistics and were quicker to recognize their weaknesses in areas such as science and technology. Even so, the Chinese fumbled in interpreting their own numbers to themselves and to us. By contrast, Schlesinger deftly handled an array of issues, calling on numbers and details to support his arguments. To wit, Schlesinger had perceptively figured out from charts of China's largest oil field, Da Qing, that the Chinese had adopted with disastrous results Soviet secondary recovery methods using water. In terms of prospects for future cooperation, the large scale of some of the suggested energy projects that we discussed with the Chinese—like a dam on the Yangtze River and joint exploration of offshore oil—indicated China's desire for strategic linkages with the U.S. over a significant period of time.

The Chinese leaders we talked with made a point of telling us that the government was in steady hands after the turbulent events of 1976. Yu Quili said, "We smashed the Gang of Four with one blow." Later, Hua echoed his deputy, almost gloating over the demise of the Gang of Four in October 1976: "Wine and liquor were sold out all over the country," he told us with a smile.

I also got the sense that China was moving away from the autocratic leadership of Mao. Hua Guofeng did not enjoy anything like the reverence that Mao had attracted, and I understood from our exposure to him and other members of the leadership that, forced to build consensus within a coterie of powerful officials, he must have found it difficult to get his way. Actually, in 1979 Deng got rid of Hua, who was never his match, and became the paramount leader of the People's Republic of China.

On a personal level, I believed that China's continuing acceptance of me, a CIA officer, as part of an official delegation signaled their willingness to cooperate on security issues. Not only did Hua personally greet me, but my photo also appeared in two Chinese newspapers.

As I wrote down my observations of the trip, I found the Chinese to be "peaceful, realistic and reasonable, not a threat." They were anti-Soviet for the time being and came across as determined for normalization. Since they were industrializing and in a building phase, "they were seeking to build foreign connections in constructive ways."

.   .   .

The establishment of official diplomatic relations with the People's Republic of China was not so much a question of when but how. As early as February 1977, President Jimmy Carter had talked of his hopes for normalization of relations with Communist China. By the spring of 1978, Carter's national security advisor, Zbigniew Brzezinski, was working hard to bring the complicated task to fruition by granting permission for China to buy infrared scanning equipment, which China had previously been denied, and by providing assistance in helping China to buy weapons from America's allies in Europe. I helped in this process by getting the CIA to write a series of memos to Brzezinski's China specialist on the National Security Council, Mike Oksenberg, who was an old friend.

A major issue in the minds of China-watchers around the world was the future of Taiwan. Specifically, what would happen to Taiwan in the context of an agreement between the U.S. and China to exchange embassies in their respective countries?

Within the Carter administration, Brzezinski had taken over China policy from Secretary of State Cyrus Vance and by 1978 dominated the making of China policy in a fashion not unlike that of his predecessor Henry Kissinger. Brzezinski's hard-charging anti-Soviet approach led him to focus on the geopolitical significance of the People's Republic of China.

When the announcement was made on December 15, 1978, that Peking and Washington had finally reached a solution, the final communiqué dealt a blow to Taiwan. The U.S. agreed to break official diplomatic representation with Taipei, terminate its mutual defense treaty with Taiwan, and remove U.S. military personnel from the island. On the crucial point of the future security of Taiwan, the U.S. skirted its way around the issue, preferring to secure agreements with China now and haggle about Taiwan later. There was no mention in the communiqué of China agreeing to allow the U.S. to sell defensive weapons to Taiwan. Rather, the U.S. agreed to make no new arms sales to Taiwan for a period of one year with the tacit understanding that after that time the U.S. could resume sales. In the midst of last-minute negotiations on the conditions for opening up official relations, the two sides agreed that any specific wording on arms sales to Taiwan would have to wait until a later date.

In the U.S., prominent Republican politicians criticized the final agreement, which called for official relations to begin on January 1, 1979. Governor Ronald Reagan of California said the agreement was a betrayal of Taiwan and quickly rushed off to visit the island nation before it lost its status as an independent country in the eyes of U.S. diplomacy. Private citizen George Bush called the communiqué on normalization a sellout of the Republic of China's security. I knew from my extensive contact with Bush that he was for the establishment of diplomatic relations with China, but he didn't want the final agreement to neglect Taiwan. Reagan, on the other hand, represented the harder line of conservative Republicans. In his mind, Taiwan was the better friend of America among the two parts of China, and it should remain so.

As the national intelligence officer on China at CIA, I watched the whole process take place but was cut out of the negotiations. I knew that normalization negotiations were going on, but Brzezinski's proprietary handling of the matter shut out virtually all government agencies. Eventually, motivated to act by the Carter administration's approach favoring mainland China, I worked with Robert Bowie, the head of the National Intelligence Office structure at CIA, to influence the process. With some help from his friend Secretary of State Cyrus Vance, Bowie gave me instructions, or terms of reference in CIA-speak, to draft an interagency report on the reaction in Asia of normalization of relations between the U.S. and China. The project polled Asian countries, including Taiwan, on their reaction to several hypothetical conditions of our imminent normalization.

In findings that I collected in a national security studies memorandum (NSSM), I discovered that our Asian allies had mixed feelings about normalization. On the whole, though, Asians didn't want us to rush into an agreement. The paper, which I presented to the National Foreign Intelligence Advising Board, headed by Director of CIA Admiral Stansfield Turner, went over very well, mostly for its broad scope and objectivity. At a time when policymaking seemed akin to a steamroller laying down a new road, the NSSM suggested that more examination of the terrain would allow us to chart a wiser path through complicated issues like the future status of arms sales to Taiwan and the nature of our diplomatic mission there.

My shepherding of the NSSM through a reluctant bureaucracy was

My father arrived in China in 1916 to work for Standard Oil. Here he is traveling up the Yangtze River, a river he would call "awe-inspiring in its massive ruggedness," on a mission for the company.

Idyllic Tsingtao, with its beautiful beaches and international community, was a wonderful place to grow up. This picture was taken in the garden of our home. I am the baby sitting with (from left to right) Frank, Jack, and Elinore.

Wash amah was the tiny woman assigned to take care of me. Her bound feet forced her to hobble around, but they didn't prevent her from taking care of my every need, while bantering to me the entire time in Shandong street talk. We were inseparable.

During the summer, swimming races for adults were held on the Strand, Tsingtao's finest beach. In 1934, thirteen-year old Frank challenged a muscular Japanese army sergeant. He swam as hard as he could but the sergeant won. I watched from the shore. Frank is in the white sweatshirt third from the left. The Japanese sergeant is far left. Jack is on the far right.

While at Yale, Frank developed into a crack swimmer. In 1942 he helped the university's 400-yard relay team set a world record.

In late 1945, I met Frank and his new bride Nan at the Copa nightclub in New York City. I was surprised when Frank, who outranked me, admonished me for pulling his ears.

In 1946, Frank was assigned to the 76th Military Government based in Kure, a suburb of Hiroshima. He took this picture of Hiroshima shortly after his arrival. Frank was deeply affected by the devastation.

Yale was exhilarating. Though I was always aware that Frank and Jack had preceded me there, I was able to carve out a space for myself, taking a wide array of courses and diving into swimming and soccer. In my senior year I was elected captain of the soccer team, and we went on to have a winning season.

Here I am as a young CIA officer, with a CIA colleague, in Japan. The photo was taken just before I went to Korea to launch a clandestine mission into Manchuria.

I met Sally Booth in 1951, and we were married in Andover, Massachusetts three years later. I had just returned from a two-year tour in Asia. That's my mother peeking over our shoulders, and Jack is standing next to Sally with Bill Washburn, Elinore's husband and Frank's classmate at Yale.

My posting to Peking in 1973 was historical; I was the first CIA officer to enter China legally in decades. Here I am with Mike, Sally, and Jeff ice-skating at the Summer Palace outside Peking.

When George H.W. Bush left China in 1975, as a parting gift Deng Xiaoping offered him a trip to wherever in China he wanted to go. I came along in 1977 when George Bush took up Deng on his offer. This is me in Tibet with Jim Baker, Ren Rong, a Chinese military commander in Tibet, Yang Jiechi, the current Chinese Ambassador to the U.S., and Lao Ma, a senior cadre.

In 1978 I returned to China with Secretary of Energy James Schlesinger and was one of a select few included in a private inspection of a Chinese submarine—the first time, I believe, that American officials had ever visited a Chinese submarine.

In April 1984, I returned to Washington to brief President Reagan on U.S.–Taiwan relations just before his first trip to China. Looking over my shoulder is my trusted fellow Asia-hand Gaston Sigur, who was on the National Security Council staff. From left to right are: Secretary of State George Shultz, Assistant National Security Adviser John Poindexter, National Security Adviser Robert "Bud" McFarlane, and Chief of Staff Jim Baker.

Before I left Washington to serve in Taiwan, President Reagan took me aside—Nancy Reagan and George Bush joined us—to make a point about Taiwan's importance to him. The personal attention meant a great deal to me and I would often remember Reagan's words about the Taiwanese, "I want you to know that I like those people."

From mid-April until early June of 1989, Tiananmen Square filled with more and more demonstrators. This crowd passes in front of three symbols of China's struggle—in the furthest background is Mao's Mausoleum, in front of that is the Monument to the Martyrs of the Revolution, then the Goddess of Democracy.

Following the massacre in Tianamen Square, the U.S. Embassy's sheltering of Chinese dissident Fang Lizhi and his wife complicated the bilateral relationship with China. I spent many hours negotiating Fang's release, which we finally obtained in June 1990. On the eve of his departure from China, Sally and I along with son Mike bade farewell to the couple.

an attempt to lend some balance to the positions being followed by the White House. As I would write several months later in a policy paper to George Bush, I personally was critical of parts of the normalization agreement of December 15, 1978, not because I was against normalization but because of the way it was handled. Secrecy, timing, and disrespect toward Taiwan had produced "a bungled, compromised agreement." Secrecy, used effectively in the national interest by Kissinger in the early 1970s, had been taken to an extreme by the Carter administration. There was no consultation with Congress, and I understood that Taiwan was notified via a 2:30 A.M. call to President Chiang Ching-kuo on the morning of the December 15 announcement. In terms of timing, whereas European nations had conducted painstaking and deliberate negotiations with China on the conditions of normalization, the U.S. had rushed into a deal. I think it was Rudyard Kipling who said, "Fools try to hustle the East." Well, we had gotten hustled by the East! In my policy paper to George Bush, I had wondered "Is this administration . . . planning a disarmed and neutralized Taiwan with its existence becoming increasingly dependent on Peking's goodwill toward it?"

In Taiwan, the U.S. had plenty of egg on its face. A mission sent to Taipei by Carter on December 27 to explain the U.S. decision on normalization became a target for unhappy Taiwanese. President Carter's emissaries, Deputy Secretary of State Warren Christopher and U.S. Ambassador to Taiwan Leonard Unger, were attacked by demonstrators as their car was driving them to a downtown Taipei hotel. Crowds pelted the car with tomatoes and then started throwing rocks. Windows of the car were broken, and in the commotion that followed Christopher suffered cuts and Unger's glasses were broken. There were some indications that there was governmental manipulation behind the attack, but we could not prove it.

The real loser in all of this, as I told Bush in my memo on normalization, was America's prestige: "I've lived in China and I know how sensitive the Chinese are to political style and nuance. If we are as incompetent as we appear or if Peking can manipulate us so easily, how can any Chinese have any real respect for us?"

A balance to our relationship with Taiwan and mainland China was restored when both houses of Congress passed the Taiwan Relations

Act (TRA) in April 1979. Having been shut out from the normalization process, Congress weighed in on the side of Taiwan—in a measured and bipartisan fashion. Passed 339–50 in the House and 85–4 in the Senate, the Taiwan Relations Act wrote into law security guarantees for Taiwan that were nearly as strong as those contained in the terminated Mutual Defense Treaty. It called on the U.S. to provide Taiwan defensive arms and in time of crisis to "make available to Taiwan such defense articles and services . . . to enable Taiwan to maintain a sufficient self-defense capability." For the hearings on the TRA, I had primed the Senate Foreign Relations Committee to ask Leonard Woodcock, the chief American representative in Peking, one key question: Had anyone to his knowledge asked the Chinese to renounce force on Taiwan? His answer was, and I paraphrase, "Not to my knowledge." I thought it important that this failure be recognized as such.

Congress had salvaged a measure of respect and badly needed security for Taiwan. But what about leadership from the executive branch? Surely America could do better than what the Carter administration had shown in its handling of normalization. "Peking houses hard-eyed realists—they are not romantic about us and they judge us more by our actions than our words," I wrote to Bush. "You do not put dilettantes up against pros and come up with favorable results. We were taken to the cleaners on Taiwan."

I wrote this policy paper to George Bush from the perspective of a private citizen. I had retired from the CIA in January 1979 after twenty-seven years and nine overseas postings. Business was interesting and paid for my rapidly increasing education expenses—my sons chose expensive colleges. But politics beckoned. George Bush was going for the presidency, and I wanted to be part of his team.

14

RIDING A WAVE

I LEFT THE CIA because I was no longer interested in the process of deliberation, bargaining, and compromise, which accompanied analytical work, and I was not trusted by many people in Jimmy Carter's entourage. Now, after spending my entire adult life working in government, I wondered what I was trained to do. I wrote to a colleague for help in writing a résumé and started to send out feelers in what I called "the great bazaar of the outside world." I targeted the American oil companies interested in China and even dashed off a letter to Hugh Liedtke of Pennzoil, whom I had met on the 1977 trip to China. I was eventually hired as an independent consultant for Hunt-Sedco Oil Company of Dallas and United Technologies of Hartford.

On August 31, 1979, Director of the CIA Stansfield Turner presented me with the Distinguished Intelligence Medal, one of CIA's highest honors, for my service to the agency. The awards ceremony at CIA headquarters in Langley, Virginia, was a highlight for me and my family. Many of us at CIA work in obscurity for years, but an occasion like this allows a person to gather around him colleagues and family to celebrate a secret profession in open fashion.

I was leaving behind a lifetime of secrecy or, as they like to say in the spy novels, I was coming in from the cold. Virtually all my professional contacts at the posts in which we had served had known me as a "diplomat." My cover applied to my family as well. Sally, of course, knew who my real employer was, but my sons didn't find out until that sunny August day at CIA when I was awarded the medal. Sally and I didn't tell the boys anything before the ceremony. Old habits die hard.

For all those years they thought that their father was a diplomat working for the State Department until, upon entering the headquarters building, they saw the floor mosaic of the crest of the CIA.

Our second son Mike actually found out in 1975 when he was at boarding school, although he had put it out of his mind. An eighth grade classmate told him that his father had read in the newspaper that I worked for the CIA. Mike didn't believe the boy but brought it up with me. Since Mike was close enough to Washington that he might well hear more mention of me in connection with my exposure, I asked a CIA colleague to explain to Mike my exposure in the newspaper when Mike was staying with family friends in the Washington suburbs during a vacation from school. For a second time Mike refused to believe the story. The newspapers were probably wrong, he thought. He was convinced that I was a diplomat.

Part of the reason I was awarded the medal from CIA was my work in setting up the first CIA unit in Peking. Another contributing factor was my role in developing intelligence sharing with China, a "brainstorming" project that was just coming to fruition at about the time that I was being honored in Langley.

This intelligence sharing with China was born of a slow day in 1975 in a fifth-floor office of CIA's main building. The Soviet National Intelligence Officer and I were looking at a map of the Soviet Union and its contiguous border with China. Both of us knew that the Soviets had been testing nuclear missiles in Soviet Central Asia and that the CIA had been at a loss to monitor the heavy Soviet missile-testing activity. My eyes came to rest upon China's enormous northwest province of Sinkiang. I observed that from the mountain ridges of Xinjiang the Chinese had a clear shot of the Soviet missile-testing area at Semipalatinsk in what was then known as the Kazakh Soviet Socialist Republic. My colleague went up to inspect the map more closely.

Turning back to me, he asked the question that we were both thinking. "Do you think the Chinese would ever cooperate with us on this?"

It sounded like a far-fetched idea—the U.S. and China, who had been fighting each other through surrogates just a few years earlier in Vietnam, working together to collect strategic technical intelligence on the Soviet Union. But since the U.S. now had diplomatic contacts with

China and USLO was functioning, these were the kinds of creative ideas that we could consider. There was, of course, an actual basis for our thinking. As early as 1973, utilizing overhead photography, we had started briefing the Chinese on Soviet military deployments along the Sino-Soviet border because the Americans wanted the Chinese to be prepared for a Soviet buildup. The Chinese seemed to be impressed. But monitoring sites would be a significant step forward in that the operation would marry American technicians and technology with Chinese geography and support personnel.

"It's worth a try," I answered my colleague.

I typed up a memo for CIA director William Colby in which I laid out a detailed plan. I named the project "Wallabee" in honor of my father-in-law, Waller B. Booth. Colby loved the concept and passed it on to Secretary of State Henry Kissinger, who briefed the Chinese on it during his October 1975 trip to China. Deng seemed to like the idea but said that we should wait for normalization. In April 1979, after normalization of relations, Vice Premier Deng Xiaoping agreed to start actual cooperation.

The agreement to pursue U.S.–China intelligence cooperation against the Soviet Union signaled an "intelligence revolution" of sorts because, after decades of mainly spying on each other, the Chinese and Americans had decided to work together in a concrete way to collect information on the Soviet Union.

Not that we ever really stopped working on each other.

.   .   .

While I was working as a private consultant, out of the side of my eye I was keeping track of George Bush and his intention to run for president of the United States. Bush had kept me notified of his thinking and wanted me aboard his campaign. In January 1979, he informed me that he would be filing the necessary papers for the Federal Election Commission. "Needless to say, I want and need your help in this," he wrote.

On May 1, 1979, George Bush officially announced his candidacy for the presidency. In between trips to China for consulting, I threw myself headlong into campaign work—donating money, ringing doorbells, and writing rebuttals to newspapers. Sally and my son Mike pitched in as well. We traveled a lot and advanced our candidate for the Republican nomination in New Hampshire and Pennsylvania.

I was also advising George Bush on his Asia policy. In February, I had flown down to Houston for his private meeting with Deng Xiaoping during the Chinese leader's historic visit to the U.S. I think that Deng requested the meeting because he sensed a bright political future for Bush.

At the Hyatt-Regency Hotel in Houston, Bush and Deng discussed the need for a more assertive U.S. role in the world, the Vietnamese invasion of Cambodia, and Taiwan. Echoing sentiments in my memo to him on U.S.–China relations, at the start of the meeting Ambassador Bush wasted little time in clarifying his statements to the press criticizing the Carter administration's approach to normalization. "I respect you and I want to clear the air," Bush told Deng. "My concern about recent events does not concern China's position but my own country's position."

For the next thirty minutes, Deng impressed upon Bush the need to "hold the line" against the Soviet Union and the importance of improving other nations' perception of America. "It is necessary for you to do solid, down-to-earth actions to establish U.S. credibility," said Deng. Bush concurred with the Chinese decision to support Cambodia against Vietnam and gave his support to China's decision to attack Vietnam, which would take place on February 17, just two weeks after the meeting with Deng. "If you do not give a bloody nose, your troubles will increase," Bush said. Referring to Vietnam as "Cuba East," Deng took Bush's support for Chinese action against Vietnam as a chance to declare the need for a front against the Soviet Union, especially in places like Angola, where Soviet-backed rebels supported by Cuban troops were trying to overthrow the Angolan government. "I believe some punishment to Cuba East or West would give them [the Soviet Union] a lesson to hold back and when we consider it, it is not just from China but from global strategy. We see the U.S. is not firm enough in various parts of the world with Cuba and the like, and now it is our time," Deng said.

On the delicate issue of Taiwan, Bush spoke carefully, drawing on personal experience to push a peaceful solution. "Because I lived there [in China], I understand as well as anyone in the U.S. the 'one China and Taiwan' problem. My only reservation is I would like to codify this 'peaceful' problem." Deng answered: "We will try to solve Taiwan by peaceful means but not tie the other hand. Can you persuade Taiwan to negotiate with us?"

"If I can ever be helpful, I will—I will help get them to negotiations— maybe someday there will be a useful role to play," Bush replied. Later, I suggested to Bush that he use caution in getting in the middle of differences between China and Taiwan. As far as I know, Bush never followed through on his hint of being an intermediary. But it's worth noting that seven months after the Deng–Bush meeting in Houston, Deng's close colleague Ye Jianying announced his nine-point proposal for reunification with Taiwan. The plan allowed Taiwan considerable independence under the sovereignty of China. Taiwan would be able to keep social, economic, and cultural relations with other countries while maintaining a free market economy and its own military. Furthermore, in a sign that China seemed to be moving away from the "liberation" theme to a more peaceful reunification theme, the Chinese stopped bombarding Quemoy Island in 1979 after twenty years of intermittent shelling.

At the time Bush and Deng met in Houston, Deng had consolidated his hold on the Chinese leadership. While his official title of Vice Premier did not show it, Deng was now calling the shots, and his seven-day trip around the United States was a way to showcase him to America. Before the start of our meeting with Deng, I got an unusual insight into the personality of the Chinese leader from Zhang Wenjin, China's Vice Foreign Minister, who was accompanying Deng. In the course of our conversation, Zhang said, "Deng is different from Chou En-lai. Deng decides so quickly. Chou was more . . ." Zhang groped for the appropriate word in English. I said, "moderate," but Zhang said, "No" and used the Chinese term "kao lu," which means "to reflect more, to consider carefully."

.　　.　　.

After losing to Governor Ronald Reagan in the Republican presidential primary, George Bush was selected by Reagan to be his running mate against President Carter in the November 1980 election. With Reagan's charisma and Bush's experience in government, the two men presented a powerful Republican ticket to the American people. But in the complex field of China policy, there was considerable work to do to get the two politicians on the same page. Reagan had long taken a hard line toward mainland China and openly favored the more democratic Taiwan. Having served in China and having dealt with the PRC/Taiwan question in his role as U.S. Ambassador to the UN, Bush had a better feel for the nuances of the issues at hand. In their respective campaigns, both men had criticized Carter for his China policy, but Reagan had gone considerably further than Bush. At a rally in Cleveland in May 1980, Governor Reagan told the audience that he looked forward to reestablishing official relations between the United States and the Republic of China. With his statement, the Republican presidential candidate put Peking on guard that, were he to become president, he might undo the efforts of the last three administrations to establish diplomatic relations.

Throughout his primary campaign, Governor Reagan continued to call Taiwan "the Republic of China," a name that was supposed to have exited the American diplomatic lexicon with the establishment of official relations with the PRC. Whether he was grandstanding or not, and I believe he was not, Reagan's actions were sending shock waves through the moderate wing of the Republican Party. So when the Reagan/Bush ticket came together in July, one of its campaign strategists' first tasks was to use George Bush's expertise to patch up the ticket's China policy.

Accordingly, it was decided that Bush would go to Japan and China on a trip designed to showcase the Republican vice presidential candidate's skill with Asian issues and his acquaintance with the Chinese and Japanese leadership. The trip was the brainchild of Richard Allen, Reagan's senior foreign policy advisor. Bush asked me to accompany him on the trip along with Allen and five others. But before Bush left, Reagan seemed to undercut his personal emissary at a press conference for Bush on August 16, 1980, the day of his departure for Asia. Reagan said that if he won the election he would set up official government-to-government relations with Taiwan by making the American Institute in Taiwan, America's nongovernmental representation there since the closing of the U.S. Embassy in January 1979, into a direct operation of the U.S. government. This put Bush in an awkward position. For damage control, Bush got me to phone the Chinese Embassy in Washington, D.C., and tell them that Reagan's words could have been taken out of context and to advise them to wait for the written text before reacting.

In Peking, we found the Chinese leadership visibly disturbed by Reagan's pronouncements. In separate meetings, both Vice Premier Deng Xiaoping and Foreign Minister Huang Hua said the statements raised doubts about the approach of a Republican administration toward China. The U.S. was going backward, they said. During a particularly unpleasant August 22 meeting with Deng in the Great Hall of the People, Bush explained the context of the remarks—that they were made in an election year at a harried press conference and that the press had distorted Reagan's views on China. Bush insisted that Reagan, while he had good friends on Taiwan, did not favor turning the clock back. But Bush had to concede the Chinese frustration and anger over the pronouncements, at one point asking the Chinese in our meeting with Huang Hua for their interpretation of the normalization treaty and then adding, "Reagan is not totally familiar [with these points], and we can explain the Chinese position."

"On more than one occasion, Reagan has said he supports official relations with Taiwan. There is no misunderstanding. And on the day you left the U.S. for China Reagan said something in this vein," Deng told us, adding later that "No matter what one's views and positions are on other international issues, if Reagan's remarks and the Republican platform should be carried out, this is bound to damage Sino-U.S. relations."

During the meeting, to make an awkward situation even worse, the Chinese aides assisting Deng were translating and reading the latest news dispatches from the Reagan/Bush camp on China/Taiwan policy. These were comments that none of the Americans in the meeting had seen or heard but were being forced to explain. It was as if we had come to defuse some mines in the U.S.–China relationship, and more were being planted as we set about our work. At one point, Deng's aides scurried around with a news dispatch, finally handing it to Deng to

read. "Who is Ke-lai-ne?" the Chinese asked us. It turns out that a
Reagan advisor, Ray Cline, had made a statement to the press that the
Bush visit to China would not have an effect on Reagan's plans to de-
velop relations with Taiwan. A few minutes later, the Chinese transla-
tor interrupted George Bush to read an Associated Press story dated
August 21 in which Reagan had told journalists that the Taiwan Rela-
tions Act permitted the establishment of a government liaison office on
Taiwan.

In the face of the interruptions, Dick Allen persisted in trying to set
the record straight with the Chinese. A Reagan administration would
not turn back the clock, but the Chinese government couldn't expect
the U.S. to abandon an old friend to gain a new one.

At the end of the meeting, Deng was unmollified. "Allen and Bush's
explanation have not put our minds at ease," he said. He closed our session with a scathing dig, part dark humor but designed to get his message across. He said that if the Republicans continued to support
Taiwan, he would be forced to stand up for the interests of one billion
Chinese. The pro-Taiwan statements were forcing him into a corner,
and he was hardly likely to "sell out" to the U.S. in response. If he did
that, said Deng, "I would no longer be qualified to be a Chinese and
should take out American citizenship."

We retreated from the meeting. Bush turned to me. "That meeting
went pretty badly, didn't it?" he said. I nodded, "Yes, it sure did."

The trip was an eye-opener for Dick Allen. He had believed, like
Reagan, that facing down the Soviet Union was the primary issue in
U.S.–China relations and that as long as we worked with the Chinese
in this direction, Taiwan would become less important. Deng talked
directly to this point in the meeting: "[Reagan's] tough stand on the
USSR will not cause China to swallow his position on Sino-U.S. relations and Taiwan." In another meeting at the Foreign Affairs Bureau of
the People's Liberation Army, we got the same line from a military
man: "If you don't get Taiwan right, nothing is going to happen," our
interlocutor from the PLA told us. It was a real education for Dick
Allen. "Don't give us this stuff about Russia and polar bears," the Chinese seemed to be saying to him. "Taiwan is a real issue, and don't forget it for one minute."

On the plane back to the U.S., Allen set about drafting a communiqué on the trip for Bush's press conference upon arrival at the Los
Angeles airport. I joined him on the second level of the Pan Am 747 jet
between Tokyo and Honolulu, where he was hunched over, pecking the
keys of a tiny typewriter. Reagan would be in Los Angeles, and we
needed a statement from the Republican presidential candidate that
would clarify the ticket's position on the sticky China–Taiwan issue.
As the plane sped toward the West Coast, Allen and I boiled down the
ticket's policy on China–Taiwan to five principles for Ronald Reagan
to read at the press conference. Above all, we wanted to allow Reagan
to put his comments into a more benign context and, equally important, take the issue out of the election spotlight. The statement said
glossy things like the U.S. will be a friend to all Chinese, whether in
China or Taiwan, and protected Reagan's conservative flank by declaring that a Reagan administration would carry out the law of the land in
the form of the Taiwan Relations Act. But it also formally acknowledged that Reagan wouldn't try to undo or renegotiate the terms of
America's formal recognition of China.

In Reagan's hotel room in Los Angeles on the morning of August
25, we found his inner sanctum of advisors milling about. Reagan had
drafted his own statement on Taiwan on a yellow pad and was prepared
to read it. It was very strong stuff and contained the kind of rhetoric we
were trying to tone down. Allen and Bush had greased the wheels a bit
by talking to Reagan in private the night before about the importance
of reading the more moderate statement. We introduced the draft
statement again in the morning. "Look at this," somebody said to Reagan. The Republican presidential nominee looked at both pieces, his
and ours, one in his right hand, one in his left, weighing them as if they
were on a scale. "You want me to say this?" Reagan said somewhat incredulously to the collection of advisors surrounding him. "Yes, it's the
best thing to do," came the reply. Then as we sat around a table, expec-
tant for a reply and wary of time passing, Ronald Reagan started to tell
jokes and stories. We continued to sit. He hadn't made his decision,
and the second hand on the clock was going around and around. The
press conference was scheduled for 10:30 A.M. At 10:25, the Republican
nominee for president still hadn't made a decision. Finally, he said,

"Well, you really want me to say this?" We all nodded our heads. "Okay," he said, and headed out to the press conference.

The astute political cartoonist Patrick Oliphant did a fine job of parodying the Reagan–Bush split on China. In an August 29, 1980, cartoon, Oliphant depicted Bush as crashing into a China shop on the back of a bucking bronco with the head of Ronald Reagan. To a bunch of irate Chinese in the shop, Bush says from his perch on the bronco and amid clattering plates, "Take it easy, gentlemen—I can explain everything." In reality, though, in his position as vice presidential nominee, Bush could try to influence Reagan quietly, but it was clear that Reagan was the one who was going to carry the election for the Republicans, and Bush couldn't overcome him.

After Bush returned from China, the Chinese press started to attack Reagan during the buildup to the election, accusing him of trying to set back relations and saying that he had insulted the Chinese people with his comments on Taiwan. The attacks were a nuisance and gave fodder to the Democrats in the heat of a presidential campaign. So, in an attempt to quell the attacks or at least open the channels of communication, on October 30 I invited Chinese journalists from the *People's Daily* to visit the Washington headquarters of the Reagan–Bush campaign. I arranged briefings for them on policy, finance, and organization. We made sure to show the Chinese the computer printouts that indicated Reagan was ahead of Carter by 8–10 percent. They responded positively. "The Reagan–Bush campaign is better organized than the Carter campaign," they said.

As they were leaving, I managed to locate two Reagan–Bush bumper stickers with "The Time Is Now" written on them in Chinese and gave them to the journalists to their surprise and pleasure.

A week later, the two journalists asked to have tea with me. We came to an implicit agreement to tone down the heated words and to stop making China a campaign issue: "If you guys don't raise this hostile approach with us, we will be less hostile toward you" was the idea.

This kind of open and productive exchange with Communist Chinese reflected the progress that had been made at higher levels. The Bush–Deng relationship set the tone. Between 1977 and 1980, the two men met three times when I was present. Having a seat at the table for their conversations convinced me of the historical importance of these three meetings. The first in 1977 formed part of Deng's economic re-form movement that transformed and is still transforming China. The second in 1979 was followed by a more subtle and effective approach to cross-strait reconciliation. The third in 1980 got the U.S. and China through potentially damaging conflicts in the American approach to China.

.   .   .

On November 6, 1980, Ronald Reagan and George Bush defeated Jimmy Carter and Walter Mondale to usher the Republicans back into power. Sally and I dashed off a congratulatory telegram, partly in angli-cized Chinese, to the Bushes in Houston. "RP and Bar, you both have made it and our country will be the better for it. Gong Xi Gong Xi to RP, now VP."

A month later I got a call from George Bush's personnel man re-questing that I come to the Reagan–Bush transition headquarters on Massachusetts Avenue. A quiet, aristocratic southerner from Virginia, the man asked me point-blank to name four jobs that I would like to have in the coming administration. I thought hard while he stared at me impatiently. Other people were waiting outside to see him. I was unprepared and a bit disturbed at the hurried nature of such important business. But I collected myself and said: National Security Council Staff for East Asia, Director of the American Institute in Taiwan, As-sistant or Deputy Assistant Secretary of State for East Asia, and finally, as a long shot, Ambassador to China.

I got the National Security Council position. Over the course of the next decade I would get the other three assignments. Was it the Chinese who said, "Watch out for what you ask because you might just get it?"

IV

DIPLOMAT IN ACTION

1982–1991

15

RIGHTING THE BALANCE

LIKE THOUSANDS of Americans, Sally and I faced the cold January air to watch the Reagan–Bush motorcade proceed up Pennsylvania Avenue on the morning of Ronald Reagan's inauguration. It was one of those winter days when frost comes out of your mouth, and people stamp their feet to stay warm. But at least we had company with whom to share the frigid temperatures. George Witwer and Sally's sister, Lee, joined us from Indiana, where George now owned several newspapers. It was fitting for George and Lee to be there at the start of what would be the most important decade in my career, for they had been there in the beginning—those early days in Washington when as CIA novices George and I had spent a good deal of time trying to master intelligence techniques while wooing the Booth girls. Almost thirty years later, the four of us waved at George and Barbara Bush as they passed by. The evenings were filled with tasteful balls, dancing, talking, and toasting. Personally, as the East Asia specialist on the National Security Council, I was pleased to be a player in the forming and carrying out of policy toward Asia.

Even in the midst of all the excitement about the inauguration, the complexity and nastiness of the U.S. relationship with China and Taiwan reared its head and snapped at the incoming administration. Sensing a chance to capitalize on President Reagan's pro-Taiwan sympathies, Anna Chennault, the Chinese-born wife of General Claire Chennault of World War II fame, and others had arranged for Senate invitations to be sent to several prominent politicians from Taiwan to attend the inauguration festivities as official guests of the new administration. It was, in effect, a symbolic move upgrading the U.S. relationship with Taiwan.

When the Chinese ambassador in Washington, Chai Zemin, caught wind of the invitations, he threatened to boycott the inauguration ceremony. Chai asked me to arrange a meeting with Vice President-elect Bush. At the meeting in the vice president's temporary quarters on Lafayette Square, Chai started off by praising Bush. Then at the end he launched into a tirade against the presence of an official Taiwan delegation.

After the Chinese ambassador left, Bush turned to me and said, "What the hell was Chai talking about?"

I briefed the vice president. He said, "Lilley, take care of it."

Despite American attempts to discourage the Taiwanese delegation from coming to Washington, the governor of Taiwan, the secretary general of the Kuomintang, and the mayor of Taipei all planned to arrive in Washington with tuxedos in tow. At the last minute, the diplomatic embarrassment was avoided when Secretary General of the KMT Y. S. Tsiang conveniently checked into a Washington-area hospital with a case of the flu. The governor canceled his trip, and the other members of the Taiwan group who did come to the gala weekend did not sit in the official section. We had dodged a bullet. But it was humiliating for our Taiwan friends. It looked as though we were already caving to Chinese pressure.

The inauguration maneuverings were an example of the diplomatic chess game between China and Taiwan that would characterize the unsettled early years of the Reagan administration.

Six months later, I found myself in the firing line of another decision, this one designed to tilt Washington policy toward Peking. In just six months as Reagan's secretary of state, Alexander Haig had made a name for himself as an outspoken "China supporter." He used the phrase "strategic imperative" to describe China. Haig wanted to give China a preferential status in the formulation of U.S. foreign policy because, like Kissinger, he saw it as a valuable counterweight to the Soviet Union. Haig's master strategy at that time centered on a plan to sell sophisticated arms to both Taiwan and China. He had a lot of self-confidence and occasionally a flair for the dramatic.

Haig traveled to Peking in June 1981 to advance ties between Peking and Washington. I went along as a member of the delegation, but I was there to represent a White House policy that called for a more gradual engagement with the Chinese. I felt like an outsider for the entire trip. In the months leading up to the visit, Haig had pretty much co-opted China policy, freezing out the National Security Council and even cutting us off from key cable traffic.

While the Reagan administration had discussed the possibility of forging closer military ties with Peking and had, in fact, eased restrictions on China's purchase of high-tech American weapons, the White House had resolved that any decision to sell arms to China had to be kept secret for two months to allow the U.S. government a chance to inform its long-standing friends in the region like Japan and Taiwan. It was the right thing to do, particularly in regard to Taiwan, which would have to face a beefed-up Chinese military. I found company in Richard Armitage, the Pentagon specialist on East Asia and a fellow "outsider" who did not fully share Haig's view of China's immediate strategic importance. Rich's loyalty was to Secretary of Defense Caspar Weinberger. We nicknamed ourselves the "bastards at the family reunion."

Haig was intent on pushing through his vision of a partnership with China. During a press conference in Peking, he revealed that Washington was considering the sale of sophisticated arms to China. Haig had jumped the gun, and I could only imagine the tremors that would hit Taipei and the rest of Asia as they heard—unprepared—that the U.S. was ready to help arm Communist China.

After Haig made his announcement, Armitage and I used the secure communications links, which had been set up during my time in Peking, to send messages back to Reagan's National Security Advisor Dick Allen and to Defense Secretary Weinberger. Allen got the policy wheels turning back in the other direction. That day President Reagan appeared at a news conference. He reaffirmed the United States' commitment to fulfilling the Taiwan Relations Act and specifically emphasized the clause regarding the continued sale of weapons to Taiwan.

Like Anna Chennault and her supporters in the White House, Haig had moved too quickly and too far in one direction, throwing out of balance what some others and I perceived should be a more carefully calibrated American policy toward the two sides of China. On the one hand, I didn't dispute the advances made in opening up relations with

Peking, nor the acknowledgement that the U.S. officially recognized one China, whose capital was in Peking where we had our embassy. But relations with Peking did not have to proceed at the expense of Taiwan's security. In navigating through incidents like the inauguration invitations and Haig's premature announcement, at times I felt as if I were standing in the middle of a seesaw, planting my feet carefully so that neither side went too high or too low.

In those first years of the Reagan presidency, however, I probably did lean to the Taiwan side over concern that U.S.–China policy had been taken over by groups of bureaucrats at State, CIA, and Defense who, like Secretary Haig, were crusaders for the strategic relationship with China. After all, it had been forbidden fruit for almost thirty years. In an attempt to counter these groups, I put a stop to a weekly intelligence report published by the CIA that highlighted Taiwan's transgressions and infractions, often in inflammatory and accusatory language. In the more notable case of Haig's breach, I advocated for a reaffirmation of support for Taiwan, not because I was necessarily "pro-Taiwan," though I could find many reasons to like the country, but because a more balanced policy would better serve America's interests, such as stability in Asia and support for democratization.

I based my thinking on the need for a more balanced policy on a reading of Chinese history and current evidence. Threats to China historically had come either from tribal forces sweeping down from the north, such as the Mongols in the twelfth century and the Manchus in the seventeenth century, or from the sea in the form of the British in the nineteenth century and the Japanese in the twentieth century. The land invaders had in large part been absorbed by China because of its superior civilization, enduring culture, and huge size. The later invasions by sea, however, were more devastating. The British and Japanese had shown little respect for Chinese culture and had destroyed the Qing dynasty and damaged China's first attempt at a republic, the Republic of China under Chiang Kai-shek. To avoid a repeat of these invasions from the sea, I reasoned, China sought control of an island chain stretching roughly from the Senkaku Islands off Okinawa down to the Paracel Islands in the South China Sea, which the PRC had seized in 1974 from a declining South Vietnamese regime. Control of the islands would form a buffer zone around China's most valuable areas on the coast, including Guangdong and Fujian Provinces, Shanghai, and the Shandong Peninsula.

For the Chinese, in the 1980s the inheritor of the threat from the sea was the United States with its powerful 7th Fleet and military bases in Japan and the Philippines. A key location for China to control was Taiwan, situated as it was between Japan and the Philippines.

I concluded that Chinese designs on Taiwan had to be dealt with because, first of all, China's occupation of Taiwan could threaten Japan, the linchpin of U.S. forward deployed military in Asia that acted as a stabilizing force in a historically volatile region. Second, Taiwan was becoming a force for stability in its own right with its growing economic strength and its tentative movement toward democracy. But without bases for the U.S. military, the island was no longer an unsinkable aircraft carrier, and it needed U.S. military support.

I was also coming to understand the paradox that was part of U.S. relations toward China and Taiwan: Positive results could come from China if the U.S. carefully managed solid backing for Taiwan. A first indication of this pattern came in September 1981 when, at a time when the U.S. was considering the sale of advanced FX fighter planes to Taiwan, China issued its nine-point peace plan, which emphasized peaceful reunification rather than liberation and offered Taiwan greater autonomy under the sovereignty of the People's Republic of China. The offer was unprecedented, and many China-watchers saw Peking's plan as an olive branch for peace in the Taiwan Strait and felt the U.S. should respond by not selling the fighter to Taiwan. I, however, interpreted the peace plan as recognition on China's part that the intimidation of Taiwan that it had been carrying on for three decades with intermittent shelling of Quemoy and Matsu had not worked. It was time, Peking realized, to try another tack—to use enticements and to stress reunification rather than liberation. That the peace missive had come on the heels of the Taiwan Relations Act of 1979 did not escape me either.

.   .   .

After I had been working at the NSC for about six months, Dick Allen approached me with a job offer. "We want to get the right man in Taiwan. You are trusted by the administration and have a good reputation on Taiwan," Allen said. I accepted the offer to become the director of the American Institute in Taiwan, which had replaced the U.S. Embassy in 1979. After working as a cog in a large machine often at odds with itself, I liked the idea of being in charge of something. But in both Taipei and Washington, D.C., things were conspiring to make the start of my tenure on Taiwan a rocky one.

To start, Taiwan lacked confidence in relations with the mainland. The island was still trying to rebound from the setback of normalization. Further signals made it appear that the balance was tipping in Peking's favor. While discussion of the sale of the FX fighter planes to Taiwan might have influenced Peking to tone down its approach, the truth was that Peking started to press hard on the U.S. to limit arms sales to the island. Even the vaunted Taiwan Relations Act, which reasserted the requirement for the U.S. to supply weapons for Taiwan's defensive needs, did not seem to be rock solid. One of its clauses hinted at past human rights abuses on Taiwan by stating that the "preservation and enhancement of the human rights of all the people on Taiwan" were objectives of U.S. policy.

Chiang Ching-kuo's Taiwanese government was especially worried about negotiations between China and the United States that were originally supposed to commemorate the tenth anniversary of the Shanghai Communiqué with a new communiqué on U.S.–PRC relations. Since the fall of 1981, the Chinese had been applying heavy pressure on the Americans to agree to a termination date on arms sales to Taiwan. Their first tack was to try to force us to acknowledge that on the eve of normalization in 1978 the Carter administration had made a commitment to end arms sales to Taiwan, but we found nothing of the sort in the NSC files.

Still sensing weakness in the Reagan administration's resolve to hold the line on arms sales to Taiwan, the Chinese then pressured Secretary of State Haig as well as U.S. Ambassador Arthur Hummel in Peking. Foreign Minister Huang Hua drove home the point to Haig that the U.S. needed to set a termination date for arms sales to Taiwan. If Washington refused, Huang Hua said, then China could downgrade relations.

Haig, who had succeeded in shutting out the NSC from the foreign policymaking process, pushed a memo past my boss Dick Allen and onto the president's desk at 6 P.M. one night in late October 1981. The memo called for the U.S. to agree not to exceed the levels of arms sales proposed by the Carter administration and even reduce their quantity and quality over time. Haig's memo purposely excluded the mention of a specific termination date, but the insertion of the "quantity and quality" clause was his response to Chinese pressure, and it surprised top aides who had been following the talks with the Chinese.

I was tipped off to the memo that afternoon by a "loyal" friend in the State Department, who said it was "bad news." I stated my concerns to Dick Allen late in the day. But by the next morning when we came to work, it was too late to do anything about the memo. The "quantity and quality" clauses became the basis for the commitment that was made to the Chinese the next day. Under pressure from Peking, Haig had gotten his way.

.   .   .

The sale of the FX fighter to Taiwan was in the pipeline before Haig had his discussions with Huang Hua. This sale to Taiwan, coupled with sales of arms to China, was at the heart of Secretary of State Haig's plan to move ahead relations with both sides.

The FX was one of a number of arms requests that the previous occupant of the China position on the National Security Council had dumped on my desk when I arrived at NSC in 1981. There had been a one-year moratorium on arms sales to Taiwan after normalization, and little had been done in 1980 on the backlog of requests. My predecessor said with a smirk, "You guys like Taiwan so you can handle this."

The agendas of the various players in the FX game led to debate among government agencies, think tanks, and politicians. Did Taiwan actually need an upgrade from its present F5E? Was the Chinese Air Force modernizing at that fast a clip? Not to mention the politics behind a decision involving California-based Northrop and Texas-based General Dynamics, which were squaring off to win the lucrative U.S. government contract to supply Taiwan with a new-generation jet fighter. In the highly politicized environment surrounding the sale of the FX, in my role as the China specialist on the NSC I thought it best to turn to an objective source—the Defense Intelligence Agency (DIA)—to provide more objective analysis on the question of the FX in light of the provisions of the Taiwan Relations Act. The truth was that I didn't trust the CIA to do an objective paper because some of its key analysts favored a strategic relationship with China over any commitments to Taiwan. In fact, by that time, Taiwan was seen as an obstacle if not an albatross to improving relations with the PRC. Taiwan became a hyphenated term with a pejorative: Taiwan-problem or Taiwan-question. And these terms were becoming part of our diplomatic language.

I commissioned a study of Taiwan's aircraft needs from the DIA. Personally, while I supported giving Taiwan better means to defend itself, the sale of the FX fighter seemed to me to be pushing China's buttons in the wrong way at the wrong time. DIA turned out a balanced report that concluded that the country's existing fleet of F5Es was good enough to defend Taiwan against China's aging and obsolete Air Force of MIG-15s, 17s, and 19s. Taiwan could extend the existing assembly line for the F5E and still be ahead of the Chinese. The sale of a more advanced fighter to Taiwan, the DIA report said, would also needlessly complicate U.S.–PRC relations. I remember when Charley DeSaulnier of DIA approached me with the results.

"Jim, I don't think you are going to like it," he said.

"Charley," I replied, "it has nothing to do with whether I like the results or not. I want to know what your findings are so we can make the right decision."

Just before I left for Taiwan in January 1982, I took a walk with Vice President Bush in the woods on the grounds of his home on Massachusetts Avenue. He asked me to give him my honest opinion: Did Taiwan need a new fighter at this time? I laid out the pros and cons. The bottom line reached by the experts, I told him, was that Taiwan did not need a new fighter now, but it might in the future if circumstances changed. Bush pressed me. "What do *you* think?" he asked. I said I could not disagree with the conclusion of the DIA report.

.   .   .

During this time, while preparing to leave Washington, we were accorded an unexpected audience with President Reagan himself. It was a fortuitous meeting that helped me to understand the commander in chief's point of view on Taiwan. Over the objections of the State Department, which was ever loyal to its own version of diplomatic protocol with the PRC, Dick Allen had finagled for me to be included in a ceremony at the White House for ambassador-designates to meet the president in the Oval Office. Technically, as a director of the American Institute in Taiwan, I didn't have ambassador status and probably shouldn't have been invited to the ceremony. But there we were: me, Sally, and two of our sons, Mike and Jeff, who had come down on the train from Princeton and boarding school in Delaware, respectively, for the chance to meet the president. We stood last in a line of about twelve other appointees waiting to have their photo op with the president. We watched him work the assembly line. As each new ambassador-designate filed into the room with his spouse and perhaps children, Ronald Reagan glanced at a 3-by-5 card with the necessary information—name, country assigned to, and maybe a personal note. Like the professional actor he was, he smiled, shook hands, and delivered a line or two.

But when it came to me, the president changed his routine.

"Please, sit down," he said to me. "I want to talk with you."

A side door to the Oval Office opened up, and Nancy Reagan happened by. Then George Bush joined us. We sat in the president's office for fifteen minutes while he entertained us with stories and anecdotes. In one anecdote, President Reagan related how he had been asked to travel to Taiwan. There he found himself explaining the reasons for our opening to China to a stone-faced President Chiang Kai-shek. Reagan gave his explanations: first, to form a stronger front against the Soviet Union—Chiang did not move; second, to open up China to positive foreign forces—Chiang was immobile; third, because it was in America's national interests—Chiang slowly nodded his head.

The photographer took our family's picture with both President Reagan and Vice President Bush in the photo. At the end of the session, Reagan turned to me and said in a clear voice, "You are going to Taiwan. I want you to know that I like those people. I want you to understand that."

This simple, direct statement was my guidance on how the boss felt and proved valuable in helping me to manage relations with Taiwan. I understood that even while we moved ahead in establishing a relationship with a new and important country, China, we would not abandon an old friend, Taiwan. It was a message that I took to heart and that I tried to deliver on during my two-and-a-half-year tenure in Taipei.

The opportunity to speak with President Reagan also gave me insight into his character. He was a master at communicating with people—the timing and the personal connection. Reagan's strength lay not in his intellectual grasp of situations but in his skill in handling people and his sense of timing and selective recall. These are traits that Jim Billington, currently the Librarian of Congress but in the 1980s an advisor to President Reagan on Soviet policy, also noticed. Billington once remarked that, although he had spent decades working on the Soviet Union, he had never seen a person manage the Russians with the instincts of President Reagan. "He could pull something out of the air that he had been told six months ago and use it with Gorbachev at just the right moment," Billington said. He had used the same instincts with me and sent me to Taiwan with the one thing I needed to know.

.　　.　　.

On January 11, 1982, just as Sally and I arrived in Taipei to take up our new post, the Reagan administration announced that it would not go through with the sale of the FX fighter to Taiwan. I had commissioned the decisive study and accepted the outcome, but the timing of the announcement opened my tenure at the American Institute in Taiwan (AIT) on a negative note. It added salt to Taiwan's wound, so to speak. From Taiwan's perspective, disappointment over the turndown of the FX was piled on top of the country's loss of diplomatic recognition and the U.S. military's presence. In addition, the government was having to contend with the island's nascent opposition movement, which chafed against martial law and the limited nature of political participation and had become more vocal in the wake of downgrading of relations by the U.S.

If the scales of favoritism were tipping away from Taiwan, I took heart from the fact that I came with credentials that made me a popular choice to right the balance. First of all, I had a personal appreciation for what Taiwan had achieved in the years since World War II. I had seen the island in the early 1950s when it was an economic and political basket case. In 1980 I had returned to Taiwan after a thirty-year absence and came away impressed by Taiwan's openness and economic growth. Compared to my tour in the PRC from 1973 to 1975, Taiwan was vibrant and alive with ideas. The people had taken in stride the U.S. normalization with the PRC and were looking at their counterparts in China less as "communist bandits" and more and more as "our suffering brethren."

Perhaps more important for the Taiwanese were my strong ties to the U.S. leadership. With the backing of the White House, my goal in Taiwan was to restore a level of confidence among the Taiwan leadership. My sense was that firm U.S. support in the form of careful policy toward the mainland as well as reliance on the Taiwan Relations Act to provide the island with necessary weapons could go a long way toward reassuring Taiwan. Taiwan knew Reagan's personal views, and this made them feel more confident. And a confident Taiwan, I thought, would be more willing to negotiate with the mainland.

In fact, the two governments were starting to reach out to one another in a small but measurable way. The two sides almost came to a compromise to allow teams from both countries to participate in the Fifth Women's World Softball Championship to be held in Taipei in February 1982, a month after my arrival. Taiwan agreed to several concessions such as not flying its flag at the event, but the Chinese in the end elected not to come. It seemed both sides were becoming more amenable to, at the least, communicating about contact. And that communication could take place through intermediaries like myself, who had contacts and experience on both sides of the Taiwan Strait.

A gesture made to me by the Chinese Communists before I left for Taiwan showed some flexibility. Cao Guisheng, a minister at the Chinese Embassy in Washington, insisted on hosting a farewell party for me. It was curious: The Chinese Communists throwing a good-bye party for the American representative on his way to Taiwan. But Cao and I had had a history of contacts going back two decades. In 1961 during my tour in Cambodia, a Chinese defector had fingered Cao as the head of China's intelligence and research branch in Phnom Penh.

We paid some attention even then to this outgoing Chinese "diplomat." At a time when diplomats of both sides were under instructions not to make contact, Cao would actually exchange comments with American diplomats in Cambodia. I ran into Cao again in 1974 during my posting in Peking when he approached me at the International Club. While the two of us watched and chatted, our sons played a game of Ping-Pong. His approach was highly unusual in my time in China as CIA chief.

Through these sporadic connections, Cao and I had developed an understanding that cut through the polarized atmosphere. In a needling way, I asked Cao if I could bring some of my friends from Taiwan to the farewell party, but we both agreed that it was still premature. Instead, I invited my sister, Elinore, and her children as well as my own to the good-bye party. With Cao as our host in a banquet room at the Chinese Embassy in Washington, we had an uproarious time drinking toasts to my upcoming assignment to Taiwan. Cao cut to the chase, suggesting that I could help in "unification" of Taiwan and China. I replied that I thought it was too early, saying I would have to first explore the situation on the ground in Taiwan. Nevertheless, it was a unique experience and foretold increasing contacts between Taiwan and China.

.   .   .

In Taiwan I had to get used to the unusual situation of conducting diplomacy in a country with which America wasn't supposed to have diplomatic relations. To wit, at AIT we were officially consultants under contract to the State Department working in an unofficial capacity at a nonembassy to advance America's interests in Taiwan. It was a mouthful, and the semantics and diplomatic gyrations that American representatives in Taiwan had to go through were at times humorous, at times frustrating.

Starting with the mundane, we had to develop a new vocabulary to conduct diplomacy. The embassy became an institute in 1979, and I was its second director, following veteran diplomat and fellow China hand Chuck Cross. At the institute, there were no American flags flying, no national days celebrated, nor Marines in red, white, and blue. Instead of a political section, we had a general affairs section or GAS, perhaps an appropriate acronym for political reporting. Rather than a consular section, there was a travel service section. In our daily lives, we had to be careful to adhere to certain rules. If I were addressed by a Taiwanese journalist as ambassador, I had to ignore him. If at some function or performance we were seated in the special section reserved for diplomats, we had to suggest that this was not quite right. Most of the time we ended up sitting there anyway. Should the agressive Taiwanese press have caught wind of any protocol slipup on our part and used it to trumpet recognition of an upgrading of the relationship, we would have caught hell from both Washington and Peking.

The most frustrating part was that we were prohibited from meeting with Taiwanese Foreign Ministry and Defense officials as well as with the president himself in their offices, nor could they visit us in ours. We could meet with a designated group of Taiwanese foreign service officers who staffed AIT's counterpart organization on the Taiwan side. But we had to transact the majority of our discussions in other venues, like restaurants, country clubs, golf courses, and private homes. Perhaps the most serious casualty of such restrictions was our waistlines. Dinners and cocktail parties—the staple of most diplomatic posts—took on added importance in Taiwan. A rich Chinese diet can wreak havoc with an American-fed body, as it did with mine.

.   .   .

In her own effective way, Sally moved the relationship forward. At our house on Yang Ming Mountain overlooking Taipei, she did a marvelous job of entertaining. Her long-standing interest in Asian art made Taiwan a superb location for exploration. The famous National Palace Museum, with its splendid collection of Chinese art, was a favorite. In fact, her affinity for Chinese culture gave her access to the elite of the island. Several times a year she was invited to join the Women's Garden and Art Club of Taipei for a get-together. The luncheon meetings were designed by the club to showcase traditional Chinese ladylike pursuits—such as calligraphy, flower arrangement, and the study of the rice plant's uses—to the diplomatic community.

The wives of some of the most influential men on Taiwan as well as a few powerful women in their own right belonged to the club. Members included the wives of the governor of Taiwan, of the minister of communications, and of high-ranking diplomats, as well as prominent banker Shirley Kuo, who would play a historic role in Taiwan–China relations several years later in 1989. The "mother hen" of the group was Metsung Yu, the wife of the president of the Central Bank of Taiwan. Though Metsung had gone to Wellesley College and had strong ties to America, she was quintessentially Chinese at the core. She had a strong sense that Taiwan women must not lose touch with traditional Chinese culture. While the Communists on the mainland were eradicating the vestiges of culture, Taiwan, the Garden and Art Club believed, had become one of the remaining bastions of Chinese culture. All the women felt a shared sense of duty to carry on cherished but endangered traditions.

To be sure, the women were mostly mainlanders, members of families who had fled China and then risen to power alongside Chiang Kai-shek in the 1950s and 1960s. At the meetings, the women were not overtly political, but, by virtue of being Chinese on Taiwan and by being married to KMT members, their very presence was political.

On occasion, Sally returned the favor of hospitality by inviting the women's club to our house for lunch. Afterward, they would watch movies like *My Fair Lady* and *The Sound of Music*. All the ladies cried at *An Affair to Remember*, a first-class tearjerker starring Cary Grant and Deborah Kerr. Such visits fostered sentiments on a person-to-person basis. In important ways, these friendships provided the structure for the business of diplomacy to be conducted in as convivial an atmosphere as possible. At a time when we as diplomats were trying to rebuild the Taiwan relationship, Sally's connections with the Garden and Art Club underscored the close ties that linked Taiwan and the U.S. Many of the women had lived in the U.S. when their husbands were studying at American universities or, like Metsung Yu, had studied there themselves. They appreciated America and continued to send their own children to study in the U.S., so there were intersecting interests, mutual friends, and common cultural affinities. Perhaps most important was that this was genuine affection, beyond contrived diplomatic niceties.

.   .   .

It was a good thing that Sally took up the social slack because my first year in Taiwan was absorbed in damage-control work. I was heavily courted by the Taiwanese, but constant complaints came along with the attention. Unfortunately, I had few carrots with which to reassure the Taiwan government, which repeatedly emphasized its fear of being isolated by U.S. moves to placate China. Far from being pleased with the U.S. decision not to sell an advanced fighter to Taiwan, the PRC was continuing to press for more concessions. In the late spring of 1982, Peking increased the pressure on the U.S. to agree to a termination date for all arms sales to Taiwan as part of the new communiqué being negotiated. China officers at the State Department reasoned that acceding to this latest request would be a significant gesture toward getting an agreement with China by the tenth anniversary of the 1972 Shanghai Communiqué. This request, with the "deadline" approaching, put the rush on, a well-known negotiating mistake.

Late in 1981, Secretary of State Haig had agreed to the "quality and quantity" restrictions, but he had held the line at naming a definite date for an end to arms sales. However, as the negotiations in Peking between Ambassador Arthur Hummel and his Chinese counterparts continued into the middle of 1982, the U.S. side started to give on that most sacrosanct of prerogatives: the right of the U.S.—as part of the Taiwan Relations Act—to sell arms to its friend Taiwan. At the State Department, the line being advanced was that if the U.S. didn't agree to a specific termination date, then the Chinese would downgrade relations. For proof of the seriousness of China's intention, the group at State pointed to China's recent downgrading of relations with Holland earlier in 1981 in retaliation for the Dutch selling two submarines to Taiwan. However, I saw the Chinese actions as "killing the chicken to scare the monkey" and didn't believe we should be swayed. We were a bit larger and more important to the Chinese than the Dutch.

Sure enough, I was called back to Washington for consultations. Forces at the State Department wanted to get me on board in support of a specific termination date on arms sales for the new communiqué. I remember an evening in April 1982 when, after quite a few drinks, high-ranking State Department officials prodded me to see if I would try to get the Taiwan government to agree to a termination date. I think the State officials thought a more relaxed atmosphere might get me to bend. I held my tongue, but I felt in my bones that the proposal was off-base, and I recalled President Reagan's words to me before I set off for Taiwan: "I want you to know that I like those people." Once back in Taiwan, I did not bring up the proposal directly with the Taiwanese. I cabled back to the State Department that it was the wrong thing to do in terms of placing Taiwan's security at risk and in the way it violated the main tenet of the Taiwan Relations Act. The State Department did not press me further, but there were mutterings that I had let them down.

I was becoming increasingly concerned with the signals that Washington was putting out. I was well aware of the tactics of a China-leaning group at State, but it seemed that the executive branch, or at least parts of it, was losing its perspective as well. After I did not raise with the Taiwanese government a termination date for arms sales, I had to face some displeasure from my patron, Vice President George Bush. In a private lunch with him during my April 1982 trip to Washington, he said forcefully, "You have got to realize where the big relationship is. It is with China, not Taiwan." Then in May the vice president traveled to Peking with the expressed purpose of assuring the Chinese leadership that the U.S. wanted to maintain strong relations with them. He carried with him three letters from President Reagan, drafted by officers at the State Department but with a tone somewhat toughened by the new national security advisor, William Clark. Bush personally delivered the letters to de facto Chinese leader Deng Xiaoping, General Secretary of the Chinese Communist Party Hu Yaobang, and Premier Zhao Ziyang. The message of the letters, though, was vintage State. The letters restated America's commitment to the "one-China" policy and emphasized that the U.S. would not "permit unofficial relations between the American people and the Chinese people on Taiwan to weaken our commitment to this principle." Finally, in terms of arms sales to Taiwan, the letter to Premier Zhao stated that the U.S. expects that "in the context of progress toward a peaceful solution" of the China–Taiwan issue "there would naturally be a decrease in the need for arms by Taiwan."

So where was President Reagan during these defining first months of 1982 when policies toward Taiwan were being shaped that were at odds with his personal convictions? Through National Security Advisor Clark, he was, no doubt, apprised of the letters. But the truth was that it was a somewhat hands-off policy. The president was aware that certain people were going in their own directions, pushing a PRC-slanted agenda. Even Vice President Bush had said to his staff that he would "save the relationship" with China in May 1982. When Clark, one of the president's oldest friends and closest advisors, replaced Dick Allen in early 1982, he became the responsible gate guard that the president needed on China policy. With Clark now in a position to correct policy variation and influence traffic, the White House was ready to take a more firm line with the Chinese in the drafting of the communiqué. By May, when Vice President Bush set off for China, he was on the same page as the president. He underscored the somewhat conciliatory message of the three letters with an important assertion: The U.S. could not possibly set a date to stop supplying Taiwan with arms.

In Taipei, I was trying to assuage an already nervous Taiwan that it wouldn't be left further out in the cold by the unpredictable patterns of a mainland China-focused policy. I was put into quite a dilemma by the vice president's trip. No one in the administration, not to mention the State Department, had informed me or, for that matter, Taiwan that Bush was going to hand-deliver three letters, which, among other things, reiterated the U.S. commitment to a "One China" policy and acknowledged U.S. recognition of the significance of Peking's nine-point proposal. The oversight was not that we had made such statements to the Chinese but that we had failed to balance them with any reassurances to Taiwan or to give any advance notification. By giving them three letters instead of one and by letting our delivery of them leak to the press, we made ourselves look incompetent and biased. The TV coverage had not helped. It caught American officials fumbling around as they looked for the letters in a meeting with the Chinese leadership. So much for subtlety and smoothness. I was blindsided by the goings-on in Peking and felt that my credibility with the Taiwanese had been damaged.

On May 11, Vice Foreign Minister Fred Chien asked for an urgent meeting with me. When I arrived, Chien, apoplectic over the blatant disregard of Taiwan, unloaded his wrath on me, careful to inject a bit of personal invective regarding my evidently feeble ties to the White House.

"Why three letters?" the vice foreign minister demanded. "Why not just one? Why the need to grovel?"

I did not respond.

"You were a friend of George Bush, Mr. Lilley," he said, substituting my surname for the more friendly "Jim" he normally used, "and you did not know this all was going to happen? Did they have to let it out to the press before we were told?"

I listened to his diatribe. Chien probably had the go-ahead from Chiang Ching-kuo, but he seemed to relish dressing me down. He explained that he was particularly worried about what he interpreted as "new language": The letters had referred to "Chinese people on Taiwan" rather than the accepted "people on Taiwan" in the Taiwan Relations Act. Did such signs indicate that America's intention was to decrease arms sales to Taiwan? Taiwan's interests had been totally ignored, and President Chiang Ching-kuo was shaking with anger, he made sure to tell me. "Is this the way to treat an old friend?" Chien asked rhetorically. "Do our U.S. friends have any credibility left?"

I had brought along a young Foreign Service officer as a note taker. When Fred Chien unleashed his anger on me, I watched the young officer's face go ashen. I was accustomed to this kind of attack because I had gotten to know Fred fairly well in the few months I had been working in Taiwan.

A bespectacled man with an intense manner, Fred was my chief interlocutor on the Taiwan side and a man close to Chiang Ching-kuo. He was a gifted scholar who had received his doctorate at Yale about ten years after I had graduated, and in Chinese fashion he treated me respectfully as his elder. Fred was a pragmatist in that he recognized that Taiwan could not waste time moping about its fate. Instead, he believed that the country had to move quickly to secure its place among the forces pushing China and the United States together.

Fred had a temper, and he made calculated use of it. In fact, his prickly manner had earned him a reputation as being "hard" on America among State Department officials, who regarded him as the antagonist. In fact, Fred was too smart for many of them. But I thought I understood him and was able to work with him. Thus, when Fred bore down on me, I felt that I knew where he was coming from.

After Fred unloaded on me, I said to his displeasure that it was basically "Xiaoti Da Zuo"—making a big thing out of a little one. It was a four-character Chinese saying—a *cheng yu*—that was intended to distance me from his rancor and earn me a little standing for being literate in Chinese. Correct use of a *cheng yu* often helped me in confrontational engagements with the Chinese in China and Taiwan. In truth, I was disturbed at what Washington had done. It was a clumsy and significant oversight; and it also made me look out of the loop. By the way, Fred did not respond well at all to my use of the *cheng yu*.

Just five days earlier, I had seen the other side of Fred—the pragmatic and broad-minded diplomat. We had met at his house for lunch and had a wide-ranging and productive discussion on cross-strait relations. I brought up reports that I had read of people across the strait in Fujian and Guangdong Provinces watching Taiwan TV programs and of a flourishing indirect trade between Taiwan and mainland China. People in China, I said to Fred, were interested in what was going on in Taiwan, and I thought that Taiwan could be creative in its response. I suggested that Taiwan should think about reducing the role of its intelligence and security agencies—which held sway over any issues dealing with Communist China—and adopt a broader approach that took into consideration the political, economic, and sociological issues involved in cross-strait relations. Our conversation was one of the earliest moves to get the China–Taiwan relationship going, and it shed light on a longer-term trend that could lead to greater peace and stability in the area.

. . .

Secretary of State Haig fired his final salvo on the arms sale issue in June. Swayed by the Chinese threat to downgrade relations if there were no resolution to arms sales to Taiwan, Haig wrote up a memo for President Reagan. Haig says in his memoirs that "the future of Sino-American relations depended on the answer [Deng] received" from Reagan. It was a last act by the secretary of state, who had long been at odds with the White House over his authority.

When Haig's memo was officially presented to him, President Reagan refused the option of ending the arms sales. He was amenable to language about a limit on sales and other concessions, but not to a cutoff. Instead, he approved what was termed a "final offer" to be inserted in the communiqué being negotiated in Peking. It was a written agreement that spoke vaguely about America's hopes for a "final resolution" of the dispute over arms sales but set no date for the sales to end.

The Chinese played hardball up until the very end, hoping to get a termination date in writing. As the late Arthur Hummel recalled in an interview shortly before he passed away, "The Chinese went kicking and screaming" toward a communiqué. George Bush's letters and the pressure of a congressional deadline (having to do, incidentally, with the continuation of the U.S. Air Force's F5E assembly line in Taiwan) convinced them to agree to sign the communiqué on August 17, 1982. Ambassador Hummel's considerable talents, particularly his ability to use indirect channels to pass messages and get results, also played an important role in getting the PRC leadership to accept the compromise deal.

The August Communiqué, as the agreement came to be called, laid out the principles by which the U.S. and China would navigate the issue of arms sales to Taiwan for the next ten years. Despite failing to get a termination date, the Chinese did not downgrade relations with the U.S. Taiwan, however, still took a big hit. The U.S. agreed to reduce the quantity and quality of arms it could sell to Taiwan, meaning that it would not exceed, either in qualitative or quantitative terms, the level of those supplied since the establishment of diplomatic relations between the United States and China in 1979. In the communiqué, while the U.S. pledged to pursue a "One China" policy, it also committed China to acknowledge in writing that it would "strive for a peaceful solution to the Taiwan question." Point 6 addressed the sensitive issue of arms sales to Taiwan. In particular, it contained a statement by the U.S. that reduced arms sales would lead "over a period of time to a final resolution."

But the agreed points of the August Communiqué were not the last words on arms sales to Taiwan. Those were reserved for President Reagan.

.   .   .

On July 14, 1982, a month before the actual signing of the communiqué, I delivered six assurances to President Chiang Ching-kuo. Drafted mostly by my friend and collaborator David Dean, chairman of AIT's Washington office, with the help of the Office of Taiwan Coordination at the State Department and with the input of Taiwan's representative staff in Washington, the assurances were designed to be a sign to Taiwan that it was not going to be abandoned by the Reagan administration. They reaffirmed that the U.S. would live up to the guidelines of the Taiwan Relations Act by not setting a specific date by which arms sales to Taiwan would end and by not pressuring Taiwan to negotiate with Peking. The assurances cushioned the anxiety and uneasiness of the Taiwan leadership over the August Communiqué and were, I think, a direct contrast to the shoddy way in which Taiwan had been handled during normalization with Communist China.

In accordance with procedures we had developed, Fred Chien picked me up at the Grand Hotel and escorted me to Chiang Ching-kuo's residence, a relatively austere house sparsely furnished in Chinese style. I found the aging president to be physically weak with diabetes. He could barely walk. But his mind was still sharp. In fact, as I recited the six assurances to him, I had the distinct feeling that he had already been briefed, that he was ahead of the game. I figured the State Department bureaucracy had leaked the assurances to him. In his clever way, he did not commit himself to accepting the assurances but quietly listened. We made sure there would be no paper trail. The assurances were delivered in the form of a blind memo. They were committed to paper but without a signature or letterhead so that there would be no evidence of its origin. In addition, I told him that the blind memo format allowed for various interpretations, including the one Taiwan preferred—that the memo was really a personal letter from President Reagan to President Chiang.

In Washington, in his own extraordinary way and in keeping with his warm sentiments for Taiwan, President Reagan dictated a presidential directive that became our guidelines for interpreting the August Communiqué as the departing point for U.S. policy on arms sales to Taiwan. In the presence of the politically astute Dr. Gaston Sigur, a short, cherublike man who was the East Asia specialist on the National

Security Council, the president drafted a statement that gave his interpretation of the communiqué. National Security Advisor Clark prepared the final version, which was then initialed by Secretary of State George Shultz and Secretary of Defense Caspar Weinberger and returned to safekeeping in the National Security files. Dated August 17, 1982, the final four-paragraph version of the statement read:

> As you know, I have agreed to the issuance of a joint communiqué with the People's Republic of China in which we express United States policy towards the matter of continuing arms sales to Taiwan.
>
> The talks leading up to the signing of the communiqué were premised on the clear understanding that any reduction of such arms sales depends upon peace in the Taiwan Strait and the continuity of China's declared "fundamental policy" of seeking a peaceful resolution of the Taiwan issue.
>
> In short, the U.S. willingness to reduce its arms sales to Taiwan is conditioned absolutely upon the continued commitment of China to the peaceful solution of the Taiwan–PRC differences. It should be clearly understood that the linkage between these two matters is a permanent imperative of U.S. foreign policy.
>
> In addition, it is essential that the quantity and quality of the arms provided Taiwan be conditioned entirely on the threat posed by the PRC. Both in quantitative and qualitative terms, Taiwan's defense capability relative to that of the PRC will be maintained.

Sigur, a close confidant of mine and a fellow supporter of maintaining balance across the Taiwan Strait, explained to me later the president's reasoning for rewriting the communiqué in his own words: "The President felt that the communiqué hit him at the last minute. He didn't like it, and his understanding of the communiqué was that if China were to become belligerent or build up power projection capability that brought insecurity or instability to the area, then the U.S. would increase arms sales to Taiwan, regardless of what the communiqué said about quantity and quality conditions on arms sales." For Reagan, maintaining the balance of power across the Taiwan Strait had to be the departure point for U.S. foreign policy.

16

THE GOLDEN YEARS

IN THE STRUGGLE over the August Communiqué between bureaucrats in the State Department and political appointees in the White House, the White House had won a partial victory by defeating attempts to set a termination date for arms sales to Taiwan. Certainly, President Reagan's liberal interpretation of the communiqué swung the diplomatic pendulum back toward Taiwan. The Taiwanese, by the way, were informed of the general contents of President Reagan's personal directive.

But as momentous as these events were in their own right, they also heralded a sea change of personnel in policymaking positions that solidified a common approach toward China and Taiwan policy. Reagan cleaned house around the time of the signing of the August Communiqué.

With the resignation of Al Haig and the rise of a more assertive national security advisor in William Clark, there was more institutional support for a balanced policy toward Taiwan and China. Clark's arrival was just part of a major staff shakeup. George Shultz took over as secretary of state in July 1982, and a few months later he recruited Paul Wolfowitz to be his assistant secretary of state for East Asia. As the State Department's director of policy and planning in the early years of the Reagan White House, Wolfowitz had made a name for himself as a brilliant and outspoken advocate of a Pan-Asian approach to U.S. foreign policy in Asia. Believing China's military, diplomatic, and economic status to be more characteristic of those of a regional, not an international, power, Wolfowitz favored more reliance on traditional allies like Japan, South Korea, and Taiwan, with whom the U.S. had more in common. In Shultz's own view, American policymakers had become overly solicitous of Chinese interests, and he understood Wolfowitz's assessment of the China situation.

Kindred spirits assumed important policy positions at other Washington agencies that were instrumental in shaping China policy. In the same month that Shultz arrived, Gaston Sigur became the National Security Council advisor on China and Taiwan. At the Defense Department, Rich Armitage, my fellow outcast on the Haig trip to China in 1981, became the assistant secretary for international security affairs, the equivalent of the Defense Department's foreign policy guru, in 1983. In June 1983, Bill Brown, a career Foreign Service officer, joined Wolfowitz's staff as his principal deputy on the East Asia desk. Brown, the same man who had worked secretly to prepare memos for Henry Kissinger during the opening to China, was a stalwart supporter of balance in the U.S. approach to Asia.

From the perspective of AIT, I felt instinctively that this group of people made a much more compatible team. We would move ahead on improving relations with China, including the development of military ties with the PRC and sending President Reagan to visit China in 1984. But at the same time we believed that Asia would be a safer place and that, ultimately, Taiwan would be a better partner for Peking if it received strong and consistent U.S. support. In Washington, the two-track approach moved forward because of the effective working relations between key subcabinet members Sigur, Wolfowitz, and Armitage. For the first time in a long while, the State Department and the White House were in agreement on China policy, and for me in Taiwan it was the heyday. I would later look at the period from 1983 to 1988 as "Golden Years" in terms of China policy.

The Pan-Asian team did a masterful job of both managing and building the relationships. At the same time that the U.S. was working on opening up China in economic fields as well as transferring military equipment like advanced avionics for China's F-8 jet fighter, it was pushing forward the development of a defense fighter for Taiwan and supporting Taiwan's continued involvement in international financial institutions.

An interagency core that included Wolfowitz and Brown from State, Armitage from Defense, Sigur from the NSC, and usually a representative from CIA used to meet weekly on Monday afternoons in Paul Wolfowitz's office at the State Department. For a wide range of policy decisions, the presidential directive proved decisive. "When it came down to a tough decision or to the latest demarches from the PRC, Gaston would pull out the president's directive in our small company and cite Ronald Reagan's subsequent interpretation of the communiqué," Brown recalled. "We knew what the president wanted concerning the quantity and quality provisions. Not too many others did know. Others would maintain that the communiqué says other things. We would pull it out to remind ourselves that behind all this was a presidential decision to let us do what was necessary to right the balance." The shrewd and avuncular Sigur never revealed the actual words of the document to the others. He just waved it around.

.　　.　　.

I began to breathe easier on Taiwan and acted to balance America's policy toward China and Taiwan. Sometimes, my actions were aimed at strictly bureaucratic procedures that were isolating AIT within the U.S. government. At other times, my efforts were directed in concert with my colleagues back in Washington. I spent many hours with the Taiwanese military determining their specific needs for American armaments, and I worked hard to keep Taiwan informed about U.S. policy prerogatives as well as engaged in international institutions.

Nonetheless I was made to feel like a second-class citizen in encounters with top U.S. diplomats in Asia. For example, for the first several years of AIT's existence, the director—because of AIT's unofficial status—was excluded from the State Department's annual Chiefs of Missions meeting for Asia. While I understood the role of careful diplomacy, I thought that keeping me out of an important internal State Department conference was going too far. I asked to be included in the 1983 Chiefs of Mission Conference in Hong Kong. In the end I wasn't allowed to attend, nor was my deputy director Stan Brooks, but we did wrangle permission for the third-ranking member of AIT, the chief of our economic and commercial section, Clarke Ellis, to go to the conference. As Clarke likes to put it, he went to Hong Kong and sat "with a paper bag" over his head.

I also encouraged AIT employees to call on their Taiwanese counterparts in the central bank, the Ministry of Economics, and the Board of Foreign Trade.

On the question of military sales to Taiwan, I walked a tightrope, employing the loose interpretation of the August Communiqué while being very careful not to let the news out or promote systems which would unnecessarily provoke the PRC. I needed a commitment from my Taiwan counterparts to carry on the delicate negotiations in a low-key manner. I underscored to them that there could be no news leaks. It turned out we were all in accord on this matter. Vice Foreign Minister Fred Chien understood the efficacy of keeping quiet in order to advance the U.S.–Taiwan relationship on the military side. General Hao Peitsun, a heavyset and bluff military man, was a chief interlocutor on the issue of arms sales. I considered him a personal friend, and we spent many hours together at social occasions. An invitation to dine with him was an opportunity to work with some of the best the island had to offer. He was proud of the Republic of China and fiercely loyal to President Chiang Ching-kuo. We worked in quiet and arranged for carefully selected weapons systems.

One of those weapons systems was the Indigenous Defense Fighter or IDF. The FX deal had fallen through, but President Reagan wanted to meet promises made in 1981 and 1982 that America would make it possible for Taiwan to obtain an advanced fighter aircraft. Relying on a liberal interpretation of the August Communiqué that excluded the transfer of technology from the treaty's "quantity and quality" provisions, policymakers in the Reagan administration searched for a way to put together a deal to provide Taiwan with its own advanced fighter.

The big breakthrough came one day when a General Dynamics representative told Brown that his company had been asked by the Taiwanese to serve as a mentor for Taiwanese engineers who would build the plane. A midlevel Defense Department team visited Taiwan in the summer of 1983 to study the feasibility of transferring technology for Taiwan to build a modern fighter and returned with a favorable recommendation.

Knowing he had allies in powerful positions, Wolfowitz's deputy Bill Brown carried the proposal to Wolfowitz, Sigur, and Armitage, at the State Department, NSC, and the Defense Department, respectively. In a decisive meeting in Secretary Shultz's office, the Pan-Asian group prevailed over State Department officials who believed the IDF deal violated the August Communiqué.

On momentous matters like the April 1984 visit of President Reagan to Peking, the State Department and White House—in the persons of Paul Wolfowitz and Gaston Sigur in particular—made sure I was kept informed and, therefore, was able to play a key role in reassuring Taiwan. Just before President Reagan's visit, I was called back to Washington where I briefed the president, Chief of Staff James Baker, and Secretary of State Shultz on the situation in Taiwan. Such high-level access allowed me to return to Taiwan and deliver statements of reassurance in private meetings with my Taiwanese counterparts: "Ronald Reagan is going to China," I told them, "but, by God, he will protect your interests." On the eve of a visit that marked the real opening of the U.S. to China, the Taiwanese remained calm. There was no cause this time to reproach me for weak links to the White House.

In a cable back to Washington in advance of President Reagan's trip, I addressed the trend that I had first discussed with Fred Chien that spring day two years earlier: the increasing cross-strait contacts between Taiwan and China. With indirect trade and personal contact between citizens of Taiwan and China growing, the trend was gaining momentum. Rather than get dragged down in the usual Chinese rancor over continuing arms sales to Taiwan and possible demands for revision of the TRA, I suggested that the president bring up these developments. "Focus on the positive aspects in PRC–Taiwan relations," I counseled. Avoid "an extended watering contest with the largest elephant around." Progress toward peaceful resolution of the Taiwan issue would lead to a natural resolution of Taiwan's need for arms. That was something the Chinese should be able to swallow.

I also felt it was important to keep Taiwan active in international organizations at a time when other nations were deserting Taiwan by moving their embassies from Taipei to Peking. In 1984, China formally applied to join the Asian Development Bank, thus setting the stage for a protracted battle to keep Taiwan, a founding member of the ADB, in the organization. China had replaced Taiwan at the UN, the World Bank, and the International Monetary Fund in the same way. The U.S. Embassy in Peking supported China's application to the ADB, believing that China's ascension to membership and Taiwan's expulsion were the natural course of events of pursuing a "One China" policy. Letting Taiwan stay, the embassy said repeatedly, would be a violation of this policy.

But in Taipei we believed differently and staked out our ground. Unlike the case of its UN and World Bank memberships, which had been granted to Taiwan with the understanding that Taiwan represented all of China, when it joined the ADB Taiwan did not claim to represent all of China for the simple reason that ADB contributions were assessed on the basis of a member country's population and size. We thought that we had a hook on which to hang dual membership of Taiwan and Peking.

As a result of the tireless work of Paul Wolfowitz, Bill Brown, and later myself, we were able to get the Chinese to agree to a compromise formula by which Taiwan would retain membership under a different name, perhaps Chinese-Taipei or Chinese-Taiwan. It was the Olympic Games formula recycled for multilateral financial institutions.

But we faced surprisingly stiff opposition from Taiwan, which didn't want to countenance any change in its status and name in one of the last important multilateral institutions in which it had membership. Reaching a compromise suitable to both sides took two and a half years.

Eventually, we convinced Taiwan through subtle methods, letting them know indirectly that the technology transfer for the IDF deal would go through more quickly if they agreed to a compromise formula.

Though there was additional wrangling over protocol and in spite of the fact that Taiwan attended ADB meetings for several years under protest, the ADB deal was historic because it allowed ambassadorial-level leaders from Taiwan and China to participate in the same official organization. In May 1989, Taiwan's representative to the ADB, Shirley Kuo, the same woman whom Sally had gotten to know at the gatherings of the Women's Garden and Art Club, would travel to Peking for the ADB's annual meeting, becoming the first cabinet-level official to visit mainland China since Chiang Kai-shek had fled in 1949. By being patient and working the corners, the Pan-Asian group had won a significant victory for Taiwan, a so-called "unofficial" country, which retained "official" member status in the ADB.

.   .   .

By mid-1983, Taiwan's security needs had been resolved to such an extent that I could direct AIT's energies toward America's commercial ties with the island. In the early 1980s, Taiwan was booming economically. It had benefited from American foreign aid in the 1950s and 1960s and put into practice a successful land reform program. Throughout the 1970s and into the 1980s, the Taiwan government focused on industrialization and export-oriented growth. Private capital flowed toward labor-intensive consumer industries, such as footwear, sporting goods, toys, and textiles. Taiwan came rightly to be known as one of the "Asian tigers." By the time of my arrival at AIT, Taiwan's economy was remaking itself once again by moving into high-technology areas.

But like other countries that had followed export-oriented development strategies, Taiwan had experienced tremendous growth at the cost of choking off domestic demand. Its markets were notoriously closed to imports, and the country enjoyed a large bilateral trade surplus with the U.S. At the same time, in its rush to grow economically, the government expended few resources on enforcing standard economic norms of behavior. Counterfeiting and copyright infringement ran rampant. Downtown Taipei stores were stocked with Apple Computer knockoffs, fake Cartier watches, and back-alley copies of bestsellers and the *Encyclopedia Britannica.*

At AIT, we set about trying to get Taiwan to open its markets and educate and pressure it about the importance of respecting intellectual property rights (IPR). These were not flashy issues; they took time and did not yield immediate results. Given the restrictions on my activities in the political arena, I had more freedom of interaction—and maybe even more influence—with Taiwan's business magnates. I will remember fondly the time I spent with the late Henry Hsu (Hsu Fengho), the founder of the Formosa Rubber Company. A short, somewhat overweight man with a drooping visage, Henry was a delightful human being. He was forward-thinking on economic issues, and he became AIT's point man in the Taiwan business community for increasing awareness of the IPR issue. In terms of relations with the mainland, he took a refreshingly practical point of view. Over monthly lunches at a Japanese restaurant in Taipei, Hsu would emphasize to me that Taiwan had to open trading relations with China. The island, he insisted, needed trade, not military confrontation. "Turn Quemoy Island into Disneyland," Henry used to say to me. "Pull those five divisions off the island and build a roller coaster and Ferris wheel." In a country that was under martial law and technically still at war with the PRC, Hsu's view was the equivalent of heresy.

Because of his progressive and unconventional views, I arranged for Henry Hsu to meet with Vice President Bush in Washington. Hsu's visit along with that of Koo Chen-fu, who was head of Taiwan Cement as well as a member of the Central Committee of the Kuomintang, occurred after White House attempts to get Taiwan's leading diplomat in Washington into the State Department had blown up in the press. Private business people, however, were less contentious visitors, not subject, as we had found in Taiwan, to the restrictions governing interactions with government officials. And Hsu and Koo's visits sent a convincing signal back to Taipei that influential but unofficial Taiwanese still had access to the highest echelons of American government.

.   .   .

The more stable situation on Taiwan also allowed me to address the need for change in Taiwan's closed, one-party political system. When I first arrived, Taiwan was still struggling to deal with the imbalance in representation that had existed since Chiang Kai-shek had fled China and set up an island government staffed with mainland Chinese. The government's treatment of the opposition was particularly sensitive because a majority of the activists were native Taiwanese who felt underrepresented in positions of power. A good number of them advocated for an independent Taiwan, a position at odds with the official line, which held out for eventual reunification of Taiwan and China. The KMT security apparatus, which was still enforcing martial law on the island, was working hard at stemming a growing opposition movement—the most glaring evidence being the government's complicity in the 1981 death of Taiwan independence supporter Chen Wencheng.

About six months before we arrived in Taiwan, Chen, a U.S. permanent resident and professor of statistics at Carnegie-Mellon University in Pittsburgh, had been found dead on the campus of National Taiwan University in Taipei. Professor Chen had allegedly taken his own life on July 31, 1981, by jumping off the roof of the university's four-story library. The night before, it was discovered, Chen, who was visiting Taiwan with his family, had been interrogated by police for thirteen hours. My predecessor as head of AIT, Chuck Cross, determined that there was clear evidence of government involvement in the case. The U.S. Congress was up in arms. During the course of congressional hearings into Chen's death, it was discovered that Taiwan National Security Bureau operatives in the U.S. had followed Chen in Pittsburgh. Congress subsequently passed a resolution that barred arms sales to a country that could be shown to be engaged in acts of intimidation or harassment against individuals in the U.S.

As America's representative in Taiwan, to effect change in the sensitive area of human rights I worked closely with President Chiang Ching-kuo, who, I knew, had his own plans to reform Taiwan.

As a rule, President Chiang—the son of Chiang Kai-shek—felt more comfortable with American CIA and military types than with those from the State Department, because he saw them as tougher, more useful, and more understanding of Taiwan's position. I think he saw me as a hardened, somewhat sympathetic American who could carry Taiwan's message back to the White House and Capitol Hill. Perhaps that's why, even before I had left Washington to take up my new post in Taipei, President Chiang opened the channels of communication by informing me through intermediaries of his plans for political reform on Taiwan. Chiang's personal envoy had confided in Gaston Sigur, and Sigur then briefed me on President Chiang's four-point program for Taiwan—democratize; begin a process of Taiwanization of the government; maintain prosperity; and open up to China.

Chiang reasoned that Taiwan had to develop successful political as well as economic institutions in order to defend its autonomy vis-à-vis the mainland. Change came in fits and starts. It was a challenge to overcome or at least temper the paranoid patterns of behavior that had shaped the Taiwan government's approach to its vocal opponents. In fact, U.S. recognition of China had actually exacerbated intolerance on Taiwan by increasing the government's sense of insecurity. Parliamentary elections for 1979 were postponed, which gave restless opposition parties fodder to mobilize. Unwilling to tolerate open dissent at a time of national insecurity, the KMT government cracked down on demonstrators in the southern port city of Kaohsiung in December 1979. A rash of arrests followed, and several prominent opposition figures were kept in jail without being sentenced or tried. There were rumors that the government expected to try the prisoners in military courts and wanted to call for the death penalty. U.S. intercession at this point, in the form of a trip to Taiwan in January 1980 by the head of AIT's Washington office, David Dean, allowed cooler heads to prevail. Dean emphasized in a meeting with President Chiang that harsh treatment of the prisoners would blacken Taiwan's reputation in the U.S. and make it even harder to rebuild some measure of trust and confidence following the break in relations. "My argument was that if they move toward removing martial law, toward civilian trials instead of military trials, and toward allowing the opposition to speak out, then they would get a great deal more support in the U.S. and elsewhere," recalled Dean. President Chiang listened to Dean. No death sentences were carried out, and the prisoners were eventually released over the next several years. But the murder of Professor Chen Wencheng a year and a half later had given Taiwan a huge black eye.

I worked with the old and new guard to advance human rights on Taiwan. My contacts with Wang Sheng, the immensely powerful political commissar of Taiwan's military and President Chiang Ching-kuo's mentor, proved helpful at the start of my tenure. My private entreaties to Wang for clemency or release got some of the opposition figures free. But General Wang was a true hardliner. In his own words, the Taiwanese feared and hated him. I got the sense during my time with him that he wanted to be helpful but that he was mired in the past, an old-thinking KMT stalwart who had a hard time seeing the world outside of his narrow focus. For this reason, Wang represented a symbol or, more bluntly, an obstacle to President Chiang's goal of democratizing Taiwan. Chiang Ching-kuo was obligated to Wang for his years of loyal service, but the general was becoming a liability.

So in June 1983, with help from AIT in the form of sending Wang on an eye-opening trip to the U.S., President Chiang started to move Wang out of the way. I sensed at that time that Chiang knew what he was doing in letting Wang travel to the U.S., and in this way the two of us were working together to advance Taiwan's interests. Since Wang was one of President Chiang's most influential advisors on internal security, the trip was meant to impress upon him the depth of U.S. public opinion about human rights on Taiwan. In the United States, General Wang heard firsthand American politicians' concerns about the treatment of political dissidents in Taiwan, including, no doubt, the death of Professor Chen two years earlier.

Shortly after Wang's return from the U.S., President Chiang shipped him off again, this time to Paraguay as ambassador. At a time when there was increasing speculation in the press about who would succeed the physically declining Chiang as leader, Chiang's demotion of Wang removed a powerful "pretender to the throne" while sending a message that the next leader of Taiwan should be a more broad-minded person.

. . .

One of my most sustained contacts with the opposition came in the form of scuba dives off Taiwan's southern coast. Through my friendship with Lin Homing, a native Taiwanese who lived on the coast south of Kaohsiung in Ping Tung, I met Chiu Lienhui, an influential member of the Taiwan opposition movement. In between scuba dives in the luscious surroundings of Taiwan's tropical south, Chiu and I had long talks about Taiwan's politics, about the opposition's policies, and about its reactions to President Chiang Ching-kuo. We would start our conversations on the boat and continue them in the evenings at Lin Homing's stone country house, where aborigines came to perform traditional dances. I remember one visit when I was with George Witwer, United States Information Agency chief Harry Britton, our wives, and my mother-in-law. The squat, middle-aged aborigine dancers asked us to join them. We did, and after a long boisterous dance, Harry said to me, "You just did the wedding dance and are now married to that little 70-year-old standing next to you."

But the undercurrent of these delightful outings into the country-side of southern Taiwan was politics and the future of Taiwan. I remember Chiu telling me his wish for Taiwan: "I hope we can become the Switzerland of the future—prosperous, hi-tech, neutral, and with our own defense."

Given what I perceived to be Chinese interest in my posting to Taipei, I thought it might be useful during one of my trips back to the U.S. to convey my impressions of Taiwan to a senior Chinese diplomat in Washington. While I may not have been able to help with reunification as I had been asked at my farewell party in 1982, I could at the least keep the mainlanders informed about Taiwan. I met covertly with Ji Chaozhu, a counselor at the Chinese Embassy. Ji had been Chou En-lai's interpreter and had studied at Harvard in the 1940s. He had also been my contact during Vice President George Bush's troubled trip to China in August 1980. When Ji and I met, I stressed that Taiwan was on a dramatic economic upturn. I pulled from my pocket a transistor made in Taiwan and presented it to him as an example of the island's extraordinary progress in technology production. I then gave him a publication of Taiwan's opposition movement, which talked about how democracy and Taiwanization were coming. Ji replied that he had his own contacts in Taiwan through his wife's family. He painted a more negative picture of conditions and emphasized corruption and continuing KMT authoritarian rule. However, I did most of the talking because my impressions were both deeper and more current.

With these encounters in mind, I suggested to the Washington powers-that-be at the NSC and State Department that change was coming but that the Chinese on both sides of the strait would determine the pace, not the Americans. Our strong support for Taiwan was paying off in that Taiwan now had more confidence in experimenting with openings to China.

·   ·   ·

There's a rock formation off the southern coast of Taiwan that bears a natural resemblance to the late President Richard Nixon's face. If you look at the formation from the right angle, you can make out Nixon's ski jump nose, long forehead, and trademark jowls. Taiwan residents have dubbed the rock, which sits in a small bay near the beach town of O Luanpi, "Nixon Rock." The legend is that after Nixon's trip to China, his head was cut off and placed in the bay, forever condemned to looking toward China.

When I arrived in Taiwan in January 1982 on the heels of the announcement that the U.S. would not sell Taiwan an advanced fighter, I could have been lambasted by my hosts, isolated, and, for all intents and purposes, made as immobile as Nixon Rock. But that didn't happen. Instead, I presided over a rebuilding of relations. With solid support from both the White House and the State Department and strong backing from President Reagan himself, AIT made sure that Taiwan's security needs were sufficiently addressed and then was able to concentrate on other parts of the relationship, like the trade surplus, American investment in Taiwan, and Taiwan's move toward a more pluralistic and democratic society. The Pan-Asian group proved that, if handled carefully, America could make military sales to both Taiwan and China.

When I left Taiwan in 1984, the country was making a clean break from its past in noticeable ways. Elections were characterized by open and lively debate among competing candidates, and there was an active opposition even though it was still in reality a one-party state. While some branches of government suspended dissenting publications, other branches just as quickly approved the operation of new ones. And in the area of Taiwanization, President Chiang chose island native Lee Tenghui as his successor. He named Lee his vice presidential candidate for upcoming elections in May and set about preparing Lee for the new position. To expose Lee to the American point of view, President Chiang asked me to travel around the island with him in January 1984, just the two of us, accompanied only by our wives and a miniscule entourage. Other officials wanted to go, but Chiang wisely said no. Chiang Ching-kuo wanted us to establish a "personal relationship," so we spent two days together, traveling to the port city of Hua Lien on Taiwan's eastern coast and then across the island through the dramatic Taroko Gorge up to Hohuan Mountain through a snowstorm. Yes, a blizzard in semitropical Taiwan.

In the shade of linden trees, Lee and I took long walks and discussed books about Taiwan. We both agreed that U.S. economic cooperation in the decades after 1949 had helped to bring prosperity to the island. I saw in him an effective politician, a man with a connection to the people who was not a conventional KMT leader. In public, he toed the party line, but in private he voiced strong opinions and was a Taiwan patriot. More so than his mainland Chinese colleagues in the Taiwan government, Lee identified with his people, and he believed in them. Yet at that time he showed no particular animus against China. In fact, he wanted greater contact with the mainland in the form of trade and tourism, but he was suspicious of China's desire to take over Taiwan, and he told me that his people would not accept China controlling Taiwan. Throughout the trip Lee was clearly politicking: shaking hands, kissing babies, and being photographed with honeymooners and youth groups. I wrote in a cable back to Washington that given Chiang Ching-kuo's declining health, "this vigorous and healthy Taiwanese could be the next president." And that he was.

Lee succeeded Chiang after his death in 1988 and continued Taiwan's peaceful transformation to a true democracy by instituting direct elections of the president and members of the Legislative Yuan. A confident Taiwan's opening to China, initiated by Chiang's policy in 1987 to allow military veterans to visit their families on the mainland, reversed forty years of isolation from the mainland. The same year President Chiang abolished martial law and allowed opposition parties to register. In the paradox that I had come to notice, a more self-assured Taiwan was a better partner for Communist China.

Taiwan's impressive growth into a full-fledged democracy continued with a historic election in 2000 that I had the privilege of observing. The country's citizens elected Chen Shuibien, a native Taiwanese and the mayor of Taipei, as the first non-Kuomintang president in the country's history. Chiang Ching-kuo's four-point program had, indeed, made great strides.

.   .   .

I left Taiwan four months after the trip with Lee Tenghui, staying on after Sally's departure to attend President Chiang's inauguration for a second term in office on May 20, 1984. Felled by acute pain in my right knee, I hobbled onto a plane bound for home. The farewell banquets, those endless affairs of tasty but too rich Chinese food and numerous toasts, had overwhelmed my Western metabolism. My uric acid count and cholesterol level went through the roof.

The May 15th issue of the *United Daily News* saluted me as I was about to leave. An article announcing my departure noted that my personal relations with Taiwan's leaders had helped me to lead the American Institute in Taiwan in "making great contributions to U.S.–Taiwan relations."

I had done my work. It was time to go home, at least for a little while.

17

PUSHING FOR CHANGE

Perched behind the transparent nose of an American bomber, I looked down at the southern part of the Korean Peninsula spread below me. It was November 1952, and I was flying down the peninsula after overseeing the infiltration of two Chinese agents into Manchuria. The city of Seoul was in ruins. Only a few buildings still stood after the North Korean attack in June 1950. Though fighting against the North Koreans and their Chinese allies had moved north of Seoul to the area around the 38th parallel, most of South Korea remained an armed encampment, full of soldiers and military equipment. As I headed back to Japan, I got an unobstructed view of the devastation—wide swaths of smashed trees and destroyed villages from Seoul to Pusan. The country was little more than a battle-scarred staging area of war inflicted on the peninsula by North Korea.

Thirty-four years later Sally and I arrived in a rejuvenated South Korea. Seoul had come a long way from the cease-fire that ended the Korean War in 1953. It was a bustling capital city of 10 million that had all the amenities of a modern metropolis. The country had become one of Asia's "Little Tigers" with an economic recovery that was the stuff of record books. South Korea was on its way to registering 12 percent annual growth in 1986, the world's best performance. The opportunity to host the Olympic Games in 1988 would be another feather in the country's cap.

The United States could be justifiably proud that it had helped South Korea rise from the ashes. It was a success story on the front lines of the Cold War, particularly in comparison to its isolated communist brother to the north. But the country still faced serious challenges. First was the threat from North Korea, which was armed to the teeth and ready to strike. On another front, tension was rising in the Korean capital. The end of President Chun Doo Hwan's term in office was approaching. A former army general, Chun had come to power in 1979 by means of a military coup. Like his authoritarian predecessors, Chun ruled South Korea with a tight fist: Opposition leaders were jailed or placed under house arrest; the press was circumscribed; and protests against the government were squelched. And like his predecessors, Chun justified his iron rule by pointing to a belligerent North Korea. It was not a healthy climate, and Chun's authoritarianism was wearing on the U.S.

By the time I arrived in November 1986 to take up the post of U.S. Ambassador to the Republic of Korea, the South Korean government's hard-line approach was being challenged not only by university students, who had a history of vocal and sometimes violent opposition, but also by a growing middle class, which wanted more political choice to go along with higher standards of living.

I hoped the experience and good fortune of having been present in Taiwan when that country laid the foundation for a more open society would help me in Korea. If the U.S. could encourage South Korea to democratize, the country could become a more vibrant example of the superiority of open economic and political systems. At the same time, I was concerned that South Korea's coming-out party at the Olympics in September 1988 could be crashed either by the country's authoritarian leadership overreacting or by provocations from the North.

· · ·

In Washington, there was a policy tug-of-war going on over how best to encourage South Korea to reform. Voices from the legislative corridors of Washington as well as from the halls of the State Department were pushing, loudly and crudely, for the primacy of democracy in the South Korean equation. However, having witnessed firsthand the collapse of governments in Southeast Asia to communist infiltration and attack from outside, I believed that security was an equal priority for a country like South Korea, separated from its hostile neighbor North Korea by the most heavily armed border in the world.

The North Koreans deserved close monitoring. They had a long and sordid history of provoking incidents along the 150-mile-long demilitarized zone (DMZ) between the two countries. And their terrorist activities included North Korean agents in Burma planting a bomb in October 1983 in a mausoleum at Burma's National Cemetery. The bomb was intended to kill South Korean president Chun while he was on a state visit to the country. All told, seventeen South Koreans—including the foreign minister, the South Korean ambassador to Burma, as well as two senior presidential advisors—and four Burmese died in the explosion at Burma's most revered ceremonial site. Because the motorcade he was riding in was behind schedule, Chun himself escaped injury. Burmese police quickly apprehended the North Korean agents. One of them made a full confession, which exposed the intricate planning in Pyongyang that had gone into the attack.

Given the historic importance of the next three years in South Korea, I believed that the U.S. could not waver in its commitment to help defend South Korea. North Korea understood the language of deterrence, and a strong message needed to be sent to Pyongyang that the U.S. stood firmly beside its ally.

People inside and outside the Reagan administration questioned my views, though. At my confirmation hearings in the Senate, Senator John Kerry of Massachusetts prodded me: "What do you place first: security or democracy?"

"I am all for bringing democracy to South Korea," I responded, "but first we have to stabilize the security perimeter in the north and make it clear to South Korea that we support them." To hammer home my point, I turned to President Reagan's invitation to South Korean president Chun in 1981 as an example of a successful approach to Korea. In a clear sign of support for South Korea, President Reagan invited Chun to visit Washington. Fresh from directing a military coup in 1979, the South Korean president was one of the first foreign leaders invited for an official visit. But before the South Korean president's invitation to the White House could be finalized, the Korean government had to agree to commute the death sentence of Chun's hated opponent Kim

Dae Jung and allow him to leave the country, whereupon he went into exile abroad. Kim would be elected president of Korea in 1997.

The lesson for me was that the U.S. had leverage to influence change if it calibrated policy wisely. In my statement to the Senate Foreign Relations Committee, I called the United States' mission in South Korea "one of the most interesting and demanding in the world."

The posting to Seoul was my first official ambassadorship. At my swearing-in ceremony at the State Department, I saw people from all parts of my life. I looked out over an audience and spotted Barbara Bush and Secretary of Defense Caspar Weinberger. I also saw family members as well as friends from the CIA and Yale. My sister Elinore, who had shared practically everything with me from the day I was born in Tsingtao, China, had come down from Massachusetts for the occasion along with her husband, Bill. And, of course, Sally was there. This was my chance to tell a large crowd in Washington about her. "If there was any joy, charm, or smattering of culture that came out of my various postings, it was because of Sally, not because of me," I said.

I finished with a tribute to two men who in their service to their country, and in my life, loomed over my appointment to Korea. Sally's father, Waller Booth, had himself operated in North Korea during the early days of the Korean War. Wally had passed away nine months before my swearing-in. My closing words recalled my older brother Frank, who, though he had died forty years earlier, continued to serve as a moral conscience for me.

> And finally there are those who are not here, who have died and served this country. I pick two: my father-in-law Wally Booth, who fought behind the lines in North Korea so that I could try to win the peace, and my brother Frank, who should and would be standing here, and perhaps he is.

.   .   .

My position on the importance of security in the democracy equation made me a target for Korean students who were violently protesting the division of the peninsula and the presence of America's 37,000-strong military contingent. I was burned in effigy even before I got to Seoul. This was the first time I had ever been so honored. I was soon to find out, however, that Korean antagonism toward America was spreading toward economic issues as well. Seoul's economic development strategy had led to positive results in Korea, but the same policies were also responsible for a huge imbalance in trade with the U.S. Back in America, cattle farmers, shippers, bankers, insurance companies, and movie producers were clamoring for the same freedom to operate in Korea that Korean businesses enjoyed in the states. American pressure on South Korea to open up its protected domestic markets was perceived as more bullying by a power-hungry America.

The Korean preoccupation with being dominated went back a thousand years at least and instilled a belief in Koreans that if left alone they could live in peace and harmony with their own sacred traditions. In 1986, however, the issue that most rankled young Koreans and irked a good number of older Koreans was President Chun Doo Hwan's brutal suppression of anti-government demonstrations in the southern city of Kwangju in May 1980. By the mid-1980s, cries of "Remember Kwangju" had become a touchstone for Koreans of all ages, who wanted a more democratic country.

In an effort to consolidate his hold on power, General Chun, with no official title other than the military rank he had when he masterminded the coup in December 1979, declared martial law throughout South Korea just before the crackdown in Kwangju. Student leaders and senior political figures were imprisoned. The National Assembly was closed and censorship imposed on the press. Under the pretext of preparing for an invasion by North Korea, which he said was the "hidden hand" behind the student protests, Chun executed, in effect, a military takeover of the country.

In Kwangju, the arrest on the night of May 17 of the region's native son, Kim Dae Jung, and the imposition of martial law sparked further angry protests. After a standoff between students and Korean special forces troops, the South Korean Army mounted an assault on the city on May 27. Around 240 people were killed according to official estimates. Unofficial estimates run as high as 2,000 dead.

The legacy of Kwangju for U.S.–South Korean relations was that many South Koreans held the U.S. partly responsible for the massacre or at least acquiescent in the face of a determined South Korean military. In the years following the Kwangju massacre, the U.S. government's reluctance to speak in depth about the incident further encouraged many Koreans to consider America culpable.

. . .

During the time I spent as the U.S. ambassador in Seoul, I became more familiar with the history of Kwangju and tried to dispel the lingering shadow that it cast over U.S.–South Korean relations. I drew two lessons. The first lesson was that in a crisis situation there could be no separation of opinion between the U.S. military in Seoul and the U.S. Embassy that might lead to ambiguity in the American position on matters of crucial importance to the U.S. and South Korea.

The second lesson was that developments inside Korea had to be "a Korean thing," meaning that Koreans themselves must decide the direction of their country. America's role was to support and, perhaps, advise but not try to control the process. This meant, especially, that America should keep a low profile. This also entailed paying close attention to perceptions, particularly the perceptions of the Korean people.

. . .

Walking the streets of Seoul I couldn't help noticing the ominous presence of Darth Vader-like policemen on street corners. Newspapers reported on large-scale demonstrations at Yonsei University and Seoul National University. The policy approach to Korea's complicated situation took some careful crafting. I wanted to reassure the government on some issues and prod them on others.

In America, Gaston Sigur, now serving as Assistant Secretary of State for East Asia and the Pacific, was more blunt in his message to the South Korean government. A committed advocate of democratic reforms who had been instrumental in getting Ferdinand Marcos out of the Philippines in 1986, Gaston became the U.S. government's point man in Washington to urge democratic reform on Korea in 1987. As Gaston put it later, "we decided to get rather bold in our policy."

Sigur headed a low-key yet firm campaign to convince Chun to agree to democratic reforms. Gaston's political instincts about people and timing were superb. His laid-back southern manner—he was of Louisiana Cajun stock—helped, as did a wonderful sense of humor. In a speech to the Korea Society in New York on February 6, 1987, he announced U.S. support for a new political framework in Korea. Specifically, Gaston's speech signaled U.S. support for democratic election of the South Korean president. He also advocated the "civilianizing" of the country's military-dominated politics. Needless to say, the speech shook both the political and military establishments in South Korea.

Though he had proclaimed his desire to step down peacefully at the end of his term in 1988, President Chun had shown signs of digging in his heels. There were rumors in Korea that, in the face of rising discontent on the part of the populace, the former general would not give up power and would, if necessary, use the military to remain in power just as he had used it to assume power. "Civilianization" was a not-so-oblique reference to getting the South Korean military's undue influence out of politics.

.   .   .

When President Chun decided in April 1987 to suspend further consideration of constitutional revision until after the 1988 Olympics, our movements and pronouncements took on more urgency. Chun's decision meant that the next president of South Korea would be elected by an electoral college that he could easily control. It was a serious setback. The opposition in Korea and some politicians back in the U.S. started to paint visions of Chun influencing the election of a loyal successor and then continuing to exercise power from behind the scenes.

In reaction to Chun's decision, demonstrations gathered momentum, and the political climate heated up quickly. In the midst of this rising tension, Gaston visited several times. Each time he made a point of meeting with Kim Dae Jung, who was under house arrest at his home in Seoul after having voluntarily returned to South Korea from exile abroad in 1985. One time as Gaston was approaching Kim's residence, the car he was traveling in was rocked so hard by South Korean security guards that it almost turned over. It was a scare tactic of the crudest form.

During the hectic months of 1987, I met with opposition leaders and even with student protesters, but I didn't go with Gaston to his meetings with Kim Dae Jung even though he asked me to. I told him that I had to preserve my position with the South Korean leaders. Branded by the government as a communist, Kim was seen as the éminence grise behind the violent student protests.

I kept more quiet about my work, reassuring leaders that they had U.S. support and then making sure they understood our hope that democratic change would come in the form of open elections, greater freedom of the press, and genuine opposition parties. I couldn't be effective as the U.S. ambassador if alienated from my Korean counterparts.

. . .

Perhaps one of my more controversial acts was to attend the electoral convention of the ruling Democratic Justice Party (DJP) in early June 1987. Even my own embassy had come out against my going and, without clearing their decision with me, had informed the press that I wouldn't be attending. The Political Section of the embassy reasoned that the DJP's candidate, Roh Tae Woo, a former four-star general, was really just Chun's anointed successor, the beneficiary of an electoral system that was rigged to keep the ruling party in power. The embassy's political counselor told me that if I went I would be blessing a false process, a new authoritarian man replacing an old one. He said that I should express disapproval by staying away. I said that just gets people angry. I saw Roh as the type of leader who could be influenced if we supported him at crucial times.

My entrance into the convention raised a few eyebrows among the media, which had not been expecting the U.S. ambassador to make such an appearance. In fact, sixty ambassadors were boycotting the convention. The affair was entirely choreographed. It reminded me of the cheering section at a Texas A&M football game. The cheerleaders lead the familiar cheers, and the fans respond en masse. After the convention, candidate Roh came to me and said he really appreciated my coming and that he knew it wasn't an easy thing for me to do.

The formal nomination on June 10 of Roh as the DJP's presidential candidate set off some of the most massive demonstrations Seoul had ever seen. Chun's decision to push Roh's candidacy through using the stacked election system meant that there would be no direct election of the president. From the rooftop of the embassy in downtown Seoul we could see 200,000 to 300,000 people massing in the square in front of City Hall. Within hours protestors were battling police in pitched battles in the streets of Seoul.

This time it wasn't just students. Housewives, merchants, and teachers joined the protests, proof that much of the Korean middle class was going to stand up and be counted. The demonstrations in Korea became the single biggest story in the U.S. press, surpassing even ongoing hearings on the growing Iran–Contra political scandal. In TV reports, Seoul looked like it was under siege.

As I watched the crisis unfold from the embassy, however, I bristled at the role of the media in inflaming the conflict. The U.S. news outlets, I thought, pandered to the need for sensationalism—the demands of the audience for "blood and gore" as I called it. "Korea is not as described in the U.S. press," I wrote to Jeff on June 28, 1987. "We go through 90% of the city without encountering a trace of violence. The other day the police were relaxing in the sun and thirty feet away the radical students were lying on the grass smoking and chatting. A television crew drove up and the students immediately jumped up and started shouting and throwing rocks—the police reacted, and we had our lead item for the evening news."

Though the media's coverage irritated me, I realized that the issues in South Korea were deep and troubling. The country was burdened with a decaying authoritarian government that was trying to hold onto power.

.   .   .

In my first months in Korea, during its sputtering march toward a more open society, I spent some time thinking about unresolved issues in my own family. A letter from my sister, Elinore, about Frank's death led me to reflect again on his life and his last days at the Allied base in Kure, Japan. The most mystifying part of Frank's suicide was the letter he left on his military cot explaining his final desperate action as one induced by isolating selfishness. More than forty years after Frank's death we were still trying to understand what happened to him. In my response to Elinore, I tried to fathom why Frank had ended his life at the age of 26.

Frank was there in 1946—one year after [the atom bomb was dropped]. Kure is right next to Hiroshima. The tragedy of Hiroshima is almost beyond belief. Then it was utterly smashed. Cynical, broken, desperate people lived there. War was at its most gruesome. Frank probably had a child's appreciation of China and Japan—possibly idealized. His childhood visions of China were smashed in Yunnan [where he served in 1945]. His younger version of Japan—clean, orderly, slightly amusing Japanese—was changed forever at Hiroshima. . . .

And finally Frank himself—very intense—living life to the fullest. His diaries reflect this and I've reread them. His highs and lows—deep depressions, vicious self-criticism and then pride, achievement and exuberance.

A combination of these factors hit him. Loneliness compounds it. He is in Hiroshima, comes from war shattered [and] corrupt China. His depression hits and letters from home make him feel more remote.

His last sentiment was—I have outlived my usefulness. Perhaps we are better off for not being able to figure it out fully. I saw him as a younger brother who idolized him. Not totally healthy but it will always be that part of how I view him.

I had said in my swearing-in speech in Washington in October 1986 that I would try to keep the peace that had been won in Asia in World War II. Korea in 1987 was at the crossroads between continuing on an authoritarian path or transforming itself into a democratic society. As Washington's man on the ground, I needed to do my best to help pull Korea back from possible disaster. The stakes were high. In South Korea, the U.S. was helping to shape a society that could stand as a bold contrast to the communist regimes in North Korea and China and perhaps prod them to change as well. It was a mission that Frank, with his high ideals of achievement, would have supported. But there seemed little room for his idealism in the way events were unfolding. We were guided by calculated diplomatic maneuvering and gut instinct in our responses to the evolving situation on the ground.

.   .   .

On the evening of June 10, a handful of students retreating from violent clashes occupied Myongdong Catholic Cathedral in downtown Seoul. Built in the 1890s by foreign missionaries, the cathedral was one of the most revered sanctuaries in Korea. By taking refuge in the cathedral, the students were bringing attention to the fact that they were largely supported in their demands by Korea's Christian clergy. Over the course of the next few days, citizens flooded the students in the cathedral with donated clothing, food, and money. But to the government, the occupation of the church was an embarrassment and a challenge. Some high-ranking officials argued for forceful eviction of the students. I envisioned a possible scenario: a violent confrontation between hard-nosed special forces and recalcitrant students in the church, leaving it covered with blood. The pictures would be sent all over the world, and the fallout would be destructive not only for the government but for the country. In a meeting with South Korean foreign minister Choi Kwang Soo on June 13 at the Foreign Ministry, I made myself clear: "Don't go into the cathedral with troops. It will reverberate all over the world." My appeal, I learned later from a high-ranking member of the government, helped to defuse the situation. Cooler heads prevailed, and the standoff was resolved peacefully through priests acting as intermediaries. In the neighborhoods around the cathedral, the students actually lost support because they were seen as loud-mouthed, ungrateful, and dirty.

Six days later, the stakes were even higher. The demonstrations against the government's policies continued throughout the country. By this time, I viewed President Chun as a man determined to hang on in the best tradition that he knew, which was not to compromise. I knew that Chun could attempt to repeat Kwangju, but we had indications that not all of the soldiers would follow an order from the president to suppress the demonstrations with military force. There remained some Korean generals who had been present at Kwangju seven years

earlier, and we had a strong sense that they didn't want more of the terrible blood and vengeance. One of them was General Chung Ho Yong,
commander of the special forces at Kwangju, who had had a change of
heart and mind about using military force in civilian disturbances. In
the worst case scenario, there was the possibility of civil war breaking
out between different parts of the military. The fate of the Olympic
Games, just sixteen months away, lay in the balance. Not to mention an
opportunistic and terrorist-minded neighbor to the north that might
take advantage of civil dislocation in the south.

On Wednesday, June 17, I was on a long-delayed tour of some of our
embassy's cultural offices in the Korean countryside when I got a
phone call from Harry Dunlop, the political counselor at the embassy.
Dunlop told me that he had gotten word from Washington that a letter that we had been expecting from President Reagan to President
Chun would be arriving that night. Dunlop said he would make an appointment for me to see President Chun to deliver the letter personally.
I cut my trip short and immediately returned to Seoul.

The letter was a coordinated strategy to sway President Chun from
using force. The South Korean ambassador to Washington, Kim
Kyung Won, counseled the State Department to let me deliver the letter personally rather than send it through the normal diplomatic channels, which would have been through the South Korean Foreign
Ministry. Kim's advice was based on instinct and experience. He was a
long-time government official who had served in the Blue House. We
didn't know each other well, and I didn't talk directly to him. He just
sensed that having me deliver the letter and then back up its contents
with my own words would be the most effective way of dissuading
President Chun from using force.

But back in Seoul Dunlop was having no luck getting through to
the president's office to make an appointment for me. The message he
left Wednesday night that I would like to meet with President Chun
the next afternoon was never returned. On Thursday, June 18, Dunlop
called the Foreign Ministry and was told that President Chun would
not receive me. Dunlop finally got a representative from the Foreign
Ministry to come to his office in the embassy. The representative politely stonewalled him. "But that cannot be," said an exasperated Dun-

lop. "This is a personal letter from my president to your president, to be delivered by my president's personal representative, who is also under instructions to have a few additional words to say." The Foreign Ministry representative said, "Oh, yes, he can refuse to receive the ambassador." Dunlop then escalated his appeal farther up the protocol ladder, but to no avail. He had a sinking feeling that he was being shut off because President Chun had already made up his mind to use force. One Korean government official told Dunlop that he could drop the letter in the mail or slip it under the door. "We'll see that President Chun gets it," the official told Dunlop.

I was riding back to Seoul on Thursday afternoon, expecting to meet President Chun. At the embassy, the radios were on so that political officers could hear security reports on the demonstrations. There were gas masks in the offices. Political officers were running in and out of the building. Dunlop finally lost his cool and shouted into the phone, "I don't believe that President Chun has made this decision [not to see the U.S. ambassador]. I will not accept that your president has made it. I don't think that he would be that stupid to make it. He couldn't have made it. Goddamn it, I want to know the name of the person who made that decision right now!"

I arrived about an hour later. Dunlop's outburst apparently paid off because soon after the phone rang. It was Foreign Minister Choi. He told me that I couldn't see President Chun today but that I could meet with him on Friday, June 19. Violent rioting continued through the night. A South Korean soldier was killed in Seoul. In Pusan the police chief called for soldiers to help maintain order. His police were too tired to go on, he reportedly said. At the embassy, the premonition that Chun had already made the decision to declare martial law appeared to be correct. Meeting at 10 A.M. Friday with his defense minister, uniformed service chiefs, and the director of the intelligence agency, Chun ordered deployment of battle-ready troops by 4 A.M. Saturday on a variety of campuses and cities. Plans were put in place for the arrest of political opponents and the opening of military courts. The country was quickly sinking into "social chaos," warned Prime Minister Lee Han Key, and an unspecified "extraordinary decision" might be needed to address the situation.

I went alone to call on President Chun at the Presidential Palace at 2 P.M. on June 19. Before I went, I was at a lunch also attended by General William J. Livesey, the U.S. military commander in Korea, at a hotel in downtown Seoul. I hadn't expected to meet him there, but I took the opportunity to tell him of my upcoming meeting with President Chun. With the lessons of Kwangju etched in my mind, I figured that if Livesey and I presented a united front, we had the best chance of persuading the South Korean government to stand down from declaring martial law and using troops. On the way out of the hotel from the luncheon, I told Livesey that I was going to deliver President Reagan's letter to President Chun and that I was going to urge Chun not to use the military to quell the protests. Livesey just listened. I took his silence as assent. In my mind, I could now go to Chun Doo Hwan and make the case that the United States, from the president on down to the country's highest-ranking general and diplomat in Seoul, were in accord.

Now I felt more confident in our approach. I knew things could still break against us, but I didn't see us as desperate in our strategy. After all, Gaston and I had been preaching the message of compromise and democracy to the South Korean government for months.

President Chun sat stone-faced during our ninety-minute meeting. Foreign Minister Choi Kwang Soo and an interpreter were the only other people in the room. In our previous meetings, Chun had been animated, dominating the conversation, often as if it were a monologue, even breaking out into laughter at what he said. But this afternoon, I sensed a deeply troubled man. I gave him the letter.

Chun read it. President Reagan had adopted a friendly tone in the letter. He reaffirmed the U.S. security commitment to President Chun in the first part. Reagan also applauded the South Korean president's commitment to a peaceful transfer of power. Then he counseled Chun to take additional steps to ensure his country's continued political development, like releasing political prisoners, prosecuting police officials who abused their power, and encouraging a free press. Such moves, Reagan wrote, would "send to the world a dramatic signal of your intent to break free of what you correctly term the 'old politics.'"

Then in my own words, I impressed on him the gravity of the situation, backing up the contents of President Reagan's amicable letter with firm and unambiguous statements about the U.S. position regarding the declaration of martial law. I emphasized first that I spoke on behalf of the U.S. military as well. "We are in agreement on the recommendation not to use force," I told President Chun. If the prime minister announces that martial law is about to be proclaimed, I ventured, he would risk undermining the U.S.–South Korea alliance and courting a repeat of the disastrous events in Kwangju in 1980. As I was leaving, Foreign Minister Choi, in my view the most accomplished diplomat in South Korea at the time, said to me, "I hope there will be a good outcome."

The staff was breathless in anticipation when I returned to the embassy. I recounted what I had said and then wrote a long cable to the State Department with my observations of the meeting. Later that afternoon, I got a phone call from Foreign Minister Choi. He said that after my meeting at the Blue House President Chun had decided not to declare martial law. When she heard the news, a Korean-American woman who worked as a secretary in the embassy front office hugged me in the hallway. "Thank you," she said. "Thank you for helping to stop it from happening." She probably should have hugged Harry Dunlop as well, who labored so hard to get me in a position to deliver the message and who was actually harder on the Koreans than I would have been. Dunlop later said that if there was anything in his career that might have had an impact on history, it was losing his temper on the telephone. He's probably right.

We had reason to be pleased for our work, though it was likely the South Koreans themselves and, oddly enough, high-ranking military men may have influenced President Chun the most in his decision not to use force. They had whispered in his ear in the crucial tension-filled days leading up to June 19. His key foreign policy advisors, meanwhile, were delivering a similar message.

Timing had been fortuitous. Ambassador Kim in Washington cabled that Reagan's letter was on the way, which may well have provided some breathing room while I was out of town. Then Dunlop struggled to set up the meeting for me. I met coincidentally with Livesey and forged a united front. And, finally, I happened to have my audience with Chun as the clock was ticking.

Livesey was not happy that I had taken license with his silence. He complained loudly to an embassy official the next day that I had acted without his approval. My short discussion with Livesey had been un-planned, and I had acted on instinct when I said Livesey and I repre-sented a united front. Just as Ambassador Kim had acted on instinct when he suggested that I deliver the letter personally to President Chun. Once the June 19 decision seemed to be working, General Livesey told me that his troops were ready to block any Korean mili-tary movements into Seoul.

. . .

The next week was a whirlwind of meetings. Sensing that South Korea was at a turning point in her history, Assistant Secretary Sigur abruptly changed his schedule at my suggestion and flew to Seoul from Singapore. Evidently, our reports from Seoul were hitting home. "I was reading all these cables [from Korea], and I couldn't sleep," recalled Gaston. "I kept thinking: Something, we've got to do something. . . . We've got to make a show that we support what we've said we support."

During Gaston's visit, he met with Chun Doo Hwan and opposition leaders. I sat in on many of the meetings, including those with Presi-dent Chun and Roh Tae Woo. The wheels were turning fast. On June 24, President Chun met with Kim Young Sam for the first time. But in his meeting with us Chun insisted that, by fueling demonstrations, the opposition was trying to scar his legacy. He didn't rule out the possibil-ity of using force if the protests spun out of control. But as the opposi-tion to his regime continued to harden in the form of street protests, Chun's options became fewer and fewer. He was a proud man, and he told us that he didn't want to blemish his legacy by declaring martial law in his last eight months in office.

Roh appeared to be more willing than Chun to acknowledge the historic tide overtaking the country. As leader of the ruling party, he was more attuned to the changing political thinking than Chun, who was sequestered in the Blue House. An aide to Roh confided to a U.S. Embassy official that Roh knows "this is a crucial period" in South Ko-rean history.

Roh, however, was the chosen successor of Chun Doo Hwan and remained beholden to the current president for his political stature. But the gap in the two men's thinking was wearing on Roh during this tense period. At a private meeting with Roh on June 25, I sensed that he feared he was going too far for Chun's liking. "I find myself in a very difficult position in a difficult time for my country," Roh confided to me. I learned later from an aide to Roh that he was so worried and fearful during these uncertain June days that on the eve of his private meeting with me he had considered the possibility of seeking refuge in the U.S. Embassy. Others deny this. I cabled Washington after our June 25 meeting that Roh might be getting wobbly. Our presence during these tense times, I believe, demonstrated our continuing support.

.   .   .

On June 29, at what was scheduled to be a routine photo op at the headquarters of the Democratic Justice Party, President-elect Roh Tae Woo asked members of the media to remain. To the astonishment of the members of the press in the room and Koreans watching live on TV, Roh then announced dramatic reforms. "I have now come to a firm conviction about the future of our nation," the DJP candidate began. In what came to be known as the June 29 Declaration, Roh said he favored granting all of the opposition's demands, chief among them being the direct election of the president, the freeing of Kim Dae Jung, and the release of all political prisoners. One senior U.S. official described it as "the damnedest thing I ever saw."

On July 1, President Chun officially endorsed Roh's package of reforms, which had been announced in the form of recommendations to the president. Debate over which man, Chun or Roh, was the initiator of the June 29 Declaration goes on to this day in South Korea, with opinions dividing sharply based on whose camp the speaker is or was in during June 1987. Since both Chun and Roh were discredited in the ensuing years following trials on corruption charges and their roles in the Kwangju Massacre, for which they received prison sentences, most of their supporters keep a low profile, but their attitudes on the June 29 Declaration still emerge when you talk directly to them. My personal reading is that Roh was the standard-bearer of the democracy message announced on June 29, while Chun shuffled along cautiously.

.   .   .

I could not imagine a better way to usher in a new era of governing in Korea than to invite leading political figures to the July 4th celebration at the U.S. Embassy residence. So we extended invitations to ruling-party candidate Roh and opposition figures Kim Young Sam and Kim Dae Jung. After all, July 4 is the defining holiday of a country that holds to democratic principles such as open elections for president, a military under command of a civilian, and separation of powers.

Before we asked Kim Dae Jung to attend the reception, I undertook some personal research into the politician's background. The South Korean government had long contended that Kim was a communist and an agent provocateur for North Korea. These were the charges used to justify his jail sentences and house arrest. I requested to see everything in State Department files, including confidential reports and police files, on the dissident politician. I concluded that, while he may well have been a leftist politician in his early days and had been involved in anti-government activities, he was not a communist. I saw no evidence that Kim had instigated an armed rebellion, as the government had alleged.

So on a muggy July afternoon at the U.S. ambassador's residence in Seoul, to the strains of a Dixieland band playing jazz, Kim Dae Jung entered our compound. Guests stopped sipping their drinks and craned their necks toward the front gate. Surrounded by followers, Kim hobbled up the long outdoor stairs on a cane. The leading dissident in a country known for its heavy-handed dealings with the opposition then shook hands with O Jae Bok, the senior military general who represented all that Kim had opposed. It had the glow of Stanley meeting Livingston in the search for the source of the Nile.

That day at the embassy residence we hosted what would turn out to be the three main candidates in the December 1987 presidential election, the freest election in the history of South Korea up to that time. Because opposition candidates Kim Young Sam and Kim Dae Jung split for personal reasons and thus could not agree on a platform for a united front, the ruling party's candidate Roh won with less than a majority, garnering only 36 percent of the vote. If the two Kims had stuck together, they probably would have won in a landslide. Roh's June 29 Declaration, though, helped him at the ballot box.

As did the Korean Airlines 858 bombing.

18

***

"THROUGH THE BLUR OF OUR TEARS"

THE NORTH KOREAN regime was a pariah in the world, and the awarding of the Olympic Games to its rival was a defining moment in the country's isolation. North Korea's actions in the lead-up to the games led to a split with its communist allies and in an ironic twist brought South Korea and China closer together.

Like a scorned child, North Korea demanded a piece of the Olympics action. Under the auspices of the International Olympic Committee (IOC), Kim Il Sung's government engaged in negotiations to cohost the games with South Korea, but it refused all of the deals that the South offered. The talks ground to a halt in August 1987 when Pyongyang refused to accept an IOC compromise proposal. Satisfied that North Korea had been given ample chance to participate, virtually all other socialist countries, including the Soviet Union and China, agreed to come to Seoul to participate in the Olympics.

In retrospect, the talks with the IOC may have been a ruse to get the South to lay down its guard. That was—and is—the North Korean modus operandi: negotiate on the one hand, appear willing to reach an agreement; meanwhile, stealthily set up an attack with the other hand or use fear of an attack to gain concessions. The hidden hand struck on November 29, 1987. That's when a powerful bomb exploded on a Korean Air Lines (KAL) jetliner over the Andaman Sea on its way from Abu Dhabi to Seoul. All 115 passengers and crewmembers were killed.

When I heard the news of the plane's disappearance, I knew the North Koreans had done it. "They've made a terrible move," I said to myself. "Let's get to the bottom of this, get the facts, and clobber them with it."

Moving swiftly after news of the plane's disappearance, the Bahrain Intelligence Service had determined that the passport of Mayumi Hachiya, a 25-year-old Japanese woman traveling with her father and registered on the first leg of KAL 858 from Baghdad to Abu Dhabi, was a fake. On November 31 at the airport in Bahrain, where the two had flown in an attempt to get home from Abu Dhabi, the suspicious pair was apprehended by Bahraini police as they were about to board a flight for Rome. The elderly man, who turned out to be a veteran North Korean secret agent, bit into a cyanide-laced cigarette and died instantly. Bahrain Police Chief Ian Henderson, however, grabbed for a similarly poisoned cigarette on the lips of the young woman. She hesitated for a moment, and Henderson flicked the cigarette out of her mouth. The young woman survived. To this day, Henderson, an Englishman by birth, shows curious visitors the scar on his finger where the young woman bit him when he reached for the "cigarette."

At first, with her interrogators the young woman stuck steadfastly to her cover story that she was a Chinese orphan who had grown up in Japan and who had had nothing to do with the bombing. But her actions belied her story. In one violent outburst in Bahrain, enraged by a line of questioning about her sexual past, she felled a female interpreter with a palm-heel strike to the nose, delivered a hammer-fist punch to the groin of Henderson, and then grabbed for his pistol. She was about to shoot herself with the pistol when she was jolted by an electric stun gun. Her rage prompted Henderson to send her to Seoul. "Get her out of here. She belongs to the South Koreans now," Henderson said.

The man who took Kim Hyun Hee—her real name—back to Seoul was Vice Foreign Minister Park Soo Kil. Park flew to Bahrain shortly after the KAL 858 explosion with three agents from the Agency for National Security Planning, also known as the KCIA, to demonstrate to the Bahrain authorities that Kim was indeed a North Korean agent. Chief among the evidence was an analysis of the cyanide-laced cigarettes, which showed them to be the same type used by North Korean agents apprehended in South Korea. Bahrain was getting pressure from unfriendly countries such as Syria to send her to China. Park told

Bahrain government officials that the longer the suspected terrorist stayed in their country, the more at risk Bahrain would be to a rescue attempt by North Korea that could leave more people dead, likely Bahrainis. Finally, after Kim's attack, the Bahrain government let her return with him.

In Seoul, under twenty-four-hour observation and subject to in-depth questioning to which she replied in either Japanese or Chinese, Kim broke and confessed. On the eighth day of her interrogation, she collapsed upon the breast of a woman interrogator and said in Korean, "Forgive me. I am sorry. I will tell you everything." The interrogation had been conducted masterfully by the South Koreans. They had ob-served the way she expertly made her bed every morning as if she had had prolonged military training, uncovered discrepancies in her story, like her incorrect use of southern Chinese words to describe life in northern China, and cajoled her by taking her on a tour of Seoul.

She admitted to helping place a radio time bomb with liquid explo-sive in the overhead luggage rack of KAL 858 while on the Baghdad to Abu Dhabi leg and then deplaning with her fellow agent. Kim revealed that the two North Koreans had been traveling overseas, disguised as father and daughter, for more than three years in preparation for the operation. Interestingly, the South Koreans used the fact that Kim had said she was originally from China to get back at the North Koreans. They communicated to Peking through the New China News Agency in Hong Kong that "your North Korean friends have put this monkey on your back." The Chinese were upset—and probably embarrassed. Just five months earlier in June, we had used diplomatic channels with the Chinese to pass a message to the North Koreans not to underesti-mate America's security commitment to the south nor to try "to take advantage of the current situation in the south."

When Park flew to Bahrain, he was under orders to get the sus-pected terrorist back to Seoul as soon as possible. He ended up escort-ing Kim back to Seoul a few days before the presidential election. The news of her arrival in Seoul made headlines around the world and probably did not harm presidential candidate Roh Tae Woo. Roh's tougher line against North Korea played better among the populace than the softer stands of his chief rivals, Kim Young Sam and Kim Dae

Jung. Roh ended up winning 8.3 million votes, with Kim Young Sam, who came in second, getting 6.4 million. A high-ranking assistant of Roh's later told Park that Kim's arrival probably brought Roh at least 1.5 million votes on election day.

.   .   .

Kim's confession exposed the North Korean regime of Kim Il Sung again: its moral bankruptcy, predilection for terror and secrecy, and suppression of basic human rights. We used to watch North Korean TV at the Demilitarized Zone. News broadcasts would show a group of generals sitting in the Supreme People's Assembly, bedecked with ribbons from their chests to their crotches. A fat kid with a pompadour and belly sticking out would walk in duck-footed in high-heeled shoes and sit down with the stone-faced generals behind him. The "fat kid" was Kim Jong Il, Kim Il Sung's son and the current leader of North Korea. According to an investigation conducted by the South Korean government, he is also the man who reportedly personally signed the order to blow up the Korean airliner in an attempt to disrupt the upcoming Olympic Games. This repeated TV spectacle was one of the most bizarre things I have ever seen. I remember asking Koreans, "What is this?" The South Korean monitors were restrained in their comments. They were reluctant, as many in South Korea are now, to downgrade fellow Koreans in front of outsiders. Nevertheless, the news clips gave us a sense of the strange—and yet highly dangerous—government we were dealing with.

On more than one occasion, the U.S. Embassy collected North Korean propaganda pamphlets that featured me; they had started to attack me in their propaganda. I guess that's one way I could tell that I was doing the right thing. These comic strips, found on university campuses, were either distributed by sympathizers or dropped by balloons sent from North Korea. The first cartoon figure bearing my name looked entirely unlike me. He was bald, smoked a cigar, and wore sports coats. I think the North Korean propaganda department must have thought all American ambassadors looked like Phil Habib, the U.S. ambassador to South Korea from 1971 to 1974. Later cartoons showing me with President Roh Tae Woo colluding against the North were more on the mark—at least in terms of physical appearance. I had glasses and more hair.

After getting a confession from the North Korean agent, South Korea held the regime accountable for its actions. At the U.S. Embassy in Seoul, we helped the State Department and the Koreans in their efforts to muster the two-thirds vote of the members of the United Nations Security Council necessary to make the issue a topic for discussion at the UN in February 1988. There was no chance of a resolution because both China and the Soviet Union would most likely veto or at best abstain. Since they didn't have relations with communist countries then, the South Koreans leaned heavily on us to convey their views to both Peking and Moscow as to Pyongyang's culpability in the terrorist bombing. Both communist powers agreed not to block discussion of the matter. In the lead-up to the discussion at the Security Council, we reemphasized to the South Koreans the importance of letting the Chinese know that Kim was trying to pass herself off as a Chinese woman in her cover story. Using the same unofficial channels that the U.S. had used in the early 1970s, the Koreans, through their consul general in Hong Kong, had passed the message about Kim's cover story to a representative of the New China News Agency in Hong Kong. Thus, it's no surprise that in a private discussion with South Korean foreign minister Choi Kwang Soo in New York, the Chinese ambassador to the UN was quite friendly.

At the UN hearing, the North Korean ambassador charged the U.S. with sponsoring sabotage and terrorism around the globe and accused the South Koreans of bribing the Bahrain authorities to bring Kim back to Seoul. During his hour-long tirade, the North Korean ambassador pointed his finger at South Korean vice foreign minister Park Soo Kil. "Here is the so-called Vice Foreign Minister Park," said the North Korean diplomat. "He took millions of dollars in jewelry to Bahrain to bribe the royal family." The atmosphere heated up. Insulted by the North Korean's unsubstantiated charge, the Bahrain ambassador to the UN jumped up and asked for the right to reply. In the midst of the heated exchanges, Choi turned to his deputy Park and said, "We are fighting a monster, but we can't become a monster in the process."

For the bombing of KAL 858, the U.S. put North Korea on its list of countries engaged in terrorism and started to assist South Korea in security arrangements for the upcoming Olympics. In a meeting with Soviet foreign minister Eduard Shevardnadze in March 1988, President Reagan received assurances that there would be no North Korean terrorist attacks at the Olympics.

.   .   .

The 1988 Olympic Games in Seoul were a crowning achievement. One hundred and fifty-nine countries, including the Soviet Union, China, and the Eastern European countries, participated. But they might as well have come to celebrate Korea's coming-out party. South Korea had much to be proud of. In the span of just two years, the country had instituted a democratic political system, withstood a terrorist attack, and kept its robust economy growing.

The country had come so far since I had first seen it. The images of a war-ravaged Korea were in my mind as I watched the opening ceremony in Seoul's magnificent new Olympic Stadium on a crisp fall evening in September. Flowing fabrics in the hands of dancers on the Olympic Stadium field lent the ceremony a distinctly Korean feel. A Korean marathoner, who had been forced to run for the Japanese at the 1936 Olympics in Berlin, carried the Olympic torch up its final steps. Except now he was running—or, rather, jogging slowly—under his Korean name, not the Japanese name he had to assume as a subject of the Japanese emperor.

Sitting several rows away from me and Sally, South Korea's ambassador to the United States, Kim Kyung Won, the man with whom I had worked to get President Chun Doo Hwan to desist from military action during those heady days a year earlier, was taking in the festivities as well. In December 1950, as a 12-year-old boy, Kim had escaped from North Korea along with his mother, grandmother, and younger brother ahead of advancing North Korean and Chinese troops. They floated for three days on a boat overflowing with refugees. When the boat ran aground on a rock off the west coast of South Korea in the pitch black of a frigid December night, his mother despaired for the lives of her two children. She grabbed her sons' hands and put her rings in their little fingers. "If we get separated, hold onto these rings, and you can buy some food," she told them. With the boat taking on water, the family climbed into the icy water and waded to shore. They made their way down the Korean Peninsula in a column of refugees and found safe haven in Pusan, the southern city at the center of the Pusan Perimeter that was still under allied control in December 1950. After the war, Kim and his family worked their way out of poverty, and he eventually won a scholarship to Williams College in Massachusetts and then earned a doctorate from Harvard.

To us, Ambassador's Kim's story is extraordinary, a true rags-to-riches tale, but in Korea, a country oppressed by the Japanese, torn apart by a civil war, and then wracked by a division of the peninsula that continues to this day, his story is all too commonplace. The Koreans even have a name for the sorrow and sense of loss associated with the country's history. That pervasive sense of melancholy is called "han." It is both a national and individual sentiment.

At a dinner party following the opening ceremony at the Sheraton-Walker Hotel in downtown Seoul, Sally sat next to Ambassador Kim. The first Olympic events were under way across the Han River, and the notes of national anthems drifted over the party. "When I looked at the glorious spectacle of the opening ceremony, I could not imagine that in these short years my country had come to this point," the soft-spoken Korean diplomat told Sally. "My life flashed before me. It was very emotional. I think I could have dealt with it, but then I looked at my wife, and the tears were streaming down her cheeks. I took her hand, and we watched the rest of the performance through the blur of our tears."

The South Korean Olympic team would go on to perform superbly throughout the Games, garnering the fourth most medals of any country, behind the traditional powerhouses of the Soviet Union, East Germany, and the U.S.

There were, however, moments that reminded Americans of the prickly side of our relations with South Korea. When NBC, the American broadcaster of the Olympics, showed extensive footage of a dour-faced Korean boxer holding a sit-down strike in the ring after an unpopular decision, the Korean press railed against American insensitivity. The whole incident reminded me of how vulnerable the Koreans are to anything that might be perceived as making fun of them. The flip side of the coin is their innate decency. When American light-middleweight boxer Roy Jones was cheated out of a gold medal in a match against South Korean Park Si Hun, Korean colleagues in influential positions called me to express their chagrin that Park had been declared the winner against the clearly superior American fighter. An investigation after the Olympics later determined that the group of three judges who scored the match had been bribed.

To be sure, we Americans also had our embarrassing moments. Sally and I were aghast when we watched the American delegation at the opening ceremony stream into Olympic Stadium and across the field in a haphazard and unorganized way. Other delegations kept in line, but the American delegation's uncontrolled exuberance cast a pall over the beautifully choreographed ceremony and the Korean sense of propriety. Ambassador Kim, watching the Americans' behavior, put his head in his hands and groaned.

During the Games, I was awakened in the middle of the night to help get two American swimmers out of a Seoul jail where they had been taken after misbehaving in a restaurant. Earlier that evening, I had come down from the stands to congratulate the swimmers on breaking the world record in the 800-meter relay. In celebration, they had taken a logo off the wall of the restaurant. The Koreans initially wanted me to make an official apology, but they relented and let the swimmers go. Kids will be kids, but it's more embarrassing when they act up in a foreign country.

As always, the Olympics were primarily a celebration of sport. While the American Embassy had to keep vigilant, particularly regarding North Korea, there was a sense that joint U.S.–South Korean security preparations had created a cocoon of safety around the athletes. Sally and I spent enjoyable days watching swimming, equestrian events, basketball, volleyball, and track and field events. I remember American swimmer Matt Biondi winning five gold medals. In the evenings, we would recall what we had seen with the many guests who had come to visit us and see the Olympics.

I found out as well that I wasn't the only high-ranking American diplomat in Northeast Asia with a passion for sports. Both Winston Lord, the American ambassador to China, and Mike Armacost, the

Undersecretary of State for Political Affairs, came to Seoul and saw the Games. Lord was an inveterate sports junkie. After a day of watching events from morning until night, he would return to the embassy compound, flick on the TV, and catch the day's final events and highlights until they went off the air.

Lord and Armacost even found time to get in some sports competition of their own. One day the two diplomats challenged my eldest son Douglas and family friend Scott Simpson, both in their twenties, to a game of two-on-two basketball. Acting like the son of a diplomat, Douglas offered to mix the teams up so that the ambassadors could partner with youth. But Lord would have nothing of it. "We're on the same team," he said, pointing to Armacost. In warm-ups, Armacost unveiled a one-handed set shot that he had honed on the courts at Carleton College in Minnesota, probably at about the time that South Korea was emerging from the Korean War. The first play caught the ambassadors flat-footed. Douglas nodded at Scott, who faked for the ball. When Armacost dutifully followed Scott on the fake, Scott cut behind him in time to catch a pass and lay the ball in the basket. Not surprisingly, youth and agility triumphed over age and diplomatic acumen. There was no rematch.

.   .   .

Winston Lord was on more familiar turf in his capacity as American ambassador in Peking during those years. Working with Lord as my teammate, I was able to help South Korea in its first tentative moves toward rapprochement with Communist China in 1988. The moves were part of Roh Tae Woo's Nordpolitik, his bold foreign policy initiative to establish diplomatic relations with communist countries. Roh's victory in the hotly contested presidential election gave him legitimacy that Chun never had and allowed him to pursue contacts with Eastern European communist countries, the Soviet Union, and China. Ironically, the explosion aboard KAL 858 also helped move forward the rapprochement between South Korea and the East bloc by discrediting North Korea and, thus, downgrading its role in the equation.

Because of my background, Roh would consult with me on China. He called me "his China expert." One day in 1988, he invited me to the

Blue House and showed me his calligraphy. I had heard he was a man of various pursuits, interested in music, poetry, and novels, and his practice of the refined art of calligraphy separated him from South Korea's previous, more hard-edged rulers. He said it soothed his mind. After drawing some characters gracefully, Roh asked me to paint some characters. I was caught off-guard by his request. I was born in China and spoke Chinese, but I had never studied calligraphy. I ended up writing my name in Chinese.

I was on safer ground when he asked me what I thought of Nordpolitik. I told him the initiative made a lot of sense. I believed that the Chinese government, guided by the more practical economic policies of Deng Xiaoping, was ready to open up to South Korea. A Chinese delegation had recently visited the state-of-the-art steel mill of the Pohang Steel Corporation and come away very impressed. "You've made a great impression on the Chinese," I told the South Korean president.

So, when Foreign Minister Choi Kwang Soo called me to see if the U.S. could help arrange a stopover for him in China in August 1988, I got in touch with Winston Lord in Peking. Foreign Minister Choi wanted to fly to Pakistan to attend the state funeral of Pakistani president Mohammad Zia ul-Haq on August 20, 1988. The shortest flight was from Tokyo to Islamabad via Peking. How would the Chinese react, he asked me, if he traveled through their country? After all, the two countries had never had diplomatic relations and had sat on different sides of the Cold War fence for as long as South Korea had existed. The Chinese reaction to Minister Choi's request would be a signal as to the future of relations between the two Asian nations.

Winston Lord cabled back to me that the Chinese Foreign Ministry had agreed to the South Korean request to spend two hours in the Peking airport in transit to Islamabad. When Choi flew to Pakistan via Peking on August 19, he became the highest-ranking South Korean official to be allowed to enter China. Lord personally met Choi at the airport and talked with him for ninety minutes. At the end of their conversation, Choi asked Lord to convey to the Chinese Foreign Ministry his government's hopes for normalization of relations with China. Within a month, the Chinese delegation to the 1988 Olympic Games arrived in Seoul and created a stir with its participation. Winston Lord

was rewarded for his role by Foreign Minister Choi with an invitation
to attend the Olympics.

.   .   .

One day in 1987 in my capacity as ambassador, I traveled to the port
city of Inchon to attend the dedication of a Christian radio station
being opened by the Far Eastern Broadcasting Company. I had known
of the company from our time in the Philippines in the 1950s. For several decades, it had been transmitting religious programming into
China from its base in the Philippines. With the help of generous do-
nations, the company had built a radio station in Korea to beam an
even stronger signal to Christians in the Chinese heartland.

During the dedication of the new facility, I heard the name Paul
Kauffman mentioned as one of the donors. In the 1930s, my family had
known a Paul Kauffman in Tsingtao. Sons of a missionary, he and his
older brother, Donald, had been pals of my older brothers, Frank and
Jack, at the same Christian boarding school in Pyongyang, Korea. I had
not seen Paul Kauffman for more than forty years. And I could still remember the last time clearly. In 1946, just after my family had learned
of Frank's death in Japan, Paul had shown up at my parents' apartment
in New York City without notice and as a young Christian evangelist
extended good feeling and sympathy in our time of need. Although we
had heard virtually nothing from him since he and his family had left
China in 1937, somehow Paul had heard of Frank's demise and tracked
my parents down. It was almost supernatural, this old high school acquaintance of Frank's appearing out of nowhere to pay respects to the
person who had taken an interest in him when no else cared.

You see, Frank had rescued Paul in a way. In 1936, Paul was floun-
dering at the Pyongyang Foreign School. He was notorious for his
slovenly appearance and bad behavior. By February 1936, the school administration and Paul's older brother, Donald, had thrown up their
hands in frustration over the recalcitrant youngster. In early February,
Frank, just a ninth grader himself, offered to take in Paul as a roommate. Perhaps Frank, who was chafing at what he saw as the school's
arbitrary guidelines over who was a good Christian, saw in Paul a fellow outcast, except that Paul was part of what Frank was chafing

against. What puzzled Frank most about Paul was that the boy said some of the longest prayers in the school but didn't change his deplorable behavior. Frank became his surrogate parent. He made sure Paul did his lessons, kept the room clean, and bathed himself. By offering to help Paul when no one else would, Frank saw himself as refuting the Christian belief he had heard at the school that you can't be worthy of salvation without faith. It was vintage Frank, pushing the envelope, believing fervently, and acting on his beliefs.

I approached Paul after the dedication was over. It had been more than half a century since Frank had taken Paul under his wing. "Are you the Paul Kauffman who was in Tsingtao with Frank and Jack Lilley?" I asked him. "Yes," he said, surprised by my question. Paul seemed pleased to see that I was the U.S. ambassador to South Korea. He related how he had gone from being a wayward teenager to a leading Christian activist in Asia. Frank would have been both proud and surprised. Paul had established a Christian outreach mission in Hong Kong and authored a number of books on China. Like other missionary children who had grown up in China, he was always looking for ways to get back. He eventually did return. When I later became ambassador to China, I saw Paul and his older brother, Donald, also a missionary, when they passed through Peking in 1990 on the way to visit their birthplace.

Reminiscences of Frank didn't always come through encounters with people who had known him. In April 1988, I attended the annual celebration of ANZAC day commemorating the Australian and New Zealand soldiers who died fighting as part of the UN forces in the Korean War. With diplomatic representatives of other countries that had fought to repel the North Koreans and Chinese, I traveled to Pusan, where we visited the UN cemetery. Rows of white crosses against a backdrop of Korean hills stretched before our eyes. An Australian then read the immortal words of English poet Laurence Binyon from his poem "For the Fallen":

> *They shall not grow old, as we that are left grow old:*
> *Age shall not weary them, nor the years condemn.*
> *At the going down of the sun and in the morning*
> *We will remember them.*

Visions of General MacArthur landing at Inchon, fighting at the Pusan perimeter, the devastated countryside of Korea, and the tough, stiff North Korean guards at the DMZ flooded my mind. I thought of Frank walking the cold hills of northern Korea in 1935. He had not grown old as I was growing old. I had been left on earth to do what I could in the unending process of change and challenges. In South Korea, one-half of the Korean Peninsula had gone from Japanese colony through civil war to democracy and prosperity, while the other half had locked itself in militancy and stagnation. And the actions of China, the great land power in Asia, were now speaking louder than communist rhetoric. It was opening up to South Korea. Four decades after fighting each other during the Korean War, the two countries established diplomatic relations.

.   .   .

One last incident from South Korea tells us a bit about America's evolving relationship with that country. These days in Seoul, newlywed couples pose for photographs and toddlers play on a patch of land near the Han River. It is called Yongsan Family Park, and it is a touch of green in the middle of downtown Seoul. The park used to be part of the land occupied by the U.S. Army Base in Seoul. In fact, the U.S. Army's golf course was laid out there. In the early period of relations, the army base had been located on the outskirts of Seoul, but with the city's growth the base and its golf course came to occupy prime real estate in the middle of one of the fastest-growing metropolises in Asia. They were visible and high-profile blemishes on the American military presence in Korea. Yet the presence of the golf course was especially galling to Koreans. It was as if the Japanese had built a golf course for their businessmen in New York's Central Park.

Shortly after taking office in 1988, President Roh Tae Woo sought my help in removing major elements of Yongsan Army Base from downtown Seoul. The South Korean president's national security advisor, Kim Jong Hui, visited me that spring. As we sat in a corner room of the residence, Kim laid out Roh's plan.

But as I saw it, Roh's plan was too ambitious, and, at the request of Foreign Minister Choi, I agreed to participate in drawing up a plan that would have a better chance of being accepted by the military establishments of both countries. We boiled the plan down from the removal of all U.S. military facilities at Yongsan to removal of the offending golf course.

I faced a lot of resistance from local U.S. military commanders because the U.S. military saw the golf course as a privilege that came with getting posted to Korea—you could play golf right outside your front door.

Unfortunately, we couldn't get the situation resolved by the time of the Olympics, but by late 1988, the golf course had been moved to a spot forty minutes from Seoul.

The decision to remove Yongsan Golf Course was one of the last major policy issues that I worked on. It reflected the changing reality that was South Korea in 1988: a budding democracy, successful host of the Olympics, and an independent nation in its own right.

In 2004, the contentious issue of American troops in downtown Seoul was finally resolved. In order to blunt criticism from South Korea and in line with a repositioning of U.S. forces around the globe, the U.S. agreed to pull out American troops from Yongsan Army base and station them farther from the DMZ. The move sent a message to China: we are not about to move into North Korea and create a unified Korean government allied to the U.S.

.   .   .

I could look back on the posting in South Korea with pride. In December 1988, Secretary of State George Shultz—no doubt with the help of my old friend Gaston Sigur, who had done so much to support democracy in Korea—wrote me a farewell cable in Seoul. Shultz was leaving his post in the Reagan administration. He zeroed in on a summer day in June 1987.

It is rare that an ambassador can identify one act, or one day, by which he made an historic contribution. You are one of those—at a most critical juncture, in June 1987 as the tragic prospect of martial law loomed over the Republic, your personal intervention with the ROK President undoubtedly made a significant contribution to his decision not to draw the sword. Your role in dissuading him from an act which would have been disastrous for his people and for our relationship can be a source of quiet pride to you and to your nation.

Sally and I returned to Washington for a short stay in January 1989, long enough to see family and for me to get through confirmation hearings for my next and last diplomatic post: U.S. Ambassador to China.

Sally, who usually left things political to me, was prescient in a farewell note to Jeffrey, who left South Korea in September 1988 after spending ten months with us while working at the Olympics as a researcher for NBC. "Change is in the air for you and Dad and me who have shared these past historic months in Korea. Active and varied as they have been, I feel in retrospect it will have been a serene time—in contrast to the unpredictable future into which we three now head."

19

STEPPING ON A VOLCANO

PRESIDENT George Herbert Walker Bush, who defeated Michael Dukakis in the 1988 election, appointed me to be Ambassador to the People's Republic of China shortly after Sally and I returned from Korea. The China position was a great honor, and it was fitting that my former boss in China had appointed me.

Reporting on my appointment as ambassador in March 1989, a Soviet radio commentator remarked that I would have my hands full dealing with the Chinese. I would have to draw on "my rich diplomatic experience," the announcer said, to keep the Sino-U.S. relationship on track. It wasn't a daring pronouncement by the Russian commentator, but it proved true sooner than I could have imagined. I met outgoing ambassador Winston Lord for dinner at the Metropolitan Club in Washington in late April before I left for Peking. As we sat down, a TV showed the latest scenes from Tiananmen Square, where tens of thousands of Chinese students had been rallying for a more open society since the death on April 15 of popular leader Hu Yaobang, the former head of the Communist Party. The Chinese leadership seemed paralyzed by the huge protests against corruption, nepotism, and special privileges for Party officials. In four decades of watching China, I had never seen anything like it—spontaneous, motivated, exuberant, idealistic protesters.

"Is this for real?" I asked Lord, who had recently returned from Peking. "Are these demonstrations really against the government?"

Yes, replied Lord, they are for real.

Truth be told, I was not up to date on China when I met Lord in Washington. The two-year tour in South Korea had kept me focused on the Korea Peninsula. Even when Winston Lord visited us in South Korea in 1988 to see the Olympics, the two of us talked sports, not China. But now China was a lead item on television screens all across the world. "Demos," I wrote to Jeff shortly before leaving for China, "seem to follow me around." Or perhaps I was following them.

.   .   .

Sally and I arrived in Peking on May 2. As a *New York Times* writer aptly put it several weeks later, we "stepped on a volcano." Stirring the pot were not only students' complaints against the government, but also a confluence of important anniversaries. The year 1989 was the 200th anniversary of the French Revolution as well as the fortieth birthday of the People's Republic of China. But it may well have been the marking of another student-led revolt—the seventieth anniversary of the May 4th Movement—that was motivating the protestors the most.

On May 4, dressed in casual clothes, I rode my bike down to Tiananmen Square—meaning Gate of Heavenly Peace—to do a little investigative work of my own. I saw young Chinese marching around the city carrying signs for "Democracy and Science," the main slogan of their predecessors in 1919. As I passed by them, they gave me the "V" sign. I detected no antiforeignism in these demonstrations.

Making sure to keep my identity as the American ambassador secret, I engaged students in conversation, querying them about their hopes and dreams for China. I was struck by their passion and enthusiasm for their causes. They were determined to rid China of corrupt rulers and practices of nepotism in the government. They wanted a better China, but not necessarily a noncommunist China. Above all, in those early weeks, I saw a protest movement, not a call for democracy. The students were not yet asking the Chinese Communist Party to give up power.

The Tiananmen demonstrations kept building in numbers. People from the countryside and other cities poured into Peking to show their support for the grassroots movement. It was both exhilarating and frightening to witness these outpourings from a Chinese populace that had a reputation for being subservient and close-mouthed unless whipped into a frenzy by forces in the government. Soon, the demonstrations would represent a genuine cross section of Chinese society, with workers, intellectuals, civil servants, and journalists joining the students on the square.

Soviet president Mikhail Gorbachev was due to arrive on May 15 for a historic visit that was supposed to cement party-to-party relations. Some people in Washington were alarmed that the visit might signal real progress in Sino-Soviet rapprochement. To take some wind out of the sails of a Sino-Soviet summit and to underscore U.S.–China military cooperation, the White House and Pentagon set up a visit to Shanghai by the U.S. Navy. I was scheduled to make a speech in Shanghai on the U.S. flagship, then accompany Vice Admiral Henry Mauz, the commander of the U.S. 7th Fleet, to Peking for more ceremonies before traveling back to Washington to accompany Wan Li, the chairman of the National People's Congress, on an official visit to the U.S.

The schedule was a full one, and on top of all the planning, I was making introductory calls on Chinese leaders. In a meeting on May 8 with President Yang Shangkun, who was the highest-ranking official in China, I told him that it was a source of pleasure to serve as ambassador to the country where I was born. I used a *cheng yu* that explained I was coming back to my roots (*ye luo gui gen*—a leaf falls and returns to its roots). The Chinese president said he expected further progress in our bilateral relations during the next decade. Deng Xiaoping, whom I did not call on, was, in fact, the most powerful person in China in his role as chairman of the Central Military Commission.

My meeting with Premier Li Peng, who ranked under Yang as head of the government, was less cordial. I had gotten to know Li when he came to the U.S. in 1985 in part to search for American partners in The Three Gorges Dam project. He had a prickly personality and came across as a man influenced by his Soviet training and steeped in the jargon of his Soviet mentors. I remember him in Los Angeles talking about the need for central planning and the importance of ideologically sound workers. He even used the Soviet term "Stakhanovite"—harking back to the hero shock worker of the Soviet Union's drive in the 1930s to increase industrial production through ideological fervor and effort—to drive his point home.

During our meeting in Peking, I did not speak directly with Li about the growing protests in central Peking, though he knew full well that we had been giving the Chinese the message through government channels not to use force. But in a not so oblique reference to the students gathered on Tiananmen, I paraphrased the author John Hersey in his book about how Yale University had responded to student demonstrations there in the 1960s. I said that at the time Yale president Kingman Brewster had said, "If you lose your youth, no amount of crisis management will make much difference in the long run." This allusion was not lost on Premier Li. He shot back, "No government in the world would tolerate this kind of disorder in the middle of its capital city." He was stating his case as a law-and-order man.

What wasn't as apparent at the time I was meeting the Chinese leaders was that the students' tactics were causing a deep fissure in the leadership ranks of the Chinese Communist Party (CCP). The General Secretary of the CCP, Zhao Ziyang, sympathized with the students' demands for accelerating reform. While Zhao maintained the primacy of the Communist Party's place in governing society, he believed the Party had to change. At a Politburo Standing Committee meeting on May 1, he said: "Times have changed, and so have people's ideological views. Democracy is a worldwide trend, and there is an international countercurrent against communism and socialism that flies under the banner of democracy and human rights. If the party doesn't hold up the banner of democracy in our country, then someone else will, and we will lose out." Zhao insisted in front of his colleagues that "the student slogans that uphold the Constitution, promote democracy, and oppose corruption all echo positions of the Party and the government."

Opposing Zhao was Premier Li Peng, who feared that the government was losing its grip on the situation and starting to panic. In response to Zhao, Li said: "Some socialist countries launch political reforms only when conflicts in society are severe and the Party is crippled. This makes control of the process nearly impossible. So our first order of business should be stability. Once that is achieved, we can talk about reforming the political system."

.   .   .

Ironically, while the Chinese leaders had their hands full with protesting students, those same students were disrupting both American and Russian plans. President Gorbachev's state visit was the first casualty. Though it had been billed by some diplomats as a first step toward Sino-Soviet rapprochement, Gorbachev's first visit to the Middle Kingdom was doomed from the start. By the time he arrived on May 15, close to half a million people filled Tiananmen Square. Protesters had set up tent villages on the square, so a grand welcoming ceremony, complete with an honor guard and twenty-one-gun salute, had to be moved from there to the airport. The students held their own welcoming placards for the Soviet leader, whose policies of "perestroika" and "glasnost" to reform the Soviet Union were music to their ears. "We Salute The Ambassador Of Democracy" read one poster, while another crowed: "In The Soviet Union They Have Gorbachev, But What Do We Have in China?"

Events throughout his visit were marginalized by the demonstrations, as was Gorbachev's final press conference on May 17. McKinney Russell, the chief of the American Embassy's press and cultural affairs office, was set to attend Gorbachev's farewell press conference at 5:30 P.M. in a ballroom in the Great Hall of the People. But the area around Tiananmen Square was choked with surging crowds. Buses filled with students from the provinces and flatbed trucks draped with banners and jammed with workers, journalists, and even Communist Party functionaries clogged Peking's main roads. After being forced to ditch their bikes halfway to the square, Russell and a colleague walked the rest of the way to the Great Hall of the People. There, after waiting twenty minutes for the press conference to start, journalists were told by a sweaty Soviet counselor that the venue had been changed to the Diaoyutai guesthouse where Gorbachev was staying because his motorcade couldn't get through the masses of protesters. The visit of Gorbachev, the so-called champion of reform from the top down in the Soviet Union, had been rendered meaningless by Chinese people power from the bottom up.

That same evening, members of the Standing Committee of the Politburo voted to impose martial law in Peking. Communist Party boss Zhao Ziyang and propaganda chief Hu Qili voted against the proposal, but they lost out to Premier Li Peng, planning czar Yao Yilin, and a vacillating Qiao Shi, the security chief. The overwhelming senti-ment among the elders on the Standing Committee was for the gov-ernment to get tough with the protestors. "Our backs are to the wall," noted President Yang Shangkun, a close comrade of paramount Chi-nese leader Deng Xiaoping. "If we retreat any further we're done for." Zhao Ziyang continued to disagree and tried to resign as general secre-tary that evening.

Deng, still China's leading authority even though he had retired from his Party posts in 1987, had effectively cast the deciding vote on the side of restoring order on the morning of May 17. "If our one billion people jumped into multiparty elections, we'd get chaos like the 'all-out civil war' we saw during the Cultural Revolution. You don't have to have guns and cannon to have a civil war; fists and clubs will do just fine. Democracy is our goal, but we'll never get there without national stability." On the morning of May 18, the eight elders, a group of party veterans who took part in crucial decisions during the April to June period, met with other high-ranking Chinese and formally declared martial law in Peking.

On May 19 in Shanghai, our joint Chinese–American motorcade struggled through hordes of students marching along the waterfront in solidarity with Peking's demonstrators. We were on our way to a wel-coming ceremony for the visiting American naval ships, which had sailed up the Huangpu River to the famous Shanghai waterfront, or Bund. Friendly Chinese waved at my car with its American flag. Along with a large cast of Chinese leaders, I met Vice Admiral Mauz on the flagship of the U.S. 7th Fleet, the USS *Blue Ridge*. I had originally been enthusiastic about the visit, in part because of its strategic implications and in part—I have to say—because it represented a continuation of my association with growing U.S.–PRC naval ties from childhood through my professional career. As a young boy, I had traveled on a U.S. Navy gunboat going down the Yangtze River on my way to board-ing school in Shanghai in 1940. While working at the State Depart-ment in 1986, I helped arrange the first port visit since 1949 by U.S. Navy ships to a Chinese port. Those ships had docked in Tsingtao, my birthplace.

But the emotions of being in Shanghai and the larger geostrategic implications of the ship docking seemed much less significant in the face of the demonstrations. Back in Peking I had sensed that the tide of popular sentiment building in the cities would eclipse the ship visit, particularly in the eyes of the international media. I knew Western TV crews angling for a story about the gathering protests could quickly turn their cameras away from the ships to the students. I tried to communicate this to Foreign Minister Qian Qichen when I met with him before going to Shanghai. "If things go wrong," I had warned him, "the Western media will go after you like a mad dog." He just smiled.

For my welcoming speech on the flagship I said the pro forma words about growing U.S.–China military ties. Meanwhile, a largely spontaneous uprising was under way across the water. In the midst of waving banners and military pomp and circumstance, I remember thinking to myself, "Here we are making nice speeches on the ship, but there is something wrong in the equation." It was even more evident by that time that neither Gorbachev, nor our ship visit, nor platitudes about U.S.–Chinese military cooperation were going to diminish or divert attention from the student demonstrations. Nor should they have. They were growing, and they were the story. My thoughts were echoed in a cable I sent to the State Department on May 21. "What is happening here in opposition to the authorities has a permanence about it. It is not going to go away," I wrote. Two months later in mid-July, I cabled back to Washington that we had not been "coping with or anticipating current realities" by going through with the ship visit when demonstrations were going on. "Our attitude," I stated in the cable to the State Department, "was a throwback to the early days of our relationship when common Soviet bashing was in vogue."

Back on shore in Shanghai, I telephoned the State Department to tell them I was not going to leave China with Wan Li at a time when the country's major cities were in turmoil. Over the Department's strong objections, I said, "It looks ugly, and I am going back to Peking." Then along with others I recommended to Admiral Mauz that he forego his visit to Peking. The best thing would be to get the American ships and sailors out of Shanghai as soon as possible. To get back to Peking as soon as possible, I took Sally's ticket, leaving her in the care of a consulate official to get to Peking on the soonest flight they could book.

As Sally and I were preparing to leave for a dinner the evening of May 19, I turned on the TV in our hotel room. We listened as CBS news anchorman Dan Rather announced from Peking that the CBS broadcast had been ordered to go off the air in ten minutes. At the airport the next day, I saw Premier Li Peng himself on TV making the declaration of martial law. It was both chilling and absurd. Right after Li's declaration, the song "Paper Moon" came across the airwaves. No doubt the TV station had pro-democracy sympathizers manning the controls. It was a jab at the increasingly unpopular premier because the song implied a phony and make-believe arrangement.

.   .   .

By now the heavyweights of the American press—NBC, ABC, CBS, as well as fledgling CNN—were devoting expanded resources to cover the growing demonstrations. With the world's attention focused on them, the Chinese students became more emboldened in their tactics. On May 13, 1,000 students had embarked on a hunger strike around the Martyr's Monument on Tiananmen Square. Student leaders like Wuer Kaixi, Chai Ling, Wang Dan, and Li Lu were becoming folk heroes among Western viewers. On May 18, to the amazement of Chinese who watched on TV, Wuer Kaixi, one of the leaders of the hunger strike, upbraided Premier Li Peng for being late to their meeting in the Great Hall of the People. Wuer was even dressed disrespectfully in pajamas. Not only were the young student leaders willing to voice their grievances, but many of them were also putting their lives on the line by engaging in a hunger strike. It was high idealism coupled with erratic and undisciplined tactics. Propelled by the combination, the student movement was gaining adherents among the general populace. People continued to stream into Peking from outlying cities and provinces.

Meanwhile, in the upper echelons of power, there was disorganization and acrimony over how to respond to the demonstrators. Paramount leader Deng Xiaoping was apparently furious at Chinese Communist Party chief Zhao for airing party secrets when he told Gorbachev during a meeting on May 16 that, despite reports to the contrary, Deng still continued to wield power from behind the scenes. In my opinion, that was Zhao Ziyang's deathknell. The fact that he was also allied with the reformist leaders of the Communist Party didn't help either. These reformers were in touch with the demonstrators and were advocating a softer line within the government. They were pushing the government to rescind a tough April 26 editorial in which it had branded the demonstrators as counterrevolutionary troublemakers inciting turmoil. They also wanted greater press freedom as well as recognition of independent student associations. In return, the reformers would convince the students to leave the square peacefully. The terms were rejected by both the old guard and the student leaders.

Like millions of Chinese and viewers around the world, we were informed by what we saw on TV. And that spoke volumes. On the night of May 19, Zhao showed up on the square. With tears in his eyes, Zhao was broadcast on television apologizing to hunger-striking students that "We have come too late." With current premier Wen Jiabao standing near him, he urged the young students to end their fast and look to the future. That night the students ended their fast. Behind Zhao on the square was Li Peng, somber and silent. His sidekick Luo Gan stood by his side. According to accounts of the time, Li followed Zhao at the last minute in an effort to offset any political advantage the reform-minded leader might gain from appearing publicly at Tiananmen. It was remarkable footage—the drama of the inner party struggles being played out on TV in front of millions of viewers. Zhao Ziyang was the loser. He was dismissed by the Party elders on May 21 and then placed under de facto house arrest, where he remains today.

The imposition of martial law did not do much to quell the demonstrators. In fact, the heavy hand of martial law fell so lightly and uncertainly on Peking that expatriates were wryly calling it "partial martial." Few troops were in evidence, and when they were around, they were hopelessly outnumbered. Crowds held convoys of soldiers on the outskirts of Peking at bay on May 20 and 21. The traffic on Peking's main thoroughfare, Chang'an Boulevard, was still being conducted by student volunteers, and despite prohibitions against demonstrations, there were impromptu speeches on street corners and even a bike parade on May 21. As for foreigners, we were told to stay in our compounds and not go downtown, but it was hard to corral curiosity, and the authorities weren't preventing people from moving around.

.   .   .

Shortly after arriving in Peking, I had made a quick survey of the embassy staff. I hadn't worked with many of the principal players before, but I was impressed with the caliber of people. We had excellent Chinese-language capability among the economic, military, and political sections of the embassy. In addition, over the past fifteen years of relations with China, our diplomatic staff in Peking had established reliable contacts with people in the military, the student movement, and the intellectual class. These two attributes—Chinese-language capability and contacts on the ground in Peking—would pay dividends in the coming months.

As the standoff between the demonstrators and government continued, we augmented the monitoring measures we had already taken. Since April, our defense attaché's office had been working closely with its counterparts in the Australian, British, Canadian, French, German, and Japanese Embassies to keep tabs on events in Peking. They divided the city into sectors and shared information obtained from patrols. At the end of May, in response to the attenuated crisis, the defense attachés of the different embassies set up full-time listening posts at designated spots around the city. In a farsighted move, General Jack Leide, the defense attaché at the U.S. Embassy, lobbied for and got permission to rent hotel rooms for the U.S. monitors. In addition to a room at the Fuxingmen Hotel on the west approach to the square, we booked two corner rooms at the Peking Hotel, just northeast of Tiananmen Square, that provided a clear line of sight to the square. Leide also equipped his men with walkie-talkies smuggled in from abroad. It was a violation of diplomatic protocol because diplomatic missions are prohibited from maintaining their own private radio communications inside China, but it was a violation I felt comfortable making.

With so many situation reports being filed back to the U.S., our political section opened a 24-hour phone line to the State Department. This line allowed us to get up-to-date reports immediately to Washington from Peking and our four consulates in Shenyang, Shanghai, Guangzhou, and Chengdu. Because of timely communication from

Shenyang, for example, we knew that Chinese troops were moving south toward the capital. Crack Foreign Service officers on the ground in Shanghai delivered excellent reports on how the Shanghai municipal government headed by Zhu Rongji and local party headed by Jiang Zemin were handling the protesters with more success.

As ambassador, responsible for all of those at the embassy, and concerned about other Americans in the city, I also had to prepare for the worst: a siege in which Americans might be harmed or trapped inside the compound. Our medical office put a disaster plan into action, making sure there were first-aid supplies at the three embassy buildings and compiling the necessary information on blood type and potential donors for blood transfusions. Families started to stockpile food, and we made sure there was enough peanut butter and candy at the embassy to keep people energized.

Already most of us were working twelve to fifteen hours a day in an attempt to keep abreast of the fast-changing situation. But the demands kept growing. For example, when martial law was declared, we made sure that embassy staffers called Americans in Peking who had registered at the embassy. Their message to the American residents and visitors was to sit tight and avoid Tiananmen Square for the present time. Unfortunately, we couldn't tell them anything more specific. We also reduced our files. My secretary, Kathy Gaseor, took several boxes of embassy files for safekeeping to Hong Kong in late May.

The previous months had already been hectic for Gaseor and most of the embassy employees. President Bush had visited Peking in February. Then an inspection team came to evaluate embassy operations in May. With annual efficiency reports on almost everyone in the mission coming due, embassy staffers had been working long hours since the start of the year. Already fatigued by the grueling schedule of the preceding months, American diplomats were now living in a capital city that appeared to be trying to break away from the control of Central Communist authorities. We were working the staff to its limits.

Sentiment among American diplomats was with the students. Their youthful enthusiasm, not to mention their clear favoritism toward America, earned them many supporters at the U.S. Embassy. "The movement has been non-violent, but passionate," I wrote back to the

State Department in a cable on May 21. "All signs indicate this is a popular uprising supporting basic principles of democracy." Chinese nationals working at the embassy were going down to the square to show solidarity with the students. Some Chinese employees would arrive for work only to linger around aimlessly before announcing, "My place is not here. I have to go down to the square." Chinese workers cooperated with Chinese nationals working at other embassies to organize a march. But among the American embassy staff, along with affinity for the Chinese people came apprehension that the Chinese government would suppress the democracy movement violently. "We lived a roller coaster," recalled Gaseor of the last weeks of May. "Would the police and military crack down? When would it happen?"

．　　．　　．

On May 26, after about three weeks of watching the dangerous dance of the students on the square with their paralyzed government, I put pen to paper or, rather, I dictated to Kathy Gaseor my thoughts on the coming crackdown. From the point of view of the Chinese government, the whole debacle had dragged on because, as I liked to put it, the "old men couldn't make up their minds." But I sensed that Deng was still in charge and that he was gathering the allies necessary to reassert control. On May 21, I had sent a cable in which I said that "[a] confrontation resulting in bloodshed is probable." But in the five days between the May 21 and May 26 cables, what looked "probable" turned to "imminent" in my reading of the situation.

During those days, plainclothes police sent to monitor the square had been accosted by residents of Peking and prevented from advancing. The repulsion of the police was the latest in a series of humiliations suffered by the Chinese authorities in their attempts to restore order. Critical editorials decrying the student movement hadn't dissuaded the demonstrators or their supporters. Meetings between government officials and student leaders only highlighted the arrogant and difficult stances of leaders like Li Peng. Both plainclothes police and unarmed troops had been subsumed by masses of people in the streets before they could even get close to the square. The appearance of armed soldiers only made the crowds more determined to convince them of their wrongdoing in moving against the people. Half-measures hadn't worked. Neither had shows of minimum force. The government had run out of options short of a military assault, I reasoned.

In my analysis, I also took account of China's history of defending "the revolution" at all costs. To a China-watcher, the capacity of the system—meaning the Communist Party—to damage the country and its people was not unfamiliar. Hundreds of thousands of people had been violently purged, killed, or driven to suicide during the Cultural Revolution, little more than a decade earlier. The attitude of the Communist leadership had long been that it would have to inflict casualties to accomplish important political objectives. I thought it especially significant that by the end of May the government-controlled press constantly referred to the demonstrators as "counterrevolutionaries." There was a specific provision in the Chinese constitution stipulating that counterrevolutionary behavior was criminal and had to be stamped out. This would give the government a semilegal basis for suppression.

Finally, there was the personality of the man in charge, Deng Xiaoping. I had studied the Chinese leader both up close and from afar for almost three decades. Though he was the father of China's economic liberalization, he was a dyed-in-the-wool communist, committed to using force to restore order. Deng had lived through the insanity of the Cultural Revolution when he had been purged. His biggest fear, as well as the biggest fear of his elderly comrades-in-arms, was chaos. In my cable, I wrote that Deng resembled an Old Testament character. Revenge was in his nature. He was being personally humiliated by the student demonstrations and the government's inability to quell it, and he would not stand for it. As for the negative repercussion in the West of a crackdown, I remember somebody quoting Deng as saying, "You carry these things out, and the Westerners forget." There would be no happy ending to the Tiananmen affair. There was going to be bloodshed, and we believed this would happen in the next couple of days. In my personal tale of two cities, Seoul and Peking, South Korea in 1987 would be no model for the Chinese.

I had a sense that the White House perceived Deng as basically a leader who sought reform and opening up and would avoid harming U.S.–China relations. Perhaps that is simplistic, but I had the feeling during the week after martial law was declared that high-level people in Washington were under the delusion that the standoff between the students and government would have a peaceful outcome. My cable resonated little in Washington, and I learned later that it never made it to the president's desk. It remained in State and with lower-level members of the National Security Council staff.

As for the role of the U.S. government in dissuading China from cracking down, I had little hope. Unlike the situation in Seoul two years earlier, we had little influence on internal decision making in China. Yes, George Bush had a personal relationship with Deng Xiaoping that stretched back fifteen years, but even then the relationship was not one in which he could send a letter to the China's de facto leader and expect results, as President Reagan had done in South Korea. Another alternative—going through the Chinese bureaucracy—was not efficacious either because information was probably doctored for the top Chinese leadership. This was one of Zhao Ziyang's chief complaints—that Deng was not getting a true sense of the democratic nature of the student movement from the reports he was reading. In the end, as history has shown, you tend to get better results when you use high-level emissaries and present to the Chinese clear choices. I sometimes think that there was a point after May 26 when we might have been able to use former President Nixon, Henry Kissinger, or even a high-level presidential envoy to convey to Deng or his longtime comrade Yang Shangkun that we care deeply and that there would be serious repercussions from a crackdown. But it probably wouldn't have worked. The Chinese leadership had by then isolated itself to such an extent that we had to use the Foreign Ministry in Peking or the diplomatic channel to the Chinese ambassador in Washington to get messages through.

The best we could do was to stay apprised of the latest developments and report them back. Fortunately, we had good contacts in Peking. On May 24, one of those contacts confirmed to an embassy staffer that Zhao had lost out. We learned that the general secretary had intended to carry out an anticorruption campaign and that he was prepared to start with an investigation of his own two sons, who had reportedly profited in business from their contacts in government.

Zhao's determination turned well-placed children of top Chinese leaders against him. During the revealing conversation, our contact got a phone call telling him to stop talking.

· · ·

Residents of Peking awoke to an extraordinary sight on Saturday, June 3. Thousands of PLA soldiers, bedraggled, befuddled, and some even weeping, were wandering through the city in a disorganized retreat from the city center. During the early morning in parts of the city, Peking residents and demonstrators had swarmed around buses carrying troops. After halting the troops' progress, they proceeded to berate the soldiers verbally. At one location, elderly women were seen scolding shame-faced soldiers, who stared at the ground. Embassy press chief McKinney Russell witnessed the people of Peking repel a column of 5,000 unarmed soldiers who had been ordered in at a "reluctant" jog to "co-occupy" the square. They looked more like a children's crusade than a military strategy. Near the square, several thousand citizens at the intersection of Chang'an Boulevard and Xidan Avenue surrounded a bus of about forty soldiers. On top of the bus, students and other citizens took turns posing for photos holding a rifle and wearing a helmet taken from the soldiers. People cried, "We have to protect Peking." The vaunted People's Liberation Army seemed to wilt in the face of people power. Jack Leide called the PLA's fiasco "a Chinese version of Napoleon's retreat from Moscow."

If U.S. diplomats weren't out on the streets witnessing such extraordinary events firsthand, they could probably see them from their balconies, at least those who lived in the main diplomatic compound at Jianguomenwai about a mile and a half east of Tiananmen. For a good part of May and into June, diplomats would return from work and watch the drama being played out below them in the streets that led to Tiananmen Square. They would invite friends over, make drinks, and observe the street scenes, transfixed by the spectacle of Chinese people standing up to their government. Pictures snapped and video cameras rolled to record history in the making. It was an exciting atmosphere, and as one embassy staffer said, it was a time when "the unusual takes on normalcy."

But by early June, normalcy had given way to serious jitters. I had already upgraded the likelihood of a crackdown from "probable" to "imminent." People on the street had ominous feelings about an impending crackdown as well. When Kathy Gaseor returned on June 2 from a few days in Hong Kong, the cab driver who picked her up at the airport told her excitedly of the new statue that had been erected on Tiananmen Square. Built by students at Peking's Art Academy, the statue took after the Statue of Liberty and had been named the Goddess of Democracy. "Do you want me to take you to see it?" the cab driver asked Gaseor. Tired from her trip, she politely declined. "Perhaps, I will go see it tomorrow," she said. The cabby turned to her. "Tomorrow, it won't be there," he said cryptically.

On June 3, I went with a group of embassy people to bowl at the Diaoyutai guesthouse at the invitation of Sinochem, one of China's largest trading companies. The head of Sinochem had invited us for an evening of relaxation and, I believe, to give us a sense that things were normalizing. I agreed to go because I wanted to stick to as normal a schedule as possible despite the abnormal circumstances in Peking. The excursion also gave me cover for openly traversing the city in the area of Tiananmen. Coming back through town in the early evening, we saw the demonstrations building up in number. Earlier that afternoon police had battled crowds with tear gas near the square. There were other altercations around the Great Hall of the People between workers and unarmed troops, and near the Minzu Hotel on the western approach to the square, an irate crowd had destroyed ten military vehicles. The atmosphere was palpably tense. I returned to the embassy and didn't leave for the next twelve hours.

.   .   .

Assistant Army Attaché Larry Wortzel struck me as a man of action from the moment I met him. A stocky and gregarious former infantry officer, Major Wortzel had excellent Chinese and was always on the prowl. He avoided sitting in his office. Upon Wortzel's arrival in Peking in 1988, his boss Jack Leide asked him about his goals for his tour. Wortzel replied that he wanted to find a group of Chinese military officers to exercise with and then drink beers with afterward. He then planned to work his network of contacts for any information he could get. "General," Wortzel told Leide, "you will probably see me, I hope, about an hour a day in the office."

On June 2, Wortzel and another assistant military attaché, Bill Mc-Givven, were investigating the northwestern suburbs of Peking. They had gotten word that a convoy of troops had been halted by civilians. Sure enough, they found an entire PLA radio battalion, with radio logs lying open and frequencies turned on, stopped on the train tracks twenty miles from Peking. The two American military officers ran up and down the length of the train shooting pictures with impunity. The PLA soldiers were too busy arguing with townspeople to notice the eavesdropping Americans. But the Americans pushed their luck and were hauled to the front of the train to see the battalion commander. The commander berated them for stealing military secrets. Wortzel and McGivven flashed their diplomatic cards but to no avail. Wortzel was expecting the townspeople to step in to save them. Instead, he got a surprising lesson in the limits of anti-government action. "You cannot be here," townspeople told the two American military attachés. "We will stop the train, but you cannot violate the national security of China." It was a telling moment and highlighted how Chinese civilians, whether they were hunger-striking on Tiananmen Square or stopping military trains on the outskirts of Peking, considered themselves patriots who, however much they might have resented the current government, strongly identified with their motherland and would defend its interests against foreign intrusion.

About forty miles outside of Peking on the following night, Wortzel and McGivven were settling in for a night of troop watching after scouting out the situation around Peking's military airport, Nanyuan Airfield. They had been coming to Nanyuan for the past couple of nights to observe troop movements in their sector, the southeast quadrant of Peking. The two assistant military attachés had watched while planes landed, troops unloaded, and armored vehicles were assembled. The night of June 3, they took a room in a small hotel in the town bordering the airfield. By the time they checked into their room, tanks, armored personnel carriers, and trucks were lined up with their motors running in a convoy on the main road into Peking. Facing the military convoy, townspeople had assembled a barricade of trucks, tractors, and buses. Wortzel and McGivven sat poised in their room, ready to call the embassy when the command was given for the convoy to move forward.

In the heart of Peking on Tiananmen Square at about 9 P.M. on June 3, Jim Huskey, an unusually adventurous embassy officer who had been pulled out of the consular section to help us with information gathering, sensed an air of relief among the people occupying the square. Despite ominous messages over the loudspeakers that Peking residents should stay off the streets and away from the square, the protesters were feeling secure. The troops had not come in sufficient numbers to do any harm, and they had been turned back with minor scuffling. In front of the History Museum on the east side of Tiananmen Square, student leaders Wang Dan, Chai Ling, and Wuer Kaixi buoyed the spirits of a gathering of 5,000 to 10,000 people with emotional and inflammatory speeches. The mood was optimistic—they believed that they would get through another night as they had gotten through other nights before.

Jim Huskey was another extraordinary member of our staff, a diplomat who had joined the Foreign Service at the late age of 39 after getting a Ph.D. in Asian Studies and studying Chinese intensively. Fortune smiled on him when he drew Peking as his first post. He had traveled all over Asia as a merchant seaman and penniless student, but had never lived in China. While most Foreign Service officers on their first tour bemoan their mandatory visa-stamping work in the consular section, Huskey had attacked his job with vigor since arriving in Peking in 1987.

Equipped with excellent Chinese-language skills, Huskey started to keep a file on the children of high-ranking Chinese officials who came to the consular section to inquire about visas for America. Huskey would spot a familiar last name or recognize a particular government ministry or institution on the back of the visa application and note the information. After making the connection, he might say to the candidate, "Please give your father my regards. I read his article in the paper recently." If the candidate had a strong academic record, Huskey would process the visa application. More often than not, he would end up getting an appreciative phone call from the father and an invitation to dinner. In this manner, he collected valuable information on influential Chinese with whom we might otherwise never have had contact. Huskey's junior-level position and seemingly innocuous consular work allowed him not only to open but also to walk through doors that were shut tight for other embassy officers. In the aftermath of Tiananmen, Huskey's list of sons and daughters of high-ranking cadre who went to the U.S. to study came in very handy.

Huskey had become a regular on the square in the preceding weeks. Along with political officer Don Yamamoto, Huskey had been drawing the 12 P.M. to 6 A.M. shift. The two men would meander among the crowds and usually end up among a clump of trees in the northwest corner of the square where they would watch the sun come up.

But on June 3, with Yamamoto having left for annual leave, Huskey was alone. After dropping off his wife at their apartment following a quiet dinner at the Palace Hotel, Huskey returned to the square via the main thoroughfare in front of the Jianguomenwai diplomatic compound. The street was packed with thousands of people milling around. Huskey's gray Honda was the only car visible on the wide road. As had become the custom, he showed the victory sign with his left hand as he drove slowly down the road. It was the sign of support and nonviolence that had been adopted by the movement. The mass of people parted, and Huskey drove straight through, accompanied by cheers from onlookers. He parked his battered 1974 Honda near the Great Hall of the People.

.　　.　　.

By purging Zhao Ziyang, Deng Xiaoping overcame a main obstacle to using force against the demonstrators. He then shored up support of the military in the last days of May and early days of June. The preceding weeks of chaos and confusion had weighed on China's paramount leader. There were rumors that he had had a heart attack and had been hospitalized. But I believed that, seething over the inability of his military to quell the anti-government movement and the personal humiliation at seeing his capital city overrun by demonstrators, he withdrew to work behind the scenes. In the evening of June 3, we had information that Deng, through Yang Shangkun, gave the final command. "End it," he said. "Hit!" Deng did not order a massacre. He wanted a minimum of bloodshed, if possible, and he cleared what he did with the eight elders. But quelling the effort came first in his thinking, and once the order was given to move, the officers and soldiers acted violently.

We sent off a cable to Washington: "We are witnessing a massive military movement into central Peking. The troops are armed unlike the troops that moved into the city early this morning. We have citizens resisting the entry of these armed troops into Peking. We have American television crews filming directly on Tiananmen Square in violation of martial law provisions. We have our own officers out observing. Many Americans and American residents are wandering around oblivious to what is happening or the potential dangers involved." It was a recipe for disaster if you were the American ambassador with a stake in protecting American lives and preserving the U.S.–China relationship.

Meanwhile, near Nanyuan Airfield, Wortzel and McGivven were taking turns pulling two-hour shifts observing the armored column when they heard the motorcade rev its engines. Wortzel knew that meant trouble because the army would have to break through the barricades put up by the townspeople. As the engines were cranking, McGivven suddenly doubled over from pain in his abdominal area. Wortzel was at a loss what to do. It was the beginning of the assault, and his partner looked as if he were going to die. With McGivven moaning in the background, Wortzel called the embassy doctor, who instructed him to bring McGivven into the embassy as soon as possible. As far as Wortzel was concerned, judging from McGivven's cries of pain, he had no other choice. He loaded McGivven into the front seat of the embassy-issue white Plymouth Fury they were driving and turned onto the only road back into town—the same road that the PLA was getting ready to blast its way through on its way to Tiananmen Square.

Wortzel pulled the Plymouth Fury into the middle of the armored PLA column that had begun to crunch its way into Peking. The tanks crashed through the jerry-built barricades, and PLA soldiers opened fire all around. When there was a pause in the onslaught, Chinese officers would turn toward the alien white car in their column and scream, "You have to get out of here!" Wortzel pointed at McGivven, buckled over in the front seat, and screamed back, "I am going to the hospital!" The incongruous back and forth between the assistant American army attaché and PLA officers continued for twenty minutes as the column made its way to Peking, shooting and smashing through anything in its sight. Finally, Wortzel reached the turnoff for the embassy and sped to the medical unit. McGivven was diagnosed with kidney stones and evacuated on the next plane out.

Down at Tiananmen Square at about 11:30 P.M., Jim Huskey heard what sounded like firecrackers going off to the west of the square. He found a phone and dutifully called back to the embassy. I picked up Huskey's call in the political affairs section on the second floor, our command post during the crisis. From a defense attaché's post on Fuxingmenwai Boulevard we had received reports that an armed PLA column was moving toward the square. I instructed Huskey to clear as many Americans as he could from the square and then to get out himself. Huskey told several foreigners to evacuate the area and then heard a big boom. When he turned around, he saw an orange glow in the sky above Chang'an Boulevard, the main avenue feeding into Tiananmen from the west. It was the afterglow of a battle being waged on the streets below. Like a wave rushing the beach, masses of Chinese on the square moved toward the glow. Huskey tucked himself into the crowds of people, pulled forward by his duty to keep Americans out of harm's way and by a powerful sense that a historic event was unfolding.

Jim Huskey fulfilled dual roles in his reporting that night. He was both a diplomat and a historian as the Chinese Army moved in to crush the spontaneous flowering of a freedom movement. "I know the history of Chinese student movements, and I realized I was watching another one of these events," he recalled later. "I realized this was a student movement being massacred, and I had to be there. But, secondly, I am an American Foreign Service officer, and I thought we should have people seeing this—to count bodies and get some sense of what was happening."

The Chinese around Huskey at the northwest corner of the square didn't believe that the troops were firing live rounds. People ran toward

the firing in an attempt to stop the columns of soldiers just as they had
done on previous nights. Then a screeching noise caught Huskey's attention. He turned around to see a lone armored personnel carrier ca-
reening through the masses of demonstrators from the east, paying no
mind to the human beings in front of it. People scattered to make way
for the reckless APC. Then stones and rocks and sticks came in waves
from bystanders and lodged in the APC's treads. The army vehicle
ground to a halt at the main intersection in front of the Great Hall of
the People. Stranded on the asphalt pavement and unable to move, the
APC sat by itself, like a hapless fish marooned on the beach. The
crowd seemed stunned by its own power to halt the APC and, silent
for a moment, appeared to pause to gather its collective will. Then,
spontaneously, a hail of wood rained down. Chairs were smashed,
branches broken off, and the pieces thrown to create a circle of kin-
dling around the beached army vehicle. Then someone ignited the
bonfire.

A CNN cameraman standing next to Huskey caught the crowd's actions. The gruesome scenes that followed were broadcast around the
world. The grainy images caught a PLA soldier jumping from the back
of the APC, no doubt to escape burning alive inside. Enraged,
whipped into a frenzy, the crowd in front of Huskey set upon the soldier and pummeled him to death.

.   .   .

At the embassy, we kept track of unfolding events via access to ABC
TV's internal radio communications, CNN broadcasts, and reports
from embassy officers. From about midnight onward, huddled around
a walkie-talkie that carried the internal communications of ABC TV's
on-the-ground crew, a group of us listened to the Chinese army launch
its assault from the west. This unusual access was a perk that McKinney Russell had rustled up by forging close ties with the U.S. press
corps in the lead-up to the crackdown. You could say it was ABC's
thank you for the embassy press conferences Russell organized starting
in late May that gave our view of events. We heard the chaos and gunfire that erupted when live fire slammed into the heart of what had
been a peaceful protest.

At the same time, we had CNN on in the snack bar. CNN's coverage of the crackdown was first-rate, and its capacity to deliver instantaneous news during the events at Tiananmen Square set the standard for TV crisis reporting. CNN's Peking bureau chief Mike Chinoy and his staff worked nonstop to deliver images that not only informed policymakers in Washington, but also came back to us in the embassy and supplemented our information. Western TV cameras may have missed Budapest in 1956 and Prague in 1968, but in 1989 CNN led a pack of broadcasters who, as far as I know, for the first time televised in depth a military crackdown on a popular uprising in a communist country.

For its part, the Chinese leadership was woefully unprepared to cope with the impact of such coverage. The government was in such disarray that it couldn't exert effective control over Western broadcasts. There were too many ways for enterprising journalists to get the story out— via phone, fax, satellite feeds, and courier service. A country that badgered America for interfering in its internal affairs inadvertently gave the major U.S. networks box seats while it aired its dirty laundry. The elderly Chinese leadership simply foundered in the face of the Western media and its ability to literally spread the news.

Reports from the embassy's outposts around Peking comprised the third source of information. Jim Huskey's reports, called in from street phones or from the Peking Hotel, filled many of our cables going back to Washington. Throughout the night of June 3, we also got timely updates from our four consulates on events in other cities in China.

·   ·   ·

Around midnight, Huskey found himself looking down Chang'an Boulevard to the west. He saw smoke rising and tanks going over the barricades. In a grim drama that would replay itself several times before the night was over, people ran toward the gunfire as it got louder and louder. It was as if they believed they could face down the guns and tanks with their willpower. Or their rage blinded them to the danger. A column of tanks and APCs, leading with headlights thrusting into the dark, smashed through barricades on its way to the square. Huskey wondered why people kept tripping on rocks in the road, but then he realized they were being felled by bullets. Huskey retreated with the crowds to the eastern part of the square. He traded words with a young man beside him about the live firing. When he turned back to speak to the man, Huskey saw a red hole appear on his forehead, and he fell with a bullet through his head. Huskey moved back to a grove of trees lining Chang'an Boulevard for safety and caught his breath. He watched as tanks and APCs came to a halt along the northwestern edge of the square.

After army loudspeakers broadcast an order to the remaining students huddled around the tents to evacuate the square, a group of students and thousands of supporters began leaving between 1:30 and 2 A.M. Others carrying cans of gasoline tried to torch the army vehicles at the northern edge of the square, but they were arrested by soldiers.

Jim Huskey stayed around the square until about 2:30 A.M., long enough to witness the start of a grisly series of events. At about 2 A.M. in the northeast corner on Chang'an Boulevard near the Peking Hotel, from a starting point about 150 yards away, Chinese citizens edged toward a line of prone soldiers, backed by jeeps with machine gun turrets on top. Huskey watched a wave of Chinese edge forward, chanting, "Don't shoot your own people" and "Chinese don't kill Chinese." Some citizens tried to cajole the troops into putting down their arms. But the machine guns opened fire on the unarmed people, cutting them down with bursts of automatic weapons fire that lasted up to forty-five seconds. The grim theater would play itself out at least four more times over the next several hours: The people retreated, then returned to aid the fallen. Enraged at the wanton killing, they became emboldened and started to curse the soldiers as they edged forward, only to be met with another hail of lethal fire.

At about 2:30 A.M., Huskey made his way to the Peking Hotel. Doormen let him in after he banged on the doors. From the embassy's seventeenth floor watch post, along with acting deputy chief of mission Ray Burghardt, Huskey watched the PLA unleash more fusillades on the defenseless citizens. Bicycle carts driven by citizens hauled the bodies away after each flurry of sirens and gunfire.

Meanwhile, a quarter mile away in the center of the square, Chinese authorities were using more peaceful means with student leaders gathered around the Monument to the People's Martyrs. Sometime around

3 A.M. negotiations ensued between student leaders and the army. By 4 A.M. only a core group of a couple of thousand demonstrators remained around the Monument to the People's Martyrs in the center of Tiananmen Square. At 4 o'clock sharp all the lights went out on the square, sending its occupiers into panic. There were more announcements to clear the square. In a voice vote, students around the monument decided to leave. A half hour later the lights came back on, and armed soldiers, their bayonets fixed, started marching across the square and pressed the students closer and closer together. At about the same time, the tanks and APCs moved in and rolled over the demonstrators' tent city. The Goddess of Democracy was pushed over by military vehicles. There was noise and gunfire and crying and screaming all around. At about 5 A.M. the last students and citizens began to file out, threading their way among the tanks and APCs toward Qian Men, the southern entrance to the square.

Jim Huskey's eyewitness reports from the square became a basis for labeling the PLA's military action on the night of June 3 a massacre. In a letter to President Bush after the dust had settled on the crackdown, I commended Huskey for his superb duty. "What he reported was accurate, timely, relevant, and made up a sizeable portion of our situation reports. Jim is a people's man with good Chinese. He is a giant among men."

Before leaving the embassy for home at about 5 A.M., military attaché Jack Leide and I had to settle another hero down. Larry Wortzel had been up the whole night since coming into town in the middle of the motorized PLA column and was determined that I should send him to the hospitals to get an accurate body count. "The Chinese are going to deny it all happened," said an exasperated Wortzel. Leide and I agreed, but we also knew that Wortzel's skills could be better used elsewhere. "That's not your job," Leide reminded Wortzel. "You are a military attaché." Wortzel's flare-up was the kind of thing we had to handle carefully, especially in the midst of a crisis situation. The welfare of hundreds of American citizens depended upon our ability to use our personnel wisely. As a "man of the streets," Wortzel would be far more useful in tracking down Americans in Peking, a task that soon became our first priority. Instead, Jim Huskey and others went to the hospitals and gave us the first reliable casualty counts, which were frightening. They indicated that, at a minimum, hundreds had been killed and thousands wounded.

.   .   .

At the San Li Tun diplomatic compound, where Sally and I were temporarily living while renovations were being completed on the ambassador's residence, the morning of June 4 broke gray and overcast. The weather was a fitting complement to the pallor of death and destruction that overhung the city. I returned to the apartment in the early morning through broken roadblocks, overturned buses, and stunned people. Military vehicles still burned at major intersections, and gunfire rang out periodically from the streets. Along the city's main avenues leading from Tiananmen, loudspeakers blared the national anthem, and the army announced that order had been restored in the city. On the square, a huge bonfire lit up the sky. Huskey and many others, myself included, suspected that the government was burning the evidence of its carnage, so that it could begin to perpetrate its version of what happened.

Sally had spent the night at our fifth-floor apartment. She had been stranded there for the last several days. The house staff had stopped showing up for work, begging off by saying it was too hard to commute. But the cook had stockpiled food before he left. Sally and I ate simple meals, and while I was at work Sally stayed in the bare apartment, reading, taking our dog, Joey, for walks around the compound, and listening for the latest news by taking a radio onto the porch to catch the faint reception of the BBC. Each time she took the elevator down to take the dog out, she found the elevator lady in tears.

At 10 A.M. on Sunday, June 4, I began the job of trying to put together the U.S. response to the Tiananmen Massacre. Special assistant to the ambassador Gerrit Gong came out to brief me on the latest developments. It was clear that the Chinese were already trying to minimize the fallout. We had reports of bonfires on Tiananmen reportedly to burn bodies, and I sensed that in the coming days the Chinese government would try to rewrite history. Indeed, on June 6, State Council spokesman Yuan Mu, who became the odious face of

the government, declared that martial law troops had shown great restraint in the face of a "counterrevolutionary rebellion." The hundreds
of thousands of citizens who had occupied Tiananmen Square were
labeled criminals.

Thus, the first order of business was to make sure that we had the
facts recorded and right. Then, at the least, the U.S. government could
make policy based on concrete evidence. I tasked Gong with this job.
"We need a detailed chronology because we aren't going to remember
this clearly afterwards," I said.

I called a meeting of the embassy's Emergency Action Committee,
and we put the embassy into crisis mode. We opened the consular section on a twenty-four-hour basis and set up an American Citizens Services phone line around the clock. Staffers started calling American
residents, embassy dependents, and hotels to tell Americans to stay inside. All embassy social functions were canceled. We advised Americans to stockpile food, and we set up a triage area in the embassy
chancery. I instructed consular officers to visit Peking hospitals to
check for injured American citizens and to get estimates of the number
of casualties. That search turned up just one injury to an American,
who had been hit on the head by a blunt instrument during the massive confusion the night before.

It was fortuitous, but also calculated, that Americans, one of the
largest foreign communities in Peking with 1,400 people, had escaped
unharmed from the chaos. The Chinese purposefully instructed their
soldiers not to shoot or attack foreigners. Even when the Chinese
wanted to kick foreigners out of Peking, as we were to learn soon, they
gave advance warning to avoid bloodshed. Later, however, an ABC
correspondent was brutally beaten by Chinese troops when he intruded
into Tiananmen Square.

While pairs of diplomats were checking the hospitals, Wortzel was
working with a political officer to scout out evacuation routes for a voluntary evacuation of American citizens and embassy dependents in
Peking. Wortzel knew the city as well as anyone and had proved he
could handle the pressure in rough spots. The PLA and People's
Armed Police had set up roadblocks all around the city and were stopping cars in menacing fashion, on occasion pointing their guns at

drivers. I instructed him to map out routes from the university district—where a number of American exchange students were living—to the embassy and hotels that we would use as collecting points. "You guys stay out of the square itself," I cautioned Wortzel before he left the embassy. "I don't need any dead Americans on the square." I relied heavily on Wortzel and didn't want to lose him to some trigger-happy Chinese soldier.

The evening of June 4, Gerrit Gong returned to his apartment exhausted. He turned on the TV to relax and found to his puzzlement a documentary being aired on the funeral practices of a minority people in the southern province of Yunnan. The program was full of clanging and banging and wailing and moaning. "Why in the world is this on TV now?" Gong thought to himself. Then it dawned on him that someone in the hierarchy of Chinese State Television was calling attention to the students and workers who had been killed the previous night. The program was a funeral for the dead since they weren't going to get any other kind of send-off. Like the broadcast of "Paper Moon" after Li Peng's announcement of martial law, this was a sign that there were people in the bureaucracy in anguish and agony over what had happened. Gong started to weep in front of the impromptu, unsanctioned funeral for the nameless "counterrevolutionaries" who had dared to dream of a new, free country. Shortly thereafter, all programming was halted on Chinese TV.

.   .   .

President Bush called me Monday morning, June 5th. Earlier that day in Washington, in his first official comment on the crackdown, the president had announced a ban on new weapons sales and suspension of military contacts. In our phone conversation, I told President Bush that things were pretty calm on the ground but that my main concern was the safety of American citizens in Peking, particularly American students living at Peking universities that were the locus of the student movements.

At the U.S. Embassy, we were already getting heat from the American press, which had gathered en masse in front of the embassy at 7 that morning, clamoring to know how the embassy was going to safeguard the lives of Americans in Peking. Fortunately for the U.S. government, McKinney Russell, a career officer at the old United States Information Agency, was an experienced hand. Russell knew that any story, once the fighting subsides, becomes a local story. He had called me at about 6:30 A.M. that morning, and we got our cue cards together. Yes, we assured the journalists, we had scouted out evacuation routes and organized buses to get students out of harm's way and take them to hotels or to the embassy. We fended off the hungry journalists, but we knew they would be coming back for more.

At this point, I should have put into place a general evacuation order as some other embassies had done, in particular the Japanese and French Embassies. I would have saved myself a lot of headache, but we went about it piecemeal We started evacuating students on Monday, and on Tuesday embassy personnel started calling all Americans to urge them to leave Peking. But we waited until Wednesday, June 7, to inform American residents of a voluntary evacuation procedure for all Americans. Initially, I relied on the Consular Section, which has the responsibility for the welfare of American citizens, to do the calling and planning. Later, at Leide's suggestion, I switched the evacuation planning to the military attaché's office because, as military men, they were better organized to handle this sort of crisis operation.

Larry Wortzel's frustration over delays was the catalyst for the change. On June 8, after scouting evacuation routes and informing American citizens of collection points, Wortzel returned to the embassy prepared to lead a convoy of embassy vehicles at 11 A.M. But he discovered that little progress had been made in assembling the convoy. Diplomats and others were haggling over insignificant details, like who would drive which car. Wortzel stormed out of the room, cursing a blue streak. He bumped right into me. Ten minutes later, I found Wortzel in his office. I dumped the batch of motor pool keys on his desk. "You are in charge," I said. "Get this convoy out of here in 30 minutes."

The delays brought all sorts of opprobrium down on our—largely, my—head. Disgruntled Americans gave the media the story they wanted: The American government wasn't performing well in a crisis. Stories appeared in the stateside press about the embassy's "failure" to assist U.S. citizens trying to get out of China. Magnifying the "failure" was news footage from Peking that showed a city under lockdown with the possibility of more clashes. There was talk of civil war between branches of the Chinese military, which had different views of the crackdown. The reports were wrong. At the embassy, we knew from accurate reporting by Wortzel that rumors of a split in the PLA were overstated. It turns out that a Canadian military attaché, who had never been trained in ground combat, asserted to the press that civil war between ground troops was imminent. The attaché had looked at tanks facing outward on a highway overpass with guns pointed in three directions and come to his erroneous conclusion. This fueled the rumor mill racing around Peking and over the airways.

Nevertheless, despite our best efforts, I was behind the curve. Hysteria set in on the other side of the Pacific Ocean. Our Citizen Services Center started getting about 2,000 calls a day from Americans concerned about family members in China, and politicians in Washington excoriated the Bush administration for failing to act to protect Americans. I had people badmouthing me in Peking and all over the U.S.

.   .   .

While we may have taken a hit on the evacuation, we fared better in saving lives of Americans in Peking. Without a mysterious phone call on the night of June 6, there could well have been tragic loss of American lives in Peking's already bloody June of 1989.

That night, Larry Wortzel, worn out from a day of scouting evacuation routes and checking troop movements, fell asleep on the floor of his office. The phone rang in the middle of the night. The voice identified itself as a young PLA officer. The voice's urgent tone roused Wortzel from his slumber.

"Major Wortzel, I have been to your home a number of times. Please do not go to your apartment between ten in the morning and two in the afternoon tomorrow," said the young officer, whom Wortzel knew. "Do not," the voice implored, "go above the second floor of your apartment building."

Wortzel explained that he had no plans to be near the diplomatic compound.

Sensing that Wortzel had not understood his message, the Chinese officer repeated himself. "This is very important. Do not be in that building above the second floor."

Wortzel's mind raced as he tried to make sense of the Chinese officer's cryptic message. "A call in the middle of the night from a Chinese military officer warning me not to be near my apartment tomorrow," thought Wortzel. It was a classic tip-off. The Chinese officer had been instructed to call, Wortzel decided. Something was going to happen tomorrow at the diplomatic compound, and Wortzel was the conduit to get Americans out of harm's way. Wortzel immediately called me, Jack Leide, and the regional security officer. "They have warned us," said Wortzel. "Something is going to happen."

To me, the call was a sign that there were elements in the Chinese military that didn't want to jeopardize the working relationship with the United States that had been built up over the last decade. Wortzel's contacts were reliable, so we conceived a plan to protect Americans. To ensure that the Jianguomenwai apartments would be empty, I scheduled a meeting at the embassy on Wednesday morning for all embassy officers and dependents, ostensibly to discuss plans for the voluntary evacuation we had been organizing, but just as much to clear the building for whatever was coming. We ended up getting all Americans out of their apartments except for seven dependents. Two small children of one of our diplomats may well have been saved by their alert Chinese amah who threw herself over the children when bullets crashed through the windows.

Through his contacts, Wortzel learned later that the Chinese Army wanted to teach the international community a lesson for reporting on the Tiananmen events from their balconies at Jianguomenwai. The idea was, we learned from a Chinese source, to "close the door to beat the dog." The PLA planned to close the door by firing on the diplomatic compound, thus chasing out the snooping foreigners, and then, in the privacy of their own country, Chinese security forces would carry out a massive crackdown on their own citizens to restore order. "Close the door to beat the dog," or "guan men da gou"—it was a *cheng-yu*, and it carried a particularly chilling message.

The PLA had used the withdrawal of the 38th Army as a convenient pretext to fire directly at our apartments. The Chinese leadership appears to have cooked up the scheme of claiming a sniper was on the roof and then machine-gunning the diplomatic compound from one end to the other. An inspection of the bullet holes indicated that some of the rounds had come from directly across the street, from the buildings that had been infiltrated by soldiers the day before.

On the afternoon of the June 7 shooting incident, we got word from the Chinese Foreign Ministry that I could meet with Vice Foreign Minister Zhu Qizhen. We had been stonewalled for several days after the massacre, but this meeting came through. I took advantage of the opportunity to drive home several points. First, I asked that he help establish contact between the U.S. Embassy and the martial law authorities. I told him there was a sense of panic in the American community after the indiscriminate shooting at Jianguomenwai. Given the anxious state of U.S. citizens in China, I also requested that the Chinese government let the U.S. land four planes in Peking to assist in evacuation. Zhu replied that the situation in Peking had still not quieted down, but that what was happening was temporary and that the government was fully capable of suppressing the riots. As for my request to establish contact with the martial law authorities, Zhu replied that it wasn't possible at this moment. I closed by noting the growing credibility gap opening between official statements and what had actually happened the night of June 3 and pointed to the fact that the June 7 edition of the *China Daily* contained no reporting on the most important story in China. "The situation in China is complex," Zhu said. "It is not easy to understand events at a single stroke."

Voluntary departure became mandatory evacuation for all dependents as a result of the incident at Jianguomenwai. Reasoning that the situation was too uncertain and that the embassy could no longer ensure the safety of American citizens, the State Department ordered the evacuation of all embassy dependents and urged American students, business people, and tourists in China to leave as soon as possible. Secretary of State James Baker called at midnight on June 7 to inform me of the president's decision to evacuate all nonessential personnel and dependents. "That means Sally, too," Baker said. Later, I talked with my counterpart from England, Ambassador Alan Donald, who explained to me why his wife was not among the British dependents being evacuated. "There is privilege in rank," he said matter-of-factly. There is no such privilege in the U.S. diplomatic corps.

In late June, I had a chance to impress upon the Chinese government my views of their behavior. The new Chinese vice foreign minister replacing Zhu, who took a position in the Chinese Embassy in Washington, called me in to chastise me for articles in the U.S. press about the shooting at the Jianguomenwai diplomatic compound on June 7. He was livid that the stories were calling the shooting a ruse to chase foreigners out of China and not an attempt to snuff out snipers. "This is a fabrication," he said. "You have insulted the Chinese government and military by saying we fired deliberately on you." I listened patiently to the high-ranking diplomat and then responded. "I was only a private in the infantry," I said to him. "But I know that you don't machine-gun a building from one end to the other and up nine stories to get one guy on the roof." As I had done in Korea with President Chun Do Hwan at a crucial point in Korea's transition to democracy, I pressed harder to make my point even more powerful. "If you had hit one of those kids," I said in reference to the two American children who were shielded by their Chinese nanny, "I wouldn't be sitting here today." It was not a blessed exchange.

.   .   .

At the embassy, we went into high gear to arrange the evacuation. Embassy officers manned the hotlines around the clock, taking calls from all over China to help Americans find transportation to Peking and evacuation flights out of China. Embassy personnel called twenty-four local bus firms in search of assistance because our drivers were no longer coming to work. They were turned down by every firm. All the buses were out on the streets, some, no doubt, smoldering. So, using every available embassy vehicle, Foreign Service personnel drove cars and vans around the city to pick up American citizens. Embassy staff made posters in Chinese saying "American Embassy" and painted American flags, which we attached to the sides of the vehicles. The deputy chief of mission's car, bedecked in flags and posters, was the lead car for convoys around town. Larry Wortzel led the operation. He became a master at getting past armed roadblocks, using bribes of cigarettes, Cokes, candy, and even money to convince fierce-looking and armed PLA guards to let the convoys through.

The evacuation was an arduous and grueling process. In some cases, we had to cajole students to take advantage of the evacuation. They were reluctant to leave their activist Chinese friends on such short notice, and some had a strong distaste for anything associated with the U.S. government. But most were eventually swayed by our argument that the situation was still dangerous. At the other end of the spectrum, consular officers had to handle crafty Chinese civilians who tried to use infant and child relatives with American passports to get themselves into the U.S. as escorts. In the midst of it all, we would get phone calls from the U.S. in which a distant voice would rant at an overworked embassy officer, "Where's my Johnny? He's disappeared!" In at least one case, Johnny turned out to be in the next town in Texas, safe and sound.

On June 8 and 9 more than 350 Americans departed on United Airlines charter flights to Tokyo, and on June 10 a convoy of American-flagged U.S. Embassy vehicles brought eighty-three Americans and other foreign nationals from Tientsin to the Peking airport. The Tientsin convoy was led by Lyn Edinger, a resourceful and tough commercial officer who came through in the clutch. The departures provided poignant moments. As the wife of one embassy official was packing her bags to leave on June 8, her amah turned to her and said of the Chinese authorities, "We'll never forgive them because they killed our children."

I went out with McKinney Russell and special assistant Gerrit Gong to say good-bye to the first group of evacuees on June 8. At the urging of the savvy Russell, I made a point of being seen. In the wake of events that had had such a thunderous impact all over the world, I had to appear to our media like an ambassador who was accessible. At the airport before the departure of the charter flight, I gave three interviews to radio, TV, and print journalists detailing the evacuation plans. Later that day, I sat down for an interview with CNN.

China was the center of world news, and I was in the spotlight, or on the hot seat, depending on your perspective. President Bush had helped to focus attention on me during his June 5 press conference by referring to me as "thoroughly experienced" and "very able." I was even the subject of an inquiry in the June 25, 1989, issue of *Parade Magazine*. "So much is going on in China," asked a reader from Seattle, "I'd like to know who our new ambassador in Peking is."

With the interviews behind me, I boarded the charter plane with Russell to bid good-bye to the first group of Americans. On either side of me sat Americans whose families were being split up and for whom the future looked uncertain. No one knew what was going to happen in Peking, once a stable and peaceful city but now the vortex of powerfully destructive political forces. There was still sporadic firing in the city, and our embassy officers were routinely getting loaded guns aimed at their heads as they went through blockades around the city. Emotions were running high and people were crying as I made my way down the aisle of the plane shaking hands and wishing passengers a safe journey. "Go home and tell the world what you have seen," I said. "Do not exaggerate. The truth speaks for itself." From the group of evacuees, David Semmes, one of my first CIA colleagues and a friend of almost forty years, stood up from his seat and walked toward me. Semmes and I had started out together in the CIA working on China projects during the Korean War. A lawyer in Washington, Semmes's business trip had been interrupted by the Tiananmen events. As an old China hand, he knew what I was going through. He said nothing and just put his arms around me.

Sally was evacuated the next day with our dog on her lap. Ambassadors may not get dispensation on evacuations for their wives, but we were able to convince the Japanese authorities to give our 14-year-old dachshund a reduced one-day quarantine before Sally and the dog went on to Korea, where they would stay for the evacuation period, which dragged on for two months. So I guess there is a little privilege in rank.

By June 23, more than 6,000 Americans had been evacuated from China in one of the largest evacuations of Americans in a crisis situation since World War II. In the end, not a single American died during the disturbances in China and only two U.S. citizens were injured, one seriously. Thanks to the efforts of a remarkable group of diplomats, military officials, and embassy workers, we got out every American citizen who wanted to go.

A word about the embassy staff during these tense times. Most of the people rose to the occasion, performing superbly in a difficult and dangerous atmosphere. A few, however, broke under the pressure. Of those who broke, some indulged in grandstanding, putting their own interests before the interests of the embassy and country. Others slipped out of town, and a few fell back into wayward behavior like excessive drinking. Those who did the best were grounded in traditional American values of hard work, subordination of self, and pride in accomplishing things as part of a team. I also noticed that the embassy staff members most shocked by the events of June 3 and 4 were often the people who had spent a good deal of time studying China but who had developed a romantic image of Chinese behavior. They felt personally let down or jilted by the Chinese government's actions to disperse the students with force.

.   .   .

On June 8, Sally went to our residence to collect things from our unpacked boxes of belongings, which had been deposited on the first floor. While fishing around for her Korean language books, she was struck by the organized fashion in which they were stacked—piled high against the guest room like a fortress wall, as if to protect someone inside.

She was dead right. Three days earlier in a semicovert operation, Chinese dissident Fang Lizhi and his wife, Li Shuxian, had slipped into the embassy and been granted protective refuge. They spent their first night in the guest quarters of the residence before being moved to a secret hideaway on the embassy compound. Our boxes had been hastily assembled into a wall around the guest room to prevent the Chinese staff at the residence from going in there.

At the time that Fang sought safety at the U.S. Embassy, he was one of the most famous dissidents in China. A renowned astrophysicist, Fang had made a name for himself by openly criticizing China's Communist leadership, and in January, in a bold move, he had written a public letter to Deng asking for a pardon for Chinese political prisoners. For his outspoken support of human rights and democracy, Fang was known as China's Andrei Sakharov. Though he did not appear on Tiananmen

Square, his effigy had been burnt by a group of pro-government demonstrators, who demonstrated infrequently and in small groups in the
lead-up to June 3. Fang was a personal thorn in the side of China's paramount leader, Deng Xiaoping. On June 6, Deng fingered Fang as one of
the "ambitious handful who were trying to subvert the People's Republic of China." It was a Chinese version of the personal enmity I had seen
in Korea between South Korean leader Chun and dissident Kim Dae
Jung.

Fang's final entry onto embassy grounds was the stuff of spy novels,
and of some suspense for the Chinese dissident. Earlier in the day,
Fang and his wife had come to the embassy seeking refuge. He was
number one on the Chinese government's black list and feared for his
safety, he told McKinney Russell and acting deputy chief of mission
Ray Burghardt. The American diplomats talked with Fang and his
wife for three hours, explaining to them the State Department's procedure for granting asylum—unless there was a threat of death, people
were encouraged to leave the embassy voluntarily and find another solution. That is what Fang did.

He and his family took temporary refuge in the hotel room of an
American journalist. Russell got the room number and cabled back to
Washington what had happened. Several hours later, a senior officer on
the China desk called back with an urgent message: Get Fang and his
family into the embassy as soon as possible.

The call overruled standard operating procedure, and Russell and
Burghardt raced to get China's most famous dissident onto American
soil. At about 11 P.M. on June 5, they snuck through the back entrance
of the Jianguo Hotel. Russell, an urbane man who speaks five languages, says he felt more like James Bond than a career diplomat. They
stealthily made their way to Fang's room. "Let's go," they said in Chinese when Fang came to the door. The group hunched down as they
passed the hotel guards, and Fang, his wife, and adult son climbed into
an unmarked American van with their American escorts. Later in June,
their son decided to leave the embassy, and in another covert operation
he was smuggled out and returned to the family's apartment in Peking.

That first night, surrounded by a wall of boxes in a dark corner of
the uninhabited embassy residence, Fang and Li got a taste of what

their lives would be like for the next thirteen months in protective American custody. During their stay at the embassy, Fang and Li lived like hermits in a sanctuary. In their hideout, they did not see the light of day for a year. As I like to say now, Fang was the man who came to dinner and stayed.

Fang's presence at the embassy was initially top-secret information that was shared with only a few people. To me, it was a sensitive situation best handled as covertly as possible until the political temperature had cooled down in Peking. So you can imagine my surprise when on June 6 White House spokesman Marlin Fitzwater announced during a press conference that Fang and his wife had taken refuge in the U.S. Embassy. While I knew the Chinese would eventually figure out where he was, I didn't think the U.S. government would be the one to tell them. Apparently there had been a misunderstanding among decision-makers in Washington regarding Fang's presence at the embassy, and Fitzwater thought he was simply being accurate. The Chinese government went ballistic. Chinese spokesmen and the official media denounced the U.S. for interfering in the country's internal affairs and for violating its sovereignty. At an already difficult time in Sino-American relations, the Fang ordeal pushed the relationship to a new low.

On June 9, Deng Xiaoping made his first public appearance since the massacre. He looked frail and articulated his words poorly. But his remarks in support of the military action on Tiananmen were unequivocal: "The aim of the small group of counterrevolutionary rebels was to overthrow the Communist Party, the socialist system, and the PRC in order to set up a bourgeois republic."

And at the U.S. Embassy, cut off from our contacts and surrounded by Marine guards with automatic weapons, we were harboring a "so-called" ringleader. The presence of Fang and his wife in our embassy was a constant reminder of our connection to "bourgeois liberalism" and made us foreign enemy number one in Peking.

U.S.–China relations were in a deep freeze.

20

SMALL VICTORIES

MUCH OF WHAT we witnessed and heard about in the weeks following Tiananmen showed that the Chinese leadership and its immense propaganda operation were at work rewriting history. The official government line in news conferences and in the press was that the military had suffered more than the civilians, a dubious claim in light of the fact that the PLA's firepower, manpower, and armored vehicles overwhelmed the unarmed people in the square. As part of an effort to glorify the military for putting down the "counterrevolutionary" rebellion, entire schools were instructed to write letters praising the soldiers. Parents were encouraged to buy presents for the "heroic" troops.

In those first weeks after the massacre, a gloom hung over Peking. The overcast weather was the silenced population's funeral dirge. Residents of Peking stayed home and largely mourned in solitude. The mood of darkness was caught most poignantly by a Chinese professor writing in mid-June to an American colleague, who had left Peking. "In China, if you don't know anything at all, you may be able to live happily. But the more you know, the more pain you feel. We are suffocating here. As I write to you now, I want to cry," he wrote. "Since the massacre, it has been either cloudy or rainy every day in Peking. It seems to me that even the heavens are saddened."

In the face of a countrywide campaign to arrest opponents of the government and a numbing, relentless propaganda campaign, a palpable fear gripped Chinese citizens. Steady propaganda tried to blur people's memory of the Tiananmen massacre, but it was etched into the minds of Chinese citizens, especially in Peking. In contrast to the turbulent years of the Cultural Revolution when Chinese citizens had little connection to the foreign media and residents of Peking, in 1989, citizens felt a bond with Peking's foreign residents who had witnessed the crackdown. Pronouncements against "U.S.-influenced bourgeois liberalization" or official statements criticizing the "U.S.-backed counterrevolutionaries" were designed to create a false perception. Yet I believed that the shared experience of Tiananmen had formed a link between foreigners and Chinese. "This is a subtle point, but makes for a remarkable difference between now and 25 years ago," I wrote to the State Department on June 15.

At times like this, I was reminded of the differences among the countries in which I had served. For example, in South Korea I was on good terms with the government but had my problems with radical students, whereas in China I was at odds with the government but popular among many of the people, judging from the favorable responses I received.

The connection that was forged between the Chinese people and resident Americans speaks to the legacy of Tiananmen. Neither the Chinese people in Peking nor foreigners who lived through the crackdown would soon forget the incident. June 4 would not slide inconsequentially into the backwater of history. Deng Xiaoping's new China was tainted because the blood of Chinese workers and students had been spilled by the People's Liberation Army.

A joke making the rounds of the residential alleys, or *hutongs*, of Peking, as well as the corridors of embassies, pointed to the loss of credibility on the part of the Chinese Communist Party. It went like this: A donkey is sitting in Tiananmen Square, not budging. Li Peng goes up to the donkey and says, "If you don't move, I'll declare martial law." The donkey doesn't move. Then Deng goes up and says to the donkey, "If you don't move, I'll call in the military." The donkey stays put. Finally, Yang Shangkun whispers something in the donkey's ear, and it bolts out of the square. "What did you say?" Deng asks Yang. "I told him," Yang says, "that if you don't leave the square, you'll be the next secretary-general of the Chinese Communist Party."

During the weeks following the Tiananmen massacre, I had little contact with the Chinese leadership. Even after Deng reappeared on

June 9, the channels of communication, which had been assiduously cultivated over the previous ten years, remained closed. My calls to the Foreign Ministry on behalf of President Bush fell on deaf ears. To my entreaties to set up a phone call or pass letters between the American president and the upper echelons of the Chinese leadership, I was told, "We'll handle it for you." But nothing materialized. In the face of the gravest crisis to the Communists' control of China, the leadership had hunkered down and pulled the shades.

In spite of the hostile political climate in Peking, in comments to the American press I tried to remain pragmatic on the subject of U.S.–China relations. While prospects for the short term certainly looked dim, I believed in the long-term benefits of Sino-U.S. cooperation. In an interview with CBS's Lesley Stahl on *Face the Nation* in mid-June, I said about the stalemate in Sino-U.S. relations, "They aren't going to change. We aren't going to change. So, we have to strike a deal." Put another way, China is as it is, not as we want it to be. In terms of America's role, I believed strongly that we could contribute in constructive ways to a more open China by promoting a free press, student exchanges, and business contacts. "Voice of America should continue broadcasting, Chinese students should continue to study in the U.S., and U.S. businesses should do business in China," I said.

The levers of influence were linked, as I indicated in a cable back to Washington on July 11. "For the Chinese, our message should be: If you want American business, you also get VOA." It was engagement but structured in a way that allowed us to get influence on a changing and opening China. Through the summer, I worked to articulate the approach and keep it in sync with President Bush's wishes.

But we also had immediate issues to deal with. Back in Washington, President Bush, who prided himself on his personal relationship with the Chinese leadership, was getting increasingly frustrated that he could not get a message through. Bush's concern over the Chinese leadership's disregard for human rights combined with reports that the Chinese security service was thinking about storming the U.S. Embassy to extract Fang and his wife led the president and his aides to contemplate sending a secret mission to Peking. What particularly concerned the president were the images of young Chinese men with their hands behind their backs and heads shaved being led to trial and probable incarceration and, in some cases, execution. If such television footage kept flowing into American living rooms, Bush feared that the public backlash would make it impossible to sustain the relationship with China.

Forced into action, on June 20 he extended the ban between military officials to include all high-level official contacts with Peking and suspended American support for all international loans to China through the World Bank and the Asian Development Bank. But as he was criticizing China publicly, Bush was trying to preserve the relationship in private. On June 23 he wrote a letter to Deng requesting that the Chinese leader receive a secret emissary. Because President Bush's latest sanctions permitted no high-level exchanges between the two governments, any mission would have to be kept confidential. Indeed, secrecy was so paramount that even I didn't know of the planning until I was suddenly recalled to Washington. Bush, National Security Advisor Brent Scowcroft, and Secretary of State James Baker feared that any cable traffic sent to me in Peking might leak.

Deng agreed through diplomatic channels on June 25 to receive Bush's emissary. In keeping with the need for secrecy, the White House instructed me to fly back to Washington undetected. Here is where a background in intelligence comes in handy. As far as anyone in the embassy knew, I was going to visit Sally in Korea for a weekend—that was my cover—but instead I caught a flight for Washington via Tokyo to attend meetings on the upcoming secret mission. I was back in Washington for a grand total of twenty hours, long enough to see that the idea of a secret mission that undermined our sanctions was not universally popular. Neither Baker nor his deputy Larry Eagleburger liked the idea, but both President Bush and Scowcroft pushed the mission forward. "Will a high-level mission of Scowcroft and Eagleburger persuade the Chinese to stop the executions?" I was asked during a meeting at the White House. I pointed out that if the U.S. pressed the issue, the Chinese would just execute the people in private. "You won't save any students' lives, but you may defuse the [tension in the] relationship," I responded. I then said that I agreed with the idea of the president sending the covert emissaries. Scowcroft and Eagleburger would be able to convey that the U.S. wanted to preserve the strategic relationship but couldn't do so unless the Chinese leadership helped out by curbing its retaliation and working toward an improved international image. That meant forgoing show trials and any public executions. President Bush's concern at this point was assuring access to Deng. With the embassy shielding Fang, I was not a popular choice for emissary. "Since you can't get at the top leadership, I am going to send him [Scowcroft] out," President Bush told me. "You are immune from this."

·   ·   ·

It was during this secret trip back to Washington that I learned of a disappointing revelation in our handling of the whole Tiananmen incident. I knew that the president had been surprised at the brutality of the crackdown on the student movement, but I attributed that to a normal human reaction, not to a lack of information. During a break in a meeting in late June, however, President Bush turned to me and mentioned a common acquaintance, a very pro-Taiwan man who had allegedly told the president that he had warned me there would be a crackdown. I got a strange sense that the president was asking me to justify myself as if I had *not* been writing cables warning of a bloody suppression of the student movement.

I now know that the president never saw my May 26 cable characterizing Deng as an Old Testament man bent on revenge and predicting a violent crackdown by the Chinese military at the end of May. A high-ranking China specialist from the State Department, who joined our embassy staff later in the year, told me that State had not forwarded my cable even though it was marked for the highest levels in the White House. Instead, I was told that the message getting to the White House from influential people at the State Department was that I was an alarmist and that, although the situation in Peking was dangerous, there was not likely to be a crackdown.

So, though I was touted as being a U.S. ambassador with good connections to the White House, my message didn't cross the president's desk during the crucial days leading up to one of the most important developments in China since the founding of the PRC in 1949. This was deflating, to say the least, partially because I realized that I should have called the president myself. I knew him, and I should have made my concerns known directly to him via secure phone rather than rely on the State bureaucracy. I should have insisted that high-level emissaries come out immediately. The Chinese would probably have rejected them, but we should have tried. For its part, State's mistake was not making sure the president saw key messages, like my cable, and the White House erred in allowing officials to persuade the president that the situation in Peking was not as explosive as it seemed to us on the ground. Later I sent the president a copy of my May 26 cable in an envelope marked for him personally. I received no reply.

From Washington I flew to Korea, and while I was visiting Sally, Scowcroft and Eagleburger carried out their secret mission, flying all night and refueling in midair to avoid landing and detection. They met with Deng on July 2 and tried to make President Bush's case that he needed some give on the part of the Chinese government to get the Congress and media off his back. Deng had little patience for the vagaries of U.S. politics and instead hammered home China's history of sacrifice during the founding of the People's Republic of China and the need to suppress chaos.

In Peking, we did not get the barrage of criticism that the administration was getting in Washington. July 4th provided a visible way for us to rally together. In my various postings around the world, July 4th celebrations have traditionally been an occasion to bring together expatriate Americans of all stripes. It is one of the times abroad when the American community collectively feels its national pride. Over a meal of hot dogs and hamburgers, diplomats mingle with exchange students, and businessmen hobnob with visiting scholars while children run around playing games. One of the highlights is always inviting local foreign citizens to a reception at the official residence and giving them a chance to witness this typical American celebration.

But in Peking in July 1989, with the embassy compounds surrounded by three rings of armed guards with AK-47s and our own strong reaction at what had happened exactly one month earlier, we reduced the size of our annual celebration and had no reception for our Chinese hosts or for the diplomatic corps. Minus the evacuated dependents, there was a rump group of about thirty to forty Americans at the main embassy compound, but I would bet that that group of Americans felt as proud as they ever have to be citizens of the United States of America. With people gathered around the flagpole in front of the embassy, I gave an impromptu speech. "The people of China have had to pull back from freedom, but we are still here," I said. "This embassy is a beacon of freedom in Peking." At that moment, I believe that each of us felt a palpable sense of standing against the guns, misinformation, and thuggery that had enveloped Peking in the past month. The embassy's Marine security guard detachment then raised the flag, and we all sang the national anthem. The hotdogs and hamburgers never tasted better.

.   .   .

Heading into the gloom of winter, the embassy carried forth the China relationship as well as it could. Tiananmen was off TV screens, but our hard work as diplomats was really just beginning. It was tricky keeping China engaged when its leadership seemed content to shut itself off, and the situation called for creative thinking and compromise, backed by effective use of leverage and pressure.

Many programs with China had been cut, such as student and scholar exchanges and the Fulbright program. President Bush's sanctions, coupled with pressure from Capitol Hill, had plunged Sino-American relations into stagnancy on the policy level. We no longer attended diplomatic functions given by the Chinese, nor did Chinese guests come to the residence for receptions. The halls of the newly remodeled residence echoed with emptiness.

I had the unpleasant duty of suspending and eventually arranging for the termination of our military cooperation with China. After Tiananmen, there was a strong movement in the U.S. against continuing the military relationship. This was bitter business. We had to suspend an F-8 avionics deal worth $550 million, known as Peace Pearl, as well as other deals for torpedoes, large-bore artillery shells, helicopters, and artillery radars.

As I set about preparing for meetings with the Chinese, I was reminded that on the military side of the equation there had always been hitches. Dealing with the Chinese on these sensitive issues required, among other things, knowledge of the past as well as a keen sense of the negotiators sitting across the table.

I remember trying to arrange the first U.S. warship visit to China in the mid-1980s. Our initial attempt at a port visit at Shanghai in 1985 was scuttled when the Chinese insisted that we identify whether the ship was carrying nuclear weapons or not. Here, the Chinese were taking a page from the experience of New Zealand, which, after a bitter fight over our "no confirm/no deny" policy regarding the presence of nuclear weapons on our naval ships, refused entry to U.S. naval ships. New Zealand ended up getting expelled from ANZUS, the U.S.–Australia–New Zealand defense pact.

In the interests of getting a port visit in 1986 and thereby strengthening U.S.–China relations, some officials in the U.S. Navy and State Department were inclined to cave into the Chinese demand and repudiate our long-standing policy of "no confirm/no deny" (NCND). In my role as the deputy assistant secretary for East Asian and Pacific Affairs at the State Department, I thought that would set a dangerous precedent. We had important naval arrangements with Australia and Japan, which hosted hundreds of our naval ships each year. If we changed our policy on NCND for China, we would provide fuel to the left-wing groups in both countries that opposed our port calls and possibly destabilize our long-standing military ties with both countries. Both the Australian and Japanese governments insisted that we hold firm on NCND in China.

To resolve the impasse, I called on my personal relations with a high-level officer in the Chinese Embassy in Washington. Over lunch at a Chinese restaurant in Washington, I explained to him that the U.S. could not bend on NCND. I made my case by saying that, although I knew China was no friend of Japan, the continued U.S. military presence in Japan precluded Japanese rearmament. The Chinese eventually accepted a compromise proposal, and the first ship visit was scheduled for Tsingtao, my birthplace.

At that time, on military matters, there was also the issue of Taiwan. In fact, we had been able to get the military relationship with the PRC off the ground, including the sale of avionics for the F-8, in part because we had balanced it by providing Taiwan comparable avionics kits for its Indigenous Defense Fighter, or IDF. That boost to Taiwan helped to convince Taiwan backers on Capitol Hill to allow the F-8 avionics deal to go through. I personally briefed an aide to Senator Jesse Helms, and the influential North Carolina senator withdrew his objection to the sale of American avionics to China.

When the Sino-U.S. relationship soured after June 1989, I took a negotiating team of experienced diplomats to a meeting with the Chinese to see what we could salvage from the military cooperation. Having dealt with the Chinese on thorny military issues before, we were better prepared to handle their barbs and negotiating tactics in the complicated post-Tiananmen period. At the time of our meeting in the fall of 1989, in accordance with President Bush's order to suspend all military programs, the U.S. was holding onto torpedoes the Chinese had already bought and to several F-8's that had already been fitted with the new avionics package as part of Peace Pearl. Needless to say, the Chinese, having paid out money, were upset. At our meeting with Liu Huaqing, the leading military figure as vice chairman of the powerful Central Military Commission, the Chinese started off with a long harangue on our support of Taiwan. I answered by saying cryptically that the Chinese Communists themselves had praised us for being good quartermasters because everything we had sold the Chinese Nationalists had ended up in the Communists' hands anyway because of defections and greed. I then focused the conversation. "Our relationship has changed since Tiananmen," I said, "and we have to deal with this new situation." My translator, an attractive Chinese American woman from our embassy, used the term "Tiananmen da tu sha," which translates as "Tiananmen massacre." The Chinese were somewhat taken aback by our frankness, but I thought it helped our negotiating position.

Judging that the Chinese were on the defensive, we suggested that they take the first step in jump-starting the stalled Peace Pearl program. If they would make the next payment, roughly $60 million, we would make our best efforts to get the program resumed by the end of the year. The Chinese agreed, but ultimately we couldn't come through on our end of the bargain. The domestic political environment in the U.S. was too hostile toward China. Then huge cost overruns on the American side increased the price tag of the F-8 avionics program almost twofold, to one billion dollars, and the Chinese took the initiative and pulled out.

The failure of the F-8 deal was especially difficult for China because it ended up losing about $200 million. The Chinese leadership's displeasure with our actions probably contributed to its decision to purchase advanced SU-27 fighters from the Soviet Union in 1991. Eventually, in September 1992 when I was working at the Defense Department, we settled the F-8 deal and refunded to the Chinese a small face-saving amount as well as the warehoused torpedoes and planes. This deal seemed to resolve our differences, and accusations receded into the background.

.   .   .

In nonmilitary matters, the relationship moved discreetly forward. For example, the security relationship, particularly as it concerned the exchange of information on the Soviet Union, continued uninterrupted. Americans at the embassy were careful not to bring up June 4 and patient enough to endure the occasional tirade on U.S. interference in China's internal affairs.

There were awkward moments, however, especially at a time of such strained relations. At a reception in Peking in March 1990, high-ranking American security officials on a visit to China told their Chinese counterparts that I had conceived the plan for improved intelligence sharing between our two countries and directed against the Soviet Union. I ended up being toasted for my role in that important planning. No doubt several high-ranking Chinese officials at the party found this toast hard to swallow because at that same time in China I was under attack for harboring Fang Lizhi and for representing a country that had imposed sanctions on China for the Tiananmen Massacre.

On business matters, in keeping with the Bush administration's belief that commercial relations should not be unduly circumscribed, the embassy worked hard to sustain contacts between the two countries. Though certain parts of the bilateral economic relationship were on hold, such as the use of the Overseas Private Investment Corporation and the U.S. Trade Development Agency to facilitate private U.S. investment in China, restrictions were not placed on the operation of private U.S. businesses in China. Loans from the U.S. Export/Import Bank were, in fact, quickly restored.

In July, I outlined our approach to the promotion of economic ties in the post-Tiananmen period. It reflected my belief that commercial and economic ties would be the long-term glue of the Sino-U.S. relationship. In my view, we were reconciling with new realities, namely, that we had to move beyond the anti-USSR stance that had, in the form of the U.S. ship visit in May, so obviously steered the administration in a wayward direction during the student demonstrations. The focus should be on the business end of the relationship. That meant we should continue to sell commercial aircraft and other goods to China. "Not only do we help the good guys [by doing business with China], but we also help ourselves financially," I wrote back to Washington. "Despite congressional feelings, which we realize are strong and must be considered, we are not rewarding the murderers of Tiananmen by selling Boeing Aircraft for hard cash." Taking a page from President Bush's campaign rhetoric, I added: "Let a thousand points of business decisions work in China based on our own businesses' realistic assessments of economics and political prospects in China."

It wasn't just I who was espousing the benefits of the commercial relationship. Increasingly, as time passed, embassy officers began to hear from Chinese leaders about the importance of the economic ties with America. In October 1989, the head of China Airlines (CAAC), Hu Yizhou, praised American business prowess while taking a swipe at the Soviets. "Americans are straightforward," said Hu. "The Soviets are totally unreliable." Other Chinese leaders, after "delivering themselves of the party line, their frustrations and perhaps their feelings of guilt," as I wrote back in the same cable, expressed a desire for increased Western investment in addition to a mutually beneficial military and strategic relationship.

In early July, President Bush approved the sale of four Boeing 757 passenger jets to CAAC despite the fact that their cockpit navigational systems were among the civilian-military dual-use technologies that had been banned by his sanctions. To sidestep violating the sanctions, we removed the black boxes from the cockpits and had them stored first in Hong Kong and only later in Peking.

The Chinese also badly wanted approval for export of a Hughes satellite that was scheduled to be launched by China in the spring of 1990, and they made a strong pitch to me to lobby for its export. We knew that the launch would herald China's entry into the international space market. In their discussions with me, the Chinese played up the business side of the deal. The launch would bode well for improved communications, they argued, noting that the satellite would carry twenty-four transponders covering the Indian Ocean to Hawaii. Precisely, I thought. The same satellite launches that would be good for China's national prestige would bring the outside world closer to China. The satellite launch was important to the whole business of opening up China. Partly for these reasons, President Bush waived a congressional prohibition on the export of U.S.-built satellites for launch by Chinese rockets in December 1989. We did, however, maintain close control over the technology of linking and decoupling our satellite from the Chinese rocket.

My attendance at the historic launch in western China in April 1990 raised a few eyebrows. On the one hand, I was greeted warmly by the Chinese scientific community for supporting the launch. The Minister of Aeronautics and head of China Airlines were particularly pleased and flew me out to the launch. But the political commissars were much less enthusiastic. I was a pariah for shielding Fang Lizhi, yet I had also facilitated a deal to help China's battered national prestige. All they could do was to slight me in a protocol sense. Rather than putting me at the first table, they seated me at the second table, a trivial, petulant move. The successful launch was, appropriately, a sweet and sour dish for the Chinese to swallow. With its myriad raisons d'être, it fit into the context of a U.S.–China bilateral relationship, whose modus operandi in the wake of Tiananmen had crystallized into definition of common interests, hard bargaining, and trade-offs.

Another side of the satellite launch, which fit into the approach of emphasizing commercial ties, was linking up with Chinese scientists, technical personnel, and business leaders. By going through with hi-tech cooperation like this, we gave this group a chance to be heard and to gain support. And we would help to create a lobbying group inside China for our interests. These personnel, I wrote back in a cable, represented "a reservoir of good feeling toward the U.S. and are a group which favors a genuine open policy toward the modern world."

In our dealings with the Chinese in the post-Tiananmen period, we had to balance our support for the future forces of change—the scientists and business leaders—with doing business with the current regime. Unlike in the business sphere, we knew that we had little leverage on the internal political situation in China primarily because we stood for values that the elder leadership of the Chinese Communist Party saw as threatening. To make our points with the top Chinese leadership, we often had to fall back on trusted friends of China to articulate our position. These personal relationships count for a lot with the Chinese, and they are effective because for the most part their missions can be carried out discreetly and quietly.

In November 1989, I called on a former high-level U.S. official known to be sympathetic to the Chinese to intervene on behalf of the U.S. government for the continuation of the valuable security relationship we had developed. I had heard from a visiting top U.S. security official that his Chinese counterpart had said the joint-security operation for intelligence sharing was in jeopardy because of China's unhappiness over Fang Lizhi and the imposition of sanctions. The American security official was upset and came to me for advice. I then turned to the former U.S. official, who by chance happened to be visiting Peking at the time. He was very close to the Chinese top leadership and had been involved in the genesis of the joint operations. I asked him to weigh in on the matter with the leadership and to point out the tremendous mutual advantage we both got from the cooperation. His appeal worked, and the Chinese threat dissipated.

President Bush, an old friend of China, turned to another old friend of China to do some of America's bidding. Former President Richard Nixon, who was acknowledged with respect in Chinese leadership circles for his role in opening up relations with the mainland, traveled to Peking in late October 1989 at Bush's behest. I always admired Nixon for his strategic way of thinking and his ability to speak directly to the Chinese. I also appreciated the way he included me in his meetings.

At a dinner party hosted by Foreign Minister Qian Qichen in his honor, Nixon showed his shrewd diplomatic skill. Combining cajolery

with blunt talk about the government's brutal suppression of the student movement, Nixon said to his Chinese host, "You have done something that has caused us great pain. I am telling you this as a friend. We
have one heckuva problem, and this is the American feeling across the
board." Some Chinese tried to object by saying that China had been
sanctioned by only twenty-four nations. Nixon would have none of it.
"I am talking to you in terms of reality," he said. "The other reality I
don't like," he continued, "is seeing my embassy surrounded by Chinese
soldiers with automatic weapons."

The automatic weapons were gone a few days later—only to return a
week after Nixon's departure. But the point is that Nixon touched a
nerve in the Chinese leadership, mostly by appealing to them as a
friend expressing deep concern. The Chinese listened to the elder
statesman, weighed what he had to say, and moved ahead when they
realized that concessions could benefit them in the give and take of
reestablishing their relationship with the United States. Shortly after
Nixon's trip, the ball got rolling on negotiating a release for Fang Lizhi,
lifting martial law, and resuming World Bank loans.

.   .   .

One bright spot in the midst of the dreariness was Sally's return on
August 15, 1989. She came back to Peking after a two-month stay in
Seoul at the same time as a group of forty other American dependents.
Fortunately for us, Sally's enforced evacuation was spent on the
grounds of the U.S. ambassador's residence in Seoul, an island of green
in the middle of downtown Seoul and our home from 1986 to 1989. She
lived in the compound's guesthouse, which had housed the first American diplomats in Korea a hundred years earlier. Built by the Japanese,
the guesthouse had beamed ceilings and sloping tiled roofs that turn
up at the corners. It provided a comfortable home away from home for
Sally and our dog, Joey.

Sally was able to visit with old friends, both Koreans and Westerners, who were still in Seoul, and take walks with Joey in our former
neighborhood. The new U.S. ambassador to South Korea, my old
friend and former CIA colleague Don Gregg, had not yet arrived, so
she didn't even inconvenience anyone.

Back in Peking, Sally tried to keep a normal routine in abnormal times. One evening in early September shortly after returning, she heard a flute behind the embassy compound. She ventured outside the compound with Joey at about 9 P.M. It was the first time she had been outside the compound after dark since June 4. What they discovered on their walk was reassuring. Sally described the scene in a letter to Jeff: "The street lights through the trees made dappled shadows on the sidewalk, and a few bikes and pedestrians passed by . . . on our corner were four old women sitting, one on a plastic stool, the others sitting on the sidewalk, feet in [the] street, one had a bun [in her hair] and bound feet. They were chewing the fat (I guess) and just taking in the scene." It was a typical Chinese gathering, ageless and peaceful. The Chinese even have a four-character expression for the scene. They call it "shang jie kan renao." Translated literally, it means "on-street-to-see-activity." The expression conveys a sense of life passing by and casually observing it in ordinary company.

Just a few days after that pleasant walk with Joey, we had to say good-bye to our furry companion. Joey, who had been with us for our last three overseas postings, passed on in early September. She was 14 years old and had lived a wonderful life in Washington, Taipei, Seoul, and now Peking. Her body just gave out, and we had to put her to sleep ourselves with help from a Chinese doctor.

When you are a diplomatic family, moving from place to place every couple of years, you look for constancy. Pets provide an anchor. And that's what Joey was for us. She was a mixture of dachshund and something else, and in her heyday would strut around with what we used to call her "sauciness," her tail up in the air and her ears flapping in the wind. On their walks, like the one that late summer evening in Peking, Sally and Joey got to know the Asian neighborhoods we lived in and made our postings in far away places more familiar. Having accompanied Sally on her enforced evacuation to Korea, Joey must have felt she had done her final faithful duty. She had been a sustaining addition to our family's itinerant lifestyle.

A high point of the year occurred when our three sons came out to join us for the Christmas holidays. Jeff flew out after finishing his first semester at graduate school. Mike, fresh from a three-year stint in the

Marine Corps, joined us for almost a whole year as he waited to get into law school, and Douglas, who was working in Silicon Valley, invited two college friends to come along for the winter break. So the house was full, a rarity in this downtime of U.S.–China relations.

In late December, I took the family to my hometown of Tsingtao on the Shandong Peninsula. Even though the city was now full of industries and spread over a much larger area, it was still easy to spot the German influence that I remembered from childhood. Badaguan, a German-style castle, still looked out over the ocean from a promontory. Closer into the city, lining one side of the crescent-shaped beach, stood the old Edgewater Mansion, which had been converted into a naval installation. It was from the beach in front of the Edgewater Mansion that my brother Frank had taken on the stronger Japanese swimmer in the summer of 1934. Faded yellow houses with red-tiled roofs climbed the hillside, and at one of the highest points of the city stood the Lutheran Church that we had attended occasionally when I was growing up. Pine boughs in the church were decked out for Christmas with cotton snow and ornaments.

We left our hotel on a crisp December morning in search of my family's Tsingtao home, one of the faded yellow buildings on the hillside. We found seven families living in the house. Coal was stacked up in the hallways, and the walls were blackened with soot from coal-burning stoves. An elderly woman and her young grandson were living in an apartment that I remembered as the main living room. She invited us all into her tiny main room. The woman said she was part of the original landlord family that had owned the house before it was made into a communal living space. "Do you have any recollection of an American family living here in the 1930s," I asked. She remembered that the house had been rented to a Standard Oil family. Glancing around the room, I saw that the grandson was playing with a model of a U.S. F-4 Phantom jet, and I noticed a cross over the fireplace, indicating that the old woman was probably a Christian. Her family once owned the whole house, and now she was confined to what had been one room while the rest of the house, now dark and disorderly, went to pieces.

When we left the house, I heard someone playing the piano nearby.

The melody floated eerily over my old neighborhood, and I had a flashback to more than fifty years earlier when my sister, Elinore, used to play Chopin on the piano in our house in Tsingtao. It was just the kind of music she used to practice.

.   .   .

As the cold winter months settled over Peking, Fang Lizhi and his wife, Li Shuxian, remained protected inside their cocoon in the U.S. Embassy. Besides me, only about six people in the embassy knew of Fang's exact whereabouts. I communicated with even fewer people about him. Judy McLaughlin, who worked as the nurse in the medical unit, and her husband Charlie, who worked for the information section of the embassy, had the most daily contact with Fang and Li. While I didn't speak to Sally initially about Fang's situation, she soon figured out on her own where he was staying.

In an odd occurrence in the spring of 1990 when my sister, Elinore, was visiting, she quite serendipitously fingered the hideout. While we were showing her the embassy grounds around the residence, she jokingly said as we passed the medical unit, "I bet that's where that dissident is living." Sally and I had to stifle our laughter. I didn't let Elinore know until several years later that she was a good spy.

In fact, Sally became an important intermediary between me and Judy McLaughlin. Because Judy and I rarely crossed paths during the course of a day, any interaction between us might heighten suspicions of Fang's whereabouts not only among the ever vigilant Chinese staff but also among the curious American staff. It was easier for Judy to communicate the couple's needs through Sally, whom she saw more often. The two would make eye contact and then, if the coast was clear, talk quickly out of earshot of the Chinese staff.

In this fashion, we were able to coordinate events like a birthday party for Fang in the couple's confined quarters. Judy brought in a cake, napkins, and a birthday card, all of which were unfamiliar to Li and Fang. In her role as cultural guide, Judy explained to Li how to sign the card. When we celebrated Li's birthday party, Fang had a harder time catching on. He just gave his wife a blank birthday card without signing it. For the pièce de résistance at Fang's party, the McLaughlins, Bill

Stanton (the political officer following Fang's case), McKinney Russell, Sally, Mike, and I sang "Happy Birthday." I gave Fang a framed calligraphy saying "zi you" or "freedom" painted by South Korean politician Kim Young Sam when he was under house arrest. I recounted for Fang Kim's rise from political pariah to presidential contender. "I hope this serves as an inspiration," I told Fang.

.   .   .

So where did we hide them? Fang and Li lived in the back of the embassy medical unit behind our residence. Their rooms were separated by just two feet of wall from armed Chinese sentries standing guard outside the embassy compound. Our two Chinese guests were so spooked by the proximity that they only used the bathroom during the day when street noise outside made the sound of the flushing toilet less audible.

Fang and Li's living quarters took shape quickly. They slept in the former examination room, and the medical laboratory was transformed into a kitchen. Since both of our "guests" were established scientists, we supplied them with computers and set up workspaces for them in the dental clinic. For security, we blacked out windows, reinforced doors, and wired the entire complex with an alarm system that included buttons at the places where Fang and Li worked and slept. We brought in an exercise cycle for Fang. Charlie McLaughlin hooked up a TV with cable and lent the couple a microwave. Fang, a physicist by training, had never seen a microwave before. "Can it cook everything?" he asked Charlie incredulously. They also got a hot plate and electric wok. With so many modern amenities, we started to joke that Fang and Li were living in a five-star gulag. An affable type, Fang got in on the act, saying that if he couldn't find work as an academic in the U.S., he could at least open a Chinese restaurant. Fang's sense of humor served him and us well. With the help of Li, he weathered his incarcerated refuge. Unlike some Soviet defectors, Fang did not drink or have sessions of morose depression.

The McLaughlins were Fang and Li's lifeline to the outside world. In a highly stressful situation, Judy and Charlie helped Fang and Li adjust to their confined quarters and to the bizarre political limbo in which they found themselves. While we could do little to ease their sense of dislocation, Judy and Charlie tried to make them as comfortable as possible. After getting their grocery list, Judy would shop for them at the Chinese markets, making sure to buy Fang's favorite Anhui tea. Occasionally, for a change of pace, Judy would ask her cook before he left in the afternoon to prepare an evening meal for four as if guests were coming over. After two Americans posing as guests had come over and then left, Judy would pack the two extra dinners into containers and take them into Fang and Li the next day. So as not to raise the eyebrows of Chinese guards who surrounded the embassy, Judy always carried a nurse's medical bag with her when she went to work in the morning. Usually, it was stuffed with clothes or food for Fang and Li. When Charlie visited, he brought Fang the latest scientific journals that the embassy library had specially ordered for him. They were delivered to the embassy via diplomatic pouch.

Fang was an accomplished academic, and he used his time at the embassy to burnish his professional credentials by writing papers. A high point for the Chinese scientist occurred when one of his articles would appear in a journal. "Charles, look!" Fang would exclaim. "One of my articles got published. Please read it and tell me what you think." Charles McLaughlin might as well have been trying to read Chinese, given all the mathematical symbols Fang used in his articles. Invariably, an understanding Li would bail Charles out. "Charles can't understand it," Li would reply to her husband. "I can't even understand what you are talking about, and I am a physicist."

The tensest time with Fang and Li was in late June and early July 1989. Still seething from our decision to grant refuge to the two dissidents, the Chinese government had issued arrest warrants for Fang and Li on June 11, accusing them of counterrevolutionary activities, a charge that is tantamount to treason and can bring life imprisonment or death. One of the CIA station's intelligence contacts in Hong Kong tipped us off that the Chinese Public Security Bureau was thinking about using a SWAT team to remove the dissidents from embassy grounds.

As a student of Chinese history, I knew that the Chinese had stormed the Soviet Embassy in the 1920s to remove a prominent Chinese communist, Li Da Zhao, who had sought refuge there. Li was promptly executed in the street for the Russians to see. So I took the intelligence tip seriously. Since I was basically cut off from contact with government officials, I advised the State Department to handle the sensitive issue in Washington. I recommended that they tell Ambassador Han Xu that if the Chinese stormed the American Embassy to get Fang, they might as well kiss the Sino-American relationship good-bye. I don't know if they used my language, but a high-level State Department official did give the Chinese ambassador a tough talk. Washington's strong demarche to the ambassador was one example of the U.S. regaining some control of the relationship after a rocky couple of weeks. Having secured the safety of Americans through evacuation, we were in a better position to stand our ground when it came to defending Fang.

On my own, I considered a possible plan to sneak Fang out of the embassy should that be required to protect his life. Drawing on my experience in clandestine operations, I sketched what is called in intelligence parlance a "black exfiltration" plan. The plan consisted of hiding Fang in a box with air holes for breathing and then shipping him out with the diplomatic pouch. Another option was to dress him up as a blonde woman. Of course, neither plan left the drawing board. I sensed they would not work, and people in Washington wisely turned them off. Nevertheless, rumors about an exfiltration plan sent the Chinese into a tizzy around Halloween. The buzz among the press corps at that time had it that we were going to spirit Fang onto a plane. It gained momentum when some tipsy newsmen, hashing over Fang's predicament, started to blather about my background in the CIA at the bar of the Sheraton Great Wall Hotel. The story kept on growing. The final version had everyone attending the embassy Halloween party wearing Fang masks with the real Fang slipping out in the crowd at the end of the evening. It reminds me of that game show in the 1970s called "What's My Line" in which three panelists pretend to be a real person, and at the end they ask the real person to stand up. That would have been a sight to see—Chinese guards in search of a round-faced academic, dashing frantically about and lifting up masks as guests streamed out the embassy gates!

The Chinese were so agitated by the rumors that they called me in to warn me not to use Halloween as a ruse to sneak him out. At the end of the meeting at the Chinese Foreign Ministry, I told my Chinese interlocutor that it would be best to keep our conversation a secret. If it got out that the Chinese government had made an official demarche on the preposterous idea of sneaking Fang out during a Halloween party, I told my counterpart, they would look ridiculous. One of my colleagues commented to me that we could probably expect the same kind of treatment from the Chinese at Easter when we would be suspected of trying to smuggle Fang out as the Easter Bunny!

For the Halloween party, the Chinese beefed up an already overwhelming security detachment around the embassy. They forced visitors through a gauntlet of armed guards. When a group of merrymakers showed up with a casket—the kind used to transport Americans who die overseas back to the U.S.—with a resuscitation dummy inside, the guards were most disturbed. But in the end the Americans convinced them that it was empty, and the casket went through.

The light moments in Fang's predicament served to distract us from a grim time in a gloomy city at the nadir of U.S.–China relations. The truth was that Fang was a living symbol of our conflict with China over human rights. It's a battle we have been fighting with the Chinese since normalization more than two decades ago. The longer he and his wife remained under protective U.S. custody, the more difficult it would be to repair the considerable damage that had already been done.

.　　.　　.

Fang and Li burrowed away in their space behind the residence. Fang liked to call their makeshift quarters his "black hole," and the lack of sunlight lent credence to the astrophysicist's characterization. The days turned into weeks, and the weeks into months. Fang read scientific journals and wrote feverishly on his computer. When she wasn't working on her computer, Li busied herself with cooking and cleaning their quarters. She devised resourceful ways to interact with the outside world. When she became frustrated at the way the clothes she ordered from the American mail-order catalogs didn't fit well, she made a chart showing the variations within the same sizes of the different clothing companies and proudly showed it off to Judy McLaughlin, their most frequent visitor.

The secret of Fang and Li's whereabouts was kept remarkably well. People in the embassy would whisper among themselves, "Where do you think he is?" But no one divulged the information, and Fang and Li remained safely wrapped in their cocoon. Even expenses generated by their stay on embassy grounds were processed separately. The budget officer came in on Saturdays to do the billing. When Fang needed a dentist, we arranged for an American dentist to be flown in from Japan under the pretext that he would be doing a screening of embassy personnel. I myself only saw Fang a couple of times a month, always late at night and after the house staff had gone home. I would slip across the passageway between the residence and the medical unit and tap several times. I would brief Fang on the latest developments in his case—on what the Chinese government was saying about him and how the U.S. government was responding. We would then banter back and forth in a mixture of Chinese and English. Most importantly, I wanted him to understand that we cared about him and wanted him to be comfortable. But that we also wanted him out.

The embassy's political counselor accompanied me on some of my visits to Fang, and the State Department was kept informed of Fang's predicament via embassy cables. But by using the NODIS channel of communication back to Washington, I restricted distribution of the cables to people inside the State Department. In rare circumstances when I didn't want the State Department in the loop, I used a back channel to communicate with the White House. Though I had no phone conversations with President Bush about Fang and conversed with him just once on the subject of Fang (during my trip back to the U.S. in late June to participate in the planning of Scowcroft and Eagleburger's secret trip to China), I kept in touch with Doug Paal, the China specialist on the National Security Council, and communicated with Brent Scowcroft.

During the meeting in Washington in June 1989, an intelligence representative said he had information that Fang's wife might be getting money from Taiwan. While some people might have been alarmed at the implications of such a connection for U.S.–China relations, I dismissed it. "We should just lump her in with the many Chinese officials in Fujian Province who are also receiving financial contributions from Taiwan," I responded. The issue did not come up again.

Only one time did I let down my guard on Fang. That was in October 1989 when I agreed to let journalist Orville Schell see the dissident. After the Chinese astrophysicist was selected as the recipient of the 1989 Robert F. Kennedy Memorial Award for Human Rights, Schell, a longtime friend of Fang's, was tasked with interviewing the Chinese scientist. With support from Capitol Hill, particularly from Senator Ted Kennedy, Schell lobbied hard in Washington to gain access to Fang. The State Department directed me to assist Schell. He flew over in October.

As expected, the Chinese government was very upset when they heard the news of Fang's award. It was a risky move on my part to grant Schell access to Fang. Any statement from Fang would inflame the Chinese and could complicate the process of getting him out of the country. I sensed that trouble could come as a result of the visit.

I invited Schell over for dinner at the residence and made sure not to mention Fang's name during the meal. After the kitchen staff bid goodnight and departed the premises, with a wave of the hand I summoned Schell to follow me, and we descended the back stairs to the outside and crossed the few feet of pavement to the medical unit. I was introducing Schell to some crude clandestine procedures. Schell remembers Fang looking like a hibernating animal just roused from a slumber. The two men talked for a couple of hours, long enough for Fang to agree to write an acceptance speech to be read when the award was presented.

Like a boomerang, Fang's speech came back to hit me. In his speech, read several months later at the awards presentation at Georgetown University in March 1990, Fang indicted the hard-liners in the Chinese government for fighting a rear-guard action against the advance of universal human values, calling them "murderers" at one point in his speech. Predictably, the Chinese government called me in for a tongue lashing. The White House was also upset about Fang's use of the embassy as a bully pulpit from which to lambaste the Chinese leadership. Fang was shrewd as well as principled, and he did think in terms of using the power of the U.S. against the Chinese government that he so despised.

Shortly after the human rights award was presented to Fang in absentia, I brought him to the residence to watch a tape of the ceremony. After the kitchen staff had left for the night, I sent for the couple. Judy McLaughlin turned on the light in the examination room to provide cover for their movement. With halting steps, Fang and Li approached the front door of the medical clinic. They had not been outside in more than eight months and were terrified at the prospect of being seen. Judy and Charles led Fang and his wife across the ten-foot distance from the medical clinic to the residence. Once inside the house, they settled onto the couches in front of the TV in the den on the second floor. Li sat bolt upright as Judy held her arm for comfort. Fang was remarkably imperturbable.

·   ·   ·

In May 1990, President Bush announced that he would unconditionally renew China's Most Favored Nation status, or MFN. It was a bold move in that Bush had taken some hard hits from Congress and the media for the first Scowcroft–Eagleburger trip after news of the secret trip leaked. The administration knew that if the president moved too fast on Chinese matters, he would be savaged for "coddling communist dictators" among other things.

Bush's MFN move was the break we needed in Peking to speed up negotiations on Fang's release. The Chinese leadership knew the economy was their weak point, and we had cards to play. We had been discussing the Fang issue with them in the context of a broader agenda since late 1989 when Brent Scowcroft and Larry Eagleburger had made their second secret trip to Peking, and Bush's move, combined with promises of a resumption of World Bank loans and disbursement of a Japanese loan package, prodded the Chinese to come to the table.

Liu Huaqiu, my counterpart at the Foreign Ministry, invited me for lunch. He wanted reassurances that the release of Fang would be met with reciprocal gestures in Washington. The lunch began a series of intense meetings to iron out the details of the release of China's most outspoken dissident.

This was a difficult negotiation. Over a series of secret, laborious, and time-consuming meetings with the Chinese in May and June, we traded verbal punches. I fended off Chinese pressure to set the agenda and, therefore, control the talks. They wanted us to agree that we had violated Chinese sovereignty by sheltering Fang, whom they called the criminal behind Tiananmen. That would have meant tacit agreement that we had interfered in China's internal affairs. I told them there was such a thing as the diplomatic principle of seeking asylum. Plus, the U.S. Embassy was American property. Besides, I added, Fang was a follower of nonviolence, like Gandhi, not an instigator of violence. I provided them with several of Fang's books in Chinese, which spelled out his peaceful approach.

At times, I felt like I was working as the middleman in a family dispute. I would report to Fang the results of discussions that I had had with the Chinese and then include his views in my next presentation to the Chinese. For their part, the Chinese said they were concerned that once Fang left China he would criticize the country and become a beacon for an anti-China movement. What they had seen at Georgetown, they feared, would be petty compared to their vision of Fang expounding against them from his haven in the West. The Chinese government wanted assurances from us that we would muzzle him or that we wouldn't use him to blast China.

"It is your responsibility to curtail his anti-Chinese government activities," they lectured me.

"If he comes to the U.S., we can't control him," I responded in defense of the First Amendment. "I can just tell you that the U.S. government won't support him in any political activities."

The Chinese then held out for a statement signed by Fang in which he promised not to level criticism at the Chinese government. Here's where we split hairs. Fang told me he would never sign anything that restricted his freedom to criticize the leadership in Peking or to engage in activities against the interests of the Chinese government. We finally settled on a general term of "China" in the statement. The choice of wording allowed Fang to leave China with his freedom to act and speak intact. "I won't do anything against China," Fang said to me, "but I am going to attack these bastards who are running China."

Fortunately, we found a hook to hang the agreement on, or, more appropriately in the Chinese context, we offered a face-saving measure to coax the Chinese to go forward with the deal. After all, they were reversing their decision to arrest Fang and charge him with counterrevolutionary crimes. They needed a justification. In the spring, we found one. Fang had complained of chest pains to Judy McLaughlin, and we immediately thought the worst—that he had heart trouble. Judy arranged for an EKG to see if he had an irregular heartbeat. In the early stages of negotiations, I raised the subject of Fang's health, deliberately playing up the severity of his condition. Fang himself objected at first to the pretext, but I prevailed upon him. "You *do* have a heart problem," I told him. Then I pursued the angle with the Chinese. I told them that they had a chance to look compassionate by letting him out on humanitarian grounds. Still somewhat entrenched in their opposition to Fang, the leadership suggested that he see a Chinese doctor. I dissembled to the Chinese, saying that Fang's condition could be life-threatening, and so he needed to be treated outside China. While Fang's tests proved negative—he really only had a case of indigestion—Fang's medical condition provided the pretext the Chinese needed to let him go.

Fang sensed that the government was giving ground, and he got emboldened. He wanted to go for the jugular and get more concessions out of them. I told him quite frankly that the U.S. was not in this to fight his battles with the Chinese government. We wanted him out of China, and he should take the deal we had crafted.

The final arrangements called for a U.S. Air Force C-135 transport plane to carry the couple to England, where Fang had a guest professorship arranged at Cambridge University's Institute of Astronomy. The night before Fang and Li's departure on June 25, 1990, they stayed in the residence's guest room where they had spent their first night under U.S. protection. We drank a toast to their upcoming release and to the agreement to let their youngest son out as well. There was a hitch in that the guest room had been occupied by a friend visiting from the U.S. This called for some small-time intelligence operations inside our own residence. To free up the guest room, we had to arrange for our houseguest to go to Shenyang on short notice. To occupy the house staff the next morning when the couple would be leaving, we invited an embassy officer, Dan Piccuta, who had an ability to spin stories for a Chinese audience. We brought Dan over ostensibly to brief the staff about the upcoming 4th of July reception preparations. Perched on the kitchen table with the house staff clustered around him on wooden stools, Dan kept them engaged for the necessary period.

Fang and Li departed the residence at about 10:30 A.M. on June 25 while a delivery truck backed up to the front door adjacent to the guest room and unloaded chairs for the upcoming reception. A Chinese police escort took them to Nanyuan Military Airport on the outskirts of Peking, the same airport that Larry Wortzel and Bill McGivven had been covering a year earlier. As instructed, I accompanied Fang and Li the whole way. At the airport, we were told that Fang and Li had to go through exit procedures alone. The airport officials pointed to an immigration booth at the end of a hallway surrounded by Public Security Bureau people. I was torn by my predicament. I was told not to let the couple out of my sight until they had boarded the C-135, but the Chinese were insisting on a face-saving measure—a final demonstration of sovereignty on their own soil—by making Fang and Li go through customs on their own. As the couple's guardian for over a year, I realized that I had become protective of them. What if the Chinese kidnapped them now? I decided to let them go, reasoning that the Chinese would lose heavily if they ruptured the carefully choreographed agreement. There was too much riding on Fang's release in terms of righting the U.S.–China relationship. Nevertheless, I watched with trepidation as Fang, a lone figure at the end of the dimly lit hallway, offered his passport to the passport control officer. But it was only the bureaucracy kicking in. Fang was asked a few questions, his passport was stamped, and he was on his way.

Upon arriving in London, in an interview with NBC News our protected guest criticized the Bush administration for a double standard on human rights that was tougher on the Soviet Union than on China. There is little doubt that the U.S. had hit the Soviets harder on human rights. Their system was more vulnerable to our pressure, and we had better information on their violations. But in Fang's case we had gone to great lengths to get him out of China and to toughen our approach and sanction China. He seemed ungrateful. I have never been able to forgive him for his comments. He may have been put up to it by goading on the part of the American media, but it was still unacceptable.

.   .   .

The consular office of an embassy or consulate is the front line of any diplomatic mission's interaction with the society around it. In China, still a somewhat closed and xenophobic country, the interaction takes on even more significance. Across a table, separated by a Plexiglas divider, Chinese citizens state their case for why they should be granted permission to visit the U.S. American visa officers do their best to judge the merits of each case. There are triumphs and disappointments every day.

One triumph concerned the case of a young art student from western China. Sally met Ning Qiang, a brilliant research fellow at the Dunhuang Institute in Gansu Province, when she traveled there in June with two family friends to see the famous Buddhist cave art. Ning had a superb knowledge of the Chinese influences behind the cave frescoes, some of which were more than 1,500 years old. But he said he lacked information about the Indian influences. His hope was to study in the West to complete his education.

But though Harvard had granted him a full scholarship to study for a Ph.D. in Art History, Ning couldn't get permission to go. The local Public Security Bureau agents had caught wind of his participation in anti-government demonstrations in June 1989 and were stonewalling his application for a passport. "I can't get a passport because the vice head of the Lanzhou Revolutionary Committee has never heard of Harvard," he told Sally. "Can you help me?" he asked.

I happened to like that Chinese cadre who had never heard of Harvard, but I had to do what I had to do.

Sally and her two friends, one a Radcliffe alumna, were moved by the plight of this aspiring art historian from the middle of China with the chance of a lifetime. What a waste if small-minded Communist Party hacks were able to derail a promising career. When they returned to the embassy, they appealed to me with the details of Ning's case. I very seldom, if ever, intervened in visa cases, but this was an exception. I got the wheels of the embassy bureaucracy pointed in the right direction. I directed Dan Piccuta to write a letter to Ning on U.S. Embassy stationery detailing some of Harvard's credentials that Ning could take to the official who was blocking him from leaving. Then I intervened by requesting that our visa section grant Ning a visa when he appeared in Peking.

Ning arrived in Peking in January 1991 to apply for his U.S. visa. We got him one on short notice. Nothing was going to stop him now. When they told him there were no seats on the plane, he said, "I'll stand." In the simplest terms, Ning's case was an example of a triumph of sense over nonsense. The forces of the pursuit of knowledge prevailed over bureaucracy and insularity.

In the months following the Tiananmen crackdown, many young Chinese like Ning were desperate to get out of the country, and some of them came from prominent backgrounds. The U.S. was popular, and the lines of visa applicants snaked around the consular building. For a student visa, applicants had to satisfy three criteria: show proof of sufficient financial resources to pay for their stay; have a good academic record, including a passing score on the TOEFL (Test of English as a Foreign Language); and be convincing that they would return to China when their visa expired.

When a young, presentable woman took her seat across from Jim Huskey in October 1989, he quickly absorbed the information on her application. At that time, with the embassy shielding Fang Lizhi and a host of bilateral issues shelved because of the Tiananmen crackdown, the diatribe directed at the U.S. from some parts of the Chinese government was particularly venomous. One of the worst offenders was Yuan Mu, the spokesman for the State Council, the key government body of China at that point. Yuan railed at the U.S. for intervening in China's internal affairs. He presented to the world the image of a retrenching China, defiant in the face of world criticism and determined to go its own way. No one had been killed on Tiananmen Square, asserted Yuan in the aftermath of the massacre, a statement that, while believed by some inside China, dismissed the obvious evidence from television cameras that scores of Chinese citizens had been killed on the streets within yards of the square. Among the press corps, Yuan was so unpopular that he earned the description "reptilian."

Huskey spotted the surname Yuan on the young woman's visa application. After checking the name of her father, Huskey leaned under his desk to turn up the volume on the microphone at the table. He wanted the Chinese employees of the consular section as well as the other Chinese waiting in line to hear his conversation. "You really are Yuan Mu's daughter," Huskey said incredulously, his voice audible to all in the room. The young woman leaned forward and whispered, "Yes, I am." In an amplified voice that boomed around the consular section, Huskey continued, "I cannot believe that Yuan Mu, who hates America so much and berates my country every day, would want his daughter to go to America to study." By this time, much of the work of the section had stopped, and people were listening intently to the conversation. "Ta shi ta. Wo shi wo," the daughter replied sheepishly in Chinese. "He is who he is. I am who I am." Huskey queried the young woman some more on how her father could allow her to go to such an evil place to study. The Chinese staff eventually broke into laughter at the whole spectacle.

Huskey eventually adjudicated the visa application because Ms. Yuan had a good academic record and had received a full scholarship from an American university. But he made her do considerable fidgeting in her seat to get his approval. Huskey was sure that by that afternoon the news was making its way down the *hutongs* of Peking that Yuan Mu's daughter was going to study in the United States.

.   .   .

During the time that I was involved in the secret negotiations over Fang's release, the Chinese ended their one-year boycott of embassy social events. For a concert by a visiting American pianist on June 15, about eighty-five Chinese involved in musical and cultural affairs showed up. It was a small but significant sign that reflected that relations were getting back on track. The operating environment in Peking improved with Fang's release. In July 1990, America and its allies cleared the way for a resumption of some World Bank loans to China. Such concrete steps toward engagement with China paid off in the fall of 1990 when we needed to get China on board at the UN to contest

Iraq's invasion of Kuwait. In hard bargaining over the next several months, the Bush administration succeeded in getting a UN resolution backing the use of force against Iraq. In the lead-up to this resolution, at a time when the U.S. still had sanctions on China, the Peking government supported eleven UN Security Council resolutions that condemned and sanctioned Iraq. But the question was: How would China vote on the decisive resolution?

In Peking, Premier Li Peng told me in October 1990 in a one-on-one conversation that China could not support a use of force resolution on Iraq as a matter of principle, but that information was ignored in Washington. Instead, Secretary of State Baker tried a carrot-and-stick approach with Foreign Minister Qian Qichen. In a late-night phone conversation from his hotel room in Paris, Baker made his pitch to Qian: If you vote with us on the use of force resolution, you will get a meeting with President Bush. China ended up abstaining from the UN resolution on Iraq. After appealing to Brent Scowcroft in the White House, the Chinese also got their meeting with the president. On November 30, 1990, Qian Qichen became the first high-ranking Chinese official to meet with President Bush since June 1989.

It might appear that China got the better of us, but as Qian's meeting with President Bush unfolded, I saw Secretary Baker's true skills as a mix of diplomat and Texas gambler emerge. Prior to Qian's visit to the White House, Baker and President Bush had reasoned that Qian, having secured his meeting with the president, might be susceptible to American approaches to establish the agenda for U.S.–China relations. It was a bold idea because historically China, by pressing Taiwan as an issue, a common front against the Soviet Union, and the need for technology transfer, had dominated the formation of the agenda. In his conversation with Qian, President Bush laid out American priorities in the Sino-U.S. relationship: human rights; trade imbalance, including intellectual property rights; and proliferation of weapons of mass destruction. And then the president said he wanted high-level visits to China by the American official in charge of each of these areas. The strategy worked, and Qian agreed to the agenda. Within the next six months, Richard Schifter, assistant secretary of state for human rights; Joe Massey, the United States trade representative; and Reginald

Bartholomew, an undersecretary of state for security management, all visited China.

Our policy of engaging China paid personal dividends for me. On January 15, 1991, the day that the UN coalition started to bomb Iraq, I found out that Iraq had a plan to assassinate me. It was my sixty-third birthday. An Iraqi hit squad had entered China and was undertaking surveillance of the embassy. In fact, the Iraqi squad sent to China was one of four teams that the Iraqis had deployed to sabotage American diplomatic compounds or assassinate American diplomats. One team went to Bangkok, another to Manila, a third to Jakarta, and the fourth to Peking. Washington dispatched a security guard to Peking to be with me at all times and advised us to hang against the back window of my car a lead-filled dummy that looked like a suit carrier. I started to wear a bullet-proof vest. Next to my bed I kept a loaded revolver at the request of our security people.

The Iraqis had targeted me because they believed that I had been President Bush's roommate at Yale and that I was in line to be the next Director of Central Intelligence. They were dead wrong on both accounts. I talked with the head of the Chinese Public Security Bureau, and he assured me that he could handle the situation. "Don't worry about it," he said. "We can take care of it." So, with the help of the Chinese—this was one time when I was grateful that I was living in a police state!—I avoided harm. At the embassy we detected some Keystone Cops, such as an Arab-looking person peering from behind a thin tree. The hit squad, which had reportedly come into China under the charge of the Iraqi Embassy's military attaché, disappeared soon after my meeting with the head of the Chinese Security Bureau. I didn't ask any questions.

In the other cities, the Iraqis were also unsuccessful. The Thailand team was caught immediately, exposed, and expelled from the country. In the Philippines, an Iraqi agent blew himself up, and in Indonesia, Iraqi agents got caught trying to plant a bomb in the U.S. Embassy.

The good news was that hundreds of Chinese citizens wrote me letters supporting U.S. actions to punish Iraqi aggression. I could see that they despised Saddam Hussein. They sent me swords, drawings, and money. A Chinese man from Yunnan, who had worked with the U.S.

in World War II, traveled more than 400 miles by train to get to the nearest U.S. consulate. There he plunked down $2,000 in life savings as a contribution to helping American soldiers wounded in the Persian Gulf. We returned the money with a letter of thanks. At the embassy, we were all greatly moved by the outpouring of support. Implicit in some of the comments in the letters we received was the thought that after you guys clean up Saddam, we have some ideas about your next target.

.　　.　　.

My tour in Peking was remarkably immune from the tirades I had encountered on Taiwan, which had contaminated other ambassadors' tenures as well. The subject of Taiwan came up, I believe, in only four instances. The first was in May 1989 just after my arrival when a leading Chinese Foreign Ministry official questioned me about the Taiwan economic success story. How had they done it, he asked. What were the lessons for China? At the time, Shirley Kuo, the finance minister from Taiwan, was in Peking for meetings of the Asian Development Bank board. She was the highest-ranking Taiwan official to have visited the mainland since Chiang Kai-shek fled forty years earlier. And she was there in part because earlier we had negotiated joint membership of Taiwan and China in the Asian Development Bank. I gave the Foreign Ministry official a copy of Minister Kuo's book on Taiwan's economic development as well as another book on the Taiwan economic miracle.

In the second instance, I brought up the subject of Taiwan with President Jiang Zemin in 1990. I told him that President Lee Tenghui of Taiwan had authorized me to pass a simple message to the Chinese president: Taiwan would not declare independence. I hope that this communication contributed to the unprecedented high-level meeting between Taiwan and China in Singapore in April 1993. The third reference to Taiwan came up in connection with GATT, the General Agreement on Trade and Tariffs that was being negotiated at the time. China insisted to me initially that after its entry, the People's Republic of China should be the sole member representing the mainland and Taiwan. I suggested that for good commercial reasons China should support Taiwan's remaining in the GATT, and I worked with European Union representatives to develop a common position that may well have helped to influence the Chinese to eventually acquiesce in joint membership.

Finally, I saw many of my Taiwan friends at the Asian Games in Peking in 1990. Taiwanese businessmen, lawyers, politicians, and private citizens came with their wives to a social occasion at our residence. I congratulated them on being in Peking and assured them that the peaceful and constructive attitude prevailing between the two sides was good for China, Taiwan, the U.S., and the rest of the world. Although Taiwan's resistance to unification was reinforced by the events on Tiananmen Square, the island's trade and exchanges with China had gone ahead almost unaffected. "PRC–Taiwan relations," I wrote in my end-of-tour cable, "have their own momentum independent of the U.S., and this momentum has defused their confrontation."

·   ·   ·

By the summer of 1990, it was clear to me that I was no longer the right person for the Bush administration to have in China. I supported the president's China policy fully, but over the long haul I knew that I was more inclined to work at cross-purposes with the Chinese leadership in power. The Tiananmen events had left behind a bitterness on both sides. In their eyes, I was associated with the unpleasant fallout from June 4, and they effectively shut me off from high-level access in the months following the Tiananmen Massacre. I was an easy target. Through the hard bargaining and trade-offs that shaped our China policy, I sensed that the Chinese would tend to blame me for policies that they didn't like and that I could lose my effectiveness.

I did, however, take some satisfaction in having given momentum to a stagnant U.S.–China relationship. The U.S. Embassy in Peking extended educational, scientific, and technological agreements, including a three-year extension of the Nanjing University–Johns Hopkins combined degree program in Nanjing. We signed a memorandum of understanding on intellectual property rights with the Chinese, and we gained access to the property of the former Bulgarian Embassy next to our embassy for enlargement purposes, something that had eluded us for years. We also got the Chinese to upgrade the facilities of our four consulates.

In the case of our properties, we played hardball with the Chinese to get things done. For years they had ignored our requests for consulate renovations and additional space for our chancery. Meanwhile, they were sending delegations to Washington to survey various properties with real estate agents, selecting what they liked, and moving ahead with little U.S. government involvement. To break the logjam, we held up granting U.S. visas for a visiting Chinese delegation. The Chinese were eager to go, with plane tickets in hand and their wives all set for a shopping tour of America. They kept asking about their visas and became increasingly irritated. We pleaded bureaucratic problems, but then eventually asked them in a low-key way how the renovations on our consulate in Chengdu were going. They exploded in anger, but got the message. We got the renovations and the Bulgarian Embassy property, and they got their visas.

We kept security and business ties going after a rough few months following Tiananmen, and in the military sphere, while we didn't salvage the relationship, we at least attenuated the bad feelings and resentment. When the media took stock of my two-year posting in China, they were generally favorable. In May 1991, just before our departure from Peking, the *New York Times* credited me with "navigating Chinese–American relations out of a stormy period."

My "end-of-tour" report started out with a comment about our "smug complacency" in playing the geopolitical game by setting up the U.S. ship visit to Shanghai in May 1989 in order to get "in collusion with those polar bear-suspicious Chinese." Meanwhile, as we were "climbing into bed with the PLA Navy on this occasion, history was being rewritten on Tiananmen Square in the coming confrontation between the PLA and the Chinese people led by Chinese youths and workers." Any entreaties from us for restraint fell on deaf ears because the aging Chinese leadership, reared in a different era and steeled by hardship, saw the conflict in Tiananmen Square as a matter of suppressing chaos. As I looked to the future of Sino-U.S. relations, I recommended reconciling with new realities in the relationship by focusing on three areas: first, strengthening the reform-minded coastal areas of China by supporting the peripheral territories and countries around China, such as Hong Kong, Taiwan, and South Korea; second, aiming programs like Voice of America and Most Favored Nation trading status at China in such a way that they blend in with genuine forces for reform and opening; and third, drawing China into the world order through the United Nations, nonproliferation efforts, and international trade regimes. "In conclusion," I wrote, "our efforts should be to try to bend China, not break it or change it fundamentally."

Throughout my tenure as ambassador, I had tried to make America's case to the Chinese, whether it was a July 4th celebration or protecting Fang Lizhi. It was the principles that we strove to live by, I believed, that would be the most powerful magnet to pull a retrenching China toward a more reform-minded path. Across the Taiwan Strait, Taiwan was setting a good example in its efforts to adopt Western democratic concepts to a basically Confucian society. I had hopes that China would follow this path.

.   .   .

In Peking, if there was an image that characterized our mission, with its ups and downs, it is of Jim Huskey—who figured so prominently in many of the pivotal events during my ambassadorship—retrieving his car from Tiananmen Square where he had parked it on the eve of the crackdown on June 3.

By mid-June, the city was under lockdown. Tanks surrounded the square, and soldiers, with rifles at their sides, stood at attention in front of the Great Hall of the People. No one was permitted on the square. Determined to get his car, Huskey walked down Chang'an Boulevard, passing armed sentries who stared at him. Inexplicably, nobody attempted to stop the solitary American diplomat as he entered Tiananmen Square. Huskey crossed the barren square, scrubbed clean except for the scorched area near the Monument to the Martyrs, where the army's bonfire had incinerated the remains of the students' tent city and, perhaps, a good many bodies too.

In front of the Great Hall of the People, two lines of PLA soldiers stood erect at attention, one line behind the other with a space of about five feet between the soldiers. Beyond them, parked against a wall at the base of the Great Hall of the People, was Huskey's lonely gray Honda. Like its American owner, the Honda had been an incongruous intruder on the assertion of Chinese military might over the square. The car had been parked on the square the entire time—through the final hours of the student protest, the violent crackdown, and the reassertion of the PLA's control. Knowing that a thousand pairs of eyes were boring in on his every move, Huskey strolled through the phalanx of soldiers to his car. He put the key in the ignition and started her up. Then he backed up between two soldiers and drove off.

Why didn't the Chinese stop him? Why hadn't they removed his car? It was the same sort of hands-off policy toward foreigners that—with the exception of the soldiers firing on the diplomatic compound on June 7—had defined the Chinese government's approach to Tiananmen before the fateful decision to bring in the troops. They knew that the car had a diplomatic license plate, and they had undoubtedly researched who the owner was.

One lesson I took away from my posting in Peking was an age-old one. There is something powerful about the individual standing up against the machine. The Tiananmen protests were a reflection of this historical struggle. It's no secret that the TV image that most captivated America and perhaps the world showed a single Chinese citizen, carrying what looks like his shopping bag, stopping a line of seventeen tanks in their tracks. When the lead tank tried to maneuver around the man, he shuffled to block its path. And so it went, a lone individual halting the powerful military, if only for a few minutes, until anxious bystanders pulled him to safety. Then, several weeks later, an undaunted American diplomat, a witness himself to the carnage of June 3 and 4, rendered the mighty military machine momentarily impotent by the simple act of reclaiming his forlorn automobile.

Another lesson was that China's business was also the world's business, and, as a result, China had to concern itself more realistically with its external image. That had been hammered home by the reporting of CNN and other networks, which appealed viscerally to viewers around the globe. Contrary to what Deng Xiaoping might have thought, you can't commit atrocities and expect Westerners to forget. Not with instant TV images being broadcast to the world.

Many of those images from 1989 were of students, the brave catalysts for the demonstrations. They came to the square very cognizant of the importance of Tiananmen in Chinese people's aspirations for a better future, and for a brief time in May and June 1989, the students and their supporters carried on these aspirations by reclaiming the square. I saw numerous parallels with the May 4th movement seventy years earlier, and I see now that stages of my life—which was begun in Tsingtao, arguably the tripwire for those 1919 demonstrations, and culminated professionally with my posting in Peking as ambassador—seem like bookends for a turbulent yet fascinating period of Chinese history.

EPILOGUE

In June 2003, I talked about my family's connection to China with members of the Yale Class of 1943, Frank's class. They were celebrating their sixtieth reunion in New Haven and invited me to speak. I have long admired these men, many of whom graduated early to fight in World War II. They are part of "the greatest generation." More than forty members of the Class of 1943 entered intelligence work, and many stayed on to form the core of the new CIA in its long struggle against communism. Now in their early eighties, a number of them are still surprisingly energetic and active.

Frank, of course, is my personal connection to the Class of '43, and Yale is one of the many threads that tied us together. As Sally and I walked across the campus to meet his classmates, we passed by some of his old haunts: the walled compound of Skull and Bones, the brick façades of Pierson College and Dwight Hall, and the legendary swimming pool in Payne Whitney gymnasium, where he trained to set a world record. Frank would have been 82 at the reunion, but it wasn't his fate to live long. His name is on the wall of Battell Chapel along with those of his classmates who died in the war.

In retrospect, my family's engagement with China seems almost preordained. The hand of destiny—or as the Chinese say, the order of heaven—kept pulling us back to the Middle Kingdom. And our involvement over almost nine decades reflected the great changes that shook the country in the twentieth century.

My father came first as the businessman, engaging in commerce and raising a family during the era of foreign dominance. We lived well, with special privileges and military protection, while most of the Chinese people suffered in the constant fighting between warlords. It was the time, paraphrasing Chairman Mao, of semifeudal, semicolonial existence. Frank's spirit and energy epitomized the good life in Tsingtao and our isolation from China's troubles. But those halcyon days soon ended, as Frank had let us know they would in his letters from occupied Korea. The Japanese invasion and chaos of war followed. The foreigners were toppled and humiliated.

Frank came second, returning as a soldier during World War II. He saw firsthand China's disintegration into chaos and corruption, and his personal decline after leaving China reflected the country's descent into civil war. The family connection also continued through Jack. After the war, he returned to China as an employee of Standard Oil and attempted to relive the "good old" days. He spent much time raising hell and collecting girlfriends. But the past was gone. The company's business was sinking, and soon international businesses, including the Americans, were forced out by Mao's successful revolution. Jack was driven out after fighting his way into trouble. He may have beaten up a Chinese man, but he was powerless in the face of the rising tide of communism.

I came on the scene a few years later, the fourth Lilley in my family to engage China. World events drew me back into Asia with the start of the Korean War, and it turned me from a Russian literature major into a new China hand. It was unexpected, yet in retrospect had an air of inevitability. I didn't become a businessman selling oil for the lamps of China, nor did I work as a soldier teaching Chinese how to man artillery. Instead, I worked against China as a CIA officer during the era of hostility. I followed the efforts of the Chinese communists to change China for the better but at a horrible cost in human lives, and I challenged them covertly in their attempts to support leftist revolutionary movements in neighboring countries.

Two decades later, confrontation gave way to rapprochement, and I became a part of the reconciliation. At the CIA, we had sensed that China had to work itself out of its straitjacket of total Communist Party control, but trial and error had taught us that military and paramilitary moves were not the answer. Blockades, embargoes, and paramilitary operations on our part had all failed. The way to access China was via economics and diplomacy, and it was through encouraging China to open up that the United States has been able to increase its influence. My active role in that journey was given a boost by George H. W. Bush in Peking, and then I had the good fortune to work with him again at the CIA. I wouldn't have gotten into government at the policy level without his support. Shortly after his loss to Bill Clinton in November 1992, I wrote to thank him and Barbara for "twelve glorious years." In the letter I also wrote that for Sally and me our involvement with the Bushes had been "an affair of the heart as well as a commitment of mind and energy."

.　　　.　　　.

When I spoke to the Class of 1943, it was from the perspective of an independent China hand. I had left government ten years earlier, and over the past decade I had been free finally to air my personal views on China. Some of what I said was critical of China's government. For example, after my return from Peking in May 1991, I made some strong statements in a speech at Pennsylvania State University. These feelings had been building inside of me for some time. Perhaps I overstated the case when I called the Communist Party leadership "a decaying dynasty" that was hanging on to its own survival with a frightful brutality. I also criticized China's militant strategy for political reunification with Taiwan.

The Chinese struck back. In August 1991, the *People's Daily* printed a blistering attack in which they accused me of "wagging a loose tongue" and of being behind a plot to split China forever. Two of the more extreme accusations came from mainland mouthpieces in Hong Kong and Shanghai in the early 1990s. One article accused me of personally organizing the demonstrations at Tiananmen. Some overseas Chinese sycophants repeated these accusations, but I could only marvel at how they had exaggerated my role. As a CIA officer, I had been involved in some political subterfuge in my career, but I couldn't organize 200,000 Chinese youths in four weeks to almost overthrow an authoritarian state. *That* was beyond my capabilities. The other exaggeration was that I had set up a vast underground network in China to sneak

Tiananmen student leaders out of the country in the months following the massacre. I wish I had, but unfortunately no such thing ever happened. It took thirteen months and countless hours of negotiations just to get three dissidents out legally (Fang Lizhi, his wife, and son).

In my retirement I may have temporarily set aside my professional detachment by getting into a catfight with the Chinese authorities. I know my verbal sparring disappointed George Bush, who probably thought my comments were not helpful to Sino-U.S. relations. He had always counseled me to think about the big picture. But there was a basis for my comments. I believed that Taiwan was outperforming the mainland in many ways. It was a new kind of Chinese society—prosperous and democratic—and American policy needed to reflect this. I also believed there was no need to choose sides between Taiwan and China. You could get along with both.

In my comments about America's security challenges in the twenty-first century, I emphasized to the Class of '43 that managing the U.S.–China relationship will be crucial to maintaining stability in Asia. From the standpoint of U.S. policy, America must stay engaged militarily in Asia. We must continue to recognize and understand China's growing military and economic power and counter it with a system of alliances with our Asian allies and with forward-deployed U.S. military units that are smaller and more mobile. Together with U.S. economic ties to the region and effective information programs, stability and prosperity should be enhanced.

The Chinese now realize that the U.S. military can be a beneficial stabilizing force. This understanding is part of what is causing Peking to pressure North Korea to abandon its decision to build a nuclear weapons force at a time when it can barely feed its people. The stakes are high. This part of the world has already seen two major wars in the last fifty years. Should North Korea push ahead with plans to develop nuclear weapons, it could lead to a domino effect with Japan, South Korea, and Taiwan following suit. This is something China does not want and has helped motivate the Peking government to work with the U.S. to squeeze Kim Jong Il's regime, which is hooked on fomenting instability to gain financial reward and propped up by external aid, much of which comes from China. The challenge will be to work multilaterally with a mix of economic aid, diplomatic enticements, and security guarantees to influence the North to give up its weapons under verification and reform its failed economic system. All of this could lead to a change in the regime, which is the ultimate solution. Our friends and allies in the area tacitly agree but simply will not admit it.

For sometime, maintaining balance in Asia has consisted of making China a major part, but not the center, of overall American policy in Asia. This served the U.S. well in the 1980s when a Pan-Asian approach won out over a Sinocentric focus in the upper echelons of the Reagan bureaucracy, and it should continue to work well. Our alliance with Japan will change but continue to be a central part of our Asia policy, with the Japan–U.S. security treaty remaining the linchpin of the American military presence in Asia.

Keeping the strategic balance demands innovative thinking based on solid intelligence. For example, in the early 1990s, we were able to address Chinese concerns by making both concrete alterations and symbolic gestures regarding the sensitive area of military sales to Taiwan. In 1992, while serving a brief tour as assistant secretary for international security affairs at the Defense Department, I proposed the sale of advanced F–16 jet fighters to Taiwan. The move was largely in response to China's purchase from Russia of surface-to-air missiles, KILO-class submarines, and sophisticated SU–27 fighters, which changed the balance of power across the Taiwan Strait. I knew the Chinese would be upset because the $6 billion price tag for sophisticated aircraft for Taiwan stretched the August Communiqué to the breaking point. As a way to salve Peking's disapproval over the eventual sale of 150 F–16s to Taiwan, I cleaned up the messy problem of cost overruns on the joint U.S.–Chinese project to modernize its F–8 fighter force that was left over from the Tiananmen aftermath. We paid the Chinese government a reasonable sum to recompense them for their losses. The gesture allowed us to move on. Not that there wasn't displeasure in Peking and at State, but China's paramount leader Deng Xiaoping pointed out that, disturbing as the sale of the F–16s was, China had more important business with the U.S.

In advancing U.S.–China relations, personal connections between high-level interlocutors facilitate a blending of each side's interests into a workable formula. Former President Richard Nixon had this kind of relationship with Mao and Chou En-lai, and Henry Kissinger still does to some extent with current Chinese leaders. The breakthrough in the early 1970s could not have happened, given our basic differences, had these four men not seized the moment. They had the wisdom to move carefully but decisively when opportunities for change arose. George Bush and Deng Xiaoping carried forward what these men started.

I was personally privileged to witness the relationship develop between George Bush and Deng Xiaoping. As I have mentioned, the two men established an unusual chemistry in the 1970s based in part on each man's perception that the other would be a future leader of his country. Their personal ties paid off in the 1980s in planning for joint U.S.–Chinese intelligence cooperation against the Soviet Union and in a conversation about oil exploration off China's coast, which preceded by fifteen months Deng's major economic reforms. Bush's conversation with Deng in Houston in 1979 was part of an effort to defuse the Taiwan situation, and the Bush–Deng connection was even instrumental in the eventual fall of the Soviet Union through their joint effort, which expanded on the Carter administration initiative, to get the Soviets out of Afghanistan, and in reviving the bilateral relationship following its nadir in 1989.

. . .

In the short term, thanks to Peking's hosting of the Olympic Games in 2008 and China's joining the World Trade Organization, American policymakers probably have a grace period of four years within which to work toward greater economic and political cooperation. Both of these events should serve over time to reduce the influence of the militant element in Chinese policymaking. Because of the Games and the WTO, we can assume that China will place more emphasis on being a productive and more reliable partner in the world. China needs a stable periphery to concentrate on its number one priority: economic growth and domestic stability. China's entrance into the WTO should also temper its behavior by requiring it to drop barriers on trade and investment and adjust its agricultural policies. China will resist this in its present mercantilist fixation, but over time we should be able to reduce the meddlesome role that the government currently plays. Joint efforts against terrorism should further improve the Chinese role in world affairs and give the U.S.–China relationship a base to build on. How the country's space program plays out remains to be seen, but it need not be confrontational. After all, Chinese rockets have already launched U.S. satellites.

Lastly, American policymakers must continue to appreciate what Taiwan stands for. The country is not an "obstacle" as the mainland Chinese and even members of our State Department and academia often insist. It is trying to be a democracy and has been a political and economic partner of the United States for nearly six decades, through good and bad times. Opposition candidate Chen Shuibien's election as president of Taiwan in March 2000 represented the first time in thousands of years that a true democratic state has emerged peacefully on Chinese territory. There is great turmoil and disagreement, the challenges are significant, and the jury is still out on whether Taiwan's testing of democracy will work. But it is an important step to demonstrate that Western democratic concepts can be adapted to a basically Confucian, authoritarian society.

Taiwan's stability should be established and supported. If need be, America should sell certain weapons systems—be they F–16s or Aegis-class destroyers—to help the island feel confident in dealing with mainland China. We should position aircraft carriers off Taiwan when China threatens and flexes its military muscles. Of course, China is going to respond, but—and here is where China's pragmatism and taking the long view come into play—China has a gigantic trade and investment relationship with Taiwan that started in 1987 and that is now essential both to China's growth and prosperity and to Taiwan's stability. It is estimated that between 750,000 and one million Taiwan businesspeople live in China today. The two areas are becoming interdependent. China's economic growth goes a long way toward keeping it stable. In Taiwan, the country's investment in China, estimated at about $100 billion, is becoming a new engine for growth.

Also, keep in mind that just seven months after the F–16 sale to Taiwan in 1992, China and Taiwan had their first formal meetings about cross-strait relations in Singapore in April 1993. When Taiwan gets

U.S. support, it becomes a more confident and creative partner in dealing with the mainland.

There is invective hurled back and forth over Peking's one-China policy and Taiwan independence, but so far this is largely political rhetoric, like voices arguing theory while the juggernaut of economic action rumbles on. I also believe that as long as China doesn't use force against Taiwan, the island will not declare independence and will move gradually toward greater integration.

Shared economic power and evolutionary political liberalization—already in place in Taiwan and emerging in China—could make Asia more stable by emphasizing economic competition more and military gamesmanship less. Gradual economic integration is clearly the most positive long-term trend in China–Taiwan relations, one we should support and nurture, but not try to manage. The details of cross-strait relations are something the Chinese themselves have to work out.

· · ·

In the Western mind, unity of opposites has characterized the East for centuries. A documentary that aired in China in the relatively open days of 1988 captured the dichotomy that colors China's dealings with the West. *Yellow River Elegy* juxtaposed China's Yellow River culture with its blue water culture. The Yellow River culture, taking its name from the long river that snakes its way up into the Chinese hinterlands, represents the country's backward and insular side, which has isolated China. The blue water culture, on the other hand, symbolizes China's access to the open seas and describes the part of China that welcomes, and benefits from, foreign relations and commerce. The six-part series' heavy political undertones supporting Zhao Ziyang's reformist line got it banned prior to the heady days of spring 1989.

The two sides of China's psyche tug at one another—yin and yang. China's state system struggles to find the right balance with its burgeoning free market sector. The Communist Party welcomes rich entrepreneurs even as it tries to preserve its monopoly on power. The U.S. is perceived in one glance as the great bully and in another as the Mecca for young, nationalistic students. China espouses noninterference in the internal affairs of other states but has a long record of fighting with its neighbors. Lastly, for problems inside the country, the Chinese government still manages to demonize the U.S. and Japan even though its leaders know the roots of their problems are domestic and internal. As I survey my life of working on China, I see there has been another unity of opposites. My brother Frank was a dreamer, pacifist, and philosopher who died young. I have been or tried to be the pragmatic, largely unsentimental officer who is now living into his eighth decade. Frank probably wouldn't have agreed with my decision to join the CIA, nor approved of my training Chinese paramilitary agents or aiding the secret guerrilla war in Laos.

But when I look back over the tapestry of my life with its confusing patchwork of events, a clearer pattern emerges. Frank and China have always been connected in my mind, and in choosing to study China and work in Asia, I remain linked with Frank. Even as the distance in years from his death became greater, he continued to be part of my life experiences. Visits to Kure, Tsingtao, and Beidaihe rekindled memories of Frank. His letters about his disappointment while serving in China in 1945 helped me to understand the chaos, cruelty, and corruption that I observed in China in the ensuing decades. Meeting people in South Korea and China who knew of Frank added a personal quality to postings that could be tense at times. And the nerve-wracking experiences of being in Seoul on the verge of major violence in 1987 and of running the embassy in Peking during the carnage of Tiananmen Square were attenuated by the most powerful lesson of his death: stay away from disillusionment.

Finally, throughout my career, there was the redeemable quality of carrying on the work of building peace and stability in Asia, and of fulfilling Frank's aspiration for a better world. I think Frank would approve of my roles in the evolution of Taiwan and South Korea into democracies. And he would have congratulated me for working my way into the first U.S. diplomatic mission in communist China, probably penning a heartfelt and philosophical note in his familiar longhand as he had done so often while I was growing up. If my efforts in intelligence and diplomacy have helped achieve the goal of a more stable Asia, then the shattered world that Frank left behind in 1946 is the beneficiary.

ACKNOWLEDGMENTS

THIS BOOK is a personal memoir. It is composed of my remembrances and reflections on China and our involvement in Asia. We do draw on State Department cables obtained through a Freedom of Information Act request, but the book is not investigative history. For thoroughly researched and documented accounts, I suggest Jim Mann's book *About Face* (Knopf) and Pat Tyler's book *A Great Wall* (PublicAffairs). They are interesting and readable.

My own memory, interviews with friends and participants, State cables, and books are the basis for the book. Thanks go to John Tkacik for making our research at the State Department easier. However, I was unable to review my May 26, 1989, cable on Tiananmen. Nor did I see the long cable I wrote on June 19, 1987, after a critical meeting with President Chun of South Korea. I could not look at operational orders issued in 1967 on the B–52 bombing of the tri-border area of Cambodia, Laos, and Vietnam. I also cannot and will not discuss certain sensitive operations I was involved in. Protection of sources and methods still applies.

First, my appreciation goes to my friends, colleagues, and mentors in the Directorate of Operations at CIA, including David "Tick" Semmes and Ted Shackley. Then there are others: Bob M., Bill W., John H., Charlie W., and Joseph L. (Candied Yam Jackson) M. Sorry, no last names. I am grateful to Jim Schlesinger, who with help from Henry Kissinger got me to China in 1973 and who immediately saw the historic importance of this move, and to David Bruce, first chief of USLO, whose OSS background and shrewdness helped me through difficult times and tough decisions.

In Taiwan (1982–1984) David Dean was my friend and partner. Paul Wolfowitz backed me against bureaucratic interference. Fred Chien,

Henry Hsu, Norman Fu, and then Governor Lee Teng-hui were my associates and collaborators in progress. And our gratitude goes to Bill Brown, who gave us excellent background on the opening to China.

In Korea (1986–1989) Gaston Sigur was wise in the ways of Washington and was committed to democracy. Rich Armitage gave essential support at critical times. Park Soo Kil, Choi Kwang Soo, O Jae Bok, and Speedy Lee were the indispensable Korean colleagues. Roh Tae Woo changed the course of Korean history in 1987–1988 with his support for democracy and his opening to the world.

In China, there were the magnificent five who performed brilliantly and courageously during Tiananmen in June 1989. McKinney Russell, Kathy Gaseor, Jim Huskey, Larry Wortzel, and Lyn Edinger. Later Don Keyser was with me during our laborious and often contentious negotiations. Yang Jiechi, Zhang Yijun, and Zhang Zai made the U.S.– Chinese relationship work during challenging times. I was privileged to witness firsthand great Chinese leaders at work—visionaries and pragmatists like Deng Xiaoping and Chiang Ching-kuo.

And there is my wife, Sally, who put up with a life of endless moves with charm and optimism. In this book, she corrected our grammar, eliminated obvious redundancies, and checked facts. And to my son Jeffrey who inspired the book with his fascination with my brother Frank whom he never met. Jeff did a good part of the interviewing, research, and drafting. My sister, Elinore, gave her moving insights into our earlier years in China, while Don Hoagland and Walt Beckjord told us of Frank's years at Exeter, Yale, and in the army. Nan Rickey, Frank's wife, allowed Jeff to interview her about her short time with Frank.

Our agent, Alex Smithline, got us the publisher we needed, and at PublicAffairs publisher Peter Osnos and editor David Patterson were the patient and experienced hands who coaxed us along. John Thomas provided a cogent copyedit. Also, a big thanks to the American Enterprise Institute for office space, communications, and plenty of time to complete the project.

And finally to George H. W. Bush, our forty-first president. His decisions to come to China in 1974, take over CIA in 1975, and move from Vice President to President had the unintended consequences of changing my life. He guided and supported me, and without him I could not have written this book.

NOTES

CHAPTER I
"WHERE THE DAISIES COVER THE COUNTRY LAND"

Interviews: Elinore Washburn and Mayna Avent.

Information on working for Standard Oil in China is from Hobart, *Oil for the Lamps of China*, 172 and 190.

"Coolie" was the commonly used term for a Chinese laborer. It was the anglicized version of two Chinese characters, "ku" meaning bitter and "li" meaning strength. Coolies did the hardest work for low pay.

Information on political developments in China during the eighteenth and early part of the nineteenth centuries is from MacMillan, *Paris 1919*, 324–325, and Fairbank, *China: A New History*, 250–256.

Along the Yangtze . . . material from Tolley, *Yangtze Patrol: The U.S. Navy in China*, 79.

Information on U.S. policy toward China during the eighteenth and early part of the nineteenth centuries and the Open Door Policy is from Davies, *Dragon by the Tail: American, British, Japanese, and Russian Encounters with China and One Another*, 71–100, and Spence, *The Search for Modern China*, 161–162.

Information on the Boxer Rebellion is from Fairbank, *China: A New History*, 230–232.

Information on the history of Tsingtao is from *Review of Tsingtao 1928–29*, The Tsingtao Times Publishing Company, 1928 (in New York Public Library); MacMillan, *Paris 1919*, 326–344; and Records of Foreign Service Posts, Consular Posts, Tsingtao, China, volumes 204 and 207, the National Archives and Records Administration, College Park, Md.

"If ever there was justification for Old World imperialism . . . ": *Review of Tsingtao 1928–29*, 1.

The description of the life and death of warlord Chang Tsungchang is from Hart, *The*

Making of an Army "Old China Hand": A Memoir of Colonel David D. Barrett, 10–12 and 21.

Information on Pyongyang Foreign School and life in Pyongyang in the 1930s is from interviews with Paul Crane. Details on Japan's pressure campaign against American missionaries in Pyongyang is from an interview with Samuel Moffet Jr.

Details on the start of the Sino-Japanese war at Lukouchiao are from Tuchman, *Stilwell and the American Experience in China, 1911–1945,* 164–165, and the *New York Times,* July 8, 10, 11, and 20, 1937.

For information on the Xian Incident, see Spence, *The Gate of Heavenly Peace: The Chinese and Their Revolution, 1895–1980,* 158–159, 307–310; Han, *The Morning Deluge: Mao Tsetung and the Chinese Revolution 1893–1954,* 326–330; and Tuchman, *Stilwell and the American Experience,* 159–161.

"the most bizarre experience ever to befall . . .": Han, *The Morning Deluge,* 159.

"a Chinese enigma . . . Chang Hsüehliang": *The Economist,* October 27, 2001.

CHAPTER 2
ONLY A MEMORY

Accounts of the battle of Tientsin are drawn from the *New York Times,* July 31 and August 1, 1937.

Accounts of the battle of Shanghai are drawn from the *New York Times,* August 10, 15, 16, 17, 20, and 31, 1937.

The account of the Japanese takeover of Tsingtao is drawn from the personal letters of Walter Palmer, whose father worked for Standard Oil in Tsingtao at the time.

For more on the American 15th Infantry in Tientsin, see Tuchman, *Stilwell and the American Experience,* 98–101, 180, and the *New York Times,* February 5, 1938.

The story of Taki is taken from an article I wrote in 1944 for *The Phillips Exeter Review,* June 1944, which we obtained from the Phillips Exeter Library.

CHAPTER 3
AMERICANIZATION

Interviews: Donald Hoagland, William Washburn, and Elinore Washburn.

Arnold's "Dover Beach" from *The Norton Anthology of Poetry,* 850.

"an awesome, pervasive presence . . . ": Ketchum, *The Borrowed Years, 1938–1941: America on the Way to War,* 241.

CHAPTER 4
AN ANGUISHED CRY

Interviews: Walt Beckjord, Zeph Stewart, Nan Viergutz, and Bill W. (CIA under cover).

Information on the Dixie Mission and on General Stilwell and Generalissimo Chiang Kai-shek is from Spence, *The Search for Modern China,* 470–479; Tuchman, *Stilwell and the American Experience,* 1–5 and 477–484; and Davies, *Dragon by the Tail,* 337–339.

Information on the Field Artillery Training Center is from Col. Donald Q. Harris, "Organizing Artillery Battalions in China," *The Field Artillery Journal,* volume 35, no. 6. (June 1945), 322, and "Six Training Centers in China Follow U.S. Army Pattern," *Christian Science Monitor,* March 10, 1945, 8.

To help put Frank Lilley's military duty in China in 1945 in context, we drew on *U.S. Army in World War II, Chronology 1941–1945,* D.769.A53, volume 8, part 5 (dates are 1/27–30/45), and *The Historical Encyclopedia of World War II,* D740.E5213.

were only just beginning to recognize . . . : In September 1942, Dr. Clement C. Fry, a psychiatrist at Yale and head of the health department's division of student mental hygiene, gave talks to freshmen in Dwight Hall and to freshmen counselors on how psychiatry was an important emerging branch of modern medicine and its application in university mental hygiene. For more information on the early role of psychiatry at Yale, see the September 1942 issue of the *Yale Alumni Magazine,* 7.

For an account of the failure of General Marshall's mission in 1945–1947, see White and Jacoby, *Thunder Out of China,* 292–297.

Details on post-war Shanghai are from an interview with Bill W., who served as a sergeant in the U.S. Army in Shanghai from October 1945 to April 1946; from "U.S. Sailors Steer for Shanghai Silks," the *New York Times,* September 10, 1945; from *Time,* November 26 and December 24, 1945; and from *The New Yorker,* "A Reporter in Shanghai: Ordeal of a Hopeful Man," March 23, 1946.

For an account of conditions in post-war Japan, see Dower, *Embracing Defeat.*

Information on Frank's death is from the official military investigation into his death, which was sent to my parents.

CHAPTER 5
A READY RECRUIT

Information on the fall of Tsingtao to the communists is from the *New York Times,* February 13 and 14, and June 4, 1949.

For Peter Braestrup's comments on the world situation, see *1951 Class Book,* 33 and 46.

For Yale's connection to the U.S. intelligence community, see Winks, *Cloak and Gown: Scholars in the Secret War, 1939–1961,* 35–59.

Waller Booth wrote an autobiography of his OSS operations behind German lines in occupied France during World War II. It is called *Mission Marcel-Proust: The Story of an Unusual OSS Undertaking* (Philadelphia: Dorrance, 1972).

CHAPTER 6
A COVERT FOOT SOLDIER

Information on the CIA's intelligence operations against China is supplemented with information from the *New York Times,* January 30 and February 2, 1952; and July 3 and July 15, 1953.

For President Truman's position on the defense of Taiwan, see Acheson, *Present at the Creation: My Years in the State Department,* 349–351.

Information on Jack Downey's mission and imprisonment in China is from written communication with him; from Kiyonaga, *My Spy: Memoir of a CIA Wife,* 112–114; from *Time,* "Twenty Years in China," March 26, 1973, 31; and from "*. . . And for Yale": 1951 Remembers on the Occasion of its 50th Reunion and Yale's Tercentenary,* 44–48.

For information on military operations on the border between Burma and China, see the *New York Times,* July 28, 1951; February 16, 1953; and March 2, 1953.

For information on Hong Kong in 1953, see the *New York Times,* "Refugee Influx Complicates Hong Kong Health Problems," September 6, 1953, and "Hong Kong's Britons Mock the Theory of Inevitability," July 20, 1953.

For details of mainland China's bombardment of Quemoy and the ensuing crisis, see the *New York Times,* August 24, 26, and 29, September 8 and 9, October 6 and 26, and December 24, 1958.

For information on the Great Leap Forward, see Fairbank, *China: A New History,* 368–372.

CHAPTER 7
ON THE EDGE OF CONFLICT

During my tours in the Philippines and Cambodia, at a time when Americans could not get into China, we worked with resourceful Chinese to report the facts on China to the United States government. Our contacts helped us to understand some of the dimensions of the tragedy of the Great Leap Forward. Meanwhile, in academic circles, the late Professor Richard Walker of the University of South Carolina documented in his booklet *Letters from Communes* some of the same kind of information we were reporting from Southeast Asia, but he was attacked for so-called exaggerations. In retrospect, we now know that Walker's only failing was in underestimating the scale of the tragedy. Today Jasper Becker's book *Hungry Ghosts: Mao's Secret Famine* (New York: The Free Press, 1996) convincingly describes the immense horrors we reported.

Information on Cambodia is supplemented by U.S. Department of State Background Notes on East Asia and the Pacific, www.state.gov/www/background_notes/cambodia.

CHAPTER 8
RUNNING THE SECRET WAR

Interviews: Ted Shackley and Sally Lilley.

Background information for incidents and personalities during the 1965–1968 period in Laos is from Thomas, *The Very Best Men: Four Who Dared: The Early Years of the CIA*; Warner, *Backfire: The CIA's Secret War in Laos and Its Link to the War in Vietnam*; Castle, *At War in the Shadow of Vietnam: U.S. Military Aid to the Royal Lao Government, 1955–1975*; and Conboy, *Shadow War: The CIA's Secret War in Laos*. We also drew on various obituaries of Tony Poe, who passed away in 2003 in San Francisco at the age of 78. Vint Lawrence returned to the U.S. in 1965 to work in a high-profile job at CIA headquarters, but he soon left and started a second career as a political cartoonist and artist.

For the Ojibway helicopter crash, see Warner, *Backfire*, 173–174.

For the Geneva agreements of 1962 and their violation, see Castle, *At War in the Shadow of Vietnam*, 42–47 and 89.

For another version of the treatment of General Vang Pao's wound, see Warner, *Backfire*, 179–180.

For information on Poe, see Thomas, *The Very Best Men*, 196 and 276; Warner, *Backfire*, 53, 146–148, and 251–252.

For information on Lawrence, see Warner, *Backfire*, 75–76 and 89.

For information on Lair, see Warner, *Backfire*, 31, 83–84, 163–164, and 180.

CHAPTER 9
OF COUPS, FLOODS, AND FAILURES

Interviews: William Maynes and Mark Pratt.

There has been discussion that the CIA was involved in the drug trade in Laos. I can say that the CIA as an organization was not involved. The closest the CIA got when I was there was the bombing raids by the T–28s under the command of the Lao commander in chief, which were done without our knowledge at the Vientiane station. If the CIA had known its resources were being used for the drug trade, it would have caught and punished the offending people.

For information on Kissinger's conversation with Chou En-lai about the Chinese road in northern Laos, see Kissinger, *Years of Upheaval*, 58–59.

Information on the flood in September 1966 is from the *Bangkok World*, "The Vientiane Floods," October 6, 1966, 12.

Information on General Thouma's attempted coup is from the *Bangkok World*, "Surprise Bomb Attack on Vientiane Airport," October 22, 1966, 1.

For information on Site 85, see Warner, *Backfire*, 220–234.

For information on the Hmong people, see www.home.earthlink.net/~laohuman-rights/1998data.html and www.stolaf.edu/peoples/cdr/hmong.

For information on Mike Deuel and Mike Maloney, see Gup, *The Book of Honor: The Secret Lives and Deaths of CIA Operatives*, 163–206.

CHAPTER 10
READING THE TEA LEAVES

Interviews: David Gries, Bill W., Stanley Bergman, and Sally Lilley.

For information on the Tibet operation, see Knauss, *Orphans of the Cold War: America and the Tibetan Struggle for Survival*, 249.

"If you want to know what's going on . . .": interview with David Gries.

Information on Father La Dany's reports is from *U.S. News & World Report*, "A New Look Inside Today's China," June 24, 1968, 86–87, and www.scrc.fju.edu.tw/Chinese.

For information on riots in Washington, see *U.S. News & World Report*, "The Second Sacking of Washington," April 22, 1968, 32.

The accounts of the Cultural Revolution are supplemented with material from Karnow's *Mao and China: From Revolution to Revolution,* 429–443. The events in Guangxi Province are supplemented with material from the *New York Times,* "Continuing Turmoil in Kwangsi Poses Major Issue for Maoists," July 14, 1968, A1; and *Time,* "The Pearl's Grisly Flotsam," July 5, 1968, 2, and "More Violent Than Imagined," July 19, 1968, 24.

Information on the border clashes in 1969 is from Tyler, *A Great Wall: Six Presidents and China,* 64.

For the text of Nixon's article in *Foreign Affairs,* see Richard M. Nixon, "Asia After Vietnam," *Foreign Affairs,* volume 46, October 1967, 121.

For more information on Secretary of State Rogers' speech and the atmosphere of conciliation that followed, see Karnow, *Mao and China,* 494–495.

CHAPTER 11
Breaking Down Walls

Interviews: Ambassador William Brown and Sally Lilley.

"That's one small step . . . ": nssdc.gsfc.nasa.gov/planetary/lunar/apollo_11_30th.html.

"As I have pointed out . . . ": *Public Papers of the Presidents of the United States, Richard Nixon, 1971,* 819–820.

"What brings us together . . . ": Burr, *The Kissinger Transcripts,* 64.

The account of Kissinger's dummy entourage in Pakistan is drawn from Mann, *About Face: A History of America's Curious Relationship with China, from Nixon to Clinton,* 29–32.

The account of Jenkins and his small secretive group is from author's interview with Ambassador William Brown.

"Henry Kissinger was having . . . ": interview with Ambassador William Brown.

For the text of the Shanghai Communiqué, see Holdridge, *Crossing the Divide: An Insider's Account of Normalization of US–China Relations,* 263–267.

"History has brought . . . ": Burr, *The Kissinger Transcripts,* 65.

"With conscientious attention . . . ": Kissinger, *Years of Upheaval,* 70.

"embassies in everything but name . . . ": Burr, *The Kissinger Transcripts,* 85.

"We will identify him . . . ": Burr, *The Kissinger Transcripts,* 160, note 2.

"Our action in seeking . . . ": *Public Papers of the Presidents of the United States, Richard Nixon, 1971,* 820.

"Yes, we have to preserve . . . ": Jenkins, *Country, Conscience and Caviar: A Diplomat's Journey in the Company of History,* 290–291.

"We should be under no illusions . . . ": Burr, *The Kissinger Transcripts,* 117.

"I can only tell you . . . ": ". . . *And for Yale,*" 48.

For more on Jack Downey and recollections of his time in prison, see ". . . *And for Yale,*" 44–48 and 313–314; and *Time,* "Twenty Years in China," March 26, 1973, 31.

CHAPTER 12
KISSINGER'S MAN IN CHINA

For more information on David Bruce and USLO, see Roberts, *Window on the Forbidden City: The Beijing Diaries of David Bruce, 1973–1974.*

"Criticize Lin, criticize Confucius": "Lin" referred to Lin Biao, a former head of defense and trusted colleague of Mao's, who had allegedly plotted to overthrow Mao in 1971 and was killed in a mysterious plane crash that year while he was supposedly escaping to the Soviet Union, the hated enemy. The famous Chinese philosopher Confucius was out of favor because at one point in his life he had called for overthrown feudal leaders to be restored to power so that China could benefit from their talents. The dig was apparently aimed at Chou En-lai for bringing back to government people like Deng Xiaoping, who had been run out of office during the Cultural Revolution.

For a good recollection of events in Beijing during the period 1973–1974, including the political infighting going on in China, the controversy over the U.S. Marines, and the fiasco with the visa applications, see Holdridge, *Crossing the Divide,* 143–147, 126, and 119–120.

"It still looks as if you need . . . ": Burr, *The Kissinger Transcripts,* p. 297.

For Jack Anderson's column, see "Firm, U.S. Pay for Officials' Trip," the *Washington Post,* October 30, 1974, C11.

Many years later, after George H. W. Bush had been president of the United States, when the George Bush Presidential Library Center was opening up at Texas A&M University in College Station, Texas, I sent George Bush's farewell letter down to the library. To me, it captured the essence of a great American leader.

CHAPTER 13
GOOD FORTUNE

Interviews: Michael Pillsbury and Richard Allen.

The lines from *Julius Caesar* are from *The Complete Works of Shakespeare,* edited by G. B. Harrison (New York: Harcourt, Brace & Company, 1968), Act 4, Scene 3, lines 218–219.

"I happen to have been a mountaineer . . . ": the *Washington Post,* "Out of Power in U.S., Republicans Still Popular in China," September 29, 1977.

For more information on the trip to China with George Bush in September 1977, see the series of articles in the *Washington Post* filed by David Broder. Dates of articles are September 29 and October 2, 5, 9, 16, and 19, 1977.

The account of the visit to Drapchi Prison in Tibet in 1977 is drawn partly from Embassy cable (Beijing), "Ambassador's Visit to Drapchi Prison in Lhasa," April 5, 1991, unclassified, released in part, obtained from the State Department through presidential appointee access, 2001.

For the text of the TASS dispatch on the Schlesinger trip to China, see Moscow World Service in English, "London Paper Reports Growing CIA–PRC Cooperation," October 31, 1978.

"make available to Taiwan . . . ": Wolff and Simon, *Legislative History of the Taiwan Relations Act,* 288–295.

CHAPTER 14
RIDING A WAVE

Details of George Bush's meetings with Deng Xiaoping in Houston in February 1980 are from the author's personal notes taken at the meeting.

For more on Governor Reagan's statement about reestablishing diplomatic relations with Taiwan, see *Time,* "A Case Study in Confusion," September 8, 1980, 21.

Details of George Bush's meeting with Deng Xiaoping in Peking in August 1980 and the trip back to the U.S. are from the author's personal notes taken at the meeting and from Tyler, *A Great Wall,* 292–295, and Mann, *About Face,* 116–118.

CHAPTER 15
Righting the Balance

Interviews: David Dean, Fred Chien, Lin Chongpin, Sally Lilley, and phone interview with Arthur Hummel.

"permit unofficial relations . . . ": Gibert and Carpenter, *America and Island China: A Documentary History,* 296.

"in the context of progress . . . ": ibid., 297.

Details of the meetings with Vice Foreign Minister Chien are from notes taken from AIT cables (Taipei), No. 02499, May 7, 1982, and No. 02577, May 11, 1982, unclassified, obtained from the State Department through presidential appointee access, 2002.

My understanding is that Haig presented two options: one, that the U.S. agree unilaterally to end arms sales in Taiwan or, two, that reduction of arms sales was, rather, dependent on there being peace in China–Taiwan relations and that it would be gradual. The second option included the important caveat that the U.S. be prepared to face a downgrading of relations by the PRC.

"The future of Sino-American . . . ": Haig, *Caveat,* 214.

"The Chinese went kicking and screaming . . . ": interview with Hummel.

"Strive for a peaceful solution . . . ": Wolff and Simon, *Legislative History of the Taiwan Relations Act,* 312.

"over a period of time . . . ": ibid., 313.

A copy of President Reagan's presidential directive about the August Communiqué was obtained from a former high-ranking member of the Reagan administration.

CHAPTER 16
The Golden Years

"When it came down to a tough decision . . . ": interview with William Brown.

"with a paper bag . . . ": interview with Clarke Ellis.

"Focus on the positive aspects . . . ": AIT cable (Taipei), "Some Suggestions for the President's Trip to the PRC," March 8, 1984, unclassified, obtained from the State Department through presidential appointee access, 2002.

For a history of Taiwan's domestic politics during the late 1970s and early 1980s, see Taylor, *The Generalissimo's Son: Chiang Ching-kuo and the Revolutions in China and Taiwan.*

"My argument was that . . . ": interview with David Dean.

"this vigorous and healthy Taiwanese . . . ": Notes taken from AIT cable (Taipei), No. 00908, February 15, 1984, unclassified, obtained from the State Department through presidential appointee access, 2002.

"making great contributions . . . ": *United Daily News* article on my departure from Taiwan is from AIT cable (Taipei), "Report for Period May 15–21, 1984," No. 03169, May 30, 1984, unclassified, obtained from the State Department through presidential appointee access, 2002.

CHAPTER 17
PUSHING FOR CHANGE

Interviews: Hyun Hong Choo and O Jae Bok.

Economic statistics about South Korea are from "U.S.–South Korean Bilateral Relations: The Impact of Korea's Growth on Political and Economic Issues," a speech by Anthony Interlandi, Department of State, at The 2nd Annual U.S.–Korea Trade Seminar, November 11, 1988.

For details on the Rangoon bombing, see Oberdorfer, *The Two Koreas: A Contemporary History*, 140–144.

"Hidden hand . . . ": Oberdorfer, *The Two Koreas*, 125. I had learned that as events in Kwangju were unfolding in May 1980 and afterward, despite their best intentions, Ambassador William Gleysteen and General John Wickham, the senior U.S. military commander in Korea, were perceived by some observers as having given conflicting signals about their views on the use of the Korean military in suppressing civilian disturbances. In early May, Gleysteen had said the U.S. would not oppose South Korean government contingency plans to use the army to reinforce Korean police, thus inadvertently giving cover to Chun's use of the military in putting down the Kwangju uprising. Wickham complicated matters by saying in an interview in August 1980 that the U.S. would support Chun if he came to power legitimately.

Wickham was also much quoted in his likening of the Korean people to lemmings in the way they were inclined to support a strong leader like Chun. American statements were then distorted by the Korean military and government to their own advantage. During the actual siege of Kwangju, in a bid, perhaps, to show evidence of a united front with the U.S., a government-controlled radio station falsely reported that the United States had approved the dispatch of Korean special forces troops into the city. Despite protestations by Gleysteen, a retraction by the Koreans was never given. See Wickham, *Korea on the Brink:*

From the "12/12 Incident" to the Kwangju Uprising, 1979–1980, 156, and Oberdorfer, *The Two Koreas,* 124–125 and 129–133.

"we decided to get rather bold . . .": Gaston Sigur, oral history interview, Georgetown University Library, 9.

"It is essential that for the future of the Republic of Korea, and for the future of our bilateral relations, that any new constitution and the laws which support representative government create a more open and legitimate political system," Gaston said pointedly at the speech in New York. *Far Eastern Economic Review,* "No More Big Brother," March 12, 1987, 24.

The statement about the demonstrations in Korea being the single biggest story is from Oberdorfer, *The Two Koreas,* 167.

"But that cannot be . . . ": Thomas P. H. Dunlop, oral history interview, Georgetown University Library, 151.

"I don't believe that President Chun . . . ": ibid., 152.

"social chaos . . . ": *The Washington Post,* "Carefully Timed U.S. Advice Played Role in S. Korean Events," July 5, 1987, A19.

"extraordinary decision . . . ": ibid., A19.

"send to the world a dramatic signal . . . ": Reagan's letter to Chun is courtesy of the personal files of Don Oberdorfer.

Dunlop's comment is from Thomas P. H. Dunlop, oral history interview, Georgetown University Library, 153.

"I was reading all these cables . . . ": Gaston Sigur, oral history interview, Georgetown University Library, 10–11.

"this is a crucial period . . . ": Embassy cable (Seoul), "Assistant Secretary Sigur's Meeting with DJP Chairman Roh Tae Woo," No. 07472, June 24, 1987, secret (declassified 1996), obtained at National Security Archives, Washington, D.C.

"I have now come to a firm conviction . . . ": Lee, *The Odyssey of Korean Democracy: Korean Politics, 1987–1990,* Appendix 1.

"the damnedest thing I ever saw . . . ": the *Washington Post,* "Carefully Timed U.S. Advice Played Role in S. Korean Events," July 5, 1987, A19.

CHAPTER 18
"THROUGH THE BLUR OF OUR TEARS"

Interviews: David Ransom, Park Soo Kil, Kim Kyung Won, Kim Kye Won, and Sally Lilley.

Details on Kim Hyun Hee's capture, imprisonment, and interrogation are from her autobiography *The Tears of My Soul;* Oberdorfer, *The Two Koreas;* a conversation with former U.S. Ambassador to Bahrain David Ransom; an interview with Park Soo Kil; and Embassy cable (Seoul), "ROKG Announcement on KAL 858, TV Appearance of 'Mayumi,'" No. 00563, January 15, 1988, unclassified, obtained at National Security Archives, Washington, D.C.

The comment about Henderson showing his scar to visitors is from author's interview with former U.S. Ambassador to Bahrain David Ransom.

"Get her out of here . . . ": Kim, *The Tears of My Soul,* 130.

Park Soo Kil's comments are from author's interview with him.

"Forgive me. I am sorry . . . ": Kim, *The Tears of My Soul,* 154.

"to take advantage of . . . ": State Department cable, "Demarche to Chinese Regarding Domestic ROK Political Situation," No. 195785, June 25, 1987, unclassified, released in part, obtained from the State Department through presidential appointee access, 2002.

The comment about Kim's arrival bringing Roh at least 1.5 million votes on election day is from author's interview with Park Soo Kil.

"Here is the so-called Vice Foreign Minister . . . ": author's interview with Park Soo Kil.

The comment on Shevardnadze assuring President Reagan about safety at the 1988 Olympics is from Oberdorfer, *The Two Koreas,* 186.

"If we get separated . . . ": author's interview with Kim Kyung Won.

"When I looked at the glorious spectacle . . . ": author's interview with Sally Lilley.

Recollection of the basketball game is from a conversation with Douglas Lilley and e-mail communication with Scott Simpson.

There were compelling reasons for South Korea to open up to China, but as an Asia hand I also wanted to remind South Koreans that they should not let the establishment of diplomatic relations with China damage the country's relations with Taiwan. In my meetings with President Roh in 1988 and later in 1991 with an audience of South Korean diplomats and security specialists, I emphasized the strong political and economic bonds linking South Korea and Taiwan. Both were emerging democracies. Both had strong technological and manufacturing bases to their economies, which they had built up themselves, and commercial relations between the two countries were steady and mutually beneficial. Finally, Taiwan had supported Korea during the Korean War. I also advised the South Koreans to be wary of Chinese negotiating techniques, such as the Chinese propensity to seize the issue of principle in negotiations and try to control the environment of the negotiations by holding them in Peking. I am not sure how much Korean policymakers listened to me. They handled negotiations their own way, and after a protracted period, in 1992, four decades after fighting each other during the Korean War, the two countries established diplomatic relations. For Taiwan, South Korea's turn to China was a slap in the face. There was bitterness on Taiwan's side, and air flights between the two countries were suspended for an indefinite time. My old Taiwan counterpart Fred Chien said to me caustically, "We can more readily accept your fumbling in negotiations with the Chinese because you are a major power. Korea, on the other hand, was a tributary state of China."

Laurence Binyon's poem *For the Fallen* can be found at www.firstworldwar.com/poetsandprose/binyon.htm.

"It is rare . . . ": State Department cable, "Letter of Appreciation," December 20, 1988, unclassified, personal files of James Lilley.

CHAPTER 19
STEPPING ON A VOLCANO

Interviews: McKinney Russell, Larry Wortzel, Jim Huskey, Gerrit Gong, Tick Semmes, and Sally Lilley. Phone interviews: Jim Ireland and Mary Ellen Ireland. E-mail communication with Kathy Gaseor.

"my rich diplomatic experience . . . ": Foreign Broadcast Information Service, March 30, 1989, 9.

"stepped on a volcano . . . ": the *New York Times*, "In U.S.–China Ties, Cordiality Is No Longer on the Agenda," June 27, 1989.

"Times have changed . . . ": *The Tiananmen Papers*, 107.

"The student slogans . . . ": ibid., 108.

"Some socialist countries . . . ": ibid., 107.

"Our backs are to the wall . . . ": *The Tiananmen Papers*, 188.

"If our one billion people . . . ": ibid., 187–188.

"What is happening here . . . ": Embassy cable (Beijing), "PLA Ready to Strike," No. 14051,

May 21, 1989, unclassified, obtained at the National Security Archives, Washington, D.C.

"coping with or anticipating . . . ": Embassy cable (Beijing), "China and the U.S.—A Protracted Engagement," No. 18706, July 11, 1989, unclassified, obtained at the National Security Archives, Washington, D.C.

"We have come too late . . . ": *The Tiananmen Papers,* 217.

Information on Leide and the walkie-talkies is from Tyler, *A Great Wall,* 353.

"The movement has been . . . ": Embassy cable (Beijing), "PLA Ready To Strike," No. 14051, May 21, 1989, unclassified, obtained at the National Security Archives, Washington, D.C.

"We lived a roller coaster . . . ": author's e-mail communication with Kathy Gaseor.

"A confrontation resulting . . . ": Embassy cable (Beijing), "PLA Ready To Strike," No. 14051, May 21, 1989, unclassified, obtained at The National Security Archives, Washington, D.C.

Information from the conversation on May 24 is from Embassy cable (Beijing), "An Account of Leadership Polarization During April–May Student Demonstrations," No. 14440, May 24, 1989, unclassified, obtained from the State Department through presidential appointee access, 2001.

"a Chinese version of Napoleon's retreat from Moscow . . . ": Embassy cable (Beijing), "Sitrep No. 27: Martial Law with Chinese Characteristics," No. 15388, June 3, 1989, unclassified, obtained from the National Security Archives.

"The unusual takes on normalcy . . . ": author's interview with Jim Ireland.

"Do you want me to take you . . . ": author's e-mail communication with Kathy Gaseor.

"General, you will . . . ": author's interview with Larry Wortzel.

"We are witnessing . . . ": Embassy cable (Beijing), "Situation Could Reach Critical Mass," No. 15405, June 3, 1989, unclassified, obtained from the National Security Archives, Washington, D.C.

"I know the history . . . ": author's interview with Jim Huskey.

The account of events on Tiananmen Square on the morning of June 4 is drawn from *The Tiananmen Papers,* 377–382; interview with Jim Huskey; and Embassy cable (Beijing), "What Happened on the Night of June 3/4," No. 16846, June 22, 1989, unclassified, obtained from the National Security Archives, Washington, D.C.

Commendation about Jim Huskey is from letter to President George Bush, September 11, 1989, James R. Lilley's personal files.

"Why in the world . . .": author's interview with Gerrit Gong.

The account about the Canadian attaché's erroneous statement to the press is from Larry Wortzel's book review of Timothy Brook's *Quelling the People: The Military Suppression of the Beijing Democracy Movement* (New York: Oxford University Press, 1992) in *The Australian Journal of Chinese Affairs,* January 1994, Issue 31, 124.

"The situation in China is complex . . . ": Embassy cable (Beijing), "Ambassador's June 7 Meeting with VFM Zhu Qizhen," No. 15686, June 7, 1989, unclassified, obtained at the National Security Archives, Washington, D.C.

"So much is going on in China . . . ": *Parade Magazine,* June 25, 1989, 2.

"ambitious handful . . . ": *The Tiananmen Papers,* 424.

"The aim of the small group . . . ": Embassy cable (Beijing), "The Long Night of the Chinese Power Struggle," No. 15832, June 11, 1989, unclassified, released in full, obtained at the National Security Archives, Washington, D.C.

"bourgeois liberalism . . . ": Embassy cable (Beijing), "China and the U.S.—A Protracted Engagement," No. 18706, July 11, 1989, unclassified, obtained at the National Security Archives, Washington, D.C.

CHAPTER 20
SMALL VICTORIES

Interviews: Charles and Judy McLaughlin, Sally Lilley, Jim Huskey. E-mail communication with Gloria Lannom.

"In China . . . ": *Children of the Dragon: The Story of Tiananmen Square,* 204.

"This is a subtle point . . . ": Embassy cable (Beijing), "Sitrep No. 53: June 15, 1600 Local," No. 16123, June 15, 1989, unclassified, obtained at the National Security Archives, Washington, D.C.

"For the Chinese, our message . . . ": Embassy cable (Beijing), "China and the U.S.—A Protracted Engagement," No. 18706, July 11, 1989, unclassified, obtained at the National Security Archives, Washington, D.C.

"Not only do we help . . . ": Embassy cable (Beijing), "China and the U.S.—A Protracted Engagement," No. 18706, July 11, 1989, unclassified, obtained at the National Security Archives, Washington, D.C.

"Americans are straightforward . . . ": Embassy cable (Beijing), "A Flavor of Dealing with

China Today," No. 28468, October 7, 1989, unclassified, released in part, obtained from the State Department through presidential appointee access, 2001

"a reservoir of good feeling . . . ": Embassy cable (Beijing), "The Mood at the Xichang Launch," No. 11098, April 10, 1990, unclassified, obtained from the State Department through presidential appointee access, 2001.

The description of Fang Lizhi is from Schell, *Mandate of Heaven: A New Generation of Entrepreneurs, Dissidents, Bohemians, and Technocrats Lays Claim to China's Future,* 203.

The summary of Fang's speech for the Robert F. Kennedy Human Rights Award is from *Children of the Dragon,* 219–220.

"reptilian . . . ": Chinoy, *China Live: Two Decades in the Heart of the Dragon,* 202.

The story about the Chinese citizen wanting to support American troops in the Gulf War is from the *New York Times International,* "As Things Ease in China, an Envoy Departs," May 10, 1991, A7.

"PRC–Taiwan relations . . . ": notes taken from Embassy cable (Beijing), "End of Tour Report," No. 12227, April 27, 1991, unclassified, obtained from the State Department through presidential appointee access, 2001.

"navigating Chinese-American relations out of a stormy period . . . ": the *New York Times International,* "As Things Ease in China, an Envoy Departs," May 10, 1991, A7.

"smug complacency . . . ": notes taken from Embassy cable (Beijing), "End of Tour Report," No. 12227, April 27, 1991, unclassified, obtained from the State Department through presidential appointee access, 2001.

EPILOGUE

Information on members of the Yale Class of 1943 entering intelligence service is from Winks, *Cloak and Gown,* 35.

Some of my sparring with the Chinese government can be found in Nicholas Kristof, "China Attacks U.S. Envoy for Stand on Taiwan," the *New York Times,* August 18, 1991, 6.

BIBLIOGRAPHY

BOOKS

". . . And for Yale": 1951 Remembers on the Occasion of Its 50th Reunion and Yale's Tercentenary. New Haven: Yale University, 2001.

1951 Class Book. New Haven: Yale University Press, 1951.

Acheson, Dean. Present at the Creation: My Years in the State Department. London: Hamish Hamilton, 1969.

Burr, William, editor. The Kissinger Transcripts. New York: The New Press, 1998.

Carter, Coralle J. Mission to Yenan: American Liaison with the Chinese Communists, 1944–1947. Lexington: University Press of Kentucky, 1997.

Castle, Timothy N. At War in the Shadow of Vietnam: U.S. Military Aid to the Royal Lao Government, 1955–1975. New York: Columbia University Press, 1993.

Children of the Dragon: The Story of Tiananmen Square. New York: Collier Books, 1990.

Chinoy, Mike. China Live: Two Decades in the Heart of the Dragon. Atlanta: Turner Publishing, 1997.

Conboy, Kenneth, with James Morrison. Shadow War: The CIA's Secret War in Laos. Boulder: Paladin Press, 1995.

Davies, John Paton, Jr. Dragon by the Tail: American, British, Japanese, and Russian Encounters with China and One Another. New York: W.W. Norton & Company, 1972.

Dower, John W. Embracing Defeat: Japan in the Wake of World War II. New York: W.W. Norton & Company, 1999.

Fairbank, John King. China: A New History. Cambridge: Harvard University Press, 1992.

Gibert, Stephen, and William Carpenter. America and Island China: A Documentary History. Lanham, Md.: University Press of America, 1989.

Gup, Ted. The Book of Honor: The Secret Lives and Deaths of CIA Operatives. New York: Anchor Books, 2001.

Haig, Alexander Jr. Caveat: Realism, Reagan and Foreign Policy. New York: Macmillan, 1984.

Han, Suyin. The Morning Deluge: Mao Tsetung and the Chinese Revolution, 1893–1954. Boston: Little, Brown, 1972.

Hart, John. The Making of an Army "Old China Hand": A Memoir of Colonel David D. Barrett. Berkeley: Institute of East Asian Studies, University of California–Berkeley, 1985.

The Historical Encyclopedia of World War II, D740.E5213. Library of Congress, Washington, D.C.

Hobart, Alice Tisdale. *Oil for the Lamps of China.* New York: Bobbs-Merrill Company, 1933.

Holdridge, John. *Crossing the Divide: An Insider's Account of Normalization of US–China Relations.* Lanham, MD: Rowman & Littlefield, 1997.

Jenkins, Alfred Lesesne. *Country, Conscience and Caviar: A Diplomat's Journey in the Company of History.* Seattle: Book Partners, 1993.

Karnow, Stanley. *Mao and China: From Revolution to Revolution.* New York: Viking Press, 1972.

Ketchum, Richard. *The Borrowed Years, 1938–1941: America on the Way to War.* New York: Random House, 1989.

Kim, Hyun Hee. *The Tears of My Soul.* New York: William Morrow & Company, 1993.

Kissinger, Henry. *Years of Upheaval.* Boston: Little, Brown, 1982.

Kiyonaga, Bina Cady. *My Spy: Memoir of a CIA Wife.* New York: Avon Press, 2000.

Knauss, John Kenneth. *Orphans of the Cold War: America and the Tibetan Struggle for Survival.* New York: PublicAffairs, 1999.

Lee, Manwoo. *The Odyssey of Korean Democracy: Korean Politics, 1987–1990.* New York: Praeger Publishers, 1990.

MacMillan, Margaret. *Paris 1919: Six Months That Changed the World.* New York: Random House, 2002.

Mann, James. *About Face: A History of America's Curious Relationship with China, from Nixon to Clinton.* New York: Alfred A. Knopf, 1999.

Naifeh, Marion. *The Last Missionary in China.* Aiken, S.C.: Woodward/White, 2003.

The Norton Anthology of Poetry. New York: W.W. Norton & Company, 1975.

Oberdorfer, Don. *The Two Koreas: A Contemporary History.* Reading, MA: Addison-Wesley, 1997.

Public Papers of the Presidents of the United States, Richard Nixon, 1971. Washington, D.C.: U.S. Government Printing Office, 1972.

Roberts, Priscilla, editor. *Window on the Forbidden City: The Beijing Diaries of David Bruce, 1973–1974.* Hong Kong: The University of Hong Kong, 2001.

Schell, Orville. *Mandate of Heaven: A New Generation of Entrepreneurs, Dissidents, Bohemians, and Technocrats Lays Claim to China's Future.* New York: Simon & Schuster, 1994.

Shultz, George. *Turmoil and Triumph: My Years as Secretary of State.* New York: Scribners, 1993.

Singlaub, John K., with Malcolm McConnell. *Hazardous Duty: An American Soldier in the Twentieth Century.* New York: Summit Books, 1991.

Spence, Jonathan. *The Gate of Heavenly Peace: The Chinese and Their Revolution, 1895–1980.* New York: Penguin Books, 1983.

———. *The Search for Modern China.* New York: W.W. Norton & Company, 1990.

Shakespeare, William. *The Complete Works of Shakespeare,* edited by G. B. Harrison. New York: Harcourt, Brace &Company, 1968.

Taylor, Jay. *The Generalissimo's Son: Chiang Ching-kuo and the Revolutions in China and Taiwan.* Cambridge: Harvard University Press, 2000.

Thomas, Evan. *The Very Best Men: Four Who Dared: The Early Years of the CIA.* New York: Simon & Schuster, 1995.

The Tiananmen Papers, compiled by Zhang Liang and edited by Andrew Nathan and Perry Link. New York: PublicAffairs, 2001.

Tolley, Kemp. *Yangtze Patrol: The U.S. Navy in China.* Annapolis, MD: United States Naval Institute, 1971, 1984.

Tuchman, Barbara. *Stilwell and the American Experience in China, 1911–1945.* New York: Macmillan, 1970, 1971.

Tyler, Patrick. *A Great Wall: Six Presidents and China.* New York: PublicAffairs, 1999.

U.S. Army in World War II, Chronology 1941–1945, D.769.A53, volume 8, part 5. Library of Congress, Washington, D.C.

Warner, Roger. *Backfire: The CIA's Secret War in Laos and Its Link to the War in Vietnam.* New York: Simon & Schuster, 1995.

White, Theodore H., and Annalee Jacoby. *Thunder Out of China.* New York: Williams Sloane Associates, 1946.

Wickham, John A. *Korea on the Brink: From the "12/12 Incident" to the Kwangju Uprising, 1979–1980.* Washington, D.C.: National Defense University Press, 1999.

Winks, Robin W. *Cloak and Gown: Scholars in the Secret War, 1939–1961.* New York: William Morrow & Company, 1987.

Wolff, Lester, and David Simon, editors. *Legislative History of the Taiwan Relations Act.* New York: American Association for Chinese Studies, 1982.

INTERVIEWS

Multiple interviews with Sally Lilley.

Interview with Walt Beckjord, August 21, 1993, Cincinnati, Ohio.

Interviews with Paul Crane, March 1997 and January 5, 1998, Chevy Chase, Md.

Phone interview with Samuel Moffet Jr., January 1998.

Interview with William and Elinore Washburn, August 1998, Andover, Mass.

Interview with Donald Hoagland, August 18, 1998, Denver, Colo.

Interview with Nan Viergutz, August 19, 1998, Denver, Colo.

Phone interview with Zeph Stewart, October 5, 1998.

Phone interview with Rev. Luther Tucker, October 26, 1998.

Interview with Bill W., December 20, 1998, and March 22, 1999.

Interview with Mark Pratt, March 11, 1999, Washington, D.C.

Interview with Ted Shackley, March 12, 1999, Bethesda, Md.

Interview with Charles W. Maynes, March 19, 1999, Washington, D.C.

Interview with David Gries, March 30, 1999, Washington, D.C.

Phone interviews with Stanley Bergman, April 12, 15, and 19, 1999.

Phone interviews with Ambassador William Brown, May 19 and December 16 and 17, 1999.

Interview with Michael Pillsbury, July 23, 1999, Washington, D.C.

Phone interview with Richard Allen, August 26, 1999.

Interview with David Dean, November 23, 1999, Great Falls, Va.

Interview with Clarke Ellis, November 24, 1999, Washington, D.C.

Phone interview with Ambassador Arthur Hummel, December 15, 1999.

Interview with Dr. Fred Chien, March 27, 2000, Taipei, Taiwan.

Interview with Dr. Lin Chongpin, March 27, 2000, Taipei, Taiwan.

Interview with Dr. Kim Kye Won, March 31, 2000, Seoul, South Korea.

Interview with Dr. Park Soo Kil, March 31, 2000, Seoul, South Korea.

Interview with Ambassador Hyun Hong Choo, March 29, 2000, Seoul, South Korea.

Interview with Ambassador Kim Kyung Won, March 31, 2000, Seoul, South Korea.

Interview with General O Jae Bok, March 31, 2000, Seoul, South Korea.

Interview with McKinney Russell, July 19, 2000, Washington, D.C.

Interview with Gerrit Gong, July 19, 2000, Washington, D.C.

Interview with Larry Wortzel, July 21, 2000, Washington, D.C.

Phone interview with Jim Ireland, July 25, 2000.

Phone interview with Mary Ellen Ireland, July 27, 2000.

Phone interview with Tick Semmes, July 27, 2000.

Interview with Charles and Judy McLaughlin, July 27, 2000.

E-mail correspondence with Kathy Gaseor, July 30, 2000.

Interview with Jim Huskey, August 1, 2000, Washington, D.C.

Interview with Elinore Washburn and Mayna Avent, August 19, 2001, Lewes, Del.

E-mail correspondence with Gloria Lannom, August 21, 2000.

E-mail correspondence with George Witwer, February 23, 2002.

ORAL HISTORY INTERVIEWS, FOREIGN AFFAIRS ORAL HISTORY COLLECTION, GEORGETOWN UNIVERSITY LIBRARY, WASHINGTON, D.C.

Dunlop, Thomas P. H.

Freeman, Charles

Holdridge, John

Hummel, Arthur

Lilley, James

Sigur, Gaston

INDEX

ADB (Asian Development Bank), 253–255, 338, 367

Allen, Richard, 218, 220–221, 229, 231–235

American Institute in Taiwan (AIT). *See* Taiwan, Lilley's American Institute in Taiwan (AIT) posting

American School in Tsingtao, 11–12

Anderson, Don, 172, 195

Anderson, Jack, 194, 196–197

Armacost, Mike, 289–290

Armitage, Richard, 229, 250, 253

Armstrong, Neil, 152

Arnold, Matthew, poem, "Dover Beach," 41

Asian Development Bank (ADB), 253–255, 338, 367

August Communiqué, 232–233, 241–242, 246–249, 251, 377

B., Ed, 154

Baker, James, III, 200, 253, 328, 338, 365

Bartholomew, Reginald, 365–366

Beckjord, Walt, 50–51

Bill (Lilley's acquaintance in Guangzhou), 169–170

Billington, Jim, 236

Binyon, Laurence, poem, "For the Fallen," 293

Biondi, Matt, 289

Blackburn, Bob, 184–185

Booth, Lee. *See* Witwer, Lee

Booth, Sally. *See* Lilley, Sally

Booth, Waller B., 74–75, 87, 215, 267

Bowie, Robert, 210

Boxer Rebellion, 8

Brace, Ernie, 113

Braestrup, Peter, 68

Brewster, Kingman, 300

Britain
 Chinese refugees in Hong Kong, 100

Hong Kong Special Branch, 83, 87, 135–136, 144
 presence in Tsingtao, 7–9, 27

Britton, Harry, 259–260

Broder, David, 201–203

Brooks, Stan, 251

Brown, Bill, 157, 250–254

Bruce, David, 172, 179–180, 187

Brzezinski, Zbigniew, 209–210

Burch, Dean, 201

Burghardt, Ray, 320, 333

Burma
 CIA covert operations on China, 82
 North Korean bombing of, 266
 U.S. command of Chinese Army in, 48

Bush, Barbara, 192–193, 200, 205, 267

Bush, George H. W.
 as head of United States Liaison Office to China, 192–193, 195–196, 216–217
 CIA head, 196–198
 friendship with Lilley, 192, 195, 223, 375
 opinion on U.S. policy toward Taiwan, 210
 as President, dealings with China
  ban on support following Tiananmen massacre, 324, 338
  commercial aircraft sales, 345
  covert emissary to Deng, 337–339, 358
  enlistment of Nixon as emissary, 347–348
  export of U.S.-built satellite, 346
  Lilley's Ambassador posting, 297, 330, 339–340
  meeting with Qian, 365–366
  Most Favored Nation status, 358
  United Nations Security Council resolution on Iraq, 365
 presidential candidacy, 199, 215–216
 Reagan running mate, 217–218, 222–223
 relationship with Deng, 204, 310, 378
 trip to China as private citizen, 198–205

as Vice President, 190–191, 234–235, 242–243, 256
Bush, Inez. *See* Lilley, Inez
Bush, Peter, 30, 36

Cambodia
anti-American government, 97
Chinese arms shipments through, 149–150
CIA intelligence operations in, 98–99, 101–102
economic conditions, 97–98
Khmer Rouge, 104–105
Lilley's CIA assignment, 97, 102–103
military coup, 150
relations with China, 98–99
Cao Guisheng, 237–238
Carter administration, 198, 209, 211, 378
CCP. *See* Chinese Communist Party
Central government. *See* Nationalist government
Central Intelligence Agency. *See* CIA
Chai Ling, 304, 314
Chai Zemin, 228
Chang Hsüehliang, 21–22
Chang Tsolin, 11
Chang Tsungchang, 11
Chen Shuibien, 262, 379
Chen Wencheng, 257–258
Chennault, Anna, 227, 229
Chiang Ching-kuo, 211, 232, 244, 247, 257–259, 261–262
Chiang Kai-shek, 20–21, 67, 235, 256. *See also* Nationalist government
Chien, Fred, 243–245, 247, 252
Chile, CIA in, 197
China
Cambodia, 98–99
civil war, 20–21, 48, 51, 53–55, 67, 77
civilians, 177, 313, 366–367
Cultural Revolution, 135–138, 140–142, 145–147, 150–151, 175
expansion of influence, 77, 84, 89–90
Great Leap Forward, 94–95, 100, 104
historical threats to, 230
imperialism in, 6–8
Laos, 122–123
North Korea, 68, 284, 376
Olympics (2008), 378
People's Republic of China, establishment of, 66
political infighting, 175–176, 199
press attacks on Lilley, 375–376
press attacks on Reagan, 222
Public Security Bureau (PSB), 144

Sino–Japanese conflict, 19–21, 24–27, 54
South Korea rapprochement, 290–291
Soviet Union rapprochement, 299, 301
Taiwan–China relations
anti-Taiwan activity in Philippines, 92
Asian Development Bank, 254–255, 367
Asian games in Peking (1990), 368
General Agreement on Trade and Tariffs (GATT), 367–368
improvement, 237–238, 245, 379–380
nine-point proposal for reunification, 93, 217, 231
Quemoy bombings, 92–93, 217
reinforcement of coastal area, 100–101
Singapore meeting (1993), 367, 379
Tiananmen Square, 1919 demonstration, 8, 28
Tiananmen Square, 1989 demonstration
Chinese Communist Party (CCP) fissure in leadership, 300, 304
Chinese government accounts, 322–323, 335, 363–364
citizen fear and bond with Americans, 335–336
extent of civilian participation, 298–299
funeral on Chinese State Television, 324
military use, 305, 311–312, 315–316, 323–324
treatment of foreigners, 323, 371
U.S. media coverage, 304, 318–319, 371
Tibet, suppression of, 201, 203
United Nations participation, 286, 364–365
U.S.–China relations
arms sales, Peace Pearl program, 228–229, 324, 341, 343–344
August Communiqué, 232–233, 241–242, 246–249, 251–252, 377
commercial aircraft sales, 345
energy-related issues, 203–205
establishment of diplomatic relations, 160, 208–212
first U.S. warship visit, 302, 342
intelligence cooperation against Soviet Union, 207, 214–215, 344, 347, 378
launch of U.S.-built satellite, 346, 379
Most Favored Nation status, 358, 370
rapprochement, 147–149, 152–153
Shanghai Communiqué, 159, 164–165
Sino–U.S. Ambassadorial Talks, 147
Truce Commission, 51, 55
World Trade Organization, 378–379
Xinhua (New China News Agency), 144–145
China, Lilley's Ambassador posting
accomplishments and final assessments, 368–372

China, Lilley's Ambassador posting *(cont.)*
  arms sales, Peace Pearl program, 341,
    343–344, 377
  Chinese boycott of diplomatic functions, 341,
    364
  commercial matters, 344–347
  consulate renovations, 368–369
  exchange of intelligence on Soviet Union,
    344, 347
  Fang Lizhi asylum at embassy
    concealment, 332–334, 351–353, 355–356
    departure, 360–361
    exfiltration plan, 354–355
    negotiations for release, 348, 358–360, 376
    repercussions for Lilley, 339, 344, 346–347
    Robert F. Kennedy Memorial Award for
      Human Rights, 358
    threat of removal by Chinese security, 337,
      353–354
  intellectual property rights, 368
  Iraqi plan to assassinate Lilley, 366–367
  satellite launch, 346–347
  student visas, 362–364
  Taiwan issues, 367–368
  Tiananmen demonstration, embassy opera-
    tions surrounding
    anticipation of government crackdown,
      308–310
    attack on diplomatic compound, 326–329
    breakdown in communication with Bush,
      339
    casualty counts, 321–322
    cooperation with other embassies,
      306–307
    Huskey eyewitness accounts, 314–315,
      317–321
    Lilley meeting with Li Peng, 299–300
    media coverage, 318–319, 371
    meeting with Lord, 297
    safety and evacuation of Americans, 307,
      323–326, 330–331
    staff conduct, 332
    stalemate in Sino–U.S. relations, 337
    Wortzel and McGivven confrontation
      with military, 316–317
  United Nations resolution on U.S. force
    against Iraq, 365
  U.S. Navy visit to Shanghai, 299, 302–303,
    369
China, Lilley's United States Liaison Office
    (USLO) posting
  arrival in China, 165–166
  association with Bush, 192–193, 195
  duties and routines, 175, 177–182

emotional detachment, 170–171
  Kissinger assistance in assignment, 160, 162
  Pakistani International School, 181
  Peking Hotel, 181–184
  secrecy and diplomatic cover, 163, 174–175,
    194–195
  U.S. Marine expulsion, 183
  visas, 184–188
  visits to sites from childhood, 188–192
"China News Analysis" (reports), 139
Chinese Communist Party (CCP)
  civil war
    control of Manchuria, 53–55
    defeat of Nationalists, 67, 77
    failed coalition with Nationalists, 48, 51, 55
    Second United Front against Japan, 20–21
    seizure of Mukden and Changchun, 55
    Xian incident, 20–21
  establishment of People's Republic of China,
    66
  See also China; Mao Tse-tung
Chinese Nationalist Air Force, 92–93
Chinese Third Force, 78, 80–83
Chinoy, Mike, 319
Chiu Lienhui, 259–260
Choi Kwang Soo, 274, 276–278, 286, 291
Chou En-lai
  appeal to Red Guards, 142
  Chinese road in Laos, 123
  failing health and death, 193, 199
  opening of dialogue with U.S., 176
  personal relationship with Nixon, 378
  political infighting, 175–176
  rescue of Chiang Kai-shek, 21
  trip to Cambodia, 98
Christopher, Warren, 211
Chun Doo Hwan
  appeal from Reagan against use of force,
    275–279
  coup and martial law, 265, 268
  election of Roh, 271–272
  endorsement of reform package, 280
  invitation to visit U.S., 266–267
  Kwangju massacre, 268, 280
  reluctance to relinquish presidency, 270
Chung Ho Yong, 275
Church, Frank, 197
CIA (Central Intelligence Agency)
  Bush head of, 196–198
  connections with Yale University, 68–69, 373
  institutional crises and low morale, 197
  Lilley's career in
    awarded Distinguished Intelligence
      Medal, 213–214

Deputy Chief of China Operations, Far
Eastern Division, 154–155
National Intelligence Officer (NIO) on
China, 197
recruitment and training, 69–70, 73, 196
retirement, 212
switch from covert to analytical side, 197
*See also Lilley's CIA assignments under specific
countries*
Clark, William, 242–243, 248–249
Cline, Ray, 220
Colby, William, 161, 197, 215
Communist Hukbalahap, 77
Communist Party, Chinese (CCP). *See* Chinese
Communist Party (CCP)
Cross, Chuck, 238, 257
Cuban Missile Crisis, 101
Cultural Revolution, 135–138, 140–142, 145–147,
150–151, 175
Cushing, Caleb, 6–7

Dalai Lama, 201
Dean, David, 247, 258
Defense Intelligence Agency (DIA), 234
Democratic Justice Party (DJP), 271–272, 280
Deng Xiaoping
and Bush, 198, 204, 216–217, 222–223, 310, 378
hostility toward Fang, 333
intelligence cooperation with U.S. against
Soviet Union, 215
letter from Reagan affirming U.S. commitment to China, 242
Lilley's analysis of, 309
negotiations with Kissinger, 193–194
political infighting, 176, 199
power of, 217, 242, 299, 302
on Reagan's intentions regarding Taiwan,
219–220
"risk contracts" with American oil compa-
nies, 203–204
Tiananmen demonstration, 302, 315–316, 334,
338–340
visa for travel to U.S., 186
Deuel, Mike, 130–131
DIA (Defense Intelligence Agency), 234
DJP (Democratic Justice Party), 271–272, 280
Donald, Alan, 328
"Dover Beach" (poem), 41
Downey, Jack, 69–70, 80–81, 131, 160, 167–168
Drapchi Prison, 203
Dulles, Allen, 69, 93
Dulles, John Foster, 93
Dunlop, Harry, 275–276, 278

Eagleburger, Larry, 338, 340, 358
Edinger, Lyn, 330
Ellis, Clarke, 251–252
Exeter Academy
Lilley, 38–39
Lilley, Frank, 23–26, 28–29, 37–38, 40–41
Lilley, Jack, 23–26, 38

Fairbank, John K, 68
Fang Lizhi
asylum at U.S. Embassy
concealment, 332–334, 351–353, 355–356
departure, 360–361
exfiltration plan, 354–355
negotiations for release, 348, 358–360, 376
repercussions for Lilley, 339, 344, 346–347
Robert F. Kennedy Memorial Award for
Human Rights, 357–358
threat of removal by Chinese security, 337,
353–354
criticism of Bush administration, 361–362
guest professorship at Cambridge University
Institute of Astronomy, 360
Fecteau, Dick, 80–81, 160, 167–168
Fenn, Henry C., 90
First United Front, 20
Fitzgerald, Desmond, 131
Fitzwater, Marlin, 334
"For the Fallen" (poem), 293
Ford, Gerald, 196
Foreign Affairs (journal), 147

Gang of Four, 199
Gaseor, Kathy, 307–308, 312
Ge, Mr. (Chinese intelligence officer), 189–191
General Agreement on Trade and Tariffs
(GATT), 367–368
General Dynamics, 233, 252
Geneva Accords (1962), 108–109, 115, 118, 128
Glassford, Admiral, 33
Gong, Gerrit, 322, 324, 330
Gorbachev, Mikhail, 299, 301, 304
Great Britain
Chinese refugees in Hong Kong, 100
Hong Kong Special Branch, 83, 87, 135–136, 144
presence in Tsingtao, 7–9, 27
Great Leap Forward, 94–95, 100, 104
Great Proletarian Cultural Revolution, 135–138,
140–142, 145–147, 150–151, 175
Gregg, Don, 168, 348

Habib, Phil, 285
Haig, Alexander, 228–229, 232–233, 241, 245–246,
249

Han Xu, 198, 354
Hao Peitsun, 252
Helms, Jesse, 343
Henderson, Ian, 283
Hersey, John, 300
Hmong tribesmen, 109–113, 128, 131–132
Ho Chi Minh Trail, 115, 117, 121
Holdridge, John, 164, 172–173, 183–185
Hong Kong
    Hong Kong Special Branch, 83, 87, 135–136, 144
    Lilley's first CIA assignment, 83–87, 95–96
    Lilley's second CIA assignment
        Chinese arms shipments through Cambodia, 149–150
        commemorative tie, 150–151
        Cultural Revolution, 141
        living conditions, 142
        rapprochement with China, 148
        recruitment of agents, 139, 144–145
        sources of intelligence, 135–139
    New China News Agency (Xinhua), 144–145, 284, 286
    Public Security Bureau (PSB), 144
    suitability for intelligence operations, 84, 135
Horowitz, Herb, 172
Hsiao, Annie, 186–188
Hsiao, Paul, 186
Hsu, Henry (Hsu Fengho), 255–256
Hu Qili, 301
Hu Yaobang, 242, 297
Hu Yizhou, 345
Hua Guofeng, 199, 205–206
Huang Hua, 162, 219, 232
Huang Zhen, 198–199
Hummel, Arthur, 232, 241, 246
Hunt-Sedco Oil Company, 213
Huskey, Jim, 314–315, 317–322, 363, 370–371

I Ho Ch'uan, 8
Indigenous Defense Fighter (IDF), 252–254, 343
Indonesia, 89–90
intelligence. *See* CIA (Central Intelligence Agency); *Lilley's CIA assignments under specific countries*
International Control Commission (ICC), 108, 112, 124
Iraq, plans to assassinate Asian diplomats, 366–367

Japan
    imperialism in China, 6–9, 15–16
    Kure, 57, 59, 88–89, 272–273

Lilley's CIA assignment, 88
Manchuria occupation, 19, 54
oppression in Korea, 18–19
people and customs, 30–31
Russo–Japanese war, 7
security treaty with U.S., 231, 377
Sino–Japanese conflict, 19–21, 24–27, 54
Jenkins, Al, 155–157, 173–175
Ji Chaozhu, 260
Jiang Qing (Madame Mao), 140, 176, 199
Jiang Zemin, 367
Joey (Lilley's dog), 331, 348–349
Johnson, Howie, 70
Johnson, Lyndon, 128, 140
Johnson, Nelson, 33
Jones, Roy, 289

Kauffman, Donald, 292–293
Kauffman, Paul, 292–293
Kelly, Dick, 70
Kennedy, Ted, 357
Kerry, John, 266
Kha tribesmen, 117, 121
Khmer Rouge, 104–105
Khrushchev, Nikita, 93
Kim Dae Jung, 266–268, 270–271, 280–281, 284–285
Kim Hyun Hee (Mayumi Hachiya), 283–284
Kim Il Sung, 54, 285
Kim Jong Hui, 294
Kim Jong Il, 285, 376
Kim Kyung Won, 275, 278–279, 287–289
Kim Young Sam, 279, 281, 284–285, 352
Kiphuth, Bob, 45, 65, 70
Kissinger, Henry
    Chinese road in Laos, 123
    intelligence cooperation with China, 215
    National Security Studies Memoranda (NSSM), 155–156
    normalization negotiations with Deng, 193–194
    "One China" policy, 164
    personal relationships with Chinese leaders, 378
    remorse over U.S. treatment of Taiwan, 165
    secret diplomacy, 153–154, 156, 175
    secret preparation for Nixon visit to China, 157–158
    on Soviet arms reduction, 159
    support of Lilley's CIA assignment to China, 160, 162, 173–174
Kiukiang, 30
Koo Chen-fu, 256
Korea. *See* North Korea; South Korea

Kuo, Shirley, 240, 254–255
Kuomintang (KMT). *See* Nationalist government
Kure, Japan, 57, 59, 88–89, 272–273

La Dany, Laszlo, 139
Lair, Bill, 109, 113, 128
Laos
  attitude toward U.S., 132
  Chinese road in, 122–123
  Geneva Accords (1962), 108, 115, 118, 128
  geography and people, 107–108
  Hmong tribesmen, 109–113, 131–132
  Ho Chi Minh Trail bombing, 115, 117
  Lilley's CIA assignment
    attempts to recruit Soviets, 124
    clandestine paramilitary work, 107
    Deuel and Maloney helicopter crash, 130–131
    documentation of North Vietnamese involvement in Laos, 129
    expansion of mission, 115–118
    focus on Laotian politics, 119–120
    helicopter crash into Mekong River, 106–107
    Hmong secret army, 109–113, 131
    Ho Chi Minh Trail sabotage, 117, 121–122
    Kha tribesmen, 117, 121
    life in Vientiane, 113–115
    Mekong River flood, 124–126
    Nung tribesmen, 122
    Sihanouk Trail sabotage, 121–122
    Site 85 protection, 128–130
    Thai Police Aerial Resupply Unit (PARU) paramilitary force, 128–130
  Pathet Lao, 107, 109, 118–119, 130–131
  Site 85, U.S. bombing of North Vietnam, 127–130
  U.S. Agency for International Development (USAID), 108–109, 125
  U.S. military presence, 108–109, 117
Lawrence, Vint, 110, 112
Lee, Miss (Lilley's acquaintance in Hong Kong), 86–87, 165
Lee Han Key, 276
Lee Tenghui, 261–262, 367
Leide, Jack, 306, 311–312, 321, 325
Li Da Zhao, 354
Li Lu, 304
Li Mi, 82
Li Peng, 299–301, 304–305, 365
Li Qiang, 203
Li Shuxian, 332–334, 337, 351–353, 355–356, 358, 360–361. *See also* Fang Lizhi

Liedtke, Hugh, 201, 203
Lilley, Douglas (Lilley's son), 103, 163, 182, 290, 350
Lilley, Elinore (Lilley's sister). *See* Washburn, Elinore
Lilley, Frank Walder II (Lilley's father)
  career with Standard Oil, 3–5, 10, 22–23, 29–30, 53
  guilt over son's death, 70–71
  marriage, 5–6
  opinion of Chinese Communists, 67
  visit to Beidaihe, 70–71
Lilley, Frank Walder III (Lilley's brother)
  birth, 6
  childhood in Tsingtao, 11–14
  education
    American School in Tsingtao, 11–12
    Phillips Exeter Academy, 23–26, 28–29, 37–38, 40–41
    Pyongyang Foreign School (PYFS), 16–17, 292–293
    School of Military Government in Far Eastern Affairs, 51, 56
    Shanghai American School, 189
    Yale University, 35–36, 39, 41, 43–46
  impressions of Japan, 18, 27–28, 56–57
  influence on Lilley, 13–14, 60–61, 170, 267
  internal conflict and religious leanings, 17, 42–43, 45, 51–52, 57, 59–60
  marriage, 52–53
  military service
    artillery training, 46
    China, 46, 374
    inner conflicts about, 40–43, 60
    Japan, 57–59
    ROTC, 41, 43, 45–46
    School of Military Government in Far Eastern Affairs, 51, 56
  suicide, 58–59, 70–73
  swimming accomplishments, 15–16, 29, 35, 37, 39, 44–45, 350, 373
Lilley, Grandpa, 36
Lilley, Inez (formerly Inez Bush, Lilley's mother), 6, 11, 14, 30, 71, 142–144
Lilley, Jack (Lilley's brother)
  birth, 6
  career, conduct, family, 72–73, 374
  dementia and death, 73
  education
    American School in Tsingtao, 11–12
    Phillips Exeter Academy, 23–26, 38
    Pyongyang Foreign School, 38
    Shanghai American School, 189
    Yale University, 35, 39

Lilley, Jack (Lilley's brother) *(cont.)*
  effect of Frank's death on, 71
  swim from Beidaihe to Qinhuangdao, 29
Lilley, James
  birth, 6
  brother Frank
    influence of, 13–14, 60–61, 170, 267, 381
    reflections on death of, 60–61, 272–274
  childhood and youth
    aboard U.S. Navy gunboat to Shanghai,
      33–34
    Beidaihe, 24, 29
    impressions of Japan, 30–31
    inferiority at sports, 14, 35
    Kiukiang, 29, 31–33
    summer jobs, 39–40, 67
    Tientsin, 23
    Tsingtao, 9–13, 15, 373–374
    United States, 34–36
  courtship, marriage, children, 75–76, 87–88,
    103
  education
    American School in Tsingtao, 11–12
    Chinese language review training, 140
    Foreign Service Institute, 160
    Institute of Far Eastern Languages Chi-
      nese Language School, 90
    National War College, 160
    Phillips Exeter Academy, 38–39
    Shanghai American School, 33, 35, 302
    Yale University, 52, 65–68, 74, 90, 196
  friendship with Bushes, 192, 195, 223, 375
  health problems, 36, 47, 66, 79, 103, 263
  independent consulting, 213
  military training and service
    Air Force, 74
    Army, 52, 59–60
    Army specialized reserve training pro-
      gram, 39, 47, 52
    ROTC, 74
Lilley, Jeffrey (Lilley's son), 125, 127, 163, 198, 235,
    349
  birth, 103
  friendship with Bush, 195
  Olympics researcher, 296
  Pakistani International School in China, 181
Lilley, Michael (Lilley's son), 127, 163, 191, 216,
    235, 352
  birth, 103
  Christmas visit to China, 349–350
  disbelief in Lilley's CIA employment, 214
  Pakistani International School in China, 181
Lilley, Nan (formerly Nan Viergutz, Lilley's
    sister-in-law), 52–53, 56–57

Lilley, Sally (formerly Sally Booth, Lilley's
    wife), 191, 213, 235, 267, 373
  aboard ship from Thailand, 103–104
  Cambodia, 104
  China, 181, 195, 298
    evacuation to South Korea, 331, 348
    Fang asylum at embassy, 332, 351–352
    life in diplomatic compound, 322
    return from evacuation, 348–349
    visa for Ning to study in U.S., 362
  courtship and marriage, 75–76, 87–88
  friendship with Bushes, 192, 195, 216, 223, 375
  language proficiency, 89, 163
  Laos, 116, 127, 132
  leg injury, 143–144
  Seoul Olympic Games, 287–289
  Taiwan, 236, 239–240, 263
  Washington, 140, 154, 227, 296
Lin Homing, 259
Linke, Miss (Lilley's teacher), 12
Lintilhac, Claire, 51
Liu, Eddie, 79–80
Liu Huaqing, 343
Liu Huaqiu, 358
Liu Shaoqi, 102, 179
Livesey, William J., 277–279
Lon Nol, 149–150
Lord, Winston, 289–292, 297
Luo Gan, 305

Macao, 85
Magsaysay, Ramón, 91
Maloney, Mike, 130–131
Manchuria, 7, 19, 53–54, 56, 80–81
Manila. *See* Philippines
Mao, Madame (Jiang Qing), 140, 176, 199
Mao Jenfeng, 79
Mao Tse-tung
  assumption of power, establishment of
    People's Republic of China, 66, 78
  Chinese civil war, 53
  Cultural Revolution, 135–138, 140–142,
    145–147, 150–151, 175
  defense against Soviet invasion, 146
  failing health and death, 176, 193, 199
  Great Leap Forward, 94–95, 100, 104
  and Nixon, 159, 378
  political manipulation, 176
  Quemoy and Matsu bombing, 93
The Marco Polo Papers (book), 138–139
Marks, John, 194
Marshall, George C., 51, 55
Massey, Joe, 365
Matsu Island, 93

Mauz, Henry, 299, 302
Maynes, Bill, 125, 130
Maynes, Gretchen, 125
McCune, Douglas, 18–19
McGivven, Bill, 313–314, 316–317, 361
McHugh, Marine Major, 33
McKinley, Brunson, 172
McKinley, William, 7
McLaughlin, Charles, 351–353, 358
McLaughlin, Judy, 351–353, 358, 360
Meifoo Shield (journal), 23
Mekong River, 124–126
Meo tribesmen (Hmong), 109–113, 128, 131–132
Metsung Yu, 240
Mongolia, 191
Most Favored Nation (MFN) status, 358, 370
Myongdong Catholic Cathedral, Seoul, 274

Nanjing, 26, 28, 67
National Security Studies Memoranda
(NSSM), 155–157, 210–211
Nationalist government (Central government,
Kuomintang)
agreement by Soviet Union to recognize, 54
civil war in China
defeat by Communists, 67, 77
failed coalition with Chinese Commu-
nists, 48, 51, 55
Manchuria loss, 53–55
Second United Front against Japan, 20–21
U.S. support of, 54–55
Xian incident, 20–21
Yenan capture, 55
reestablishment of Republic of China, 67,
256
See also Taiwan
NCND (no confirm/no deny) policy on nuclear weapons, 342
Nelson, Miss (Lilley's teacher), 12
New China News Agency (Xinhua), 144–145,
284, 286
Ning Qiang, 362–363
Nixon, Richard
admission of CIA operations in China, 167
ambiguous support of Taiwan, 163–165
enlistment by Bush as emissary to China,
347–348
meeting with Mao, 159
personal relationship with Chinese leaders,
348, 378
rapprochement with China, 147, 152–153
no confirm/no deny (NCND) policy on nuclear weapons, 342
Norodom Sihanouk, 97, 102, 105, 150

North Korea
Japanese occupation of, 18–19
Kim Il Sung, 54, 285
Kim Jong Il, 285, 376
Korean Airlines (KAL) bombing, 282–286
nuclear weapons, 376–377
Olympic Games (1988), 282
propaganda against Lilley, 285–286
Pyongyang Foreign School (PYFS), 16–17
terrorism, 266, 282–287
war against South Korea, 65
North Vietnam
attack on U.S. Site 85 in Laos, 129–130
Geneva Accords (1962) violations in Laos,
108–109
Ho Chi Minh Trail, 115, 117, 121
Lilley's assignment to CIA war against, 107,
121–122
Tet offensive, 130, 140
U.S. military buildup in, 115, 117
Northrop, 233
NSSM (National Security Studies Memo-
randa), 155–157, 210–211
Nunez, Bob, 106
Nung tribesmen, 122

O Jae Bok, 281
Office of Strategic Services (OSS), 69
Ojibway, Lewis, 106
Okinawa and Saipan, CIA guerrilla training,
78, 82
Oliphant, Patrick, 222
Olympic Games
1998, in South Korea, 265, 275, 282, 285,
287–289, 291
2008, in China, 378
"One China" policy, 159, 164, 242–243, 246, 254
Open Door Policy, 7
OSS (Office of Strategic Services), 69
The Other Side of the River (book), 94–95
Overesch, Commander, 33

Paal, Doug, 356
Paget, King, 12
Pakistan, 153–154
Pakistani International School, 181
Pan-Asian approach to U.S. foreign policy,
249–251, 253, 377
Paris Peace Conference (1919), 8
Park Si Hun, 289
Park Soo Kil, 283–284, 286
Pascoe, Lynn, 172
Pathet Lao, 107, 109, 118–119, 130–131
Peace Pearl program, 341, 343–344

Peking. *See* China
People's Liberation Army
   attack on U.S. diplomatic compound,
      326–329
   in Cultural Revolution, 140–141
   resistance of Chinese Third Force from
      Burma, 82
   in Tiananmen Square, 311, 316–321, 326
People's Republic of China. *See* China
Phasouk Somly, 121
Philippines
   Chinese clandestine forces in, 89–90
   Communist Hukbalahap attack on govern-
      ment, 77
   Lilley's CIA assignment, 90–95
Phillips Exeter Academy
   Lilley, 38–39
   Lilley, Frank, 23–26, 28–29, 37–38, 40–41
   Lilley, Jack, 23–26, 38
Phnom Penh. *See* Cambodia
Phoumi Nosavan, 127
Piccuta, Dan, 363
"Ping-Pong diplomacy," 152
Platt, Nick, 172
Pope, Ed, 70
Poshepny, Anthony "Tony Poe," 110–113
Pratt, Mark, 124
President Hoover (ocean liner), 25–26
Pu Yi, 5
Pyongyang. *See* North Korea
Pyongyang Foreign School (PYFS), 16–17, 38,
   292–293

Qian Qichen, 303, 365–366
Qiao Shi, 302
Quemoy Island, 92–93, 217

Rather, Dan, 304
Reagan, Nancy, 235–236
Reagan, Ronald
   administration personnel changes, 249–250
   China and Taiwan policy
      August Communiqué, 232–233, 241–242,
         246–249, 251, 377
      Haig announcement of arms sale to
         China, 228–229
      letters affirming "One China" policy,
         242–243
      pro-Taiwan sympathies, 210, 218–220, 227
      Reagan–Bush split, 217–218, 221–222
   Lilley audience with, 234–235
   South Korea, 266–267, 275–277
Red Guards, 137–138, 140–142. *See also* Cultural
   Revolution

Red Star Over China (book), 67
Reischauer, Edwin, 68
Republic of China. *See* Taiwan
Republic of Korea. *See* South Korea
Robert F. Kennedy Memorial Award for
   Human Rights awarded to Fang,
   357–358
Rogers, William, 148, 157
Roh Tae Woo, 271–272, 279–281, 284–285, 290,
   294
Romania, 153, 158–159
Roosevelt, Franklin D., 48
Rowe, David Nelson, 67–68
Russell, McKinney, 301, 311, 318, 324–325, 330,
   333, 352
Russia, presence in Tsingtao, 9. *See also* Soviet
   Union

Saipan and Okinawa, CIA guerrilla train-
   ing, 78, 82
Schafer, Virginia, 172
Schell, Orville, 357
Schifter, Richard, 365
Schlesinger, James, 146, 161–162, 205–208
Scowcroft, Brent, 338–340, 356, 358, 365
Second United Front, 20–21, 48
Semmes, David, 80, 331
Seoul. *See* South Korea
Seymour, Charles, 69
Shackley, Ted, 116–119, 128–129, 143, 163
Shanghai
   Communist takeover, 67
   revitalization, 55–56
   Shanghai American School (SAS), 189
   Sino–Japanese battle for, 24–26
   U.S. military posts, 54
   U.S. Navy visit, 299, 302–303, 369
Shanghai Communiqué, 159, 164–165
Shevardnadze, Eduard, 287
Shultz, George, 248–249, 253, 295–296
Siberia, 191–192
Sigur, Gaston, 247–248, 250–251, 253, 256,
   269–271, 279
Sihanouk Trail, 121
Simpson, Scott, 290
Sino-. *See* China
Sinochem, 312
Sisowath Sirik Matak, 150
Smith, Whitney, 13
Snow, Edgar
   The Other Side of the River, 94–95
   Red Star Over China, 67
SOCONY (Standard Oil Company), 3–5, 23,
   29–30

Solomon, Richard, 163
Souphanouvong, 119
South Korea
  Chun Doo Hwan, 265–266, 270–272, 280
  Democratic Justice Party (DJP), 271–272,
    280
  June 29 Declaration of reforms, 280–281
  Kim Dae Jung, 266–268, 270–271, 280–281,
    284–285
  Korean Airlines (KAL) bombing, 281,
    284–285, 290
  Kwangju massacre, 268–269, 280
  Sally Lilley evacuation to, 331, 348
  Lilley's Ambassador posting
    appeal to Chun against declaration of
      martial law, 274–279
    Democratic Justice Party (DJP) conven-
      tion, 271–272
    farewell cable from Shultz, 295–296
    July 4 party, South Korean presidential
      candidates at, 281
    lessons from Kwangju massacre, 269
    meeting with Roh on changes in South
      Korea, 279–280
    North Korean propaganda attacks,
      285–286
    Olympic Games (1998), 287–289
    policy approach, 265–267, 269
    rapprochement with China, 290–292
    recollections of brother Frank, 292–294
    swearing-in as Ambassador, 267
    United Nations discussion of Korean Air-
      lines bombing, 286
    Yongsan Golf Course, 294–295
  Nordpolitik foreign policy, 290
  Olympic Games (1988), 265, 275, 282, 285,
    287–289, 291
  protests and riots, 265, 269, 271–272, 274, 276
  rejuvenation following war, 264–265
  Roh Tae Woo, 271–272, 279–281, 284–285, 290
  trade imbalance, 268
  U.S. policy toward, 265–266, 269–270
  war against North Korea, 65
Southeast Asia. *See specific countries*
Souvanna Phouma, 119, 131
Soviet Union
  assurances against terrorism at Olympics, 287
  Brezhnev Doctrine, 145
  China–U.S. Intelligence cooperation against,
    207, 214–215, 344, 347, 378
  Cuban Missile Crisis, 101
  in Czechoslovakia, 145
  nuclear missile testing, 214
  pillage of industrial assets in Manchuria, 54

  South Korean foreign policy toward, 290
  threat of attack on China, 145–147
  United Nations presence, 66, 286
  Yalta Conference, 54
Stahl, Lesley, 337
Standard Oil Company (SOCONY), 3–5, 23,
  29–30
Stanton, Bill, 351–352
State Department
  Kissinger sidestepping of, 153, 174
  Nixon position papers, 156–157
  objection to Lilley visit to China, 200
  position on arms sales to China, 241–242
  South Korea policy, 265
  withholding of Lilley's memos on Tianan-
    men situation, 339–340
Stilwell, Joseph, 48
Sullivan, Roger, 157
Sullivan, William, 113–114, 120
Swank, Coby, 125

Tai Li, 79
Taiwan
  Cambodia, 98
  China–Taiwan relations
    Asian Development Bank, 254–255, 367
    Asian games in Peking (1990), 368
    Chinese anti-Taiwan activity Philippines,
      92
    Chinese reinforcement of coastal area
      across from Taiwan, 100–101
    General Agreement on Trade and Tariffs
      (GATT), 367–368
    improvement, 237–238, 245, 379–380
    nine-point proposal for reunification, 93,
      217, 231, 243
    Quemoy bombings, 92–93, 217
    Singapore meeting (1993), 367, 379
  democratic election, 262, 379
  Indochina, 82
  Kuomintang, 67, 257, 260
  Lee succession to presidency, 262
  Lilley's CIA assignment, 79–80, 82
  "Nixon Rock," 260–261
  opposition movement and human rights,
    232, 236, 257–259
  Republic of China, reestablishment of, 67,
    256
  U.S.–China relations concerning Taiwan
    August Communiqué, 232–233, 241–242,
      246–249, 251–252, 377
    normalization, 159, 193–194, 209–211
    "One China" policy, 159, 164, 242–243, 246,
      254

Taiwan *(cont.)*
  Shanghai Communiqué, 159, 164–165
  threatened boycott of Reagan inaugura-
    tion, 227–228
  U.S.–Taiwan relations
    ambiguous support from Nixon, 163–165
    arms sales, 231–234, 236, 252–254, 343, 377
    commercial ties, 255–256
    Indigenous Defense Fighter (IDF),
      252–254, 343
    intelligence collaboration against China,
      79–80, 82–83, 85–86
    Pan-Asian approach to foreign policy,
      249–250, 253
    Reagan intention to establish official rela-
      tions, 218–219, 221–222
    Taiwan Relations Act (TRA), 211–212, 232,
      234, 241–242, 244, 247
    termination of diplomatic and military in-
      volvement, 209, 236
    Truman policy, 78–79
  Women's Garden and Art Club of Taipei,
    239–240
Taiwan, Lilley's American Institute in Taiwan
    (AIT) posting
  acceptance, credentials, duties of job,
    232–233, 236–239, 251–252
  accomplishments, 261, 263
  Asian Development Bank (ADB), 253–255
  business and economic issues, 255–256
  contacts with opposition movement, 259–260
  human rights, 256–259
  intellectual property rights and open trading,
    255–256
  personal relationship with Lee, 261–262
  Reagan guidance in managing U.S.–Taiwan
    relations, 235–236
  Reagan interpretation of August Commu-
    niqué, 247–248, 252
  six assurances to Chiang affirming U.S. sup-
    port, 247
  three Reagan letters of commitment to
    China, 243–245
  weapons systems selection, 251–252
Taiwan Relations Act (TRA), 211–212, 232, 234,
    241–242, 244, 247
Takahashi, Lieutenant (liaison officer), 32–33
Takahashi, Mr. (Standard Oil client), 22, 27–28
Taki (Lilley's friend), 31–33
Talbott, Strobe, 206
Thailand, 107–108
Thomas, Lowell, 200–202
Thomas, Marianna, 200
Thompson, Jim, 126

Thouma, General, 127
Tiananmen Square
  1919 demonstration, 8, 28
  1989 demonstration
    Chinese Communist Party (CCP) fissure
      in leadership, 300, 304
    Chinese government accounts, 322–323,
      335, 363–364
    citizen fear and bond with Americans,
      335–336
    extent of civilian participation, 298–299
    funeral on Chinese State Television, 324
    military use, 305, 311–312, 315–316, 323–324
    treatment of foreigners, 323, 371
    U.S. media coverage, 304, 318–319, 371
  1989 demonstration, U.S. Embassy opera-
    tions surrounding
    anticipation of government crackdown,
      308–310
    attack on diplomatic compound, 326–329
    breakdown in communication with Bush,
      339
    casualty counts, 321–322
    cooperation with other embassies,
      306–307
    Huskey eyewitness accounts, 314–315,
      317–321
    Lilley meeting with Li, 299–300
    media coverage, 318–319, 371
    meeting with Lord, 297
    safety and evacuation of Americans, 307,
      323–326, 330–331
    staff conduct, 332
    stalemate in Sino–U.S. relations, 337
    Wortzel and McGivven confrontation
      with military, 316–317
Tibet, 201–203
Tibetan guerrilla operation, 136–138
Tientsin, 8, 23–25, 28, 67
TRA (Taiwan Relations Act), 211–212, 232, 234,
    241–242, 244, 247
Truman administration, 78–79
Tsingtao
  fall to communism, 66–67
  first U.S. warship visit, 342
  history, 6–9
  Japanese presence, 26–28
  Lilley childhood, 6, 9–12, 15, 350
  revitalization, 55–56
  U.S. Navy headquarters, 54
Turner, Stansfield, 210, 213–214
Twogood, Fred, 23

Unger, Leonard, 211

United Nations, 66, 82, 286, 364–365
United States, relations with foreign countries.
    See specific counties
United States Liaison Office (USLO), 172–173.
    See also China, Lilley's United States
    Liaison Office (USLO) posting
United Technologies, 213
Untermeyer, Chase, 200–201
U.S.S. *Augusta*, 12, 25
U.S.S. *Luzon*, 33–34

Vance, Cyrus, 200, 210
Vang Pao, 109–110, 120, 131
Vientaine. *See* Laos
Viergutz, Nan. *See* Lilley, Nan
Vietnam. *See* North Vietnam
Voice of America, 201, 337, 370
Vongrasamy Thong, 110

W., Bill, 138–139, 174
W., Charley, 144, 161–162
Wan Li, 299
Wang Dan, 304, 314
Wang Sheng, 258–259
Warsaw Talks, 153
Washburn, Bill, 61, 267
Washburn, Elinore (formerly Elinore Lilley,
    Lilley's sister), 10, 163, 195, 238, 267
    birth, 6
    education, 11–12, 30
    on Fang asylum in Peking embassy, 351
    letter recollecting brother's death, 272
    marriage, 61
    poem, 34
Washington, D.C., Lilley's assignments
    CIA Deputy Chief of China Operations, Far
        Eastern Division, 154–155
    CIA National Intelligence Officer (NIO) on
        China, 197
    CIA training, 73
    National Security Council East Asia special-
        ist, 223, 227
    National Security Studies Memoranda
        (NSSM), 155–157, 210–211
Washington Conference, 8–9

Wedemeyer, Albert, 48
Weigle, Dick, 50–51
Weinberger, Caspar, 229, 248, 267
Welch, Richard, 197
Wen Jiabao, 305
Wilson, Woodrow, 8
Witwer, George, 70, 73–76, 88, 195, 227, 259
Witwer, Lee (formerly Lee Booth), 75–76, 195,
    227
Wolfowitz, Paul, 250, 253–254
Woodcock, Leonard, 212
World Bank, 338
World Trade Organization, 378
Wortzel, Larry, 312–314, 316–317, 321, 323–327,
    329–330, 361
Wuer Kaixi, 304, 314

Xian Incident, 20–21
Xie Qimei, 162
Xinhua (New China News Agency), 144–145,
    284, 286

Yale University
    connections with CIA, 68–69, 373
    Lilley, 52, 65–68, 74, 90, 196
    Lilley, Frank, 35–36, 39, 41, 43–46
    Lilley, Jack, 35, 39
    Lilley speech to class reunion, 373, 375–376
    memorial service for Frank Lilley, 61
Yalta Conference, 54
Yamamoto, Don, 315
Yang Jiechi "Tiger," 201
Yang Shangkun, 299, 302, 310, 316
Yao Yilin, 301
Ye Jianying, 93, 217
Yellow River Elegy (documentary), 380
Yu Qiuli, 206
Yu Zhensan, 190–191
Yuan Mu, 322–323, 363–364

Zhang Wenjin, 217
Zhao Ziyang, 242, 300–302, 304–305
Zhu Qizhen, 328–329
Zinoman, Joy, 117

PublicAffairs is a publishing house founded in 1997. It is a tribute to the standards, values, and flair of three persons who have served as mentors to countless reporters, writers, editors, and book people of all kinds, including me.

I. F. Stone, proprietor of *I. F. Stone's Weekly,* combined a commitment to the First Amendment with entrepreneurial zeal and reporting skill and became one of the great independent journalists in American history. At the age of eighty, Izzy published *The Trial of Socrates,* which was a national bestseller. He wrote the book after he taught himself ancient Greek.

Benjamin C. Bradlee was for nearly thirty years the charismatic editorial leader of *The Washington Post.* It was Ben who gave the *Post* the range and courage to pursue such historic issues as Watergate. He supported his reporters with a tenacity that made them fearless, and it is no accident that so many became authors of influential, best-selling books.

Robert L. Bernstein, the chief executive of Random House for more than a quarter century, guided one of the nation's premier publishing houses. Bob was personally responsible for many books of political dissent and argument that challenged tyranny around the globe. He is also the founder and was the longtime chair of Human Rights Watch, one of the most respected human rights organizations in the world.

· · ·

For fifty years, the banner of Public Affairs Press was carried by its owner Morris B. Schnapper, who published Gandhi, Nasser, Toynbee, Truman, and about 1,500 other authors. In 1983 Schnapper was described by *The Washington Post* as "a redoubtable gadfly." His legacy will endure in the books to come.

Peter Osnos, *Publisher*